Hong Kong for Kids

Hong Kong for Kids

A Parent's Guide

Cindy Miller Stephens

BLACKSMITH BOOKS

Hong Kong for Kids
ISBN 978-988-19003-2-6

Published by Blacksmith Books
5th Floor, 24 Hollywood Road, Central, Hong Kong
Tel: (+852) 2877 7899
www.blacksmithbooks.com

Copyright © Cindy Miller Stephens 2011
The author asserts the moral right to be identified
as the author of this work.

Editorial assistance by Mandy Lam
Cover design and icons by Nick Street
Maps by Wincy Lam

Dedication

For my Grandmother, Rosa, who truly *lived* every single day of her 87 years. No one in this world was more excited about this book's release than she was. She was a warm, spirited, caring, incredibly intelligent and loving human being who touched every person who ever met her. This world is a better place because she lived, *fully*, in it.

Foreword

Hong Kong has changed so much since my husband and I arrived here as a newly married couple in 1996. When we had our first child in 1998, I struggled at first to find fun and exciting adventures that we could do as a family. It was not so much that these opportunities did not exist, but more that I did not know about them and had no idea how to get the information I needed or the directions. When child number two was born in 2000, it became a passion of mine to explore this amazing city with my family. After compiling the notes on those adventures, the first edition of *Hong Kong for Kids: A Parent's Guide* (2004) was born.

Little girl number three came along in 2005 and with her a whole new set of challenges and two slightly older children who wanted to explore more stuff! Now we have a six year old, a ten year old and a teenager (13) and we are out on the town once more! The highlights from our last five years of exploration can be found in this new edition of *Hong Kong for Kids*.

Hong Kong is a much more family-friendly place than it used to be. Sit-down toilets (cleaner ones), baby-changing facilities, nursing rooms, indoor playrooms, malls with stroller lending facilities, and more, are all present in Hong Kong today and they were a RARE find when the first edition was written. Things are just easier than they were and the options for families are better, safer and have reached world-class status. Hong Kong Disneyland is here, Ocean Park has morphed into an international-level ocean-themed amusement park, we have bike parks, skateboarding venues, indoor ice skating rinks, 3D movie theatres, and the list goes on and on.

There are many wonderful adventures available throughout the territory, but when you are toting strollers, backpacks stuffed with bottles, snacks, nappies and toys and kids, most parents understandably don't want the added challenge of FINDING the place. It is my passionate hope that this book becomes the tool that helps your family explore and enjoy Hong Kong to its fullest. The biggest obstacles between you and a great outing I hope will be eliminated by this book – namely how to identify and then locate a fun-filled outing – because while things in Hong Kong for families have improved greatly, directions can still be difficult and daunting.

The venues selected for inclusion in this book are those our family found worthy of a visit. Every site has been "Stephens Family tested" in the hopes of eliminating the possibility of hauling your children around Hong Kong only to be disappointed once you arrive (we have done this and it's no fun!) This book is not about rating venues or ranking activities in Hong Kong – it is about identifying the best things that are currently here to be explored.

When I first arrived in Hong Kong, I was fortunate enough to meet some lovely ladies who took it upon themselves to show me around. Their most memorable mantra went something like this: "We can't tell you how to get there, but we can show you the way and next time you will be able to find it on your own." It only took one or two outings for me to realize exactly what they meant, but no statement was ever more true: Locations in Hong Kong can be very hard to find. In the spirit of those women who were so very helpful to me, I present to you this book which I hope will be your family's personal guide to finding the most enjoyable things to do in Hong Kong with your children.

Happy trails!

Cindy Miller Stephens

Acknowledgements

For more than 20 years I have been blessed to have the love of the most generous person I know, my friend, my confidant, the father of my children and my husband – Chris. Without all the time, energy, computer expertise, superb navigational instincts and co-parenting skills he brought to the project, I could never have finished this second book or even started the first one. When you have someone on your side who really believes in you, anything is possible. Thanks for being my other and better half and giving me all the time I needed to do this while you did the heavy lifting.

I am also very grateful to my children Lara, Hailey and Audrey for being great explorers and for their boundless energy and enthusiasm. Thank you so much for giving me the time (even reluctantly) to work on the computer all those days when you really wanted my attention. All three of you were ready to go out there and try out new places and give your honest opinions about our outings. You all brought with you very special gifts. Lara, you were so organized, computer savvy and willing to help. Hailey, you embraced every outing with equal passion and enthusiasm and brought your contagious giggle on every journey. Audrey, you taught me what would work for the 'younger' set and were always very expressive about what you saw and did, running up every mountain with your little feet taking four steps for our every two. The three of you are the reason for this book, and indeed the reason for everything I do.

A special thanks to my mother Marlene Miller and my sister Stephanie Miller who have always supported me in all my endeavours (no matter how crazy). My many and varied career ideas have always been greeted with "You can do it!" or "That sounds great, you would be great at that…" That kind of support makes doing out-of-the-box things possible (like giving up law school and becoming a professional singer and other wild choices).

Being a mom is not a career path for the weak, the passive or the squeamish. Once on the journey, it's best to take the trip with a co-pilot, another mother with whom you can share your deepest fears and biggest triumphs. For me that person is Anne Sawyer. Not only has she been taking this wild "mommy" ride with me for the past 13 years, she was also willing to go on almost every outing for the book in the first edition, and as many as she could fit in for the second edition as well. Enthusiasm, support, encouragement and a kick in the pants when needed have been provided daily on the book and other subjects by this very special woman who I am proud to call my friend. Thank you also to Anne's children Zachary and Ceilidh Tesluk for being such great explorers. They have been so enthusiastic about the research for this book and all of the outings that were needed that we have done together over the years.

This second edition of *Hong Kong for Kids* required revisiting every one of the 56 outings in the old version and more than 30 possibilities for the new book. A giant thank you to all the following people and families who helped identify and/or visit all of the outings (in alphabetic order):

Rachel, Lorne, Jasmine, Felix and Jemima Ali
Mary-Jean Bayogos
Michael Birley
Karen and Christian Bradbury
Siobhan Byrne and Sienna and Clara Read
Kathleen, Peter, Annika, Trey, Zach and Drew Carlson
Liz, Annabelle and Jackson Derrick
Rachael, Sophie and Jean-Luis Desgouttes
Ellen and Chloe Fagan
Angela Ang, James, Madeleine and Max Griffiths
Carolyn Griffin
MaryAnne Gucciardi, Ted and Charlotte Waechter
Angelina Escobar Herrera
Malia Hirshmann and Family
Emilie Lawrence and Family
Kristin, Courtney, Emeline, Quinlan and Imogen Lowe
Jennifer Lu

The Patrat Family
Annie, Steven, Alyssa and Austin Pelayo
Noel, Heather, Edwina and Annabel Preston
Tammy Purner and Family
Joan Albite Reynes
Caroline Rhodes
Dafna, Oran, Gal and Libi Sokol
Emma Vijayaratnam and Family
Olivia Weise

The first edition was the foundation for this second book and took more than three years to research. Thank you to all of the following people for their contributions to the first edition (in alphabetic order):

Herrina Bayedbed, Tally Ben Sira, the Bradley Family, Helen Brooks, the Burnett Family, the Channon Family, the Desgouttes Family, the Dickie Family, Sue Dockstader, the Gucciardi & Waechter Family, the Hawksworth Family, Angelina Herrera, Angel Y. Ho, Kavita Jindal, Andrew Kemp, Simon Kemp, Jeannie Cho Lee, Sarah Leventhorpe, Fiona McGregor, Ellen McNally, Robyn and Christopher Meredith, the Nash Family, Rachel Penton, the Quaranta Family, the Pinkel Family, the Soutar Family, Eddie Tam, Tim Tesluk, the Trahan Family, the Tso and Muh Family, Henry Wong Kwong Wah and the Won-Patterson Family.

Table of Contents

4. Fun in the Sand – Hong Kong's Beaches

5. Fun Shopping – Hong Kong's Markets

6. Amusements Kids Will Love

How to Use This Book

All of the essential information parents will need for a successful outing with children in Hong Kong is contained in the description of each destination. For simplicity and ease of use, all descriptions cover information in the same format. Please refer to the sample template below as a guide.

Name of Destination
- Address
- Location in Hong Kong
- Telephone number(s)
- Website(s)
- Where to find an area map on the Internet (if applicable)

Written Description
This section provides the reason for visiting the destination with vivid descriptions of exactly what can be found there and what fun things there are to do there for children. In some cases a suggested itinerary is provided.

Seasons and Times
Opening hours, closing times and days of closure for destination and other relevant areas.

Admission
Information regarding cost of entry and/or availability and cost of special passes (where applicable).

The Best Ways of Getting There
Detailed directions to each destination. There are generally a variety of ways to get to each place. The BEST ways to go have been included. As it was impossible to list directions from every location in Hong Kong, Central and Admiralty were chosen as starting points. ALL DIRECTIONS BEGIN FROM EITHER CENTRAL OR ADMIRALTY OR BOTH.

Here is a complete list of possible "ways of getting there":

- By MTR
- By KCR
- By Bus
- By Mini Bus
- By City Tram
- By Peak Tram
- By Star Ferry
- By Ferry
- Walking
- By Car
- By Taxi

Please see "Transportation Information" for details regarding each of these modes of transport.

Getting a Bite
Dining or snacking options at or near your destination including restaurants, snack bars and vending machines.

What's Close?
List of nearby child-friendly areas to consider if you wish to extend your visit beyond the initial destination. Those that are underlined are destinations that are covered in greater detail elsewhere in the book.

Comments
This section answers all the following CRUCIAL parental questions:
- What is the suitable age range for the outing?
- How long should one spend there?
- Is the site crowded? If so, when?
- Toilets – Are there any? If so, where are they and are they the squat or sit-down variety?
- Baby-changing tables – Are there any? If so, where?
- Strollers – Is the location stroller-friendly?
- Gift shops – Is there one on the premises?

Extra Info

This special section provides any additional information that is not covered by the other headings. These topics might include any of the following: Discounts, special performances/programs/events, special transport, tours, maps, films, news and architecture.

Special Programs and Tours

Details on special programs and tours offered to the public at the venue.

For Educators

Contact details and program information (where applicable) for educators wishing to take students on educational field trips to the destination.

Word of Mouth

From one parent to another – personal comments, tips and planning ideas.

Additional Aids

In addition to all of the above, this book also aims to provide some useful tools to help save time in terms of choosing an appropriate outing, arriving at your destination without getting lost and accessing useful information.

Maps

There is nothing more discouraging than heading out with your kids for a fun day out and finding yourself lost and surrounded by unhappy faces (and voices). To help lessen the chances of any directional mishap, you can rely on the detailed directions given in every destination description and on the maps at the back of the book.

Chinese Characters

In the margin of each destination description you will find the name and address of each venue written in Chinese. This translation will have a multitude of purposes including: asking for directions from strangers, giving destination names to non-

English speaking taxi drivers, and once you get to the site, checking that you have arrived at the correct destination.

Icons

The icons located in the margin are there to help speed up the process of choosing a destination. For instance, if by chance the weather outdoors is inhospitable (rain, heat, wind, etc.), you may want to skim the book for indoor outings only; or perhaps you have a newborn in tow and want to be sure to head to a destination that is both stroller friendly and has baby changing facilities. Whatever your needs, the icons are there to help save time and energy.

Stroller Friendly   Outdoor   Baby Changing

Restaurant   Indoor   Parking

Snack Stand   Playground   Age Range

0-99

Useful Telephone Numbers and Websites

At the back of the book you will find an index of useful telephone numbers and websites. When you are seeking information or to confirm openings, prices and location, this is a good place to start.

A Word of Caution

Hong Kong is well known to be a vibrant and very fast moving city. Things change here constantly. Businesses come and go. Times, dates and fares change. Please check information on your chosen venue BEFORE you go by consulting its website or by calling the telephone number listed at the top of each destination description.

17

Transportation Information

Hong Kong has one of the best public transport systems in the world. Almost the entirety of the territory can be accessed by using one or two public transport systems. The majority of services are both efficient and reasonably priced and, best of all, they can be a great way to view Hong Kong as you get from one place to the next. In this city, with all the various interesting modes of transport, getting there really is half the fun.

MTR (Mass Transit Railway)

This is Hong Kong's version of New York's Subway or London's Tube but cleaner, newer, more efficient and air-conditioned. The MTR is a great way to get around Hong Kong. Many of the outings listed in the book are accessible very easily by MTR. If you are visiting sites on the north side of Hong Kong Island or venues in Kowloon, the New Territories or Lantau, chances are the MTR can get you there easily and quickly.
All MTR stations are marked by this symbol [INSERT MTR SYMBOL HERE]. There are normally multiple entries and exits for every MTR station, so if you are near one, it should be relatively easy to find an entrance by looking for the symbol.

MTR stations have automatic ticketing machines where you can buy single journey tickets. They all have customer service counters as well where you can purchase tickets, get information or ask for change. Octopus cards are on sale at all MTR station customer service counters (please see **Octopus Card** details below for more information). Children under the age of three ride free. Children ages three to 12 must have their own ticket, but are entitled to a discounted fare. Ages 12 and over require the purchase of an adult single journey ticket or, if they are Hong Kong full time students, they are entitled to purchase a student Octopus card which provides them a discounted rate.

Strollers can be difficult to manoeuvre in MTR stations. Stations are often crowded and filled with steps that need to be negotiated. If you do have a stroller with you, make sure to look for the elevators and escalators to help make your journey easier. Keep in mind however that elevators are not always available or easy to find.

For more information on the MTR visit their website at www. MTR.com.hk.

*Please note that in December 2007, the MTR merged with the KCR (Kowloon-Canton Railway) which has been serving passengers between Kowloon and the border of Guangdong province (the current name for what was once Canton) since 1910. Since the merger, all of the trains operate as a single transport network under the MTR umbrella.

Buses
Using the bus system in Hong Kong is a great way to see the city. Many of the vehicles are double decker style, which provides excellent views of Hong Kong from above it all. There are numerous bus companies in Hong Kong which service all areas from Hong Kong Island to Kowloon to the New Territories. Lantau even has its own bus company.

For the purposes of this book, bus routes have been emphasized mostly in locations where the MTR and/or ferries do not operate or can only take you part of the way to the venue, but not right to it. A very good example of this is the south side of Hong Kong. Trains and ferries do not service the south side of the island and therefore buses are a great option. The New Territories outings might also involve a bus trip as part of the journey, generally in combination with the MTR.

Children under the age of three ride free. Children ages three to 12 must have their own ticket but are entitled to a discounted fare. Ages 12 and over require the purchase of an adult ticket.

For more information on buses and bus routes please visit the following websites:
Citybus and New World First Bus: www.nwstbus.com.hk

Kowloon Motor Bus Company: www.kmb.com.hk
New Lantao Bus Company: www.newlantaobus.com

Mini Buses (also called public or private light buses – PLBs)

Mini buses are privately run, small, 16-seater buses that are almost akin to a shared taxi service. There are two kinds: green topped and red topped. The green topped ones have set routes and the red topped ones do not. Mini buses are not often mentioned in the book because other modes of transport can generally be used just as easily to the venues. There are some sites however that are not serviced by regular buses where mini buses might be your best option, particularly if a private taxi is not easily found.

If a child occupies a seat in a mini bus, they must pay full fare.

For more information on Hong Kong's green mini bus routes go to:
http://www.td.gov.hk/en/transport_in_hong_kong/public_transport/minibuses/green/gmb_online_guide/hong_kong_island_gmb_routes/index.html

The Star Ferry

The journey across Victoria Harbour aboard the Star Ferry Company's very distinctive green and white ships, operating since 1888, has become one of Hong Kong's most famous attractions. Some things don't change overly much in a century – this is still a wonderful way to reach Tsim Sha Tsui from Hong Kong Island (or vice versa) and get a breathtaking view of the city.

The main Star Ferry Terminal in Central is located near to the IFC Mall and the Airport Express Station. The fare is still unbelievably reasonable:
Weekdays Upper Deck: Adults: HK$2.50, Children (3-11): HK$1.50, and under-threes are free.
Weekdays Lower Deck: Adults: HK$2.00, Children (3-11): HK$1.40, and under-threes are free.

Weekends Upper Deck: Adults: HK$3.00, Children (3-11): HK$1.80
Weekends Lower Deck: Adults: HK$2.40, Children (3-11): HK$1.70, and under-threes are free.

If you are pushing a stroller you may wish to opt for the lower deck of the Star Ferry. You can then push the stroller on and off the ship without having to climb the stairs necessary to reach the upper deck.

Beyond the landmark route from Central to Tsim Sha Tsui and back, the Star Ferry also runs other routes including:
Wanchai ↔ Tsim Sha Tsui
Tsim Sha Tsui ↔ Wanchai

Please check the Star Ferry Company's website for more information at www.starferry.com.hk

Island Ferries
For visits to Hong Kong's outlying islands, the island ferries are the way to get there. The majority of the ferries leave from Central's Outlying Island Ferry Piers, located very near the IFC complex (just beyond Central Exchange Square Bus Terminus). Outlying island ferry destinations include Lantau (both Discovery Bay and Mui Wo), Lamma (both Sok Kwu Wan and Yung Shue Wan), Cheung Chau, Peng Chau and Park Island. There are also Lamma Island ferries located at the Aberdeen Waterfront Promenade.

Fares vary depending on the destination, type of ferry (fast or ordinary), class of service and whether it is a Sunday or public holiday (when the fares go up). There are generally two different fare classes on the regular (as in non-high speed) island ferries – ordinary and deluxe. The advantage of sailing in deluxe is the ability to access the deck seats at the back of the ship. On a day without rain it is lovely to sit out on the deck in one of the chairs provided. The deluxe cabin also has a snack bar and is generally less crowded.

For more information on ferry schedules and fares please check the following websites:
New World First Ferry: www.nwff.com.hk
Hong Kong & Kowloon Ferry Limited: http://www.hkkf.com.hk
Chuen Kee Ferry Co. Ltd. (from Aberdeen): http://www.ferry.com.hk
For Discovery Bay Ferry (schedule): http://db.tdw.hk

The City Tram

This century-old mode of transportation is the only one of its kind left in the world. These old-fashioned narrow street trams operate on roughly 10 miles of track running along Hong Kong Island's north coast and are set in the middle of some of the city's busiest streets. You can ride this double decker marvel from Kennedy Town (west of Central) all the way to Shau Kei Wan. Make sure you sit on the upper deck of the tram car to get the most out of your experience.

When riding the tram there are a few things to be aware of. Firstly, the tram fare is HK$2.30 for adults and HK$1.20 for kids, which is a real bargain, but the great value also makes this a very popular (read crowded) option. Trams come very frequently, making the possibility of waiting for a less crowded one very doable. Be aware that most of the trams are not air-conditioned which can be a problem if it is very hot and humid; however they do keep all the windows open and there is a breeze. Though the tram is likely to be the most time-consuming way to arrive at your destination, it may also be the most fun for your kids.

For more information on the City Tram: http://www.hktramways.com/en/tourist/index.html

The Peak Tram

The Peak Tram is the territory's most popular tourist attraction. Built in 1888, it is the world's steepest funicular railway, measuring at its most vertical point 27 degrees to the horizontal. You will feel as though you are going straight up the mountain while you take in some of the most spectacular views of Hong Kong, Kowloon and Victoria Harbour.

Though short in duration, taking only 7-8 minutes to get from the bottom to the top, it is long on thrills. The ride is equally stunning at night as it is during the day. Try to sit on the right hand side as you go skyward for a better view, or left hand side as you ride down. A wonderful way to extend the fun is to take the double decker, open-topped Peak Tram Shuttle Bus #15C from Star Ferry Pier 8 (at the Outlying Island Ferry Terminus near IFC Mall) to the Peak Tram Central Terminus. The kids will love riding in the open air, above it all, in the middle of Central.

The Peak Tram runs daily, including Sundays and public holidays, between 7:00am and midnight. The tram departs every 10-15 minutes. One way fares are: HK$28 for adults, HK$11 for kids (3-12); Round trip: HK$40 for adults, HK$18 for kids. Under-threes ride free.

The Peak Tram journey begins in Central and finishes at the Peak, but you can alight at one of the stops in between should you wish to. These stops include Kennedy Road, MacDonnell Road and May Road (all three of which are in Mid Levels) and Barker Road which is located on the Peak. Should you wish to alight the tram at an interim stop, be sure to push the designated button as soon as you board the tram. For extra assurance you can also let your tram operator know where you intend to alight.

For more information on the Peak Tram check the Peak's website at: www.thepeak.com.hk

Airport Express Train
This special express train to the airport is run by the MTR Corporation and is a great way to reach the airport from Hong Kong Island or Kowloon. Trains depart about every 12 minutes and arrive at the airport in 24 minutes (from Central). The train itself is very new and comfortable and even has individual televisions for each seat. Though the TVs do not have sound

or headphones, they will keep the kids entertained on the short journey to the airport.

The train departs from the Hong Kong Central Airport Express Terminal which is located on the ground floor of the IFC building in Central (this terminal is connected to the Central MTR station and can be accessed through the underground subway). This train station is also a check-in terminal for the airlines, so you can check-in for your flight and check your bags BEFORE you board the train. Keep in mind, you must check in no later than two hours before your flight's scheduled departure time. Most people who travel with children travel with lots of luggage. Lightening your load early in the trip is a great way to start your journey. Check with your travel agent BEFORE you leave for the train to be sure that your flight will accommodate an "in-town" check-in. Many North American destinations and others have added special security checks since 9/11 and might not allow you to check-in at the Airport Express Station (though of course you can still ride the train with your luggage and check-in at the airport). Trains make two stops en route to the airport – Kowloon Station and Tsing Yi Station. The airport train terminal is very conveniently located right *in* the airport, very near the airport check-in counters. Luggage carts are provided free of charge on either end of the journey and there are baggage handlers on the train that will help you free of charge (please note that baggage handlers are not allowed to accept tips).

For more information see the MTR website: www.mtr.com.hk

Hong Kong International Airport – Chek Lap Kok
This fantastic new airport (opened in 1998) has been voted "World's Best Airport" eight times since 2001. It is spacious, clean and family friendly. There are two play areas in the airport to take note of: One between Gate 23 and 25, Departures Level, Terminal 1 and one located between Gate 509 and 510, Departures Level, North Satellite Concourse. There are also 33 nursing stations/baby-changing stations located in convenient places all around the airport. Restaurants, fast food places and shops abound.

For older kids (and adults) Terminal 2 has a PlayStation Gateway, the only dedicated special gaming area to be found within an airport in Asia, which lets passengers play free of charge with the latest PSP games. There is also a high-definition family cinema playing the latest movies and game trailers. Also at Terminal 2, Level 6 is the Aviation Discovery Centre, an entertainment area which has aviation-themed attractions which include a visitor centre, a sky deck, interactive kiosks, a cockpit simulator, a full-motion plane-cabin ride simulator, a 4-D Motion Ride and many more.

For more information see the airport's website: www.hongkongairport.com.

Taxis

Taxis are a cheap and easy way to get around Hong Kong. Compared to other major world cities, Hong Kong taxis are a bargain. Taxi queues can be found in most major areas such as shopping plazas, MTR stations, bus terminals and ferry terminals. You can also hail a taxi fairly easily, but keep in mind they are not allowed to stop just anywhere. For instance, a double yellow line on the road is not a legal place for any car to stop, including taxis.

All regular taxis can accommodate up to five people (including the driver). Most taxis have seatbelts in the front seat, as well as the window seats in the back. Some have seat belts in the middle of the back seat as well, but not all. It is required by law for any person travelling in a taxi which has working seat belts to wear those seat belts. Failure to do so can result in fines.

Red taxis are the most prevalent and can be found on Hong Kong Island and Kowloon. Green taxis service the rural areas of the New Territories and blue taxis operate on Lantau Island.

A taxi with a round, red "HIRE" sign in its window and a lit sign on its roof is for hire. If you see an empty red taxi which has its interior "for hire" sign covered by an "out of service" sign, normally the driver is attempting to catch a fare back across the harbour. If you are on Hong Kong Island side and you see a taxi with its light covered, that taxi is a "Kowloon taxi" and will only take a fare that is headed in that direction. If you are on Kowloon and see a taxi with its light covered, this taxi will only take a fare that is headed to Hong Kong Island. Also, if you telephone for a taxi, the taxi driver will have the "for hire" sign covered in this same manner, as he waits for his pre-designated fare.

Extra charges will be levied for:
• Luggage: HK$5 per bag. There should be no charge for strollers or other luggage that does not require use of the luggage compartment.
• Telephone bookings: HK$5
• Tunnels: If you travel through the Cross Harbour, Western Harbour or Eastern Harbour tunnels in a taxi you will be charged a return toll on top of the taxi fare which ranges from HK$10 to HK$15 depending on which tunnel is used.

It is always a good idea to carry with you the telephone numbers of taxi services, particularly if you are travelling to less populated areas. Please check at the back of the book in the **Useful Numbers and Websites** section for a list of taxi booking telephone numbers.

When exiting a taxi in Hong Kong it is always a good idea to get a receipt from the driver so that if you have lost something or you have a complaint you will have the taxi's license number on the receipt as a reference. If you have a complaint about a taxi, call the Transport Complaints Unit hotline – Tel: 2889-9999. If you have lost property in a taxi call the Lost and Found hotline – Tel: 1872-920.

Red Taxi Fare Information:
• Flag fall and up to the first two kilometres: HK$20
• Every subsequent 200 metres or part thereof and/or every period of one minute waiting time or part thereof, HK$1.50 (for fares below $72.50) or HK$1 (for fares above $72.50).

Green Taxi Fare Information:
- Flag fall and up to the first two kilometres: HK$16.50
- Every subsequent 200 metres or part thereof and/or every period of one minute waiting time or part thereof, HK$1.30 (for fares below HK$55.50) or HK$1 (for fares above HK$55.50).

Blue Taxi Fare Information:
- Flag fall and up to the first two kilometres: HK$15.00
- Every subsequent 200 metres or part thereof and/or every period of one minute waiting time or part thereof, HK$1.30 (for fares below HK$132) or HK$1.20 (for fares above HK$132).

For more information about Hong Kong taxi fares and charges visit the Hong Kong Transport Department website: http://www.td.gov.hk/en/transport_in_hong_kong/public_transport/taxi/taxi_fare_of_hong_kong/index.html

***Special note: All taxi fares quoted in this book should be considered estimated fares. Prices will vary depending on traffic and other factors.*

Cars
For those families who have their own vehicle, the **By Car** directions are there to help guide you through the sometimes unforgiving roads in and around the city (except the outlying islands, of course). Hong Kong has some of the most efficient roadways of any major world city, but as most of you have already discovered, this efficiency translates to problems if you miss your turn. In order to help reduce the stress of finding your way, the directions are very explicit in terms of which lane to be in and when and what turns to make and landmarks you should be looking for en route.

All of the directions begin in Central and are as clear and concise as possible at each juncture so that if you are in fact leaving from another location you can join the route in the middle and follow the directions as they suit your location.

Car Rental

There are many rental car companies operating in Hong Kong. For an abbreviated list of options please see **Useful Numbers and Websites** section at the back of the book. If you are not overly familiar with Hong Kong, hiring a car might not be your best option as public transport here is more than adequate and navigating unknown territory might prove to be very frustrating.

OCTOPUS CARDS

One major suggestion for everyone, whether you are a tourist, new to Hong Kong or a permanent resident: PURCHASE AN OCTOPUS CARD FOR EVERY FAMILY MEMBER WHO IS THREE OR OLDER.

What is an Octopus Card?
An Octopus Card is an electronic debit card, the size of a credit card, which can be used instead of cash on all public transport, parking meters, vending machines and many retail outlets in and around Hong Kong. It is a very handy thing to have on your person when you are out and about in the city, as most modes of transport otherwise require you to have exact change. Octopus cards are easily attainable and are for sale at all major transport centres including all MTR stations. And best of all, using the Octopus card entitles you to a discounted fare.

For the standard Octopus card, there are different pricing schemes for adult cards and children's cards and they are as follows:
Adult Card:
HK$50 refundable deposit + HK$100 in stored value = total cost: HK$150
Child Card (for ages 3-11):
HK$50 refundable deposit + HK$20 in stored value = total cost: HK$70.
Children under three ride free on public transport.
*Full Time Student Card:
HK$90 application fee which consists of a HK$50 refundable deposit + HK$20 application fee to the MTR + HK$20 non-

refundable service charge to Octopus (this is a "Personalized Card" with student status).
*This card is only available to Hong Kong Full Time Students.

It is very easy to add value to your Octopus card should your balance run low. Value adding can be accomplished at any transport service counter, add-value machine or at any retail outlet that accepts the card – 7-Eleven convenience stores, Circle K convenience stores, ParknShop grocery stores, Wellcome grocery stores, Watson's drug stores and Starbucks coffee shops, just to name a few. You can store up to HK$1,000 in value on your card at one time.

Refunds on unused portions of Octopus cards can be had at any customer service centre at MTR stations or New World First Ferry piers. If your card has a remaining value of less than HK$500, the refund can be given on the spot. For refund values of more than HK$500 an application process to the Octopus main office is required and within five days of receipt, a refund check will be sent to you.

For more information on Octopus cards please visit their website at: www.octopuscards.com.

SPECIAL NOTES TO CAR OWNERS

1. All Hong Kong parking meters are Octopus card payment only, as are many parking garages. Please make sure you have an Octopus card with you if you are driving to any of the venues which are listed in this book.

2. Google Maps is a great tool. If you are a driver anywhere in the world, chances are you have used it. It can work wonderfully well in Hong Kong as well, but NOT ALWAYS. The roads in the New Territories in particular HAVE DIFFERENT NAMES TO THE ONES THAT GOOGLE USES so please be aware that you will need a second or third resource when venturing out. Google Maps may not be enough to get you there.

3. Similarly, iPhone apps are only as good as the source they depend on and occasionally sources are not up to date.

4. Keep a road map in your car when driving in Hong Kong. An invaluable resource to have when driving in the territory is *The Hong Kong Guide: Gazetteer of Street and Place Names*. It is a government publication that can be purchased at the Government Bookstore located at Room 402, Murray Building, Garden Road, Central. For more information contact them on 2537-1910.

Chapter 1

Exploring the Territory and Outlying Islands

Hong Kong is a very exciting place to explore. Though relatively small in size, it has an exceptionally diverse landscape, covering everything from mountains to beaches, from state-of-the-art skyscrapers to ancient temples, from the most crowded streets in the world to the quietest country parks. There is so much to see, in fact, that it can be hard to decide how to spend your time.

The sights in this chapter are some of the best places in Hong Kong to take your kids. These areas are as varied as the territory itself, covering everything from Hong Kong's number one tourist attraction (Victoria Peak) to a remote beach accessible only by kaido (a small boat for hire). Whatever you choose to do, there is fun to be had.

For achieving the most success in your outings, be sure to double check ferry times, opening hours and other important information before you set out. All the guidance you will need is provided within each destination description. Be sure to leave yourself plenty of time to get there and back, as most of these sites require a minimum of a half-day stay to do them justice. Hong Kong's natural beauty will be all around you, so don't forget to bring the camera!

1. Victoria Peak (The Peak)
2. Stanley Village
3. The Giant Buddha, Po Lin Monastery, Ngong Ping 360 and Tai O Village (Lantau Island)
4. Sai Kung Town and Hap Mun Bay Beach
5. Sok Kwu Wan Village and Fisherfolk Village (Lamma Island)
6. Yung Shue Wan Village (Lamma Island)
7. Bike Riding in the New Territories
8. Cheung Chau Island
9. Bike Riding in Mui Wo (Silvermine Bay, Lantau Island)
10. Discovery Bay – Beach, Plaza and Rock Pool
11. Peng Chau Island

Victoria Peak (The Peak)
and Madame Tussauds Wax Museum
Peak Road, Hong Kong Island

香港 山頂道 山頂

Tel: 2522-0922
Website: www.thepeak.com.hk
Email: info@thepeak.com.hk
For area map: Go to the above website, click on "The Peak Experience"
and then click on "Nature Walks."
Madame Tussauds – Tel: 2849-6966
Website for Madame Tussauds: www.madame-tussauds.com.hk

On a mountain top overlooking Victoria Harbour, 'The Peak', as it is locally known, is Hong Kong's most popular tourist destination. Join the crowd and head right on up there for a day of fun, thrills, views and great food.

The fastest and most exciting way to begin your journey is on the Peak Tram, the world's steepest funicular railway. The eight-minute ride from the Central Terminus to the Peak Terminus will have your kids "oohing" and "aahing" both because of the ride's steep gradient and the views of the harbour and beyond, which are awe-inspiring even for the most sophisticated traveller.

The tram will drop you in the centre of all the action at the Peak. Basically made up of three parts, the Peak Tower, the Peak Galleria and the Peak Walk, there are a plethora of things for children to do here. When you exit the tram you will be in the Peak Tower, a shopping plaza built in the shape of a wok, which houses the Sky Terrace, Madame Tussauds Wax Museum (see below for details), a make-your-own wax hand boutique, a multiple of child-friendly restaurants, coffee shops, and one of Hong Kong's only pick-a-mix candy shops. If you can pull your kids away, enter shopping plaza number two, the Peak Galleria, which boasts a nice outdoor playground on the first floor along with other kid-friendly stuff like toy stores, book shops, ice cream shops, a creperie and many curios shops that kids will enjoy. The Peak Galleria also has several viewing terraces with panoramic views of Central, Victoria Harbour and, on a clear day, Kowloon and its surrounding mountains.

0-99

When you have had enough of the crowds, head for the Peak Walk, a circular, paved, pedestrian trail that will take you in a loop around Victoria Peak. The views from the path are some of the best anywhere on Hong Kong Island. To start your walk, look for the signs for Harlech Road or Lugard Road, both of which can be found very easily next to the Peak Lookout restaurant. Moving clockwise on the 3.5 km trail (starting on Harlech Road), you will first discover views of the south side of the island and, later, views of Victoria Harbour and Kowloon. Surrounded by local flora and fauna, this walk is a breath of fresh air for weary urbanites where you can expect to find a mix of locals walking their dogs or going for their daily constitutionals, as well as tourists from every country on earth. There are grassy patches along the way where you can stop and have a rest. This walk is stroller friendly.

(Tip: If you are too tired, weary or have little kids in tow and don't want to do the entire 3.5K loop, just head into the loop clockwise from Harlech Road next to the Peak Lookout restaurant and in about 5 to 10 minutes you will arrive at a small natural waterfall on your right hand side. Kids will like discovering it and parents will like the beautiful photo op it presents.)

Don't leave the Peak area without having a meal here. There are a wide variety of restaurants to choose from, many with stunning views, and several which are very child-friendly. (Please see **Getting a Bite**.)

Madame Tussauds Wax Museum

This very well done wax museum is a great place for your kids to see their favourite movie or sports stars up close and in person (well, sort of). Housing over 100 life-size and lifelike wax statues, this famous museum (also located in London, New York, Amsterdam and Las Vegas) is sure to entertain and maybe even educate your kids. The museum is divided into six sections: Hong Kong Glamour, Historical and National Heroes, World Premiere, The Champions, Music Icons and Scream. The rule here is 'hands on', so your kids can feel free to pose with Madonna or compare muscles with Arnold Schwarzenegger. The experience is mostly on an entertainment level but there are some educational things to take away as well. The Historical and National Heroes section focuses on political figures of both modern and historical times. Lots of good discussion can ensue from a close-up look at Gandhi, Henry VIII or former US President Bill Clinton. Photographs are not only allowed, they are encouraged, so make sure to bring your camera. Do be aware that the Scream section of the museum is not for the squeamish or the very young, or kids who are easily frightened. This part of the museum is cordoned off, so skipping this part is very easily accomplished.

Seasons and Times
The Peak area – Year-round.
Shops – 10:00am-10:00pm daily. (Shops in the Peak Galleria open at 10:30am.)
The Peak Tram – runs every 10 to 15 minutes from 7:00am to midnight.
Madame Tussauds Wax Museum – 10:00am-10:00pm daily.

Admission
The Peak is free and open to the public; however, the Peak Tram, the Sky Terrace and Madame Tussauds all require the purchase of a ticket (see the websites for pricing and package options).

The Best Ways of Getting There
By Peak Tram
- Take the Peak Tram from the **Peak Tram Central Terminus** located in **St. John's Building** on **Garden Road** in **Central**.
- To get there you can either take a **taxi** or a special <u>double decker bus **#15C**</u> from **Star Ferry Pier Bus Terminus** to the **Peak Tram Central Terminus**.
  (*Tip: The bus is loads of fun for kids because the top is open. This special bus runs every 10-20 minutes from 10:00am to 11:40pm. Please note that the open top double decker comes only every other time so you may wish to let one bus pass, if you have time, to wait for the open topped bus.*)
- The Peak Tram drops you off in the **Peak Tower**.
↔ Travel time: 5 mins (taxi) or 10 mins (bus) to the Peak Tram Terminus in Central + 8 mins (tram).

By Bus
- Take bus <u>**#15**</u> from **Central Exchange Square Bus Terminus** or from **Admiralty Garden** on **Queensway** to the Peak Bus Terminus.
↔ Travel time: 20-25 mins (bus).

By Mini Bus
- Take mini bus **#1** from **City Hall** in **Central** to the **Peak Bus Terminus**.
- ↔ Travel time: 20-25 mins (mini bus).

By Car
- From **Central** take **Garden Road** up to **Magazine Gap Road**.
- At the roundabout on **Magazine Gap Road** make a right and you will be on **Peak Road**.
- Take **Peak Road** all the way until you reach the parking garage signs in the **Peak Galleria Building** (a right turn).
- **P** There is a large underground car park in the Peak Galleria Building.

By Taxi
A taxi from Central will cost HK$80-$100 and take 15-20 mins.

Getting a Bite
There are so many child-friendly restaurants here to choose from it might be hard to decide where to go. The following is a list of fun places where you can get a bite:

Opposite the Piazza on Peak Road
The Peak Lookout – a Hong Kong landmark, this restaurant has a large and scenic outdoor terrace for dining, with kids' menus and colouring. Even dogs are welcome here!

In the Peak Galleria
Ground Floor
L16 – a Thai restaurant with outdoor seating.
Tsui Wah Restaurant – local Hong Kong diner chain that is famous for their French toast made with condensed milk. Kids will enjoy this specialty and parents can try their equally famous milk tea.
Mak's Noodle – Chinese noodle restaurant.
NY Fries – the ultimate fast food, right on the Piazza. Take your loaded fries outside and enjoy an impromptu picnic.
Delifrance – patio overlooking the piazza area.
Starbucks Coffee – outdoor seating in piazza area.
Haagen Dazs Ice Cream shop – outdoor seating in the piazza.

1st floor
Cafe Deco – Art Deco style 15,000-square-feet, 600-seater restaurant with stunning views and huge menu. On weekends, their brunch is served up with a special children's play area so parents can relax while they dine.
Berrygood – frozen yogurt.

2nd Floor
ParknShop International – grocer to get picnic needs.
Marion Crepes – take-away crepes both sweet and savoury.
McDonald's – outdoor dining on terrace with spectacular views.
Oliver's Sandwich Shop – outdoor seating.
Spaghetti 360 – outdoor seating.

In the Peak Tower
Bubba Gump Shrimp Co. Restaurant and Market – kids' menu and amusements, amazing views from the top of the Peak Tower, plus fun little gift shop attached.
Pacific Coffee Company – great views, terrace and big comfy couches.
Burger King – nice views.
Hong Kong Day – casual HK café with noodles and other light snacks.
Candy Haus – great place to get sweets. Kids will love this small but well stocked pick-a-mix candy shop.
Gino's Gelato – serving a wide variety of gelato. A great way to cap off a meal. Located on the outside of the Peak Tower facing the piazza.

At the Dairy Farm Shopping Centre, 100 Peak Road (three minutes' walk from the Peak Galleria down Peak Road toward the traffic lights)
Saffron Bakery – a lovely child-friendly bakeshop, candy store and breakfast/luncheon spot with comfy couches and great baked treats.

What's Close?
Pokfulam Country Park Walk and Victoria Peak Garden
Mt. Austin Road Playground – this outdoor playground, situated inside a nice little garden, can be found five minutes' walk from the piazza, up steep Mt. Austin Road. When you get to the top of the hill turn right and you will find the park and playground.

Comments

- Suitable for all ages.
- Plan at least half a day here including a meal.
- It can get crowded here on weekends and public holidays.
- There are great child-friendly toilets in the Peak Galleria. The first stall in the ladies' bathrooms has a special toddler-sized toilet with lovely small toilet seat.
- There are baby-changing stations in the ladies' bathrooms in the Peak Galleria.
- The Peak is a stroller-friendly place.

Extra Info

At major holiday times such as Chinese New Year, Christmas and Easter, there are usually special events planned up at the Peak. Check the website for details if you are heading up there during a holiday.

Word of Mouth

- The terraces at the Peak Galleria have beautiful views and are FREE to enter. Both Victoria Harbour on one side and the South China Sea on the other are visible in all their splendour. These terraces are not quite as 'jazzed' up as their neighbours over at the Sky Terrace but they don't require the purchase of a ticket and therefore may be a great budget-conscious alternative.
- It is always a few degrees cooler and windier up here than down below. In the summer, this is a wonderful asset. In winter, it means you may need to bring a heavy sweater or jacket.

Stanley Village
Stanley, Hong Kong Island

Tel: 2807-6543 (Hong Kong Tourism Board)
Website: http://www.discoverhongkong.com/eng/attractions/hk-stanley-market.html
For area map: http://www.housingauthority.gov.hk/en/commercial/shoppingcentres/stanleyplaza/
Stanley Main Beach
Tel: 2813-0217
Website: http://www.lcsd.gov.hk/beach/en/index.php
St. Stephen's Beach
Tel: 2813-1872
Website: http://www.lcsd.gov.hk/beach/en/index.php

香港 赤柱 赤柱村

If you and the kids need a break from the frantic pace of the Hong Kong metropolis, why not plan a visit to Stanley Village? Though not quite the sleepy fishing village it once was, Stanley still provides a lovely seaside Mediterranean-feel retreat for tourists and residents alike.

Relaxing yes, idle no – there are loads of things to do here. Stanley has a great open-air market, a shopping plaza, two beaches, the Hong Kong Maritime Museum (see **Hong Kong Maritime Museum** chapter for details), an array of dining options, many of which are alfresco style, and some historical sites to see. Anywhere you begin there is fun to be had. The market here is one of the most popular tourist spots in Hong Kong. The range of items for sale includes a large variety of merchandise that will be popular with kids (and adults) such as casual clothing, jewellery, footwear, toys, Chinese silk garments in children's sizes, and all sorts of souvenirs, to name just a few. After or even before shopping, having a meal here is a "must do" part of the Stanley experience. There are so many choices it might be hard to decide where to dine (see **Getting a Bite** below), but if the weather is good you can't go wrong opting for a table somewhere overlooking the sea.

0-99

If you are planning a full day here, why not also take in the beach? One option is Stanley Main Beach, a small stretch of sand, the greatest asset of which is its proximity to the market. (For walking directions, see **By Bus**.) It also has facilities that make it very user-friendly: changing rooms, showers, toilets, a swimmers' raft and Stanley Beach Club, a casual kid-friendly restaurant with outside seating overlooking the sea. For a more secluded beach, try St. Stephen's Beach, a 15-minute walk from the market (head south along Stanley Village Road until it turns into Wong Ma Kok Road, then make a right at the sign for the beach until you see the water). This little beach is a quiet place where few come even during the high season. It too has good facilities including showers, toilets, changing rooms, a swim raft, a refreshment kiosk, a BBQ area and a small fishing pier (with lots of little fish to see).

Stanley also has some historical sites worth noting. Visit the Tin Hau Temple located at the very end of Stanley Main Street (just behind the amphitheatre). Dedicated to the Taoist Goddess of the Sea, this temple was built in 1767 and houses the image of Tin Hau and other gods, along with noteworthy decor of old model ships, lanterns, and the pelt of a tiger that was shot by police in 1942.

If you travel the length of Stanley Main Street to its conclusion, make a sharp left and you will find Murray House. This old colonial building, first constructed in 1884, once stood where the Bank of China Tower now stands in Central. It was taken apart brick by brick in 1982 to make room for its more modern successor, preserved, stored and reset on this spot in Stanley in 1998. Beyond its historical significance, it also houses the **Hong Kong Maritime Museum** as well as a series of child-friendly restaurants (see **Getting a Bite** below). Just next door to Murray House is Blake Pier, originally constructed in Central in 1900. The old steel buttress style pavilion and roof were dismantled and moved to Stanley in 2007. Today, it is once more a functioning pier with kaido (small private ferry) service to Po Toi Island (see **Extra Info** below).

If after a full day of the market, beach, museum and a meal you still have the energy for more, have a look around Stanley Plaza. This shopping arcade located at the end of Stanley Main Street, next to the Tin Hau Temple – and currently under renovation (2011) – has an upscale grocery store, restaurants, retail shops, a bakery, Starbucks, McDonald's and an ice cream shop and will soon have a kids' play structure in a maritime theme on the ground floor (completion is set for 2013). There is also a lovely library and toddler playroom in the community building opposite the bus station that might be worth a visit. Further afield near St. Stephen's Beach are the Stanley Military

Cemetery and Stanley Prison, which was used as an internment camp in World War II.

On weekends and public holidays, Stanley takes on a festive atmosphere. Stanley Main Street is closed to traffic, leaving room for pedestrians and more alfresco dining. The village square, located between Murray House and Stanley Plaza, offers free entertainment in a shaded open forum. For current presentations, check at the village square when you arrive in Stanley.

Seasons and Times
Stanley Market: 10:00am-6:30pm daily.

Admission
Free

The Best Ways of Getting There
By Bus
- From **Central Exchange Square Bus Terminus** take bus **#6**, **#6A**, **#6X**, or **#260** to **Stanley Village Bus Terminus**. You can also take bus **#66** from **Central** to **Stanley Plaza**. *(Tip: Bus #6, #6A, #6X and #66 are double decker buses and are a great way to see the island if you sit on the top deck on the right-hand side as you go toward Stanley, left side as you head back to Central.)*
- ↔ Travel time: 35-40 mins (bus).
- From the Stanley Village Bus Terminus to the market is a very short walk down the hill. *(Tip: Follow the crowd.)*
- **To head to Stanley Beach**, turn right on Stanley Beach Road with the bus terminus at your back (away from the market). It is a five-minute walk to the sand.

By Car
- From Central: Connaught Road→ Harcourt Road→ Gloucester Road→ **Island Eastern Corridor**.
- Once on the expressway, stay in the far right lane. It will be labelled **Happy Valley/Causeway Bay**. The far right lane will dead-end into a circular overpass. Here you will stay in the far right lane following the signs for the **Aberdeen Tunnel**.
- Once through the tunnel, take one of the tollbooths on the **left side** (HK$5) then get in the far left lane. This lane will force you to make a left turn. You will now be on **Wong Chuk Hang Road** which will turn into **Island Road**.

- Island Road changes names to **Repulse Bay Road** and then to **Stanley Gap Road**, though the road remains constant.

Option #1 (to the beach and the market)
- Stay on **Stanley Gap Road** – you will come to a roundabout. Follow it around to the right and you will be on **Stanley Village Road**.

P There is metered parking on the street at **Stanley Mound Road** (a left off Stanley Village Road) or follow Stanley Mound Road until it dead-ends into **Stanley Beach Road**. Make a **right turn** and you will find two parking lots on your left side. Both lots have metered parking.

Option #2 (to Stanley Plaza and the market)
- Stay on **Stanley Gap Road** until you see the right turnoff for **Chung Hom Kok Road** (there will be a sign there with an arrow for Stanley Plaza).
- Follow **Chung Hom Kok Road** until the left turn for **Cape Road**. Follow **Cape Road** as it turns into **Carmel Road**.

P There is a paid private parking lot on the left, a few minutes' walk from **Stanley Plaza** or you can park in the parking garage at Stanley Plaza on your right side.

By Taxi
A taxi from Central will cost HK$90+ and take 30+ mins.

Getting a Bite
Part of your outing in Stanley should include a meal here. There are many options to choose from. Here are just a few:

In Stanley Market
Lucy's Restaurant (64 Stanley Main Street, inside the market; tel: 2813-9055) – French/International, boutique style, warm decor, indoor, kids' menu, high chairs.
Delifrance (LG/F 17 Stanley New Street, entrance to market) – Deli-style bake shop, great pastries, soft drinks, coffee, casual, indoor.
Pacific Coffee Company (G/F & 1/F, 80 Stanley Village Road, above the market; tel: 2813-0008) – Coffee shop, comfy chairs, computers, TV, kids' corner with a few books and toys.
Haagen Dazs Ice Cream Shop (74 Stanley Main Street).

On Stanley Main Street

Pizza Express (90B Stanley Main Street; tel: 2813-7363) – Pizza, salads, mains, casual, indoor/outdoor, kid-friendly, high chairs, activity books.

The Boathouse (86-88 Stanley Main Street; tel: 2813-4467) – International cuisine, boutique style, indoor/outdoor, kids' menu, booster seats.

Spiaggia (G/F, 92B Stanley Main Street; tel: 2813-7313) – Pizza, pasta, casual, indoor/outdoor, kid-friendly, high chairs.

Rock Salt (25 Stanley Market Street; tel: 2899-0818) – Seafood brasserie, fusion cuisine, kids' menu and high chairs.

In Murray House

Wildfire (2/F; tel: 2813 6161) – Wood stove oven pizza, pastas, salads, casual, indoor/outdoor, kids' menu, high chairs, booster seats, kids' play area on Sundays and public holidays.

Saigon in Stanley (Shop No. 101; tel: 2899-0147) – Southeast Asian cuisine, casual, indoor/outdoor, kid-friendly, high chairs, booster seats.

Mijas Spanish Restaurant (Shop No. 102; tel: 2899 0858) – Spanish cuisine, casual, indoor/outdoor, kids' menu (on Saturdays and Sundays), high chairs.

In Stanley Plaza

Saffron Bakery (Shop No. 102; tel: 2813-0270) – Great baked goods, lunch items, cakes and cookies, sit-down area with high chairs. The bakery also sells candy.

Starbucks Coffee (Shop No. 201).

Stanley Beach

Stanley Beach Club – Pizzas, pasta, casual, outdoor overlooking the sea, kid-friendly, kids' play area.

What's Close?
The end of the **Tai Tam Reservoir Walk**.

Comments
- Suitable for all ages.
- Plan to spend at least half a day here.
- Crowded on weekends and public holidays.
- There are several good sit-down toilets in Stanley to take note of:
    Stanley Plaza – second floor by the Taste grocery store.
    Stanley Main Beach.

At the far eastern end of Stanley Market (a left at the dead end).

Between Stanley Main Street and the market, at the water's edge there is a colourful building that has clean public toilets.

Ground floor next to the community building.

- There is a baby-changing station at the toilet near the public library.
- Stroller-friendly (though it may be hard to push a stroller in the market at peak times).

Extra Info

Po Toi, a small scenic island three kilometres off of the southern tip of Hong Kong Island, is a lovely place to spend a Sunday or holiday. The island is known for its hiking trails and a Chinese restaurant called **Ming Kee Seafood Restaurant** right off its ferry pier, which specializes in black peppered squid. They also serve kid-friendly fare such as fried rice and noodles, and ice cream. There is a non-swimming beach right next to the restaurant which makes for a nice distraction for the kids to look for shells or toss a ball while the adults are finishing their coffee or wine. If you don't want to venture too far on a hike with the kids, you can wander up to a temple near the pier, have a meal and then head back on the ferry. Kaido ferry service is available from Stanley's Blake Pier on Sundays and public holidays. For ferry schedule and information go to the Tsui Wah Ferry Service website: http://www.traway.com.hk/pdf/Potoi.pdf. Please note that the ferry can also be accessed in Aberdeen.

Word of Mouth

Right next to the bus terminus on Stanley Beach Road is a small but well located playground. This is a good place to go for a break from the market if you need one.

The Giant Buddha and Po Lin Monastery
Ngong Ping 360 (Cable Car) and Tai O Village
Lantau Island

大嶼山　昂坪
天壇天佛及寶蓮寺

8+

Po Lin Monastery Information – Tel: 2985-5248 or 2985-5426
Hong Kong Tourism Board – Tel: 2508-1234
Ngong Ping 360 – Tel: 3666-0606
New Lantao Bus Company – Tel: 2984-9848
Website: http://www.discoverhongkong.com/eng/attractions/outlying-giant-buddha.html
For general area map: Go to above website and find the google map attached.
First Ferry – Tel: 2131-8181
First Ferry website: http://www.nwff.com.hk/
Ngong Ping 360: http://www.np360.com.hk/html/eng/visitor/promotion.asp
New Lantao Bus Company website: http://www.newlantaobus.com/nlb.html

The Giant Buddha and Po Lin Monastery

Up on a beautiful mountaintop on Lantau Island sits a 250-ton, 34-metre-high bronze outdoor statue of Buddha. This is one of Hong Kong's top ten tourist attractions and among its most notable landmarks. Completed in 1993 on the grounds of the peaceful Po Lin (Precious Lotus) Monastery, this impressive statue is said to be the largest seated outdoor Buddha in the world.

When you arrive at the Tian Tan Buddha you will immediately feel the peacefulness of this spot. The impressive copper-bronze statue towers over you from above, beckoning you to climb the 268 steps (which the kids will enjoy counting) to its feet. The 360-degree views from the walkway around the statue are some of the most amazing in all of Hong Kong (provided it is not a foggy day). Inside this enormous bronze monument is an exhibition hall that covers some art and history relating to Buddhism, with some written explanations in English and Chinese as to the meaning and significance of the exhibits.

When you are finished at the top, head back down the stairs and over to the adjacent monastery. Founded in the early

1900s, this serene spot is still a functioning religious enclave where many monks live and pray. There are several temples, pavilions, gardens and other interesting exhibition areas in and around the grounds. There are also several restaurants, all run by the monks, that serve tasty and very reasonably priced vegetarian meals.

Ngong Ping 360 Cable Car Ride and Ngong Ping Village

As with so many sights that are an effort to get to, the journey to the Buddha is as much a part of the experience as the destination itself. One of the three ways to travel to the Giant Buddha is by taking the Ngong Ping 360, a 5.7-kilometre cable car ride that runs from the town of Tung Chung, near the airport, over the mountains of Lantau to the village of Ngong Ping where the Giant Buddha is located. This 25-minute ride has breathtaking views of the South China Sea, North Lantau Island, the Giant Buddha and Chek Lap Kok (Hong Kong International Airport). The cabins have windows on all sides which makes for great photo opportunities. At extra cost, you can select to ride in a special "Crystal Cabin" which has a glass floor as well as glass windows, a bit like a glass-bottomed boat ride but without the water beneath you.

When the Ngong Ping 360 cable car ride was built in 2005, it was part of a larger project which included the development of a small tourist village at the cable car alighting point. This new village, a five-minute walk from the Giant Buddha, is a reproduction of a traditional Chinese mountain town which houses more than a dozen restaurants, many shops and a few themed attractions. Kids might enjoy one of the entertainment options called Monkey's Tale Theatre, which is the tale of three monkey friends and their experience with greed, gluttony and friendship, told in an animated format with special effects and surround sound. The added attractions all require the purchase of a ticket.

The Village of Tai O

If you are very ambitious and wish to take on more of Lantau Island, the visit to the Buddha can be easily combined with a trip to Tai O, a quaint old fishing village where the houses sit on stilts. Sometimes referred to as "The Venice of the East" (though I personally feel this is not an appropriate reference), this quaint village is home to a community of fisherfolk who have built their homes on the water. Narrow little streets with bakeries, traditional Chinese shops with dried fish, a market, a few temples, and a few small bridges which connect some of the streets give visitors a glimpse into another way of life.

In Tai O you will also find numerous long, narrow boats for hire that offer tours around the waters of Lantau. These tours head to a geographic area that is home to the Chinese Pink Dolphin (also called the Indo-Pacific Humpback Dolphin). It is possible to hop on board one of these boats for a short trip to have a look at the pink dolphins. (Please note that there is a chapter in this book on the dolphin-watching tour which is run by scientists whose work it is to protect these endangered creatures. That tour is a much better option if you have a strong interest in these beautiful creatures.) If you are interested in adding Tai O Village to your day in Lantau, you can catch a bus from Ngong Ping Village which goes directly to Tai O (see **By Bus to Tai O** below).

Alternative Ways to Arrive at the Big Buddha:
Another very enjoyable way to reach Lantau is by ferry from Central. The ride is very picturesque as it takes you past the sights of Hong Kong and Kowloon along Victoria Harbour as well as along the coastlines of some of Hong Kong's outlying islands. Once you exit the ferry in Lantau in the village of Mui Wo, you will then need to board a bus to reach the Buddha. This 45-minute ride along a narrow and winding road affords amazing views of the South China Sea and the mountainous regions of this large outlying island.

For those who don't like heights or get sea sick, it is possible to avoid both the cable car and the ferry and arrive here by a combined option of MTR and bus. Please see "**The Best Ways of Getting There**" below for all the information on this option.

Seasons and Times
Giant Buddha: 10:00am-6:00pm daily.
Po Lin Monastery: 9:00am-6:00pm daily.
Ngong Ping 360: Monday to Friday 10:00am-6:00pm, Weekends and public holidays 9:00am-6:30pm.

Admission
Giant Buddha and Po Lin Monastery
Free; however, during peak visiting times (and sometimes other periods as well) you will need to buy a "meal" ticket from

the box office before you go up to the Buddha and access the exhibition halls located inside the monument. Charges seem to vary depending on the crowds but are roughly as follows:

Adult "snack" ticket – HK$23-$28

Adult vegetarian regular meal – HK$50-$55

Adult VIP vegetarian meal – HK$100

Two children's tickets will cost the price of one adult ticket. One child will likely not pay unless over 12. Once you have visited the Giant Buddha, proceed to the monastery for a meal at the time designated on your meal ticket.

Ngong Ping 360 and Ngong Ping Village

Tickets for the Cable Car Round Trip: Adults – HK$155, Children – HK$58

Tickets for the Cable Car Single Journey: Adults – HK$80, Children – HK$41

Tickets for Crystal Cabin Round Trip: Adults – HK$169, Children – HK$112

Tickets for Crystal Cabin Single Journey: Adults – HK$118, Children – HK$79

Village Entry – Free

Monkey Tale Theatre: Adults – HK$36, Children – HK$18

Walking with Buddha (show): Adults – HK$36, Children – HK$18

*Please check at Ngong Ping ticket window for special combined pricing and package deals.

Tai O Village – Free

Tai O Long Boat Rides – Prices starting at HK$20 per person. Negotiate your terms based on the number of people in your party.

The Best Ways of Getting There

By MTR/Ngong Ping Cable Car

- Take the MTR from **Central to Tung Chung** on the **Tung Chung Line** and exit the station at exit "**B**".
- At street level, look for signs for **Ngong Ping Cable Car** and walk five minutes through the plaza outside until you get to the escalator that takes you up to the ticket counter.
- ↔ Travel time: 35 mins (MTR) + 25 mins (cable car).

By Ferry/Bus

- Catch the ferry from **Outlying Island Ferry Pier #6 in Central** going to **Mui Wo**. The pier is located on the waterfront **behind** the **IFC complex** where the airport express train is located.

- The Lantau ferry has its own pier and is quite easy to find once you reach the harbour.

↔ Travel time: 30 mins ("fast" ferry) and 40 mins ("ordinary" ferry).

Once you arrive in Mui Wo you can either take a bus or a taxi to the Buddha.

By Bus

- When you exit the pier look for the bus terminus located directly in front of the ferry terminus. **Bus #2** will be marked: "**Po Lin Monastery/Big Buddha/Ngong Ping**".
- Buses are generally scheduled to meet the ferry as it arrives, so make sure you head directly to the bus stop.
- Alight the bus immediately in front of the Giant Buddha (Ngong Ping).

↔ Travel time: 40 mins (bus).

By Taxi

- A taxi from the Mui Wo Ferry Pier to the Big Buddha will cost HK$200+ and take 35-40 mins.

By MTR/Bus

- Take the MTR from **Central to Tung Chung** on the **Tung Chung Line** and exit the station at exit "**B**".
- At street level, look for **Bus #23** (New Lantao Bus Company) **to Ngong Ping**.

↔ Travel time: 35 mins (MTR) + 50 mins (bus).

***Alternatively:

- Take a taxi from Tung Chung MTR station to Ngong Ping.
- A taxi will cost HK$200+ and take 35-40 mins.

By Bus to Tai O from Ngong Ping

- Take bus **#21** from **Ngong Ping to Tai O**.
- The bus runs on the quarter-hour.

↔ Travel time: 20 mins (bus).

Getting a Bite

Po Lin Monastery:

For religious reasons, food at the Po Lin Monastery is vegetarian. There is a restaurant on the premises that is well known for its simple but tasty Chinese vegetarian cuisine. The menu is pre-selected for the day and is served to you without need for ordering. You simply buy a ticket and then go to the restaurant and your meal will be served. For picky eaters or toddlers, this is not a great option. The only other choice within the Monastery is the snack stand, which serves bowls of noodles and Chinese desserts.

Ngong Ping Village:
There are a dozen eateries and snack shops at this quaint stylized village including all of the following:
Ngong Ping Garden – Chinese restaurant
Zen Taiwanese Bistro – Taiwanese fare
Zen Noodle Café – Noodle shop
Ebeneezer's – Kebabs and pizza place
Subway – Sandwiches
Phoenix – Tea house
Euro Go Go – Coffee shop
Starbucks – Coffee shop
Sweet Paradise – Candy store
7-Eleven – Drinks and snacks

Mui Wo:
If you would like to go to Mui Wo and have a meal before your ferry back to Central then refer to the Mui Wo chapter "**Getting a Bite**" section for details on options.

What's Close?
Pui O Beach, **Cheung Sha Beach** and **Mui Wo and Bike Riding**.

Comments
- Best suited to children aged seven or older.
- Plan to spend a full day.
- Can get very crowded on Sundays and public holidays.
- The toilets at Ngong Ping Village at the base of the cable car are new and clean and sit-down style. The toilets at the base of the Buddha are the squat kind, though there is a sit-down one in the handicapped toilet. Some of the toilets inside the monastery are the sit-down variety.
- There is a baby-changing station in the handicapped toilet at the base of the Buddha as well as one in the village of Ngong Ping near the cable car terminus.
- A stroller will be useful in visiting Po Lin Monastery and the grounds surrounding it, Ngong Ping, and Tai O *but* to climb up to the Buddha, you will have to carry the stroller up 260+ steps or try to leave it below.
- There are many gift kiosks at the Monastery and in Ngong Ping Village where you can buy souvenirs of your visit.

Extra Info

The taxis on Lantau are blue and service the major sites on the island. The fares are posted at the Ngong Ping Bus Terminus for destinations including Mui Wo Ferry Pier and Tai O Village. If the bus line is very long, you may want to just take a taxi. Should you need to call a taxi from any location, the Lantau taxi service tel. is 2984-1328. Bear in mind it might be hard to get one at peak times, even if you call them.

Special Programs and Tours

Ngong Ping Nature Centre was opened in 2008 to promote "the green treasures of Hong Kong". They offer free guided walks featuring ecology and sightseeing spots in the general area of Ngong Ping. Their opening hours are: Monday to Friday 10:00am-6:00pm and Saturday, Sundays and public holidays 9:00am-6:30pm. Call 2259-3916 to book in advance or register in person. For more information: www.afcd.gov.hk or www.hkwalkers.net.

Word of Mouth

This is a good outing for adults and older children or children who are good travellers. However, though the Buddha is one of Hong Kong's most popular tourist attractions, it is not a great place to take very young children. If you are going to take them, the Ngong Ping Cable Car is the best option for the younger set as it is likely to take the shortest amount of time and it will be the most entertaining. Other options might be too long for them. The ferry ride can take up to 40 minutes and the bus ride is a 45-minute journey up a mountain. When you arrive at your destination, the attraction you have come to see is a 250-ton Buddha and a monastery complete with vegetarian restaurant. Most young children are not going to appreciate the serenity of the place or the natural beauty of the surroundings.

Sai Kung Town and Hap Mun Bay Beach
Sai Kung, New Territories

Tel: 2508-1234 (Hong Kong Tourism Board)
Website: http://www.travelinsaikung.org.hk/english/intro/index.aspx
Hap Mun Bay Beach, Sharp Island (Kaido from pier in Sai Kung)
Tel: 2796-6788
Website: http://www.lcsd.gov.hk/beach/en/beach-address-sk.php

Sai Kung Town

A combination old fishing village and modern weekend retreat for busy urbanites, this lovely seaside town is a wonderful place to come and spend a very laid-back afternoon (or morning or whole day) with the kids. Sai Kung Town is very easily navigated on foot, making it relaxing and easy to take in all the attractions the village has to offer, including: a strip of alfresco harbour-side Chinese seafood restaurants, Western-style pubs, restaurants and bakeries, an old Tin Hau Temple, a market square with a playground, a morning seafood market, an old village (within the town), narrow streets with craft and antique shops and a scenic harbour where you can hire kaidos (small, privately-operated boats) to take you across to some charming outlying islands.

A good place to start your exploration might be the Tin Hau Temple, located near the town's main thoroughfare called Po Tung Road. Built in the 13th century, it is one of the most important temples of its kind in Hong Kong and definitely worth a stop. From here, head down toward the water. On your right side you will find the "old town" of Sai Kung. The streets here are very narrow and provide a glimpse into the history of this century-old village. To the left of the temple (as you face the water) is the small town square with shops and pubs and a playground immediately in its centre, where local children recreate. As you approach the water, you will pass many side streets that have interesting little shops to peek into, including local crafts and antiques stores, as well as shops selling everything one might need for a beach outing.

The small harbour in Sai Kung is picturesque and can be appreciated in many ways. One idea would be to have lunch or dinner at one of the many Chinese outdoor seafood restaurants that line the waterfront. Kids will enjoy viewing the copious amounts of live mussels, crabs, prawns, squid, coloured fish and other interesting seafood displayed in tanks at each establishment. Another option is to take a walk on the pier. There are nice views from here and kids will enjoy seeing all the fishermen hard at work. For the best views, take the family out onto the water on a sampan (traditional Chinese work boat) for a toddle around the numerous small islands that make this area so special. Sampan rides are easy to come by near the pier, but make sure you negotiate a good rate before getting aboard.

Hap Mun Bay Beach

A great way to make a full day's outing out of a trip to this area is to visit this lovely beach located on Sharp Island off the coast of Sai Kung. In 2011, Hap Mun Bay was ranked by the *South China Morning Post* as having the #1 best water quality in all of Hong Kong. This secluded stretch of sand can only be reached by taking a kaido from the harbourfront in Sai Kung (see instructions). The adventure of getting to Hap Mun Bay Beach is part of the fun and affords you fantastic views of the surrounding mountains and rocky coastline. Well equipped, Hap Mun Bay has a refreshment kiosk, lifeguard service, a first aid station, changing rooms, toilets, outdoor showers and a swim raft. There are also several sitting-out areas with benches in the shade. Best of all, located just behind the beach is a grassy area with tables and BBQ pits for cooking out. Even if you are not interested in a barbecue, the kids might enjoy a run around on the grass.

Seasons and Times

Year-round, although lifeguards are only on duty from April to October.

Admission

Free

The Best Ways of Getting There

To Sai Kung
By MTR/Bus

- From Central or Admiralty to **Diamond Hill** station, take the red line to **Mongkok**. Transfer to the green line (across the platform at Mongkok station) to Diamond Hill, exit "**C2**".

0-99

新界　西貢
西貢市中心及廈門灣

- At street level catch KMB bus **#92** or **#96R** (only on Sundays and public holidays) going to **Sai Kung Bus Terminus**, located in front of the pier.
↔ Travel time: 25 mins (MTR) + 35-45 mins (bus).

By MTR/Mini Bus
- From Central or Admiralty to **Choi Hung** station, take the red line to **Mongkok**. Transfer to the green line (across the platform at Mongkok station) to Choi Hung, exit "**C2**".
- At street level catch minibus **#1A** or **#1M** to **Sai Kung Minibus Terminus**, located in front of the pier.
↔ Travel time: 25 mins (MTR) + 30 mins (minibus).

By Car
- From Central: Connaught Road→Harcourt Road→Gloucester Road→**Island Eastern Corridor (Route 4)→Eastern Harbour Tunnel.**
- In **tunnel** (**Route 2**) stay in **far right lane**. Once through tollbooth (HK$25) look for **Kwun Tong/Tseung Kwan O Tunnel** to your **right**.
- Once past the first sign get to the **far left lane** and follow signs to **Kwun Tong/Tseung Kwan O, left to Exit 2A**. After the exit, the **road splits** and you will **stay right** following signs for **Route 7** and **Tseung Kwan O Tunnel**. Make a **right at the light** and follow signs for the tunnel. You are now on **Tseung Kwan O Road**. Go through the toll (HK$3) and **stay left in the tunnel**.
- You will take **Exit 2A** to the left with signs for **Po Lam, Hang Hau and Sai Kung**.
- The road will split again, **stay right** and follow signs for **Sai Kung and Hang Hau**.
- You will come to your first of MANY roundabouts.
- At the **1st roundabout**, follow the sign for **Sai Kung**.
- At the **2nd roundabout** take the **1st left exit for Sai Kung**.
- At the **3rd roundabout** take the 1st exit with a sign marked "**University, Kowloon, Sai Kung**". You are now on Hiram's Highway.
- At the **4th roundabout** take the first left marked "**Kowloon and Sai Kung**". **Stay right** and **follow signs to Sai Kung** when the road splits. You are still on **Hiram's Highway**.
- At the **5th roundabout**, follow signs for **Ho Chung and Sai Kung**. You will pass Marina Cove and Hebe Haven Marina on your right. Hiram's Highway will turn into **Po Tung Road** which runs right into **Sai Kung Town**.

P 2-hour metered parking→off **Po Tung Road** (to your right as you enter town).

P For parking garages on **Chan Man Street**→right at the roundabout (the first one you come to once in the centre of town) to **Fuk Man Road**→right onto Chan Man Street. Look for the big blue **"P"** signs for parking.

By Taxi
A taxi from Central will cost HK$190-$230 and take 45-55 mins.

To Hap Mun Bay Beach
By Kaido
- Head to the **harbourfront** in **Sai Kung**. Approach any of the kaido services stands.
- Buy a ticket to **Hap Mun Bay Beach**. Round trip ticket – approximately HK$20-$22.
  (*Tip: Make sure you keep your ticket for your return journey and note the colour of the flag your kaido is flying as you must return on the same colour boat. Kaidos return to town every 20-30 minutes, or more frequently on Sundays and public holidays.*)
- On the way to Hap Mun Bay, you will pass rocky Kiu Tsui Beach.

↔ Travel time: 20 mins (kaido).

Getting a Bite
Sai Kung is a diner's paradise. There are many different cuisines to choose from. On the main street, Po Tung Road (or just off of it), you will find fast food, Korean, Indian, Japanese and Italian (including a popular pizza joint called *Pepperoni's*, tel: 2792-2083). In the centre of town (near and around the town square), there are many Western-style restaurants and pubs including *Jaspa's Restaurant* (tel: 2792-6388) which has a kids' menu. Down by the pier are more than a dozen outdoor Chinese seafood restaurants. The food in Sai Kung is generally both fresh and tasty, so you can't really go wrong. If you want to grab some great snacks for the beach, stop in at the *Ali-Oli Bakery Café* (tel: 2792-2655) in the town square for tasty bread, pastries and cookies. (This bakery is well known for their delicious bread rolls.) There is also a highly-rated Chinese snack bar on Po Tung Road, *Honeymoon Dessert House* or "Mun Kee" in Chinese, that sells unique local desserts.

What's Close?
Trio Beach/Hebe Haven, Sai Kung Country Park Walk at Pak Tam Chung and Kiu Tsui Beach.

Comments
- Suitable for all ages.
- Plan to spend half a day here, more if you are going to the beach.
- The town and beach can be very crowded on Sundays and public holidays, particularly in the summer months.
- There are public toilets in and around Sai Kung Town. For a sit-down one, you may need to go to the handicapped toilet inside the wet market in the government building. The beach has toilets, though only one stall has a sit-down one.
- There are no baby-changing tables in the public toilets in town or on the beach. The beach changing room has benches that could serve the purpose.
- Sai Kung Town is stroller-friendly. The beach is harder with a stroller, though not impossible. The walk from the pier to the sand is 80% flat and paved but there are a few steps every so often.

Extra Info
Should you find yourself in Sai Kung Town early in the morning, go down to the waterfront area and have a look at the wholesale fish market.

Word of Mouth
There is a branch of the **Hong Kong SPCA (Society for the Prevention of Cruelty to Animals)** around the corner from the seafood restaurants near the pier. The kids will LOVE playing with the puppies that are waiting for adoption. Don't forget the hand wipes and be forewarned that if you do go for a visit, kids will be asking to take one of these lovelies home! The address if you want to brave it is: No.7, Sha Tsui Path, Sai Kung, 2792-1535.

Sok Kwu Wan Village
Lamma Island, Outlying Islands

南丫島　索罟灣

Tel: 2508-1234 (Hong Kong Tourism Board)
Website: http://www.lamma.com.hk/
For area map: http://www.compunicate.com/Lamma/Blog/Map-DC-1.jpg
Central ferry (HKKF Co.) Tel: 2815-6063
Central ferry website: www.hkkf.com.hk
Aberdeen ferry (Chuen Kee Ferry Co. Ltd.) Tel: 2375-7883
Aberdeen ferry website: http://www.ferry.com.hk/eng/service.htm
Lo So Shing Beach Tel: 2982-8252
Lo So Shing Beach website:
http://www.lcsd.gov.hk/beach/en/beach-address-is.php
Lamma Fisherfolk Village
Sok Kwu Wan Fish Raft, Lamma Island
Reception: Ground Floor, 5 First Street, next to Sok Kwu Wan Pier #1.
Tel: 2982-8585
Website: www.fisherfolks.com.hk

0-99

Take the kids on a dining adventure at the seafood haven of Sok Kwu Wan. The ferry is fun and quick and drops you immediately in the heart of the village. There are no cars here, or roads for that matter, just a narrow covered sidewalk that runs the length of a lane of restaurants. Kids will enjoy looking at the seafood tanks in front of each eatery that are filled with everything edible that lives in the sea. Live fish, shrimp, crabs, lobsters, mussels, clams, sea cucumbers and other delicacies are on display just waiting for their turn to be chosen (read: Eaten!). These restaurants are all reasonably priced (especially for groups), although there are some items that are very expensive (like spotted garoupa) so be sure to ask the price before you make your selection, especially if on the menu it reads "Market Price".

All the eateries here overlook the water, are covered though not enclosed, and have multiple fans moving air around from the ceiling to keep the place comfortable even in the hot summer months. Dominating the views from the restaurants are multiple fish farming rafts that for some kids will be very interesting to observe. After your meal, walk to the southernmost end of the strip and check out the Tin Hau Temple. Make sure to hit one of the ice cream stands on the way back toward the ferry, as this too is part of the experience.

A wonderful add-on to any trip with kids to Sok Kwu Wan is the **Lamma Fisherfolk Village**, located on a series of large rafts floating near the main ferry pier. This 2,000-square-metre exhibit was designed to promote the history and way of life of Hong Kong's fisherfolk people and their culture as well as the history of the local fishing industry. A variety of both passive and active exhibits bring the old ways of fishing and living to life. Kids can enter an authentic fishing junk and get a view of a floating home, watch a demonstration and learn the fishing tricks of traditional Hong Kong fisherfolk, learn about dragon boating and beat the dragon boating drums, and best of all do some actual FISHING themselves! The reception and ticket booth for this exhibit is on land just in front of the exit of Pier 1 on Sok Kwu Wan. Tickets can be purchased there and a boat arranged to access the floating village.

If you wish to make more out of your journey here, there are a few options. Lo So Shing Beach, located just 20 minutes away on a footpath, is a good choice for a quiet visit to the beach. This secluded stretch of sand has lifeguard service, a swim raft, showers, toilets, changing facilities, shaded picnic benches and a beautiful new BBQ area that is on a small peninsula which juts out into the sea. What is missing, however, is a refreshment kiosk so be sure to stop in town and load up on provisions, or bring them from your home base. To get to Lo So Shing Beach, walk north through town past the Tin Hau Temple and follow the signs for Lo So Shing and Yung Shue Wan. About 10 minutes into the walk you will come to a school. Here the road forks and you will want to go to the left. Follow the path and signs to the beach. One point of interest en route is Cave Kamikaze, a series of grottos used by the Japanese in World War II to hide boats meant for suicide missions against Allied naval vessels. There are informational plaques on site.

If you have a whole day on the island, why not walk/hike from Sok Kwu Wan to Yung Shue Wan? For those with older kids or loads of energy this is a beautiful way to see the island. To access the path, head toward the temple and follow the paved path toward Lo So Shing Beach (as above) but veer right at the fork in the road. The journey takes 90 minutes or so. The road is paved for the entire length, and has pretty views along the way though beware that it is NOT flat and will be a challenge for some kids and adults too. (See the **Yung Shue Wan** chapter for more details.)

Seasons and Times
Lo So Shing Beach: Year-round although lifeguards are only on duty from April to October.
Lamma Fisherfolk Village: 10:00am-7:00pm daily.

Admission
Lamma Fisherfolk Village:
Adult HK$60, Children and Seniors HK$50
For some of the fishing on board there is an extra charge.

The Best Ways of Getting There
By Ferry
There are two places on Hong Kong Island where you can catch the ferry to **Sok Kwu Wan: Central Outlying Island Ferry Pier** and **Aberdeen Promenade**.

From Central
- Catch the modern, enclosed and air-conditioned ferry at **Outlying Island Ferry Pier #4** in Central. The pier is located on the waterfront, behind the IFC complex, where the airport express train is located.
- The Lamma ferry has its own pier and is quite easy to find once you reach the harbour.
- The ferry leaves roughly every half-hour (see website for schedules).
- ↔ Travel time: 20 mins (ferry).

From Aberdeen
- Catch this old-fashioned, two-tiered ferry from the **Aberdeen Pier** located at the waterfront promenade in Aberdeen, very near the **Aberdeen fish market**.
- Look for a small pier with a time schedule and sign that reads Sok Kwu Wan – Chuen Kee Ferry.
- The ferry from Aberdeen leaves roughly hourly on the weekends and less frequently during the weekdays.
- ↔ Travel time: 25-30 mins (ferry).
  (Tip: The Sok Kwu Wan ferry pier is located in the heart of this small village.)

By Kaido
- Go to the **Aberdeen waterfront promenade** and hire a privately-operated little boat (kaido) to take you across to Lamma.
- There are many people milling about at the promenade just waiting for someone who wants to be taken across, so don't worry about finding them, they will find you.

- Make sure to negotiate a price before getting aboard.
- ↔ Travel time: 20-25 mins (kaido).

Getting a Bite
The entire village is all about eating so you should walk the strip and pick a place that looks good to you. ***Rainbow Seafood Restaurant***, one of the largest and most well known eateries, offers free ferry service to and from Central for its customers. You must first call them to make a reservation if you would like to use this special service (tel: 2982-8100).

What's Close?
Yung Shue Wan Village

Comments
- Suitable for all ages.
- Plan to spend at least two hours here.
- The area can get very crowded on weekends and public holidays.
- There are two public toilets en route worth noting. One is located immediately next to the exit of the pier for the Central ferry at Sok Kwu Wan. (There are two piers here, one for the Central ferry, one for the Aberdeen ferry.) The other is located at the beach. Both have sit-down toilets in some of the stalls.
- There is a baby-changing table at the public toilet located at the pier.
- The area is stroller-friendly, though crowds might make it difficult at times as the main walk is narrow. The last few portions of the walk down to the beach are not paved and have some steps to navigate just before you hit the sand.

Extra Info
All the restaurants on the island offer the ferry schedules (usually printed on the back of their business cards), so you can check with them to try to time the ending of your meal.

Word of Mouth
If you plan on going to the beach, try going first thing in the morning and wind up in the village for an early lunch. This way you will not only beat the restaurant crowds, but also the heat, as mornings are generally cooler than afternoons.

Yung Shue Wan Village
Lamma Island, Outlying Islands

南丫島

榕樹灣

Tel: 2508-1234 (Hong Kong Tourism Board)
Website for downloadable basic map of Lamma:
http://www.discoverhongkong.com/eng/attractions/outlying-lamma-island.html
HKKF ferry Tel: 2815-6063 (24-hour service hotline)
Ferry website: http://www.hkkf.com.hk/
Hung Shing Yeh Beach Tel: 2982-0352 or 2852-3220
Hung Shing Yeh Beach website:
http://www.lcsd.gov.hk/beach/en/beach-address-is.php

Hop aboard the ferry and head out to Yung Shue Wan, a village that marches to the beat of its own drummer. Part old Chinese fishing village, part Western bohemia circa early 1970s and part holiday retreat, this island town offers a laid-back outing that all members of the family will enjoy.

You can have a full day out here by taking in the village sights, having a walk and relaxing on the beach, or do much less and just take a stroll and have a meal. The pace is slow here. There is no traffic, except for bicycles and perhaps the odd motorized cart, and the buildings are all low-rise and near the sea. Kids will enjoy walking the narrow lanes and stopping to have a look in the craft shops and other local stalls selling everything from beach toys to dried fish. At the very end of Yung Shue Wan Main Street is a small Tin Hau Temple dating back to the 1870s. If you do nothing else here, you must have a meal. The island is known for its Cantonese seafood restaurants, most of which are right on the water with outdoor seating. If seafood is not popular with your group, there are plenty of other options available.

0-99

For a more adventurous day, see the village and then have a walk that leads you to a lovely beach. To access the path, walk through town, following the signs for Hung Shing Yeh Beach. You will stay on Yung Shue Wan Main Street until it intersects with Yung Shue Wan Back Street and then make a left. (If you find yourself at the temple, you have gone too far.) From here it is a 20-minute walk on a paved narrow lane through greenery and a few clusters of residences before you reach the beach.

Hung Shing Yeh Beach has a resort-like feel to it. There are snack stands that rent umbrellas, an inn right on the beach that has an alfresco restaurant, and, at the very far end, a small but quaint organic farm called **Herboland** (tel: 9094-6206) that grows, displays and sells its healthy produce. It has a bunny hutch that is sure to make the little ones happy. Amenities at this beach include lifeguards, a first aid station, showers, changing rooms, BBQ areas and toilets, making it very easy to have a relaxing time.

If you have older kids and/or are feeling very energetic, you can walk from this beach to the other main village on Lamma called Sok Kwu Wan. (Total distance between towns is around 3km.) You can pick up the family trail on the opposite end of the beach from where you came. This 60+ minute walk will take you past lovely scenic vistas and, about halfway between town en route, there is often a brave man with a cart selling ice cream and cold drinks in a rest area. Aim for him and take a break there with the kids. It is mostly downhill from the man onward (even if the man is not there, this spot is a great place to sit down, take in the view and have some water). Once you get to Sok Kwu Wan, there are many seafood restaurants to choose from. (See the **Sok Kwu Wan** chapter for more information.) You can also get a ferry from here back to Hong Kong Island, making the hike a one-way affair. You can push a stroller on the trail, many people do, but there are a few steep parts and a few areas of the path that have uneven stones.

Seasons and Times
Year-round, although lifeguards are only on duty from April to October.

Admission
Free

The Best Ways of Getting There
By Ferry
There are two places on Hong Kong Island where you can catch the ferry to Yung Shue Wan: **Central Outlying Island Ferry Pier** and **Aberdeen Promenade**.
From Central
• Catch the ferry from **Outlying Island Ferry Pier #4 in Central**. The pier is located on the waterfront, behind the IFC complex, where the airport express train is located.

- The Lamma ferry has its own pier and is quite easy to find once you reach the harbour.
- The ferry departs roughly hourly or more frequently depending on the time of day. (See website or telephone number for schedules.)

↔ Travel time: 20-30 mins (depending on whether or not you take the high-speed ferry).

From Aberdeen

- Catch the ferry from the **Aberdeen Pier** located at the waterfront promenade in Aberdeen, near the **Aberdeen fish market.** *(Tip: Look for a small playground as a marker.)*
- The pier is well marked with a **HKKF ferry banner** in white and blue (check to make sure the posted time table reads "to Yung Shue Wan").
- The ferry from Aberdeen leaves roughly hourly or more frequently depending on the time of day.

↔ Travel time: 20 mins (ferry)

(Tip: The Yung Shue Wan ferry pier is located in the heart of this small village.)

Getting a Bite

Yung Shue Wan Village is known for its outdoor Cantonese-style seafood restaurants and in fact many local Hong Kong residents come here just for the food. The restaurants are too numerous to name, but a good bet would be to pick one with an outdoor area overlooking the water. Other restaurant fare in the village includes Indian, Japanese, Thai, Italian, vegetarian and international cuisine. There is even a restaurant which specializes in pigeon, called *Han Lok Yuen Pigeon Restaurant* (tel: 2982-0608) on the way to the beach. (Look for the signs as you approach the beach.)

Hung Shing Yeh Beach has a restaurant called the *Concerto Inn Garden Cafe* (tel: 2982-1662). The restaurant offers kid-friendly food options such as pasta and pizza and also serves a variety of both international and Asian food. The side terrace of the lovely café has an outdoor toddler play area for kids to enjoy while parents take in a leisurely meal by the sea. The restaurant is a small operation, so if you plan to eat there, make sure you call ahead to see if they can accommodate you.

What's Close?
Sok Kwu Wan Village

Comments

- Suitable for all ages.
- Plan to spend at least half a day here.
- The area can get very crowded on weekends and public holidays. Try to come in the morning, as it is much less crowded then.
- There are two public toilets en route. One is located near the pier on your left. The other is located at the beach. Both have sit-down toilets in some of the stalls.
- There is a baby-changing table at the public toilet located three minutes from the pier on your left side as you head toward town.
- The area is stroller-friendly, though crowds might make it difficult at times, as the main walkway is narrow.

Extra Info

There is a large power station on Lamma Island which is clearly visible from this beach. Kids probably won't care about their view of the sea being obstructed, but parents might. One way to minimize the unsightliness is to stay on the north side of the beach (very near the entrance to the beach from the trail). From there the station is not visible.

Word of Mouth

- At the beach, children will enjoy frolicking in the water, especially the small rock outcropping that juts into the sea and has a few small pools that collect water between the boulders. Be aware, though, that at the edges of the rocks are some small molluscs with sharp edges that can cut feet very easily.
- On the way to the beach, on Yung Shue Wan Back Street before the village ends and before the path turns into more of a trail, there is a shop on the right hand side that has bikes for rent. Look for the bikes and the bike rental sign. Remember there are no cars here so this is a great place to ride around.

Bike Riding in the New Territories

Sha Tin Park to Tai Po Waterfront Park
No. 2 Yuen Wo Road, Sha Tin Park, Sha Tin, New Territories

Tel: 2695-9253 (Sha Tin Park)
Tel: 2664-2107 (Tai Po Waterfront Park)
Website for Sha Tin Park: http://www.lcsd.gov.hk/parks/stp/en/index.php
For map of Sha Tin Park: Go to the above website and click on "Location Map"
Website for Tai Po Waterfront Park: http://www.lcsd.gov.hk/parks/tpwp/en/index.php
For map of Tai Po Waterfront Park: Go to the above website and click on "Location Map".
Tel: In Sha Tin Park, Bike Kiosk #1 and #2: 2602-6862, Bike Kiosk #3: 2603-0498, 6201-6852 (mobile number) – website: www.power3cycle.com.hk

新界 沙田
源禾路2號 沙田
沙田公園

0-99

Around the scenic Tolo Harbour area is a (nearly) flat, designated bike path that runs between two outstanding parks, offering a fantastic way to enjoy the beauty of the New Territories with your kids. This special outing is relatively hassle-free and will be fun for everyone. You don't even need to invest in your own bikes; they can be rented cheaply and easily on the spot!

Sha Tin Park and Tai Po Waterfront Park both have bike kiosks where you can hire bicycles to meet each family member's needs. The bikes come in all sizes and kinds, including small kids' bikes with training wheels, mid-sized bikes, adult bikes (which can be fitted with child seats in the back), tandem bikes and family bikes which are large three-wheelers with bench seats and tops for shade. The bike shops in both parks are related to one another, allowing the luxury of a one-way ride, starting at one park and returning the bikes at another (with a small drop-off fee per bike).

The path itself is designed for bicycles, making it a very peaceful ride without the noise and worry that comes with car traffic (though you will need to look out for bike traffic en route). The trail is quite scenic. From Sha Tin you will be riding along the Shing Mun River, passing Yuen Wo Playground and the Sha Tin Racecourse. The middle section is more industrial but as you approach Tai Po you will be riding along the very picturesque Tolo Harbour with views of Ma On Shan, one of Hong Kong's highest mountain peaks.

The parks on either end of this lovely trail are half the reason to come here. Sha Tin Park's more than eight hectares of land are jam-packed with kid-friendly stuff, including two themed playgrounds with castles, dinosaurs and sand pits, a rock garden, an azalea garden, an aviary, a waterfall, lawns designated for "family games" and a refreshment kiosk along the river. It is also a five-minute walk to Sha Tin New Town Plaza and Snoopy's World, which makes a visit here even more attractive (see the **Snoopy's World and Sha Tin New Town Plaza** chapter). Tai Po Waterfront Park offers similar fare and is an outstanding park worthy of its own entry in this book. (See the **Tai Po Waterfront Park** chapter.) The distance between the two parks is 11.1 kilometres and will take around 70 minutes if you bike at a leisurely pace without making any stops along the way.

To go from Sha Tin Park to Tai Po Waterfront Park is relatively straightforward. Follow the river and signs for Tai Po Waterfront Park. When you reach a fork in the road (about 4 km into the trip) you will head off to the left. If you go to the right, you will be crossing the river and heading for Ma On Shan, which is also a lovely ride but is more hilly and for some kids might be too much of a challenge. As you carry on toward Tai Po, the route is well marked until you get to the park itself. It is important that, once you pass Yuen Chau Tsai Park on your right side, you begin looking for the bridge to cross the Lam Tsuen River. Once across the river, make an immediate right turn into the park. (Though the sign will tell you to carry on straight ahead, this will not lead you to the bike kiosks to return the bikes.) This path, which runs along the Lam Tsuen River's edge (the river that will be on your right once you make the right turn), takes you to the bike rental kiosks about 1 km ahead on your left.

There are other places in the New Territories to rent bikes and access these paths, including Tai Wai, Tai Po Market and Plover Cove. (Bike rental shops in these areas are all located within walking distance of the MTR stations.) The path described in this chapter is in my opinion the best choice for families because of the two parks on either end and because of the one-way bike drop-off option it provides. If your family is big on biking, why not pave your own way and begin from another location? Happy trails.

Seasons and Times
Though available year-round, this activity is most enjoyable from October to April before the heat is at its worst.
Bike shops are open from 9:00am-7:00pm daily.

Admission
Park admission is free.
For bike rentals, use the following price list as a guideline ONLY as prices vary from vendor to vendor and from day to day*:
Kids Bikes – 12"-16" wheels:
HK$15 per hour (Mon-Sat) + HK$5 (Sun & public holidays).
+ Training wheels: HK$20
Bikes 16"-20" wheels:
HK$20 per hour (Mon-Sat) + HK$5 (Sun & public holidays).
Bikes 24"-26" wheels:
HK$25 per hour (Mon-Sat) + HK$5 (Sun & public holidays).
Two seaters (tandem bikes):
HK$40 per hour (Mon-Sat) + HK$5 (Sun & public holidays).
Family bikes (three-wheelers):
HK$60 per hour (Mon-Sat) + HK$5 (Sun & public holidays).
Quality speed bikes:
HK$40 per hour (Mon-Sat) + HK$5 (Sun & public holidays).
Basket or seat:
HK$5
Helmet or bike lock or lights:
All HK$10 per option
PLEASE NOTE: If you plan to ride only one way there will be a small surcharge to return the bikes at another location.
*Price by the day for ALL bikes is negotiable.

The Best Ways of Getting There
By MTR
• From **Central** or **Admiralty** to **Kowloon Tong Station**, take the red line to **Mongkok**. **Transfer to the green line** (across the platform at Mongkok Station) to **Kowloon Tong**.
• In Kowloon Tong Station look for the **East Rail**. Ride it to **Sha Tin**.
• When you exit the MTR station look for exit **"A"** marked "**New Town Plaza**".

Walking (from MTR station)

• Follow signs for **Sha Tin Plaza and Sha Tin Town Hall** (through the eastern turnstiles to the concourse lined with shops). Walk through the mall, past the Marks & Spencer Department Store toward Snoopy's World (you will now be outdoors).

• From here **cross the pedestrian walkover** to **Sha Tin Town Hall**. When you see the front doors of the Hall **turn right, walking around the building perimeter** then turn left and walk toward the **Sha Tin Marriage Registry**.

• You will see a set of **stairs** to **the right of the Registry**, which will take you down to street level and then straight into the park.

• **Walk toward the water**, directly ahead, and make a left and walk along the riverfront until you see the **bike kiosks on your left**.

↔ Travel time: 20 mins (MTR) + 10-15 mins (East Rail) + 10 mins (walk).

(Tip: Walk toward the water and you will find the park).

By Car

• From **Central**: Connaught Road→Harcourt Road→Gloucester Road→**Island Eastern Corridor (Route 4)**→ **Cross Harbour Tunnel (Route 1).**

• In tunnel stay in right lane. Once through tollbooth (HK$20) stay right and follow signs for **Ho Man Tin and Sha Tin**.

• Stay in centre lane, you are now on **Princess Margaret Road**. Follow signs for **Sha Tin** and **Lion Rock Tunnel (Route 1)**. Go through tunnel (HK$8). You are now on **Lion Rock Tunnel Road**.

• Take the **exit** on the left for "**Sha Tin Central**" Exit 11A. Follow this road around across a small bridge over the **Shing Mun River Channel**.

• After you pass the **Heritage Museum on your left**, make a right turn on **Sha Tin Centre Street and this road will curve around to the left** and you will see the various phases of **New Town Plaza on both the right and the left**. There are many underground car parks in the nearby area to choose from. Look for the **"P"** signs and park in any one of them.

*Follow the **Walking** directions above from the MTR station to Sha Tin Park.*

By Taxi
A taxi from Central will cost HK$150-$170 and take 35-40 mins.

Getting a Bite
If you are planning to bicycle one way from Sha Tin Park to Tai Po Waterfront Park, it might be best to have a meal before you head out because Tai Po Waterfront Park does not have any restaurant options, though there are refreshment kiosks. Try the eateries in Sha Tin New Town Plaza Mall (see **Getting a Bite** in the **Snoopy's World/Sha Tin New Town Plaza** chapter). Another option is to bring a picnic with you in a backpack and enjoy it in Tai Po. Alternatively, there is a floating restaurant on the opposite side of the Shing Mun River in Sha Tin (where there is also a bike path) called *Star Seafood Floating Restaurant* (tel: 2635-3788) which you could stop at on the way. To get to the floating restaurant, you will have to bike across one of the many bridges that cross the Shing Mun River. It is easy to spot as it is a marble-looking barge right on the riverbank.

What's Close?
Hong Kong Heritage Museum, **Snoopy's World and Sha Tin New Town Plaza**, **Penfold Park,** **10,000 Buddhas Monastery** (see **Snoopy's World and Sha Tin New Town Plaza Chapter** for details) and IKEA.

Comments
- Suitable for all ages, but best for children who are competent at bike riding.
- Plan to spend two to three hours biking and/or touring around the parks.
- The bike path can get crowded on Sundays and public holidays, try to get here early to have your pick of bikes.
- There are toilets in Sha Tin Park and Tai Po Waterfront Park that are the sit-down variety. There is one other toilet en route just outside Sha Tin Park near the Yuen Wo Playground.
- There are baby-changing stations in both Sha Tin Park and Tai Po Waterfront Park.
- It is best not to bring your stroller if you are biking. Instead, rent a family bike or put your child in a bike seat on the back of an adult bicycle.

Extra Info

Make sure you ask at your chosen bike kiosk for a free printed map of the bike trail.

Word of Mouth

If you have very little kids, or kids who can ride but not for long distances, then why not rent bikes for one hour only and ride around either of the two parks along the river or harbour? The most interesting parts of this 11-kilometre bike path lie within or near the boundaries of Sha Tin Park and Tai Po Waterfront Park.

Cheung Chau Island
Cheung Chau, Outlying Islands

長
洲

Tel: 2508-1234 (Hong Kong Tourism Board)
Website: http://www.discoverhongkong.com/eng/local-tours/outlying-cheungchau-island.html
Ferry Tel: 2131-8181
Ferry website: www.nwff.com.hk
Tung Wan Beach Tel: 2981-8389
Tung Wan Beach website:
http://www.lcsd.gov.hk/beach/en/beach-address-is.php
For area map: Go to website above and click on "Location Map".

0-99

Feel like taking the kids on an adventure? Why not try one of Hong Kong's most popular outlying islands, Cheung Chau? This small picturesque island has something for everyone, including beaches, walking trails, temples and, best of all, a real pirate's cave that can be explored. There are no cars here, which not only provides for a peaceful environment, but also helps to preserve the timeless nature of the place (and gives parents one thing less to worry about).

Cheung Chau is shaped like a dumbbell. The village sits smack in the middle on the narrowest area of the island, essentially the handle of the dumbbell, so it only takes minutes from this juncture to walk from the west side (where the ferry docks) to the east side where Tung Wan Beach lies. To arrive at the seashore, walk off the ferry pier (located on Pak She Praya Road) and find Tung Wan Road directly opposite the exit. From ferry to sand is about a five-minute walk. At the entrance to the beach are several small stands that sell snacks, beach toys and mats and will rent beach umbrellas for a small fee and a deposit.

When your little ones need a break from sand castle building, go for a walk on Cheung Chau Beach Road (the fancy name for the sidewalk that runs parallel to the beach). A short walk north is a monument dedicated to Lee Lai-shan (locally known as San San), a female windsurfer who won Hong Kong's first Olympic gold medal in Atlanta in 1996. It is notable because she honed her skills right here. The centre where she practiced is on the far south side of the beach (to your right as you face the water). Walk toward the Windsurfing Centre, where they rent windsurfers and ocean kayaks by the hour, and stop in at the cafe for a drink. On the way, there is a small playground on the right side.

The village itself is very quaint and easily negotiated. Head back from the beach to the pier on Tung Wan Road and bear right onto San Hing Street. San Hing, which turns into Pak She Street, is the main street in town and is filled with interesting little shops which tell a good story about the way life is lived on Cheung Chau. Here there are vegetable stands, barber shops, local grocers, clothing stores, fish stalls, bakeries and candy stores. Of particular interest to the children will be the fish stalls where the goods are displayed live, the candy stores which are easily accessible to small hands and the bakeries which are essential to stop in and have a Chinese egg tart (a small yellow custard tart which is a local specialty and almost always served warm – fabulous!)

Situated at the very end of Pak She Street (north) is the Pak Tai Temple. Colourful statuettes of the Green Dragon and the White Tiger will be a draw for the whole family in this 18th-century Taoist shrine. When Cheung Chau hosts its famous "Bun Festival" in the late spring, this holy place is the centre of the action.

The south side of the island is well worth exploring with kids, but be sure to warn them ahead of time that there is significant walking involved. Start your hike at the south end of Tung Wan Beach. Find the steep path behind the Warwick Hotel and climb upwards toward Kwan Kung Pavilion located on Kwun Yam Wan Road (a right turn at the top of the hill). The colourful Kwan Kung Pavilion is dedicated to the Taoist God of War and Righteousness. After visiting the shrine, exit left and then immediately afterward bear left again and find the main path heading south (away from town) called Peak Road. This countryside trail permits a leisurely stroll through the heart of the residential part of the island as you head toward a lovely remote beach and a pirate's cave. Along the way is an unusual cemetery that has lovely views of the waters below.

Anywhere from 30 to 60 minutes later, depending on how fast little feet will move, will be a sign for Pak Tso Wan Beach. Following the path to the left for several minutes, you will come upon a beautiful, isolated beach with stunning seaside vistas from the trail above. If a picnic on Cheung Chau were a part of your plans, then this would be the ideal spot to set up your blanket.

From Pak Tso Wan Beach, it is possible to continue toward Cheung Po Tsai Cave by taking a side path that is interesting and challenging. Follow the steps up on the right, keeping the water on the left. As you climb, you will find large flat stones sticking out over the edge of the cliffs. The views from these stones are arresting, but bear in mind there is no railing, so exercise extreme caution should you wish to stand on the rocks for a photo. At the end of the paved part of the trail is yet another beach called Po Yue Wan. To pick up the remains of the trail, navigate very carefully to the other side of the beach by crossing the sand and then skipping over the stones. (Be sure to wear good walking shoes.) Stay on the trail and walk up the hill to find Cheung Po Tsai Cave on your right side.

> *NOTE: If you are not interested in the more challenging route to the Cave, then do not make the left turn at the sign for Pak Tso Wan Beach. Instead, stay on the main path until you see the signs for Cheung Po Tsai Cave.*

There is no doubt that this old pirate's cave will be the highlight of your children's visit to Cheung Chau if they are adventurers at heart. This small cave is said to have belonged to a notorious pirate back in the Ching dynasty. A flashlight is needed to get through this narrow cavern. Bring one along, or sometimes one can be rented from a local villager who smartly sets up in front of the cave to "lend" one out for around HK$10 with a HK$20 deposit. Those carrying backpacks or bags may wish to leave them with someone from the group who is not going through. The time it takes to get from one end of the cave to the other is only about five minutes.

After cave exploration, head to the main trail (not the beach path you came from) and within five minutes you should spot the pier at Sai Wan. Here you can get a kaido (a small motorized ferry boat) to take you back to the village. They run about every 20 minutes. The cost of the ride will be anywhere from HK$3 to HK$15, depending on the boat that takes you, but do make sure to determine the price before you get aboard. The 10-minute boat ride back to town weaves through Cheung Chau's small but crowded harbour filled with fishing junks that also serve as houseboats for some of the island's residents.

Even if your kids aren't walkers, you can still get to the cave without too much trouble. Take a kaido from the main ferry pier in Cheung Chau village to Sai Wan. From there, follow the signs to the cave (about 5-10 minutes' walk). When you have explored the cave and taken in the views from this side of the island, head back to the kaido ferry pier and wait for the boat back to the main part of town.

There are many more temples, shrines, beaches and landmarks on the island than what has been described above. Why not explore and find your own path and interesting sights? The island is small, so it is hard to get more than a little lost. Enjoy!

Seasons and Times
Year-round, though lifeguards are only on duty at the beach from April to end of October.

Admission
Free

The Best Ways of Getting There
By "Ordinary" Ferry
- Catch the ferry to **Cheung Chau** from **Outlying Island Ferry Pier #5 in Central**. The pier is located on the waterfront behind the IFC complex where the airport express train is located.
- There are **two speeds of ferries** that go to the island from the same pier: **the Ordinary Ferry (slow) and the Fast Ferry**. The schedule **alternates every other departure**.
- For the **Ordinary Ferry there are two classes of tickets**: Ordinary and deluxe (only marginally more expensive).
  Tip: The advantage of sailing in deluxe is the ability to access the outside deck seats at the back of the ship, though there is indoor deluxe seating as well. On a day without rain, it is lovely to sit out on the deck in one of the chairs provided while sipping a refreshment from the snack bar. It is also less crowded in the deluxe cabin whether you are inside or out.
- The ferries generally run every half-hour on the hour, but it would be best to call for details before you set out. The ferry schedule can be obtained by calling the ferry's hotline or checking the website.

↔ Travel time: 30-35 mins (fast ferry) or 50-55 mins (ordinary ferry).

Tip: The Cheung Chau Island ferry pier is located right in the middle of the island's main village.

Getting a Bite

Do not leave the island without enjoying a meal here. Casual is the theme and the food is fresh and delicious. Along Pak She Praya Road, north or south, are a number of alfresco style restaurants to choose from which are very popular and serve Cantonese style seafood in a very casual environment. Here are a list of some of the other options:

Alan Café – Breakfast, lunch and tea – 39 Hoi Pong Street

Bay View Chinese Restaurant – Warwick Hotel on Tung Wan Beach

Cheung Kee Fish Ball Noodles – Most popular noodle place in Cheung Chau – G/F, 83A Tai Sun Back Street

East Lake Restaurant – serves international fare, located on Tung Wan Road – G/F, 85 Tung Wan Road

Hometown Tea House – Japanese restaurant with sushi and other specialties. 12 Tung Wan Road, between Main Beach Road and Tung Wan Road. First left before you get to the beach

Long Island Restaurant – Dim sum, located just to the left of the pier as you exit the ferry

McDonalds Restaurant – immediately opposite the ferry terminus

Morocco's – Indian bar and restaurant – 71 Sun Hing Praya Street

New Baccarat Seafood Restaurant – Chinese food near the Pak Tai Temple, turn left from the ferry and walk along the Praya for a few minutes

Seaside Café – A great spot on a perch overlooking Tung Wan Beach, located at the Cheung Chau Windsurfing Centre (CCWC). Serves lots of BBQ type items such as spare ribs and sausages

Comments

- Suitable for all ages.
- Plan to spend at least half a day here.
- The area can be very crowded on weekends and public holidays especially in the area right around the ferry pier.
- The best toilets on the island are located at the McDonald's Restaurant immediately opposite the exit for the ferry, and at Tung Wan Beach. It would be a good idea for everyone

in the family to make a pit stop at one of these toilets before exploring the island.
- There are no baby-changing stations but at the beach there are changing rooms and benches in the stalls that could serve the purpose if you have a very young baby (probably not big enough for the toddlers though).
- Stroller-friendly.

Word of Mouth
With very young children in tow, limiting your exploration to the village and the beach may be prudent.

Mui Wo and Bike Riding
Mui Wo (Silvermine Bay), Lantau Island

大嶼山
梅窩

Silvermine Bay Beach Tel: 2984-8229 or 2852-3220
First Ferry Tel: 2131-8181
New Lantao Bus Company Tel: 2984-9848
Ark Eden Tel: 9277-4025
Website for Silvermine Bay Beach: http://www.lcsd.gov.hk/beach/en/
beach-address-is.php
Website for First Ferry: http://www.nwff.com.hk/
Website for New Lantao Bus Company: http://www.newlantaobus.com/
nlb.html
Website for Ark Eden: http://www.arkedenonlantau.com/
For area map: Go to website for Silvermine Bay Beach and click on
"location map".

It is easy to come here in the morning and spend the entire day as a family enjoying the laid-back lifestyle of the South China Sea island of Lantau. Mui Wo is a lovely cross between traditional Chinese village life and expat low-key living. You can do so much, or choose to do nothing at all; either way a wonderful time can be had here and everyone will be glad they came.

Many people come through Mui Wo everyday, most on their way to famous Lantau sightseeing areas such as the Big Buddha, Tai O and South Lantau's glorious beaches and hiking trails. But this seaside town has a charm all its own and for those willing to explore, it comes with great rewards.

When you exit the ferry, realize that you have arrived in a different world than the one you left behind 30 minutes earlier in Central. Here the pace is slow and in fact locals refer to this phenomenon as "Lantau Time". If everyone in your party takes that to heart, you and your children will go back to "the City" relaxed and with renewed energy and vigour. A long stretch of beach, bike paths, bike rental shops, great restaurants, a waterfall, a cave, an environmental learning centre, an organic farm, water buffalo, traditional temples, castle-like lookout towers and playgrounds await you.

0-99

The town itself is little more than 3-4 bustling small streets with restaurants and shops. You can't get lost in town. If all you want to do is take in a meal and laze at the beach, this is easily done on foot. The beach is rarely if ever crowded and the choice of restaurants for such a small town is both plentiful and varied. One constant is the family friendliness of all establishments. There is even a small toy shop in town called Bizzie Lizzies which sells unusual toys and has a tiny little playspace for kids to enjoy while parents shop around.

If you want to get out and explore, this is better done by renting a bike which is easy and inexpensive. Though there are some cars in this village, the main mode of transport for everyone here from babies to grandmas is the bicycle. Once you get out of the main part of this tiny town (five minutes), you will be riding on bike and pedestrian paths. It would be best to bring a map with you, though getting lost is part of the fun as you can't really go very wrong no matter which route you choose. One thing that might help is to picture the centre of town as the midsection of an octopus. There are several spurs (think tentacles) that you can explore to various small villages and sites though all roads (tentacles) have a direct connection to the body (main part of town) and can be followed back to town straight to the ferry pier.

One suggested route would be to head toward the beach and find Mui Wo Rural Committee Road over on the far side of the river and behind the beach. Off of Rural Committee Road you will find Olympic Path, which is well marked, to the Silvermine Waterfall and the Silvermine Cave, both of which are at the end of the same path. You will pass a Man Mo Temple along the way. You will need to lock up your bikes at the waterfall area and walk uphill for a couple of minutes to find the cave (make sure when you rent the bikes that you ask for bike locks to take along with you). If the weather is nice, bring the kids' swimsuits as they might want to splash around in the rock pools at the base of the waterfall (do so at your own risk and not in rainy season). The area is very rural so there will be grassy fields, water buffalo and rural landscapes to enjoy along the way. Depending on the age of your children, the journey by bike can take anywhere from 15 to 30 minutes. It is basically flat so it's not difficult at all.

The path that runs parallel to the beach is another choice: a breezy ride from one end to the other and back. There is a playground at the near end of the beach which you can stop at after you have done your exercise. Yet another option is to ride along the banks of the river (the far side closer to the beach), passing Hung Shing Temple and heading for the small village of Luk Tei Tong where you can find an old watchtower and take in the rural Chinese village ambience. None of these little trips down the 'tentacles' take overly long and if you are moderately ambitious you can do them all easily in 1-2 hours. Don't be afraid to just charge ahead and explore. There are around 4,000 permanent and friendly residents in this area and most will be more than willing to direct you anywhere you wish to go.

Ark Eden, a privately owned and operated environmental learning centre with multiple programs, is also in this area (see **Extra Info** and **Special Programs and Tours** below). Ark Eden deals mainly with schools and other organizations, but if you are interested in visiting during your trip, first contact the centre in advance of your visit to the island to see what programs or events might be available.

Have a meal in Mui Wo. Whether you come for breakfast and go to Caffe Paradiso or the China Bear Pub and then head out for a ride, lunch at China Beach Club overlooking the surf, or dinner at any one of the wonderful eateries here after a big day out, enjoying a meal on this island is part of the experience. Once you discover the peaceful and down-to-earth ambience that Mui Wo provides, you will be back again and again.

***Please be aware that there are some water buffalo in the villages around Mui Wo. They are normally gentle creatures but do not go up to them and do not feed them as they are wild animals. There was a recent (but rare) report of someone being gored by a buffalo after it had been teased by a group of boys.**

Seasons and Times

Beach: Year-round, but lifeguards are only on duty from April to October.

Restaurants: Most open by 11:30am, some open for breakfast (see **Getting a Bite**).

Bike Shops: Usually open by 10:00am or 10:30am.
> *Friendly Bike Shop*: (2984-2278) Shop B, 13 Mui Wo Ferry Pier Road. Open daily 10:00am-7:00pm. Closed on Tuesdays.
> *Bikes Mui Wo Shop*: (2134-1234) Across the street from Park n Shop. Open daily 10:00am-7:00pm.

Merida Bike Shop: (2984-9761) Shop 14, Mui Wo Centre, 1 Ngan Wan Road. Tends to open later than the other shops.

Admission
Free

Bike Rental: Please use this as a rough guide only. $20 per hour or $40 per day for regular bikes, $150 for mountain bikes. Family bikes and other specialized bikes such as tandems: negotiable depending on how long you will be renting for.

The Best Ways of Getting There
By Ferry/Bus or Taxi
• Catch the ferry from **Central Outlying Island Ferry Pier #6** going to Mui Wo, Lantau. The pier is located on the waterfront behind the IFC complex where the Airport Express Train is located.
• The Lantau ferry has its own **Pier (#6)** and is quite easy to find once you reach the harbour.
↔ Travel time: 30 mins ("fast" ferry) or 50 mins ("ordinary" ferry).

By MTR/Bus
• Take the MTR from **Hong Kong Station in Central** to **Tung Chung Station** on the Tung Chung Yellow Line.
• Get off the train at Tung Chung and **exit the station at Exit B**. When you get outdoors, walk straight ahead to the bus terminus. *(Tip: The bus terminus is in the same direction as the Ngong Ping 360 cable car.)*
• Take New Lantao Bus **#3M** or **#A35** to **Mui Wo** (this will be the final stop).
↔ Travel time: 35 mins (MTR) + 30 mins (bus)

Getting a Bite
Tom's Caffe Paradiso: (2984-0498) G/F, Shop 8, Mui Wo Centre, 3 Ngan Wan Road. Open for breakfast at 7:45am daily. Closed 4:00pm weekdays and 6:00pm weekends and public holidays. Great small café, family friendly. Tom will make your kids' food to order if they have special requests. Kids' books and GREAT hand ground coffee. Look for him around the corner from China Bear Pub, one street over from the bus terminus.
China Bear (Pub): (2984-9720) G/F, Mui Wo Centre, 3 Ngan Wan Road. Open for breakfast, lunch and dinner. Just to the left

of the pier as you head out and behind the McDonald's. Open-air pub, very family-friendly. Staff loves kids!

China Beach Club: (2983-8931) 18 Tung Wan Tau Road. Open Thursday-Sunday and public holidays only. On the far side of the path that runs parallel to Silvermine Bay Beach. Look for a two-story white building (it's an ancestral hall on the bottom floor). This casual place has excellent food, a kids' play area and you can even bring your dog!

Bahce Turkish Restaurant: (2984-0222) G/F, Shop 19, Mui Wo Centre. Family-friendly popular locals' spot for lunch and dinner. Wraps, mezze, salads and some alfresco seating. Just opposite the ferry and bus terminus. On Friday night they have live music. All are welcome.

The Pizzeria: (2984-8933) G/F, Shop C, Grandview Mansion. Family-friendly pizza joint just past the bus terminus, near the HSBC sign.

Rome: (2984-7982) G/F, Grandview Mansion. Local Chinese fare near The Pizzeria.

Bombay Café: (2984-1847) Local Indian take-out (very few seats) with versatile chef who is happy to cater whatever you need for your party; just call him in advance for special orders. Take it out to the beach!

Tak Juk Kee Restaurant: (2984-1265) No.1 Chung Hau Road. Open-air, family-friendly Chinese fare known locally as "The Ramp". Alfresco seating with views of the beach. Take the traffic circle turn toward the beach to the right as you exit the ferry and you will see it above you (up a ramp) to your left facing the sea.

Deer Horn: (3484-3095) Nepalese and North Indian food, opposite the bus terminus.

McDonald's Restaurant: G/F, Mui Wo Centre – to the left of the pier.

Dai Pai Dongs: Local noodle shops and local fare, VERY casual, to the right of the pier as you exit.

What's Close?
Pui O Beach, **Cheung Sha Beach,** and **The Giant Buddha, Po Lin Monastery and Tai O**.

Comments
- This outing is suitable for all ages.
- Plan to spend a minimum of three hours here.
- The town and beach are generally not crowded except sometimes around the ferry and bus terminus.

- There are toilets all around town. The nearest one to the ferry pier is off to the right as you exit the ferry terminus.
- There are few if any baby-changing stations in Mui Wo but there are plenty of benches around town that will work for the purpose.
- You can bring your stroller here though if you are planning to ride bikes, you will have to leave it at the bike rental shop.

Extra Info
It might be very useful to have taxi numbers on hand if you want to go exploring the island further. Here are two Lantau taxi numbers: 2984-1328 and 2984-1368.

For Educators
Ark Eden is a special place on Lantau which aims to present the island as a natural wonderland and explain how its natural beauty and features can be used to benefit everyone in the Hong Kong community and beyond. Their focus is on preserving Lantau's ecological, geographical, historical and cultural heritage by holding inspirational workshops, field trips and camps. These focus on a creating an understanding of the environment as well as furthering education of each individual's role in its conservation and sustainability. Ark Eden offers programs specifically designed for both local and international children. For further information, check their website, call Jenny Quinton on 9277-4025 or email her on jenny@arkedenonlantau. com.

Word of Mouth
What is meant by the word "village"? On Lantau, as in the New Territories, a village generally means a strip of houses clustered together, often with a small temple in the centre, run by a village head. It does not usually mean a village as one might find in the countryside in Europe. If you go bike riding around the Mui Wo area you will find many "villages" but expect them to be of limited scope. They will be interesting areas that you will cycle through on the pathways.

Discovery Bay Beach, Plaza and Hidden Rock Pool
Discovery Bay, Lantau Island

Tel: 2987-7351 (for ferry schedule and information).
Website: www.hkri.com or www.dbay.com.hk (for ferry schedule and other useful information).
For area map: Go to www.dbay.com.hk and click on "Useful Information" and then click on "Discovery Bay Maps."

Beach and Plaza:

It's easy to get to; there's a beach, kid-friendly food, and not a car in sight! Discovery Bay is a good outing option when you want to get away from it all but don't want the hassle of spending too much time or energy getting there.

This self-contained, laid-back expat enclave, commonly referred to by residents as 'DB' or 'Disco Bay', has a neighbourhood feeling that is unique and particularly enjoyable for families with young children. When disembarking from the ferry, you will find yourself directly upon the centre of activity for this area: a large circular plaza. Filled with restaurants and shops, the plaza has a fountain in its centre which acts as a kid magnet. Everywhere you look you will find children frolicking about with dogs or riding their trikes and scooters. The fact that there are no cars allowed in the community means parents can relax and enjoy the outing too. In fact, kids might get a kick out of seeing the mode of transport on the roads here – the golf cart.

Just north of the ferry dock and the plaza is a large stretch of sand called Tai Pak Beach, which only takes five to seven minutes to reach on foot. At the far end of the beach is a great playground, right on the sand, which is equipped with all manner of toys including two sets of swings – one for the older set, one for toddlers. You can either walk the length of the beach, through the sand, to get to the play area or, if you have a stroller with you, there is a paved walkway that runs to the playground from the beach entrance.

0-99

Do not leave DB without having a meal here. Choices abound with the majority of outlets being both casual and alfresco. (See **Getting a Bite** below for a list of options.)

Rock Pool and Waterfall:

These rock pools are a hidden gem. Only 15 minutes' walk from the ferry pier (uphill) there is a little piece of fresh water heaven just waiting to be found. Exit the ferry pier, turn left, go past the DB Bus Terminus, and you are now on Discovery Bay Road. Turn right, you will pass the tennis courts, which will be on your right, and look for a left turn heading uphill on Discovery Valley Road (which ultimately leads up to the Discovery Bay Golf Club). Walk 10 minutes up the hill and you will soon come to a sign before a bridge on your right hand side that says "PROCEED AT YOUR OWN RISK – DUE TO FLASH FLOODING". Behind the sign is a small carved-out trail that leads to the stream on the left. You can walk up the boulders that flank the stream for five minutes or less until you reach the small fresh water rock pool and waterfall. It is peaceful here and the water is swimmable, though beware that the rocks under the water are covered in algae and are slippery. In fact the whole outing to the rock pool is a risk-taking endeavour. DO NOT ENTER when there has been moderate to heavy rainfall. Proceed at YOUR OWN RISK!

Seasons and Times
Year-round

Admission
Free

The Best Ways of Getting There
By Ferry
- Catch this speedy ferry from the **Outlying Island Ferry Piers in Central**. The pier is located on the waterfront, behind the IFC complex, where the airport express train is located.
- The **Discovery Bay Ferry** leaves from **Pier #3** and is quite easy to find once you reach the harbour.
- The ferry runs frequently and the Discovery Bay Ferry Pier is only a two-minute walk from the Plaza. (See the website or call the company directly for a detailed schedule.)
↔ Travel time: 25 mins (ferry).

Getting a Bite
Having a meal here is part of the experience and there are many options to choose from, all of which are located in the

plaza area. The building that overlooks Tai Pak Beach is called D-Deck and it is filled with eateries:

Ground Floor:
Pacific Coffee Company Ltd. – Coffee shop with outdoor seating overlooking the beach.
Moorings – East Coast American cuisine.
Wildfire – Pizza place.
McDonald's Restaurant and McCafe – Fast food with outdoor seating.
Subway – Sandwich shop with outdoor seating on plaza side.
La Creation – Bakery.
Ebeneezer's – European fast food, kebabs.
Zaks – International cuisine, large alfresco space.
Ippu Japanese Restaurant – Japanese.
Café Duvet – Tapas and desserts served on outdoor day-beds.
Sopranos – Family style Italian restaurant serving home-cooked food, alfresco.
Caramba Mexican Cantina – Mexican grill, alfresco.
22 North – Brasserie, alfresco.
Hemingway's By the Bay – Caribbean BBQ grill, alfresco.
McSorley's Ale House – Guinness pie and Indian curries (and ale too, of course).

First Floor:
Dymocks and Gallery Café – Bookshop with café and kids corner.
Island Café – Fast food.
First Korean Restaurant – Korean BBQ and other delicacies.
Koh Tomyums – Contemporary Thai cuisine.

**SPECIAL NOTE: The 13 restaurants with ** marking denote D-Deck eateries offering free ferry tickets back to Central if you present your dining receipt for over HK$100 at the redemption centre on DB. The counter is located on the ground floor of D-Deck on the walk back to the DB Ferry Pier. Each $100 you spend can be redeemed for one ferry ticket.

Ground Floor – South Side (other side of the Plaza from D-Deck):
Il Bel Paese – Italian grocer and restaurant with table on the plaza.
7-11 – Convenience store, good place for ice cream.

Uncle Russ Coffee – Coffee shop on the plaza.
Fusion – Large grocery store chain (great for picking up picnic options for the beach or plaza tables).

Comments
- Best suited to little ones who like the beach and the playground, but suitable for all ages.
- Plan to spend half a day to a full day here.
- In general, Discovery Bay is not a crowded place.
- There are great toilets here, one by the ferry pier on your left as you exit and one near the playground at the beach.
- Both toilets have baby-changing stations.
- Stroller-friendly.

Extra Info
On the last Saturday and Sunday of the month there is a market in the Plaza. DB periodically hosts events and festivals such as an Easter Party in the plaza area for kids with bouncy castles and games. For more information on what is coming up, check the calendar page at www.dbay.com.hk or go to www.dbnplaza.hk.

Word of Mouth
There is no shade at the beach or the playground and therefore both can become unbearably hot in the summer months.

Peng Chau Island

坪
洲

Hong Kong Kowloon Ferry Tel: 2131-8181
New World First Ferry Tel: 2131-8181 (same as above)
Discovery Bay Ferry Tel: 2987-7351 (for ferry schedule and information)
Sunroom Studios – 38A Wing Hing Street, Peng Chau Tel: 6303-1426
E.A.R.T.H. (Geology) Shop – 38B Wing Hing Street, Peng Chau Tel: 9182-6031
Website for Hong Kong Kowloon Ferry: http://www.hkkf.com.hk/
Website for Discovery Bay Ferry: www.hkri.com or www.dbay.com.hk
Website for Inter-island Ferry from Mui Wo to Peng Chau: http://www.nwff.com.hk/eng/fare_table/island_hopping/
For area map: Go to the following website and click on New Peng Chau Map - http://www.greenpengchau.org.hk/

Peng Chau is a laid-back, tiny island that offers a wonderful way to spend a Sunday or a public holiday as a family. Locally known as "Level Island" (as at its highest point it rises to only 98 metres), this peaceful charming place of only one square kilometre has no vehicles, a quaint village centre, multiple temples, a family trail, a panoramic lookout point, a wide array of low-key restaurants, small shops, two playgrounds, a bike rental shop, a beach (though not for swimming), a great geology shop (complete with expert) and a ceramics studio which offers ad hoc classes for kids.

Only 25 minutes by fast ferry from Central, this place is *truly* a gem just waiting to be discovered. The ferry drops you right in the heart of the small village. It is easy to navigate if you picture the island as an hourglass. The main village is in the centre and the family trail follows a figure eight with the top of it to the north and the bottom loop to the south. The pier is to the west in the centre, and the beach called Tung Wan is on the east in the centre. You could walk the entire island in 2-2½ hours if you chose to do so or you can just choose an activity and head for it.

0-99

If you stay in the centre of the island you can walk around the village, visit the local temples of which there are many, walk over to the beach or enjoy the two playgrounds: one to the west, near the waterfront and opposite the ferry, and one closer to the beach on the east side. If you have older kids, rent bikes for an hour at the wet market building and tootle around the mostly flat roads. Having a meal here is fun and should be part of your itinerary.

If you would like to add a hike to your plans, going either north or south has great things to see and experience. Finger Hill is the highest point on the island and is part of the Family Trail to the south. Head for Nam Shan Road by walking through the main village along Wing On Street, which turns into Shing Ka Road. Follow the informational signposts to Finger Hill and you will find the pathway that leads you up the steps to the hilltop. Lovely views await you, plus a pavilion and some benches where you can rest and enjoy a snack (pick one up at the bakery in the village to incentivize the kids to hike to the top). Head back to the main village by retracing your steps; or take the steps down the north side of Finger Hill which will lead you to a crumbling old pier, back inland through an organic farm, then on toward Nam Wan, the southernmost area, past a Taoist temple and back to town.

If you decide to explore to the north from the ferry pier, head up Peng Lei Road which runs parallel to the sea and you will come across an old closed-down factory which was once the largest match factory in Asia, and in the same area three tiny temples. You can carry on over the bridge from here to a small island which is a dead end. Turn around, head back toward the tiny temples and follow the Family Walk Trail that skirts the hillside. It rises above the rocky shore to a very large stone on a point overlooking the sea which is called Old Fishermen's Rock because it looks just like one from afar. Enjoy great views along the way. The path will turn sharply toward the south and head into Tung Wan Bay. At Tung Wan Beach is the Lung Mo Temple which is well worth a visit. Then reward yourself with a meal or a treat in town.

Perhaps the most fun your kids will have on Peng Chau has nothing to do with taking in the island's natural beauty but in fact making something beautiful of their own! Sunroom Studios, a lovely little ceramic studio located on the island, offers pottery lessons for kids and adults on a regular basis for those that live in the area but it also *offers ad hoc one-hour classes which include a lesson, materials, painting and firing of their work.* Kids will learn how to craft a mug or a figurine in a single one-hour session (you will have to come back on another day to pick up their artwork). These classes are reasonably priced and need to be booked in advance of your visit to Peng Chau. Call the studio to set up your appointment. To add to this wonderful experience, next door to the ceramic studio is a geology store called E.A.R.T.H. It's filled with interesting stones and fossils and is run by a great enthusiast who is more than willing to share his knowledge with those children and adults who are interested in learning about stones, fossils and other fascinating geological topics. Call the shop in advance to find out when they will be open.

This island and all it has to offer is one of my family's all-time favourite places to go on an outing!

Seasons and Times

The island is accessible year-round but best to visit on the weekend or public holidays when all the businesses and restaurants are open.

Sunroom Studio: Call Conrad Li (owner) to find out when he is open and available for workshops.

E.A.R.T.H. (Geology) Shop: Normally open on Sundays and public holidays but call first to check.

Admission

Free

Sunroom Studio: One-hour ad hoc course including materials costs around $150 per person per hour but check with the studio for up-to-date pricing information.

E.A.R.T.H. (Geology) Shop: Kevin Laurie, owner and geology expert, will share his knowledge and answer your questions whenever the shop is open, free of charge. He sells some of his rocks, minerals and special items at very reasonable prices.

The Best Ways of Getting There

By Ferry from Central

- Catch the ferry from **Central Outlying Island Ferry Pier #6** going to **Peng Chau**. The pier is located on the waterfront, behind the IFC complex, where the Airport Express Train is located.
- The Peng Chau ferry shares **Pier #6** with the Lantau ferry and is quite easy to find once you reach the harbour.

↔ Travel time: 25 mins ("fast" ferry) or 40 mins ("ordinary" ferry).

By Ferry then Kaido from Discovery Bay

- Catch this speedy ferry from the **Outlying Island Ferry Piers in Central**. The pier is located on the waterfront, behind the IFC complex, where the airport express train is located.
- The **Discovery Bay Ferry** leaves from **Pier #3** and is quite easy to find once you reach the harbour. The ferry runs frequently.
- Once you reach the **Discovery Bay Ferry Pier make a left** and find the small privately-operated boats called kaidos and hire one to take you over to Peng Chau. Prices are negotiable.

↔ Travel time: 25 mins (ferry) + 15 mins (kaido).

By Ferry to Mui Wo, Lantau then on to Peng Chau via Inter-Island Ferry Service

- Catch the ferry from **Central Outlying Island Ferry Pier #6** going to **Mui Wo, Lantau**. The pier is located on the waterfront, behind the IFC complex, where the Airport Express Train is located.
- The Lantau ferry has its own **Pier (#6)** and is quite easy to find once you reach the harbour.
- From *Mui Wo catch an Inter-Island Ferry at the Mui Wo Ferry Pier to Peng Chau.*

↔ Travel time: 30 mins ("fast" ferry) or 50 mins ("ordinary" ferry) + 25 mins (Inter-Island Ferry).

Getting a Bite

For such a small island there are actually quite a number of choices for food.

Obbao – G/F, 40 Wing On Street (2983-1030): Burgers, pizza and crepes. Family-friendly with alfresco dining.

Chimays – Wing On Street (next door to Obbao on corner): Alfresco pub, very light fare.

Good Luck Restaurant – Located on Po Peng Street right near the pier, opposite the Peng Chau waterfront playground. Chinese restaurant (large for this size of island) with limited alfresco seating.

Chinese Fast Food – Just as you exit the ferry, make a right hand turn onto Lo Peng Street and you will find a local outdoor Chinese fast food café with outdoor seating. Order at the counter and then find a seat. Inexpensive and fresh food.

Thai food (two restaurants) – One is on Wing Hing Street next door to Sunroom Studio and E.A.R.T.H. The other is on a corner near the wet market building.

Local bakery – Just as you exit the ferry, make a right hand turn onto Lo Peng Street and you will find a GREAT bakery for take-away treats on your left.

Gelatiamo – 8A Wing On Street (9171-3762): Ice cream shop.

Wellcome Supermarket – On the corner of Lo Peng and Po Peng Streets, very conveniently located near the ferry pier. Great place to stop and get some drinks and snacks for your walk around or laze at the playground.

What's Close?
Discovery Bay

Comments
- This outing is suitable for all ages.
- Plan to spend a minimum of three hours here.
- The town is generally not crowded.
- There are toilets around town. The nearest one to the ferry pier is off to the right as you exit the ferry terminus on the ground floor of the wet market building. There is also one next to the playground close to Tung Wan Beach.
- There are no baby-changing stations on Peng Chau but there are plenty of benches around town that will work for the purpose.
- This is a stroller-friendly island with lots of paved roads to push a stroller.

Extra Info
It is very helpful, though not completely necessary, to have a map with you when you explore Peng Chau. There is a large one posted at the Peng Chau Ferry Pier. Try to take a photo of it with your camera then you can refer to it while you are hiking.

Word of Mouth
Ferries run to Peng Chau daily and you can bring your children anytime, however be aware that the island does not get many visitors apart from weekends and holidays and therefore some shops and restaurants might not be open during the week.

Chapter 2

Child-Friendly Museums

For a great family outing on a very hot or very wet day (or indeed any day), try one of the 10 Hong Kong museums covered in this chapter. Curators have gone to great lengths at these museums to impart knowledge in a way that will be fun and interesting to children. Your kids can learn about Hong Kong's history and heritage, science, art, space, trains and even tea. The museum creators have used all manner of tools at their disposal to make every visit exciting including: films, interactive exhibits, computer games, demonstrations, and participatory activities. Parents will love the inexpensive nature of these excursions, as all Hong Kong museums have either free admission or charge a very nominal fee.

For local residents who would like to become more regular museum goers, there is a Museum Pass available that is reasonably priced and has great benefits. The pass will provide access to all of the following museums: Hong Kong Science Museum (excluding some special exhibitions), Hong Kong Space Museum (excluding the Space Theatre), Hong Kong Museum of Art, Hong Kong Museum of History, Hong Kong Museum of Coastal Defence and Hong Kong Heritage Museum. The pass also comes with special privileges including: 10% discount on cash purchases of selected items at museum gift shops, 10% discount on participation in museum extension activities, and 10% discount on an Ocean Park SmartFun Annual Pass. Costs for annual passes are as follows: HK$100 for individuals, HK$200 for families of four and HK$50 for students. Six-month passes are also available: HK$50 for individuals and HK$25 for students. You can contact any one of the above museums for details on how to purchase a Museum Pass.

There is always something exciting going on at these museums. A good way to stay informed is to check museum websites for current activities and events.

1. Hong Kong Science Museum
2. Hong Kong Space Museum
3. Hong Kong Heritage Museum
4. Hong Kong Museum of Coastal Defence
5. Hong Kong Museum of History
6. Hong Kong Railway Museum
7. Hong Kong Maritime Museum
8. Police Museum and Coombe Road / Wanchai Gap Playgrounds
9. Hong Kong Museum of Art
10. Flagstaff House Museum of Tea Ware

Other chapters that include museums:
Sai Kung Country Park at Pak Tam Chung – The Sheung Yiu Folk Museum
Victoria Peak – Madame Tussauds Wax Museum

Hong Kong Science Museum

2 Science Museum Road
(off Chatham Road)
Tsim Sha Tsui East, Kowloon

Tel: 2732-3232
Website: http://hk.science.museum/eindex.php
For area map: See website above, click on "Visitor Information" and
then on "Location Map".

九龍　尖沙咀

科學館道 2 號

香港科學館

It is not hard to understand why children love this place – it is
made for touching, feeling and experiencing and you will not go
away disappointed! Five hundred exhibits, the majority of which
are interactive, create an atmosphere where education is so
much fun kids won't even notice how much they are learning.

This four-story museum uses its more than 13,000 square
metres of floor area to dazzle kids with 'science' excitement.
The 16 gallery topics include: conservation, life science, light,
mathematics, motion, sounds, world of mirrors, electricity and
magnetism, food science, home technology and transportation.
Each gallery has multiple hands-on exhibits; in fact more than
70% of the museum is interactive. Kids will love the brain
teasers in the mathematics area, the special mirrors exhibits
in the world of mirrors, the wide variety of 'tests' to check their
memory and hand/eye coordination and many, many more.
There are also special live shows where the museum staff
demonstrate interesting scientific phenomena like the way hair
stands up on end when static electricity is present and how
lightning is created. Check at the front desk for demonstration
times and topics when you arrive at the museum.

3+

The curators here are very proud of a unique exhibit called "The
Energy Machine" which is the largest of its kind in the world.
This 22-metre-high giant takes up all four stories of the museum
and can be seen from almost anywhere in the space. This
exhibit was created to demonstrate the relationship between
energy conversion and movement. A series of balls are set
in motion in this mega structure, creating a series of exciting
noises and visual effects as they roll around this specially
created, rollercoaster-like structure.

Beyond the wonderful permanent exhibits, this museum also offers periodic special installations worth noting. Over the years these offerings have included: "Candy Unwrapped", "Soaring Dinosaurs", "Mission Earthling", "Optical Illusion", "The Robot Zoo", "Whodunit? The Mysteries of Forensic Science" and "Grossology – The Impolite Science of the Human Body", to name just a few. These special exhibits require the purchase of a ticket which is normally priced around HK$20. Tickets often sell out. Call the museum or check the website for current event details.

Seasons and Times

Mondays-Wednesdays and Fridays – 1:00pm-9:00pm. Saturdays, Sundays and public holidays – 10:00am-9:00pm. Closed on Thursdays (except public holidays) and the first two days of the Chinese New Year. Closed at 5:00pm on Christmas Eve and New Year's Eve. Box office closes one hour before the museum's closing time.

Admission

Adults: HK$25; children (four and older): HK$12.50. Free admission on Wednesdays (except for special extra-cost exhibitions).

The Best Ways of Getting There

By Star Ferry
- From **Central to Tsim Sha Tsui** (TST) take the **Star Ferry** from the **Star Ferry Central pier**.
↔ Travel time: 10 mins (ferry).
- Once you exit the ferry in TST you can either take a bus or a taxi to the museum.

> **By Bus**
> - Take bus number **#5** or **#5C** at the **bus terminal** right in front of the **TST Star Ferry pier** and get off the bus in front of the **Ramada Hotel** on **Chatham Road** (called 'Science Museum stop'). Walk across the overpass and follow the signs for the Museum of History and the Hong Kong Science Museum (they are part of the same complex).
> ↔ Travel time: 10 mins (bus) + 5 mins (walk).
>
> **By Taxi**
> A taxi from right outside the **TST Star Ferry Pier** will cost HK$20.
> ↔ Travel time: 5-10 mins (taxi).

By MTR

- From Central or Admiralty to **Tsim Sha Tsui Station**, take the red line. Exit the MTR station at exit "**B2**" marked "**Tsim Sha Tsui East**".
- Walk 10-15 minutes along **Cameron Road** going east. Cameron Road dead-ends into **Chatham Road**. Make a left here and walk five minutes until you see the museum on your right side.
- ↔ Travel time: 10 mins (MTR) + 15-20 mins (walk).

By Car

- From Central take the **Cross Harbour Tunnel**: Connaught Road→ Harcourt Road→ Gloucester Road→**Island Eastern Corridor**.
- In tunnel and tollbooths (HK$20) stay to the far left. Follow signs for **Tsim Sha Tsui** and **Kwai Chung**. From here there is a series of three left hand turns all marked for either **TST** or the **Hong Kong Coliseum/Railway Terminus**. These turns all lead you to **Chatham Road South**.
- You will pass the Polytechnic University on your left side and at the next street you will see the Museum of History on your left which is in the same complex as the Science Museum. **P** Make the next left turn onto **Granville Road** and an immediate right hand turn into **Granville Square** where you will see the blue "**P**" sign for the car park. Please note that there is no parking provided by the museum; this is a private paid car park.

By Taxi

A taxi from Central will cost HK$75-$85 and take 20-25 mins.

Getting a Bite

There are vending machines in the lobby of the museum and a few tables where you can eat a snack you might have brought along. Otherwise there are many restaurants and hotel coffee shops in the immediate area to choose from as well as bakeries and some local coffee shops. Another option is to go immediately across the podium level to the Museum of History where the ground floor café has some child-friendly fare such as pasta, noodle soup, fried rice, chicken wings and ice cream. Note though that you may have to pay the $10 entry fee for the Hong Kong Museum of History in order to get to the café.

What's Close?
Hong Kong History Museum.

Comments
- Suitable for children aged two and older.
- Plan a two- to three-hour visit.
- Generally not overcrowded.
- There are sit-down style toilets on every floor.
- Stroller-friendly.
- There are baby-changing stations in the ladies' rooms.
- There is a gift shop on the first floor.

Special Programs and Tours
The museum offers free guided tours in English for groups of 20 or more. Call 2732-3219 two weeks before your date of visit.

For Educators
During the school year, the museum organizes monthly themes specifically for schools. The special tours offer programs including laboratory activities and science films. School groups with 20 students or above can apply for an admissions charge waiver. For more information and/or booking call 2732-3220.

Word of Mouth
The Science Museum shares the same complex with the Museum of History. If you want to plan a very full day with older kids, you could try to do both.

Hong Kong Space Museum
10 Salisbury Road, Tsim Sha Tsui, Kowloon

九龍 尖沙咀
梳士巴利道10號
香港太空館

Tel: 2721-0226
Website: www.lcsd.gov.hk/hkspm/
For area map: See website above. (Click on "Site Map" then "About Us" then "The Museum – Introduction" and scroll down to the bottom of the page.)

When inquiring minds – and bodies – have questions about space science, as well as the travel and exploration of space, here is a great place to come for fun and answers. Located at the waterfront in Tsim Sha Tsui and housed in a very distinctive 'egg-shaped' dome, the Space Museum was designed for hands-on learning and has plenty to offer kids. Do bear in mind that the museum was commissioned in 1980 and is somewhat dated in its appearance, but less so in its content.

The museum is divided into three main galleries: the Hall of Space Science, the Hall of Astronomy and the Space Theatre. To begin your exploration, head for the Hall of Space Science located on the ground floor. The study of rockets, gravity, motion and history all come alive with the aid of push-button displays, videos and other fun activity-driven exhibits. The bigger kids can take a walk on the moon in a virtual 1/6th gravity environment, take a 3-D trip on a virtual glider over the Grand Canyon or take a turn operating a gyroscope.

One flight up you will find the Hall of Astronomy. As you might expect, the exhibits here revolve around the sun, the moon and the stars. There are video presentations and some interactive exhibits as well. The subject matter may be too difficult for the younger children to understand, but older children, especially those that are studying astronomy in school, will find this hall very interesting.

The most exciting part of your trip to the museum will most likely be taking in a show at the Space Theatre. Located inside the dome of the museum, the screen is 23 metres high and wraps itself halfway around the theatre, providing a truly multi-sensory experience. Two very different kinds of shows are on offer each day. One is called a Sky Show, which can be categorized as

5+

99

a more traditional planetarium presentation. The other type is an Omnimax film generally covering a scientific topic not necessarily related to space science, such as Cave Exploring, Dolphins, the Continent of Antarctica, Arabia, Legends of Flight and the Hubble Telescope, to name just a few.

Seasons and Times
Mondays, Wednesdays-Fridays – 1:00pm-9:00pm
Saturdays, Sundays and public holidays – 10:00am-9:00pm.
Closed Tuesdays (except public holidays) and the first two days of the Chinese New Year. On Christmas Eve and Chinese New Year's Eve the closing time is 5:00pm.

Admission
Museum: Adults: HK$10. Children (four and older)/full time students: HK$5. Free admission on Wednesdays (excluding shows).
Sky Shows/Omnimax Shows: Front stalls – Adults: HK$24; Children/full time students: HK$12. Regular stalls – Adults: HK$32; Children/full time students: HK$16. Please note that children under three years of age will not be admitted.

The Best Ways of Getting There
By Star Ferry
- From **Central** to **Tsim Sha Tsui (TST)** take the Star Ferry from the **Star Ferry Central Pier**.
- When you exit the ferry pier in TST walk straight ahead and you will be on **Salisbury Road**. The museum is on the **harbour side of Salisbury Road**, a 5-10 minute walk from the pier.
  (Tip: Look for the Space Museum's distinctive egg-shaped dome as a guide.)
- ↔ Travel time: 10 mins (ferry) + 5-10 mins (walk).

By MTR
- From **Central** or **Admiralty** to **Tsim Sha Tsui Station**, take the red line. Exit the MTR station at **Exit "E"**. This exit is marked The Peninsula Hotel, not the Hong Kong Space Museum, but take it anyway. You will now be on **Nathan Road**.
- Walk down **Nathan Road one block** toward the harbour and you will dead-end into **Salisbury Road**.
- Directly in front of you will see the distinctive dome of the Space Museum.

*(Tip: If it is raining, stay underground and follow the signs for Hong Kong Space Museum which will take you underground to the **TST EAST** station. In this case you will walk 5-10 mins underground from exit **"J"** onward to exit **"J4"** which will take you through Sogo Department Store and then onto the street and put you one minute from the museum entrance. It is much faster to walk over ground from the first set of directions above, however in inclement weather, take this second route.)*
↔ Travel time: 10 mins (MTR) + 10 mins (walk).

By Car

- From Central: Connaught Road→Harcourt Road→ Gloucester Road→Island Eastern Corridor **(Route 4)**→**Cross Harbour Tunnel (Route 1)**.
- In tunnel and tollbooth (HK$20) stay to the far left. Follow signs for **Tsim Sha Tsui and Kwai Chung**. From here there is a series of **three left hand turns** all marked for either TST or the Hong Kong Coliseum/Railway Terminus. These turns all lead you to **Chatham Road South**.
- Stay on **Chatham Road South** until it dead-ends into **Salisbury Road**. (You will pass the HK Polytechnic University and the History Museum on your left.) Turn right on Salisbury Road and then turn left and directly into **New World Centre Mall driveway**.

P New World Centre Mall has an underground car park. This is the nearest place to park. From here it is a five-minute walk down Salisbury Road to the museum.

By Taxi

A taxi from Central will cost HK$75-$85 and take 20-30 mins.

Getting a Bite

The Hong Kong Art Museum, 10 steps away from the Space Museum, has a café called **Museum Café** which is accessed through the gift shop or immediately before you enter the main doors of the Hong Kong Art Museum. It has both an outdoor and indoor seating area and overlooks the harbour. This eatery does not have a specific kids' menu, but there are many items on offer which are very suitable to children's tastes, such as jumbo hot dogs, fish and chips, pasta, sandwiches and pizza, all at very reasonable prices. If all you want is a snack, they also offer a variety of desserts which are especially nice to enjoy while you are sitting outside overlooking Victoria Harbour.

There are several other restaurant options in this large municipal complex (consisting of the Art and Space Museums and the Cultural Centre):

Starbucks – Inside the foyer of the Cultural Centre.
Deli and Wine – Just outside the Cultural Centre doors – casual upscale deli which serves noodles, burgers, sandwiches, curries, bakery items and has a frozen yogurt counter.
Café Muse – On the ground floor behind the Space Museum – serves international fare.
Serenade – On the 1st floor behind the Space Museum – serves Chinese fare.

Keep in mind that the HK Space Museum is in the heart of TST, so if you are willing to walk for a few minutes you will have your choice of dozens of restaurants for lunch or dinner. One possibility might be to walk over to Ocean Terminal for a meal (see the **Kowloon Park** chapter, **Getting a Bite** section, for more info) or for yet another option, check out the newly restored 1881 Heritage complex across Salisbury Road from the museum.

What's Close?
Hong Kong Museum of Art, the Cultural Centre, the Peninsula Hotel, 1881 Heritage and Ocean Terminal.

Comments
- Best suited for children five and above (though little kids will enjoy pushing buttons and touching everything).
- Plan a one- to two-hour visit, or more if you will take in a movie.
- Generally not overcrowded, except on Wednesdays when admission is free.
- The bathrooms here have sit-down toilets.
- There is a baby-changing table in the ground floor handicapped toilet.
- You can bring a stroller here and use the elevator to get to the upper floor.
- There is a small museum gift shop.

Extra Info
Omnimax shows are normally 40-45 minutes in length and require the purchase of a separate ticket. Most presentations are in Cantonese unless otherwise noted on the schedule.

However, other languages including English can be heard by using the headphones located under the seats. Sky shows are presented twice a day and Omnimax films are presented five times a day with two to three different movies to choose from. To check the Space Theatre show schedule in advance of your visit, consult the museum website, or call the museum box office on 2734-9009. Tickets can be purchased over the internet at http://www.urbtix.hk or telephone on 2111-5999.

Special Programs and Tours

Every year the Space Museum organizes many extra activities which are not on their daily schedule. Fun astronomy classes, workshops, astronomy happy hours and a lecture series are on offer. To check the times and dates of these extra activities, please call the museum directly or check their website or online newsletter.

For Educators

- The Space Museum offers special shows for schools in the Space Theatre. Please call 2734-2711 for school show bookings and inquiries.
- If you cannot bring your school to the planetarium, the planetarium can come to you! There is a private enterprise in Hong Kong called **Discovery Dome HK** which brings the magic of the stars into schools in Hong Kong. This mobile planetarium run by two qualified international school teachers is an educational and fun-filled experience which helps bring the wonder of astronomy to children of all ages. For more information contact them directly: www.discoverydome.hk Email: enquiries@discoverydome.hk Tel: 9042-6396 / 2819-3420.

Word of Mouth

- Be forewarned that the interactive exhibits in many cases have a height requirement. The littlest ones might therefore be disappointed if they cannot have the same experiences as their older counterparts (though there is still plenty for the younger set to enjoy at the museum).
- If your child is crazy about the stars, check out the Discovery Dome HK website (above) for information on having a Discovery Dome birthday party or joining their after-school programs or camps.

Hong Kong Heritage Museum
1 Man Lam Road
Shatin, New Territories

Tel: 2180-8188

Website: http://www.heritagemuseum.gov.hk

For area map: See website above. (Click on "About Us", then "Plan Your Visit.")

This fantastic museum might be the best-kept secret in the territory. The curators had families with young children in mind when they designed this open and spacious place. Hong Kong's heritage comes alive here with over 7,500 square metres of exhibition area and 12 thematic galleries aimed at teaching students of all ages about the very rich legacy of this area, both geologically and anthropologically.

Six of the 12 galleries house permanent exhibitions which include all of the following: the Orientation Theatre, Children's Discovery Gallery, New Territories Heritage Hall, Cantonese Opera Heritage Hall, Chao Shao-An Gallery and the T.T. Tsui Gallery of Chinese Art. The other six galleries are host to a variety of short-term exhibits, many of which will appeal to children. At the time of writing, the temporary exhibit was an extremely popular child-friendly offer: Pixar – 25 Years of Animation. Hailing from California, this wonderful display shared an inside view of Pixar's animation works with such favourites as Woody and Buzz Lightyear from *Toy Story*, Sulley and Boo from *Monsters Inc.*, and Nemo and his dad, the clownfish from *Finding Nemo*. The visiting exhibitions change frequently; check the website for the current offering before you head out.

Though the whole museum is worth exploring, if you have kids between the ages of two and 10, you will likely spend the majority of your time in the children's discovery gallery. This very special place has eight play zones, each designed to teach something about Hong Kong's cultural heritage in a fun way. Virtually everything here is interactive. There is a Mai Po wetlands zone where kids can learn about animal species of the area, a deep ocean zone covering underwater creatures of the South China Sea, an area where they can play 'archaeologist' and discover artifacts found in the Hong Kong area, and a New

Territories village zone where they can learn about traditional village life by play-acting within a reconstructed dwelling. There are kid-sized tables and chairs where parents and children can amuse themselves with games that were popular locally decades ago. There is also a toy exhibition called "The Hong Kong Toy Story" which displays toys that were both manufactured and used in Hong Kong in the 1960s and 1970s.

Don't forget to leave time for the Cantonese Opera Gallery! This very colourful large gallery is both eye-catching and interactive. Kids will love using the computers to generate an image of themselves in full make-up and headdress as well as viewing all of the beautiful costumes and watching the videos on this fascinating part of Hong Kong's cultural history.

Seasons and Times
Mondays, Wednesdays-Saturdays: 10:00am-6:00pm
Sundays and public holidays: 10:00am-7:00pm
Closed on Tuesdays (except public holidays) and the first two days of the Chinese New Year. Closed at 5:00pm on Christmas Eve and Chinese New Year's Eve.

Admission
Adults: HK$10; Children (aged four and older): HK$5. On Wednesdays only: Free admission. Tickets for the visiting exhibits may have a small entry fee on top of the ticket price to the museum.

The Best Ways of Getting There
By MTR
- From Central or Admiralty to **Kowloon Tong Station**, take the red line to **Mongkok**. Transfer to the green line (across the platform at Mongkok Station) to **Kowloon Tong**.
- In Kowloon Tong station look for the **East Rail**. Ride it one stop to **Tai Wai.**
- Then transfer to the **Ma On Shan Line** and go one stop and alight at **Che Kung Temple Station**.
- Take exit "**A**" to your right and look to your right on the path for a post with an arrow pointing across the small river to the museum. **Cross the pedestrian bridge** following signs, make **a right after crossing the bridge** and the museum will be three minutes down the path on your left.
↔ Travel time: 20 mins (MTR) + 10-15 mins (East Rail) + 5-7 min (walk).

新界　沙田　大圍　香港文化博物館
文林路１號

3+

By Car

- From Central take the **Cross Harbour Tunnel**: Connaught Road→Harcourt Road→Gloucester Road→**Island Eastern Corridor**.
- In tunnel stay in right lane. Once through tollbooth (HK$20) stay right and follow signs for **Ho Man Tin and Sha Tin**.
- Stay in centre lane, you are now on **Princess Margaret Road**. Follow signs for **Lion Rock Tunnel**. Go through tunnel (HK$8), you are now on **Lion Rock Tunnel Road**.
- Take the exit on the left for **Sha Tin Central**.
- Follow this road around **across a small bridge** over the Shing Mun River Channel. Immediately after the bridge make a left turn onto **Man Lam Road**.

P The Heritage Museum parking lot will be on your left side just in front of the museum.

There is a small parking fee.

By Taxi

A taxi from Central will cost HK$150-$170 and take 35-40 mins.

Getting a Bite

There are snack tables and drink vending machines in a covered outdoor area to the left of the front entrance to the museum, facing the river. Unfortunately there is no longer a restaurant or snack stand to purchase food from on the premises, so it would be advisable to bring your own snacks and/or lunch with you and make your own picnic. Alternatively, combine this visit with a stop at Sha Tin New Town Plaza (see Getting a Bite in the **Snoopy's World/New Town Plaza** chapter) which has many child-friendly eateries to choose from and is only a 15-minute walk from the museum.

What's Close?

Sha Tin New Town Plaza, Snoopy's World, Ikea, Penfold Park, Sha Tin Park (**Biking in the New Territories** chapter).

Comments

- Suitable for all ages, but best for ages three and up.
- Plan to spend at least two hours here.
- Generally not overcrowded.
- There are toilets on every floor and they are clean, nice and the sit-down kind.

- There is a separate room here, near the toilets on the ground floor near the escalators, especially made for baby changing and baby nursing.
- Stroller-friendly.
- There is a nice gift shop on the premises.

Special Programs and Tours

The museum runs a program called MuseKids which has special events (normally centred around holiday periods) for children. Check the website or call the museum for more information.

For Educators

Schools and charitable non-profit organizations are all welcome to contact the museum for free guided tours. Call the Education and Volunteer Services Team for more details on 2180-8180. The museum has a variety of programs that cater to teachers and students.

Word of Mouth

You could easily make a full day's outing out of a trip to this museum by taking in the amusements at Sha Tin New Town Plaza or by taking a walk or bike ride along the promenade which runs parallel to the Shing Mun River. Bike rentals are available at Sha Tin Park along the river promenade.

Hong Kong Museum of Coastal Defence

175 Tung Hei Road
Shau Kei Wan, Hong Kong Island

Tel: 2569-1500
Website: http://hk.coastaldefence.museum
For area map: Go to the above website and click on "Location Map"

If your kids like tanks, guns, military uniforms, toy soldiers or just running through secret underground tunnels, this military museum is THE place to take them. Beautifully restored and set in and on the grounds of a more than 100-year-old fort, this museum covers 600 years of Hong Kong's coastal defence history from the Ming Dynasty to the present.

The inside, the outside and the way to get from place to place in this museum are all well designed and hold interesting things for visitors to see and do. You will need to begin your visit by necessity at the first of the three museum subdivisions – the Reception area. Beyond the perfunctory ticket taking, this area is where you will find the military vehicle and gun displays and the old gunpowder factory. Then make your way by elevator up to the top of a very large hill, where the fort, otherwise referred to as the Redoubt, is located. This is the main exhibition area and is divided into 13 galleries, each depicting a different period of Hong Kong's military history. There are some fascinating things to see here, including full-scale military uniforms from the Ming period through colonial times to the People's Liberation Army, complete battle scenes illustrated with the use of toy soldiers, miniature replicas of battleships, war photographs and multiple video presentations covering subjects from the Opium War to the Japanese occupation of Hong Kong.

Easily accessible from just outside the Redoubt is the third museum subdivision: the Historical Trail. As you follow this outdoor walk, you will find 15 restored military relics, including a torpedo station and underground magazines. The trail affords you not only a view of the fort from outside, but more importantly a breathtaking view of Victoria Harbour.

Though this museum is best suited to school-age children, there is a small play area here that will appeal to toddlers too. On the second floor of the Redoubt are half a dozen little tables and chairs with toys, books, crayons for drawing and a bank of computers with interactive educational games. The museum runs some special creative activities for young children in this play area; check the website under "Educational Programs" for more information on the current offerings.

Seasons and Times

Mondays-Wednesdays, Fridays-Sundays: 10:00am-5:00pm. Closed on Thursdays. Closed on the first two days of the Chinese New Year.

Admission

Adults: HK$10; Children (four and older)/full time students: HK$5. Free admission on Wednesdays.

The Best Ways of Getting There

By City Tram
- From **Central's Des Voeux Road** or from **Admiralty's Queensway** to **Shau Kei Wan**, take the **tram heading east**. Stops are located in the middle of the road about every three blocks.

    (Tip: Make sure the tram front reads "Shau Kei Wan" or it won't get you all the way to where you want to go.)

↔ Travel time: 60+ mins (tram).

Once you exit the tram you can either walk to the museum or take a short taxi ride.

  ### Walking
  - Walk north on **Shau Kei Wan Road** (where the tram lets you out) until you intersect with Tung Hei Road heading north.

  ↔ Travel time: 15 mins (walk)

  ### By Taxi
  - A taxi will cost HK$20.

  ↔ Travel time: 5 mins (taxi).

NOTE: Keep in mind, the City Tram is the "scenic" way to get there. Though it is by far the most time-consuming way to arrive at the museum, it may also be the most fun for your kids. Established about 100 years ago, this mode of transportation is the only one of its kind left in the world. These old-fashioned street trams operate on roughly 10 miles of track set in the middle of some of the busiest streets in Hong Kong. Make

香港　筲箕灣　東喜道１７５號

香港海防博物館

3+

sure you sit on the upper deck to get the most out of your experience. Please note the trams are not air-conditioned, though they do keep all the windows open and there is a breeze. Fares are HK$2.30 for adults and HK$1.20 for kids. A real bargain!!!

By MTR
- From **Central** or **Admiralty** take the blue line to **Shau Kei Wan Station**. Exit the station at exit **"B2"**.

↔ Travel time: 20 mins (MTR).

From **Shau Kei Wan Station** you have two options to get to the museum.

Walking
- Take **Tung Hei Road heading north**.

↔ Travel time: 15 mins (walk).

By Taxi
- A taxi will cost HK$20.

↔ Travel time 5 mins (taxi).

By Car
- From Central: Connaught Road→Harcourt Road→Gloucester Road→**Island Eastern Corridor (Route 4).**
- Follow signs for **North Point** until you start seeing signs for **Chai Wan** and **Shau Kei Wan**, then follow those signs.
- Take the **exit marked "Shau Kei Wan"** which is <u>**Exit 3B**</u>. You are now on **Tung Hei Road**.
- Follow the road around until you see the museum's car park on your **left hand side**. (*Tip: You will first spot two black-and-white signs for the museum en route and then two blue-and-white signs directing you along Tung Hei Road.*)
- The turn for the museum is **just before the re-entrance** to the expressway (Route 4).

P The museum car park is open to the public between 10:00am and 5:00pm, except Thursday and the first two days of Chinese New Year. Visitors may park their car free of charge for up to three hours. You will need to get your car park ticket chopped at the ticketing area when you pick up your ticket for the museum.

By Taxi
A taxi from Central will cost around HK$100+ and take 20 mins.

Getting a Bite
If the kids need a snack or a meal, there is a cafeteria east of the Redoubt which serves sandwiches, snacks, noodles and ice

cream. Even if you are not hungry or thirsty, the view from the balcony of the restaurant is worth the trip. Another option is to bring a picnic and take in the sights of the harbour below.

Comments

- Best suited to ages five and older.
- You should plan a two-hour visit, shorter if your children are very young.
- Generally not crowded.
- There are three modern toilets in the museum, one in each subdivision.
- There is a baby-changing facility near the entrance to the Redoubt. It is well signposted.
- Mostly stroller-friendly, though there are a few areas with steps.
- There is a souvenir shop.

Extra Info

The fort itself is a very attractive piece of architecture, enhanced by the tent-like covering that was added to enclose the museum. Parents will enjoy the panoramic views provided from both inside and out. Don't forget the camera!

Special Programs and Tours

Guided tours are available on Wednesdays, Saturdays, Sundays and public holidays at 11:00am, 2:15pm and 3:30pm. The first two of the day are of the Redoubt, the last one covers the Walking Trail.

For Educators

All kindergartens, primary schools, tertiary institutions, universities and registered charitable and non-profit-making organizations can apply for a free guided tour. For more information contact the Education Unit on 2569-1248.

Word of Mouth

The exhibitions inside the Redoubt may be a bit scary for little kids. On the top floor of the Redoubt, very near the Children's Corner, is a small but very difficult to experience photographic display called "The Cost of War". It would be best to avoid showing children these photographs of the atrocities of war, as it may scare and upset them.

Hong Kong Museum of History
100 Chatham Road South
Tsim Sha Tsui, Kowloon

Tel: 2724-9042
Website: www.lcsd.gov.hk/hkmh/
For area map:
http://www.lcsd.gov.hk/CE/Museum/History/en/location.php

This is not a boring, stuffy old relic that you will have to drag your kids to. Instead you can expect a spacious and modern museum offering a very enjoyable historical and cultural journey. As you walk through 7,000 square metres of history you will be seeing, hearing and experiencing "The Hong Kong Story." Your encounter will begin in the Devonian Period (400 million years ago) and take you through to 1997 and the return of Hong Kong's sovereignty to China.

Each of the eight galleries has something to amuse and delight the younger set (and the older set as well). The Natural Environment Gallery has a special film which simulates a volcanic atmosphere complete with lava effects. There is a walk-through mini ecosystem which has deceptively real-looking animals like a tiger, a bear and a snake representing those creatures that roamed Hong Kong before us. The Folk Culture Gallery offers a life-size replica of a fishing junk used by boat dwellers which can be freely explored. This area also has a Hakka peasant family dwelling and a reconstruction of the events of the Bun Festival. Full-sized bun mountains, a Taoist altar, the costumes for the lion dance, and last but not least a replica of a Cantonese opera theatre all help to recreate the environment of one of Hong Kong's most exciting cultural events.

The highlight of your trip to the History Museum will no doubt be the Birth and Early Growth of the City Gallery which does a fabulous job of depicting life in Hong Kong before 1941. Here the curators have created a small city complete with a traditional tea shop, a grocery store, a post office, a pawnshop, a bank and a Chinese herbal medicine shop. There is also an old-fashioned double decker tram which kids can pretend to drive.

In all of the galleries there is at least one short video pertaining to the subject matter of that section of the museum. The films are given in three languages including English. Check outside each theatre for the posted show times.

Seasons and Times

Mondays, Wednesdays-Saturdays – 10:00am-6:00pm.
Sundays and public holidays – 10:00am-7:00pm.
Closed on Tuesdays (except for public holidays) and also closed on the first two days of the Chinese New Year. Closes early at 5:00pm on Christmas Eve and Chinese New Year's Eve.

Admission

Adults: HK$10; children (four and older): HK$5. Free admission on Wednesdays (except for some thematic exhibitions).

The Best Ways of Getting There

By Star Ferry
• From **Central to Tsim Sha Tsui** (TST) take the **Star Ferry** from the **Star Ferry Central pier**.
↔ Travel time: 10 mins (ferry).
• Once you exit the ferry in TST you can either take a bus or a taxi to the museum.
> **By Bus**
> • Take bus number **#5** or **#5C** at the **bus terminal** right in front of the **TST Star Ferry Pier** and get off the bus in front of the **Ramada Hotel** on **Chatham Road** (called 'Science Museum stop'). Walk across the overpass and follow the signs for the Museum of History and the Hong Kong Science Museum (they are part of the same complex).
> ↔ Travel time: 10 mins (bus) + 5 mins (walk).
> **By Taxi**
> A taxi from right outside the **TST Star Ferry Pier** will cost HK$20.
> ↔ Travel time: 5-10 mins (taxi).

By MTR
• From Central or Admiralty to **Tsim Sha Tsui Station**, take the red line. Exit the MTR station at exit "**B2**" marked "**Tsim Sha Tsui East**".
• Walk 10-15 minutes along **Cameron Road** going east. Cameron Road dead-ends into **Chatham Road**. Make a left

香港歷史博物館 九龍 尖沙咀 漆咸道南100號

5+

here and walk five minutes until you see the museum on your right side.

↔ Travel time: 10 mins (MTR) + 15-20 mins (walk).

By Car

- From Central take the **Cross Harbour Tunnel**: Connaught Road→ Harcourt Road→ Gloucester Road→**Island Eastern Corridor**.
- In tunnel and tollbooths (HK$20) stay to the far left. Follow signs for **Tsim Sha Tsui** and **Kwai Chung**. From here there is a series of three left hand turns all marked for either **TST** or the **Hong Kong Coliseum/Railway Terminus**. These turns all lead you to **Chatham Road South**.
- You will pass the Polytechnic University on your left side and at the next street you will see the Museum of History on your left which is the same complex as the Science Museum. P Make the next left turn onto **Granville Road** and an immediate right hand turn into **Granville Square** where you will see the blue "**P**" sign for the car park. Please note that there is no parking provided by the museum, this is a private paid car park.

By Taxi

A taxi from Central will cost HK$75-$85 and take 20-25 mins.

Getting a Bite

There is a café on the ground floor which offers drinks, light snacks, meals such as pasta, chicken wings, fried rice and noodles in soup as well as ice cream and sweets.

What's Close?

Hong Kong Science Museum.

Comments

- Suitable for ages four and older.
- Plan at least a two-hour visit.
- The museum is generally not overcrowded.
- The toilets here are clean, sit-down style and located on every floor.
- The museum has a baby care station on the ground floor.
- Stroller-friendly.
- There is a gift shop.

For Educators

The Museum of History provides special educational group tours. Call 2724-9080 for booking. Reservations should be made no less than two weeks before the date of the visit.

Word of Mouth

The Museum of History shares the same complex with the Science Museum. If you want to plan a very full day with older kids, you could try to do both.

Hong Kong Maritime Museum
Ground Floor, Murray House, Stanley Plaza
Stanley, Hong Kong Island

Tel: 2813-2322
Website: http://www.hkmaritimemuseum.org/
For area map: See website above (click on "Location and Information")
Please note that in mid-2012 this museum will move to Pier 8 in Central.
In 2012 and beyond, please call or check the website before you go.

This museum might be small, but it certainly makes a big impression on kids. When visiting Stanley Village, this should be a 'must-do' part of your itinerary, but it is also interesting enough to be a draw in itself. Curators, recognizing the attraction today's children have to electronic interactive games and computerized activities, have gone to significant effort to create a learning environment that feels like fun and play.

Located in historic Murray House, the Maritime Museum is dedicated to the evolution of maritime trade and naval warfare on the South China coast and beyond. There are two galleries here – the Ancient Gallery and the Modern Gallery. The first is dedicated to the turbulent ups and downs of Chinese maritime trade in ancient times and the second to the modernization of ships and trade in the 20th and 21st centuries. Sounds dry? It's not. There is a game where kids are physically standing on a replica of a ship's bridge and, using a combination of traditional ship's equipment and modern computer screens, play the 'captain' to manoeuvre either a tanker or an ocean liner through a very uncanny likeness of Victoria Harbour. There is also a replica of an old radio room, where the engineer (i.e. child) must use a real, but old, Morse code machine to send a signal to shore that there has been a fire or a pirate attack. Without them even knowing it, kids will be learning true Morse code and its value in pre-mobile phone times. At every turn, there are touch screens and games, as well as interesting models of ships and other visually stimulating exhibits.

The two galleries house the permanent exhibits, but the museum also has temporary exhibitions as well. At the time of printing of this book the program on offer, "Fathoming the Sea", was about the wonders of the underwater world and the development of deep sea diving. Check the website for details on the current visiting exhibit.

This museum is best visited during the week or at 10:00am on weekends when it first opens its doors. Most of the interactive exhibits can only take one child at a time and if the museum is crowded your child may not be able to experience all the museum has to offer.

Seasons and Times
Tuesday-Sunday and public holidays: 10am-6pm
Closed on Mondays and the first two days of the Lunar New Year.

Admission
Adults: HK$20; children (aged under 18), full time students, and people with disabilities: HK$10; senior citizens (aged 65 or above): HK$10; groups of 10 people or above: standard rate less 20% discount (a form must be filled out for groups). Annual Family Pass: HK$130 for unlimited entries. Each pass admits registered family members only, maximum four members.

The Best Ways of Getting There
By Bus
• From **Central Exchange Square Bus Terminus** take bus **#6** (Stanley Prison via Ma Hang only), **#6X,** or **#66** for **Stanley Plaza**.
(*Tip: These three bus routes are all run with double decker buses and are a great way to see the island if you sit on the top deck on the right side as you go toward Stanley, left side as you head back to Central.*)
• From the bus terminus at **Stanley Plaza** take the escalators or elevators down to the ground floor, walk across the piazza and toward the sea and you will find the **Murray Building** on your right hand side past the temple.
↔ Travel time: 35-40 mins (bus).

By Car
• From Central: Connaught Road→Harcourt Road→Gloucester Road→**Island Eastern Corridor**.
Once on the expressway, stay in the far right lane. It will be labelled **Happy Valley/Causeway Bay**. The far right lane will

香港　赤柱
香港　赤柱
美利樓地下　赤柱廣場
香港海事博物館

5+

dead-end into a circular overpass. Here you will stay in the far right lane following the signs for the **Aberdeen Tunnel**.

- Once through the tunnel, take one of the tollbooths on the **left side** (HK$5) then get in the far left lane. This lane will force you to make a left turn. You will now be on **Wong Chuk Hang Road** which will turn into **Island Road**.
- Island Road changes names to **Repulse Bay Road** and then to **Stanley Gap Road**, though the road remains constant.
- Stay on **Stanley Road** until you see the right turnoff for **Chung Hom Kok Road** (there will be a sign there with an arrow for Stanley Plaza).
- Follow **Chung Hom Kok Road** until the left turn for **Cape Road**. Follow Cape Road as it turns into **Carmel Road**.

P There is a paid private parking lot on the left or you can park in the parking garage at Stanley Plaza on your right side.

By Taxi
A taxi from Central will cost HK$90+ and take 25-30 mins.

Getting a Bite
Please see **Stanley Village** chapter, Getting a Bite section for options.

What's Close?
Stanley Village, Stanley Beach, St. Stephen's Beach, Tai Tam Reservoir Walk (short taxi ride away).

Comments
- This museum is best suited to children ages five and up.
- You should plan at least a one-hour visit.
- Generally not crowded during the week unless there is a school visit going on. Very crowded at weekends.
- There are sit-down toilets in the museum.
- There is no baby-changing station in the museum but you could use the benches outside if you needed to.
- Stroller-friendly, though it would be hard to move around with one if it was crowded as the museum is small.
- There is a great gift shop on the premises.

Special Programs and Tours
Guided tours for groups can be provided by appointment. Call 2813-2322 or email info@hkmaritimemuseum.org for details.

For Educators

The museum curators have prepared a comprehensive teacher's guide with information on their permanent exhibition and students' visits. A set of worksheets in both Chinese and English is available and downloadable on their website. For educators who would like to organize a tour for their students please write to: education@hkmaritimemuseum.org.

Word of Mouth

The current museum has only two galleries. When they move to Central, near the Star Ferry, in 2012 they will be expanding fivefold and will have 10 galleries.

Hong Kong Railway Museum
13 Shung Tak Street
Tai Po Market, New Territories

Tel: 2653-3455
Website: www.heritagemuseum.gov.hk (under "Branch Museums", "Tai Po").
For area map: See website above, click on "Railway Museum" and then "Location Map."

Do your kids love trains? If so, this small but very quaint open-air museum is a lovely place to take them. The museum is located on the site of the old Tai Po Market KCR station built in 1913. After being declared a historical monument, it was refurbished and opened to the public in 1985 as the Railway Museum.

When you enter the front gates, you will first come to the very small but lovely depot which houses Kowloon-Canton Railway (KCR) memorabilia. Inside, kids will most likely gravitate to the miniature train sets, the ticket windows and a few interactive computer screens. You won't be indoors for long. The major attraction of this museum is to be found outside on the train tracks. Numerous old train cars are here to be explored. Kids will love running up and down the aisles, pretending to take tickets, conducting the train, holding up passengers, or any other train fantasy they wish to indulge in. They will also be allowed to play on the stretch of track that is not covered by the trains, a dream come true for some kids (and maybe some adults too). All aboard, everyone!

Why not extend your visit to the Tai Po Market area by taking in a few of the other interesting sights? The Tai Po market itself will be fascinating for some kids. Here you will find live chickens, eels, fish and all kinds of interesting fruits and vegetables. The market is located on Heung Sze Wui Street on the way to the museum from the MTR station. You could also visit the Man Mo Temple located just a few blocks from the museum. Built in the late 19th century, this temple is very popular with local residents and tourists. To reach the temple, walk straight up the street from the museum's exit and turn left on Fu Shin Street (the second left hand turn from the exit), and walk through the Fu Shin Market until you reach Man Mo Temple on your left.

Seasons and Times
Mondays, Wednesdays-Sundays, public holidays: 9:00am-5:00pm. Closed Tuesdays, Christmas Day, Boxing Day, New Year's Day and the first three days of the Chinese New Year.

Admission
Free

The Best Ways of Getting There
By MTR
- From **Central** or **Admiralty** to **Kowloon Tong Station**, take the red line to **Mongkok**. **Transfer to the green line** (across the platform at Mongkok station) to **Kowloon Tong**.
- In Kowloon Tong Station look for the **East Rail Line**. Ride it to **Tai Po Market Station**. Look for the **exit** marked "**Hong Kong Railway Museum**", exit **"A3".**
↔ Travel time: 20 mins (MTR) + 20-25 mins (East Rail).
- From Tai Po Market station you have two choices to get to the museum:
    #### Walking
    - Once you **exit the MTR** station taking **Exit A3,** you will make **a right turn onto a pedestrian walkway**.
    - At the end of the walkway, **turn right onto Wan Tau Street** (the first street you come to).
    - At the first intersection turn left onto **Heung Sze Wui Street**.
    - **Follow Heung Sze Wui Street** until you get to Po **Heung Street**. **Cross Po Heung Street** at the light and once across the road, **turn right on Po Heung Street and walk to the next corner**.
    - Here you will find **Wai Yi Street**. Turn left onto **Wai Yi Street**.
    - You will come to a junction and up ahead, heading slightly uphill, you will see **Shung Tak Street.**
    - **Walk up Shung Tak Street** and the gate of the museum is directly ahead. (*Tip: This walk is short but convoluted. Look for the large blue-and-white museum signs to help guide you along the way. If that fails, ask someone nearby to help lead you there.*)
    ↔ Travel time: 10-15 mins (walk).
    #### By Taxi
    - A taxi from Tai Po Market Station will cost HK$16.50.
    ↔ Travel time: 5 mins (taxi).

3+

By Car

While getting to Tai Po is straightforward, finding the museum once you get there is NOT. Follow these directions very carefully with a MAP in hand to guide you.

- From Central: Connaught Road→Harcourt Road→Gloucester Road→**Island Eastern Corridor (Route 4)**→**Cross Harbour Tunnel (Route 1)**:
- In tunnel stay in right lane. Once through tollbooth (HK$20) stay right and follow signs for **Ho Man Tin and Sha Tin**. **You are on Route 1**.
- Stay on Route 1 and follow signs for **Sha Tin and Kowloon Tong**. **Stay in centre lane**, you are now on **Princess Margaret Road**.
- Follow signs for **Lion Rock Tunnel**. Go through tunnel (HK$8). You are now **on Lion Rock Tunnel Road.**
- You are still on **Route 1**. Follow signs for **Sha Tin, Ma On Shan and Tai Po**, then signs for **Ma On Shan and Tai Po**.
- You will **merge with Route 9** as you continue to follow signs for **Tai Po and Fanling**. You are now on **Route 9**.
- You will be looking for exit to **Tai Po Market (NOT Tai Po)!**
- This exit is **Exit #5** to **Tai Po Market. Stay to the left at the exit following the signs, as there is a juncture here**.
- You will come to a **roundabout**; exit the roundabout at the sign for **Tai Po Market**.
- You are now on **Kwong Fuk Road** which will take you into the town of Tai Po.
- At the second traffic signal from the roundabout (in town) make a left turn onto **Wan Tau Street – there is a 7-Eleven on this corner**.
- Then a **right turn** onto **Heung Sze Wui Street**.
- Then a **right turn** onto **Po Heung Street** and then immediately **a left turn following the blue-and-white museum signs** onto **Wai Yi Street**.
- Cross **On Fu Road** to **Shung Tak Street**. The museum gate is dead ahead.

P For parking, turn right at the dead end onto **Yan Hing Street** and you will find two-hour metered parking on the street.

By Taxi

A taxi from Central will cost HK$250-$300+ and take 50-55 mins.

Getting a Bite

There is a wonderful Italian restaurant called **Lanciano's**, Ground Floor, 31-33 Yan Hing Street, 2651-6660, two blocks from the Railway Museum. They have pasta, pizza and other main dishes that kids will enjoy and it is very reasonably priced and child-friendly. To find it, walk out the gate of the museum, turn left and walk two blocks straight ahead. You will find Lanciano's on the second corner on your left (very near the back of the Man Mo Temple). Alternatively, if you want a Chinese meal, head to **Great Day Restaurant**, 9 Heung Sze Wui Street, which is on the way back to the Tai Po Market MTR Station if you are walking.

What's Close?

Tai Po Market, Man Mo Temple and **Tai Po Waterfront Park**.

Comments

- Suitable for ages three and older.
- If you are only going to take in the museum, plan a one-hour visit or less; if you are also planning to explore the Tai Po Market attractions, plan on 2-3 hours.
- Generally not crowded.
- The toilets at the museum are very nice and clean and are the sit-down kind. You should encourage your children to use them before you go on to explore Tai Po or get back on the MTR, as they are the nicest toilets in the area.
- There is no baby-changing station at the museum.
- The museum and the market are not the best places to bring a stroller (though you can do it). A backpack or baby carrier will be much easier.

For Educators

Guided museum tours are available for schools and community groups. Contact the Leisure and Cultural Services Department for more information on 2414-5551. They have a pledge to respond to your request within seven working days.

Word of Mouth

Keep in mind that this might be a long way to come from Hong Kong Island for a small museum and therefore you may wish to plan a half day or full day trip to enjoy the museum, the Tai Po Market, the Man Mo Temple and other Tai Po attractions while

you are out here.

Police Museum and Coombe Road/Wanchai Gap Playgrounds

27 Coombe Road (between Stubbs Road and Peak Road), Wanchai Gap, Hong Kong Island

Tel: 2849-7019
Website: http://www.police.gov.hk/ppp_en/01_about_us/pm.html
For area map: Go to the website above and click on: "A pamphlet of the museum", here you will find a map of the general area.

The one-two combination of an interesting little museum in immediate proximity to two wonderful playgrounds is a hard draw to resist! Set high up above Mid Levels, away from the crowds and noise, this tranquil area offers an experience both kids and parents can enjoy.

Recently restored and reopened (October 2010), the Police Museum, though small in size (570 square metres) has some interesting exhibits that will intrigue the kids. Along with historical photographs and police uniforms, you will find guns, knives, home-made weapons, bomb detectors, drug trafficking paraphernalia, triad ceremonial robes, counterfeiting machines, a replica of a heroin manufacturing laboratory and the head of the infamous Sheung Shui tiger, to name just a few. Most of the things on exhibition are at their most fascinating when combined with the stories of the events they represent. For instance, the displayed tiger head is a part of the true legend of a charging tiger found in the New Territories in 1915. It had killed one officer and seriously wounded another before being shot by a police squad. The history here, from 1844 to the present, will require reading and explaining so be prepared to be actively involved in the whole experience. Make sure you see all four galleries – the Orientation Gallery, the Triad Societies and Narcotics Gallery, the 'Hong Kong Police Then and Now' Gallery, and the Current Exhibition Gallery – to get the most out of your visit. Check the website to see the latest offering at the Current Exhibition Gallery; sometimes the topics are very kid-friendly such as the recent "Police Dog Unit".

When you have had your fill of police history, head down to the two playgrounds below for some rest and relaxation. Coombe Road Playground, located directly beneath the museum, has a large jungle gym and riding toys and a path where young children can ride their little bikes (though not suitable for older children with larger bikes). Across the street, Wanchai Gap Playground and Park offers swings, slides, monkey bars, jungle gyms and shaded picnic tables. Both playgrounds have benches, some even in the shade.

Seasons and Times
Police Museum – Tuesdays: 2:00pm-5:00pm, Wednesdays-Sundays: 9:00am-5:00pm.
Closed Mondays and public holidays.
Playgrounds – 7:00am-11:00pm daily.

Admission
Free

The Best Ways of Getting There
By Bus
- From **Central Exchange Square Bus Terminus**, take bus **#15** going toward **The Peak**.
- Alight the bus at the **Wanchai Gap Road** bus stop, at the juncture of Stubbs Road and Peak Road. On your left, as you approach the bus stop, you will see a large blue-and-white police museum sign with an arrow pointing you in the right direction.
- Follow the arrow to **Coombe Road**. You will pass Wanchai Gap playground on your left and Coombe Road playground on your right. Make a right at the Coombe Road parking lot and you will see the museum on the hill above to the right.
- The steps to climb up to the museum are located at the back of the parking lot. (*Tip: This bus is a double decker so be sure to get a seat on the top deck for the best view.*)
↔ Travel time: 15-20 mins (bus) + 5 mins (walk)

By Car
- From Central take **Garden Road** up to **Magazine Gap Road**.
- Follow Magazine Gap Road until it dead-ends into the intersection with **Peak Road**.
- At this juncture, make a left hand turn onto **Peak Road**. Follow the road around (about 5-8 mins) until you reach the **juncture of Peak Road, Coombe Road and Stubbs Road**.

5+
museum
0-99
playground

- Make a right hand turn here onto **Coombe Road**.
- Stay on Coombe Road until you see the parking lot for the Police Museum on your right side.

P Metered parking is available in the Coombe Road parking lot.

P For free parking, turn right onto **Mount Cameron Road** from Peak Road. You can park on the street here next to the Wanchai Gap Playground and then walk five minutes back to the museum.

By Taxi
A taxi from Central will cost HK$40-$50 and take 15 mins.

Getting a Bite
Bring snacks and drinks or a picnic lunch or dinner with you as the Wanchai Gap playground has several tables set up under the shade of trees that make an ideal spot for "alfresco" dining. There are no stalls or vending machines in the park, so come prepared.

What's Close?
Bowen Road Walk, Black's Link Walk and Lady Clementi's Ride Walk.

Comments
- The museum is best suited to children aged five and older.
- Plan to spend one hour or less at the museum depending on whether your kids can read or not. The playgrounds in combination with the museum can amuse for two to three hours.
- There are sit-down style toilets in the museum and also in the ladies and disabled toilets at Wanchai Gap playground.
- There is a baby-changing station at the museum. The toilet at the Wanchai Gap Playground has a counter top that can be used as a baby-changing area.
- Do not bring a stroller up to the museum as it is located at the top of a hill accessed by a set of steep steps.
- There is no formal gift shop at the museum but the front desk has a few souvenirs for sale (including a Police Museum key ring for HK$3, which makes a great kids' souvenir at the right price).

For Educators
Group visits to the museum can be arranged. Call the general number 2849-7019 for inquiries.

Word of Mouth
The material in this museum is going to provoke questions from your kids about difficult issues. Be prepared, if you decide to visit, to discuss concepts such as crime, triads, drugs, guns and war.

Hong Kong Museum of Art
10 Salisbury Road
Tsim Sha Tsui, Kowloon

Tel: 2721-0116

Website: www.lcsd.gov.hk/hkma

For area map: Click on the above website and then "About Us" and then "Location Map".

For kids interested in the fine arts, there are few better Hong Kong experiences than a visit to this lovely art museum. The collection of art objects held here is northward of 15,000, of which only the best of the best are displayed. The museum aims to preserve Chinese cultural heritage and promote interest in local art.

The first floor of the museum has an incredible collection of Chinese jade and gold in the Chinese Antiquities Gallery. The second floor is the home of the Contemporary Hong Kong Art Gallery, the Xubaizhai Gallery of Painting and Calligraphy, and the first of two special exhibition galleries. Generally the special exhibitions contain an interactive area which will be a hit with kids. At the time of printing of this book, the special exhibition on this floor was called "From Common to Uncommon," exhibiting the work of artist Ha Bik-chuen. The art featured here centred around the theme of making common everyday objects and scenes into uncommon art. At the end of the exhibit, guests were invited to create paper prints using common objects. Children of all ages were enjoying giving it a try, adults too!

The third floor has the Chinese Antiquities Gallery and the second special exhibition hall as well as the Education Corner. This corner is a dedicated interactive area with varying artistic themes and a ceramics demonstration area. At the time of our visit, children were invited to design cards using ink and ancient Chinese symbols. The curators here are clearly very keen to introduce children to the fun elements of viewing and appreciating art.

The top and final floor houses the Chinese Fine Arts Gallery which covers the various schools of traditional Chinese painting. The museum also offers international exhibitions which cover both classical and contemporary art of the West and Chinese antiquities from outside their collection. Examples of previously offered exhibitions include Egyptian Treasures, Buddhist Sculptures and Louis Vuitton: A Passion for Creating.

Seasons and Times

Monday to Friday: 10:00am-8:00pm
Saturdays: 10:00am-6:00pm
Closed on Thursdays (except public holidays) and the first two days of Chinese New Year. Closed at 5:00pm on Christmas Eve and Chinese New Year's Eve.
Museum Café – 10:00am-8:00pm daily. Closed on Thursdays (except public holidays) and the first two days of Chinese New Year. Tel: 2370-3860.
Museum Book Shop – 10:00am-6:30pm daily. Saturdays 10:00am-8:00pm. Closed on the first two days of Chinese New Year.

Admission

Adults: HK$10; Children (four and older)/full time students: HK$5. Free admission on Wednesdays.

The Best Ways of Getting There

By Star Ferry

- From **Central** to **Tsim Sha Tsui (TST)** take the Star Ferry from the **Star Ferry Central Pier**.
- When you exit the ferry pier in TST walk straight ahead and you will be on **Salisbury Road**. The museum is on the **harbour side of Salisbury Road**, a 5-10 minute walk from the pier.
  (Tip: The Museum of Art is directly across from the Space Museum. Look for the Space Museum's egg-shaped dome as a guide.)
- ↔ Travel time: 10 mins (ferry) + 10 mins (walk).

By MTR

- From **Central** or **Admiralty** to **Tsim Sha Tsui Station**, take the red line. Exit the MTR station at exit **"E"**. This exit is marked The Peninsula Hotel, not the Museum of Art, but take it anyway. You will now be on **Nathan Road**.
- Walk down **Nathan Road one block** toward the harbour and you will dead-end into **Salisbury Road**.

6+

- Directly in front you will see the dome of the Space Museum. **The Museum of Art is located just behind the Space Museum.**
  *(Tip: If it is raining, stay underground and follow the signs for the Museum of Art, which will take you underground to the **TST East Station**. In this case you will walk 5-10 mins underground from exit **"J"** onward to exit **"J4"** which will take you through Sogo Department Store and then onto the street, one minute from the museum entrance. It is much faster to walk over ground from the first set of directions above, however in inclement weather, take this second route.)*
- ↔ Travel time: 10 mins (MTR) + 10 mins (walk).

By Car
- From Central: Connaught Road→Harcourt Road→ Gloucester Road→Island Eastern Corridor **(Route 4)**→**Cross Harbour Tunnel (Route 1)**.
- In tunnel and tollbooth (HK$20) stay to the far left. Follow signs for **Tsim Sha Tsui and Kwai Chung**. From here there is a series of **three left hand turns** all marked for either TST or the Hong Kong Coliseum/Railway Terminus. These turns all lead you to **Chatham Road South**.
- Stay on **Chatham Road South** until it dead-ends into **Salisbury Road**. (You will pass the HK Polytechnic University and the History Museum on your left.) Turn right on Salisbury Road and then turn left and directly into **New World Centre Mall driveway**.

🅿 New World Centre Mall has an underground car park. This is the nearest place to park. From here it is a five-minute walk down Salisbury Road to the museum.

By Taxi
A taxi from Central will cost HK$75-$85 and take 20-30 mins.

Getting a Bite

The museum has its own café, called *Museum Café*, which is accessed through the gift shop or immediately before you enter the main doors of the museum. It has both an outdoor and indoor seating area and overlooks the harbour. This eatery does not have a specific kids' menu, but there are many items on offer which are very suitable to children's tastes, such as jumbo hot dogs, fish and chips, pasta, sandwiches and pizza, all at very reasonable prices. If all you want is a snack, they also offer

a variety of desserts which are especially nice to enjoy while you are sitting outside overlooking Victoria Harbour.
There are several other restaurant options in this large municipal complex (consisting of the Art and Space Museums and the Cultural Centre):

Starbucks – Inside the foyer of the Cultural Centre.
Deli and Wine – Just outside the Cultural Centre doors – casual upscale deli which serves noodles, burgers, sandwiches, curries, bakery items and has a frozen yogurt counter.
Café Muse – On the ground floor behind the Space Museum - serves international fare.
Serenade – On the 1st floor behind the Space Museum – serves Chinese fare.

Keep in mind that the Art Museum is in the heart of TST, so if you are willing to walk for a few minutes you will have your choice of dozens of restaurants for lunch or dinner. One possibility might be to walk over to Ocean Terminal for a meal (see the **Kowloon Park** chapter, **Getting a Bite** section, for more info) or for yet another option, check out the newly restored 1881 Heritage complex across Salisbury Road from the museum.

What's Close?
The Space Museum, The Cultural Centre, The Peninsula Hotel, 1881 Heritage and Ocean Terminal.

Comments
- This museum is best suited for children ages six and above.
- Plan to spend one to two hours here.
- Generally not overcrowded except on Wednesdays when admission is free.
- The toilets are clean and nice.
- There are no baby-changing stations.
- Stroller-friendly.
- The gift shop on the first floor is filled with art, music, cards, books, paper, stickers and traditional Chinese gift items.

Special Programs and Tours
The museum offers a free introductory service as well as free guided tours. Please see the information desk upon your arrival for more information. In the basement of the museum, there are a variety of rooms to further one's art education, including

a ceramic studio, a painting studio, a print-making studio, a resources centre and a lecture hall. The museum stages many special events here including lectures, gallery talks, open demonstrations, activities for parents and children, activities exclusively for children and thematic video presentations. A program of events is released quarterly. Check the information desk for a free catalogue of the special programs currently on offer.

For Educators

If you would like to set up a group visit for a school, please contact the special tours department on 2734-2154 or 2734-2070. Application forms must be filled out online but call first to check availability.

Word of Mouth

If you have older children (or even younger children with patience), stop off at the audio service guide counter before you begin your tour. There you can rent an audio player with headphones that will give you a running commentary as you walk through the museum galleries. The audio guides are available in English, Mandarin and Cantonese. The cost of this service is HK$10 per person.

Flagstaff House Museum of Tea Ware

(and the K.S. Lo Gallery)
10 Cotton Tree Drive (inside Hong Kong Park)
Central, Hong Kong Island

Tel: 2869-0690, 2869-6690 (The K.S. Lo Gallery)
Website: http://www.lcsd.gov.hk/ce/Museum/Arts/english/tea/tea.html
For area map (of Hong Kong Park): http://www.lcsd.gov.hk/parks/hkp/
en/index.php then click on 'Layout Plan'.

香港　中區

紅棉路10號

茶具文物館

Okay – admittedly the name of this museum is not likely to draw immediate excitement from the little ones, but it is worth getting past any objections they may have and going for a visit. This museum is a unexpected gem, especially in conjunction with a visit to Hong Kong Park.

The curators of the Museum of Art, of which this museum is a branch, want your children to be interested in tea and everything to do with tea: how it is made, how it is exported, what foods should accompany it and most importantly the beauty and variety of the vessels that hold it – the teapot and the teacup. They have created an interactive playroom dedicated to making learning about tea and its ceramic-ware fun! This dedicated space on the ground floor has four computers each with fun programs, several child-sized tables with theme-related activities, and even building blocks in the shape of the colonial building that houses the museum, for the kids to do some reconstruction of their own.

It is a true bonus that the museum is located in a beautiful mid-19th century Greek revival building, the oldest and one of the few of its kind still standing in Hong Kong. The charm of the architecture creates a special sensory experience, uniquely matched to the essence of the tradition of tea drinking, which is hard to find anywhere else in the city. Dozens of teacups and teapots, some dating as far back as the 11th century BC, are on display. Each of the artifacts is accompanied by a detailed written explanation of its origins and use, although perhaps for kids a better way to take in the information is by viewing the video on offer.

6+

When you venture up the sweeping staircase to the first-floor galleries you are in for a real treat. All of the top-floor rooms are dedicated to an exhibit of the Hong Kong Tea Ware Potters Competition, an annual event. These are not your grandmother's teapots or cups. The tea set themes, which include irons, purses, shells, trees, rams, chess, cards, buildings and old newspapers, are bound to spark conversation and interest from the little ones. This exhibit is a truly interesting show of ceramic art that everyone will enjoy.

The museum is split into two buildings, Flagstaff House and the K.S. Lo Gallery right next door. Flagstaff House has the majority of the permanent collection as well as the competition entries and winners. The K.S. Lo Gallery is dedicated to Chinese cultural relics, including a collection of ceramics dating back to 960 AD and selected ancient Chinese seals. The K.S. Lo Gallery is also home to the Tea House, a great place to stop and get tea and dim sum after your visit if the kids are hungry.

Seasons and Times
10:00am-5:00pm daily. Closed on Tuesdays, Christmas Day, Boxing Day (Dec. 26th), New Year's Day, and the first three days of the Chinese New Year.

Admission
Free

The Best Ways of Getting There
Walking
- From **Pacific Place** (shopping plaza) you can access the park using a series of escalators on the west side of the mall.
- At the top of the **escalator**, cross the street and you will see a **fountain** directly in front of you which marks the entrance to the park.
- Once in the park, turn right at the fountain and shortly you will see the museum on your right hand side.
- ↔ Travel time: 5 mins (walk - from park entrance).

By MTR
- From Central to **Admiralty Station**, exit "**C**" to exit "**C1**" marked "**Hong Kong Park**".
- When you get to street level, continue up the escalators into **Queensway Plaza**. Turn right and walk across the glass sky

bridge into **Pacific Place** following overhead signs to Hong Kong Park.

- Look for the Pacific Place west side **escalators** on your right and follow <u>walking</u> directions above.

↔ Travel time: 10 mins (MTR) + 10 mins (walk).

By Bus

- From **Exchange Square** or **City Hall** in Central take bus <u>**#12**</u> or from **Jardine House** on **Connaught Road** or **City Hall** on **Connaught Road** bus <u>**#3B**</u>.
- Exit either bus on **Cotton Tree Drive** just outside Hong Kong Park.
- Once inside the park, walk down the slope to your left and follow the signs for the museum.

↔ Travel time: 10 mins (bus) + 5 mins (walk).

By Car

- From Central take **Des Voeux Road** to **Queensway**.
- Stay in left lane and exit Queensway at the **Supreme Court Road** exit.
- You are now on **Justice Drive**. Follow the road around and make a right turn into Pacific Place. From Pacific Place follow the <u>walking</u> directions above.

P Pacific Place has a large underground car park.

By Taxi

A taxi from Central will cost HK$20 and take 5-10 mins.

Getting a Bite

See **Hong Kong Park** chapter for full details.

What's Close?

<u>Hong Kong Park</u>, <u>Hong Kong Zoological and Botanical Gardens</u>, Pacific Place and <u>The Peak Tram</u>.

Comments

- This museum is best suited to children ages five and up.
- You should plan a one-hour visit (or less).
- Generally not crowded.
- There are very nice, newly remodelled sit-down toilets here.
- There is a baby-changing station in the ladies toilet.
- Stroller-friendly (though there is a flight of stairs to the second floor).
- There is a gift shop on the premises.

Special Programs and Tours
Tea drinking demonstrations are given every Saturday from 11:30am-12:30pm at the K.S. Lo Gallery.

For Educators
Free guided tours are available for schools. Call 2849-9604 or 2849-9605 for bookings. Tour bookings need to be made at least three weeks but not more than three months in advance.

Word of Mouth
A great way to help keep the children interested in what they are observing is to let them know that they can 'vote' for their favourite entry in the Tea Ware exhibition at the end of their visit. Check the last gallery upstairs for the 'voting' board.

Chapter 3

Outdoor Fun - Hong Kong's Parks and Gardens

Parks and gardens are natural draws for families with young children and Hong Kong's offerings in this area are sure to please. What these areas lack in wide-open green spaces, they make up for with wonderful playgrounds and child-friendly activities. All manner of fun can be had at the 10 destinations covered in this chapter as the range of possibilities includes insect houses, animal enclosures, aviaries, paddle boating, model boat pools, biking, lookout towers, promenades, mazes, skateboard arenas, sand pits, lawns, and play areas.

The outings covered in this chapter are by no means a comprehensive list of all the parks and gardens in Hong Kong that are worthy of a visit. The Leisure and Cultural Services Department does a fantastic job of maintaining more than 32 parks in the territory. For more information, please call them on 2414-5555 or check their user-friendly and informative website on http://www.lcsd.gov.hk/. Whichever park you decide to visit, make sure you bring along four essential items: mosquito repellent, sun block, sun hats and drinking water. All parks are exposed to the sun and heat and mosquitoes are everywhere, particularly in the hot summer months.

1. Hong Kong Park
2. Victoria Park
3. Paddle Boating at Wong Nai Chung Reservoir Park
4. Inspiration Lake
5. Victoria Peak Garden
6. Hong Kong Zoological and Botanical Gardens
7. Kowloon Park
8. Tai Po Waterfront Park
9. Lai Chi Kok Park
10. Ma Wan Park and Noah's Ark

Hong Kong Park
Cotton Tree Drive
Central, Hong Kong Island

Tel: 2521-5041
Website: http://www.lcsd.gov.hk/parks/hkp/en/index.php
For a printable map of the park: Click on "layout plan" at the above website

Just a short distance from the heart of Central, this lovely eight-hectare park is an interesting mix of nature, modern design and old colonial Hong Kong. Opened in 1991 on the site of the former Victoria Barracks, this park's aim is to create a natural and serene space in the heart of Hong Kong where children and adults alike can come to commune with nature. There is something for every age group and interest here, including: a padded six-level children's playground, a walk-through aviary, a conservatory, a tea ware museum, a foot massage path, a Tai Chi garden, an indoor games hall, a visual arts centre, a tower with incredible views of Central and beyond, and a lovely "lake" (more like a large pond) area complete with waterfalls, goldfish, ducks and turtles.

The park's playground is a must for young children. Not only will they be thrilled by the six play platforms, but parents will be able to relax as the entire play space is padded! If the kids can be dragged away, head to the aviary for a walk through a rainforest. Set under a giant mesh tent, this 3,000 square metre aviary is filled with 600 birds from 90 different species. A wooden elevated walkway which winds its way through the whole structure will give visitors a close look at all the aviary has to offer. After bird life, take a stroll along the "lakes" area which has cascading waterfalls and ponds with goldfish and turtles, or walk up to the 1,400 square metre Conservatory (the largest in Southeast Asia) for a look at the Dry Plant House and the Humid Plant House.

Some of the other attractions of the park, the Vantage Point Tower, the Sports and Squash Centres and the Hong Kong Visual Arts Centre are all better suited to older children. The Vantage Point Tower, with its panoramic 360-degree view, is 30 metres high and can be accessed only by a 105-step spiral staircase (best climbed by the physically fit).

Make sure before leaving the park that you have a tour around the Museum of Tea Ware. Whilst the name of this museum might not ignite much enthusiasm in the little ones, it is in fact a wonderful, interesting and educational experience that caters to kids. (See the **Flagstaff House Museum of Tea Ware** chapter for more detailed information). Just behind the museum is a foot reflexology garden with a massage footpath which everyone might enjoy after a long walk through the hills of the park.

Seasons and Times

The Park – 6:00am-11:00pm daily.
Information Booth – Mondays-Fridays: 9:00am-5:00pm. Closed on Saturdays, Sundays and public holidays.
Conservatory – 9:00am-5:00pm daily.
Aviary – 9:00am-5:00pm daily.
Sports Centre and Squash Centre – 6:45am-11:15pm daily (call 2521-5072 for information on booking courts).
Visual Arts Centre – 10:00am-9:00pm daily. Closed on Tuesdays (check the website for information on classes and exhibitions: or call 2521-3008).
http://www.lcsd.gov.hk/CE/Museum/Apo/en/vac.html
L16 Restaurant – 11:00am-11:00pm daily.

Admission

Free

The Best Ways of Getting There

Walking:
- From **Pacific Place** (shopping plaza) you can access the park using a series of escalators on the west side of the mall.
- At the top of the escalator, cross the street and you will see a fountain directly in front of you which marks the entrance to the park.
- ↔ Travel time: 5 mins (walk).

By MTR
- From Central to **Admiralty** Station, exit "**C**" to exit "**C1**" marked "**Hong Kong Park**".
- When you get to street level, continue up the escalators into **Queensway Plaza**. Turn right and walk across the glass sky bridge into **Pacific Place** following overhead signs to Hong Kong Park.
- Look for the Pacific Place west side escalators on your right and follow <u>walking</u> directions above.

0-99

↔ Travel time: 10 mins (MTR) + 10 mins (walk).

By Bus
- From **Exchange Square** or **City Hall** in Central take bus **#12** – or from **Jardine House** on **Connaught Road** or **City Hall** on **Connaught Road** bus **#3B**.
- Exit either bus on **Cotton Tree Drive** just outside Hong Kong Park.

↔ Travel time: 10 mins (bus).

By Car
- From Central take **Des Voeux Road** to **Queensway**.
- Stay in left lane and exit Queensway at the **Supreme Court Road** exit.
- You are now on **Justice Drive**. Follow the road around and make a right turn into Pacific Place. From Pacific Place follow the **walking** directions above.

P Pacific Place has a large underground car park.

By Taxi
A taxi from Central will cost HK$20 and take 5-10 mins.

Getting a Bite
The park has a lovely indoor/outdoor Thai restaurant, located near the cascading waterfall, called *L16* (tel: 2522-6333) – perfect for a drink, snack or meal after a day at the park. The restaurant does not have a kids' menu but they do serve the top two kiddie favourites of pasta and pizza, and high chairs are provided upon request. If eating at the Thai place does not appeal to your kids, try one of the many restaurants in Pacific Place mall or walk across the pedestrian sky bridge at the west side of the park which connects you to the Great Eagle office tower (with a Citibank sign on its top). Once you are in the building, take the escalator down and you will find *Starbucks Coffee*, *Pacific Coffee Company* and several casual restaurants.

Another great option for a meal is in the Museum of Tea Ware. The K.S. Lo Gallery has a lovely tea and dim sum restaurant. (See **Getting a Bite** section of the **Museum of Tea Ware** chapter for details.)

There are also several snack stands around the park where you can get a drink or buy popcorn to feed yourselves or perhaps the fish.

What's Close?
The Peak Tram (in the Victoria Peak chapter), The Hong Kong Zoological and Botanical Gardens and Pacific Place mall.

Comments
- Suitable for all ages.
- Plan to spend a minimum of two hours at the park, more if you have older kids.
- There are five different toilet locations in the park; the ones near and around the playground have both sit-down style toilets and baby changing stations. The nicest toilets by far are inside the museum.
- The park is built on a steep hill so you will likely want your stroller with you, however, there are also many stairs to negotiate in places that can be tough for baby strolling. There are paths that are easier but you will need a map to find some of them.

Extra Info
To get a map, stop at the information booth located near the Cotton Tree Drive entrance on the west side of the park. Follow wheelchair access paths marked on the map if you have a stroller with you.

For Educators
Hong Kong Park has an Education Programs and Guided Tours Department. They offer special tours of the conservatory and the aviary to primary age students as well as special conservation-related tours for kindergarteners. Please call 2521-5068 for more information.

Word of Mouth
The playground has a very large sand pit complete with mechanical diggers that children can sit on and pretend to be Bob-the-Builder. These toys are not really suitable for infants and/or toddlers, so it might be better to bring your own shovel and pail if you intend a visit to the sand pit. If your child really likes to grovel in the gravel, you should bring a change of pants, as the sand can be dirty.

Victoria Park
Causeway Road
Causeway Bay, Hong Kong Island

Tel: 2890-5824
Website: http://www.lcsd.gov.hk/parks/vp/en/index.php
For printable map of the park: Go to above website and click on "Layout Map".

This lovely city park (the largest on Hong Kong Island), set in the heart of bustling Causeway Bay, is a great place to take your children to play. Victoria Park was built in the late 1950s on a 17-hectare parcel of reclaimed land, and was given a facelift from 2000-2002 with fantastic results. Attractions here include: a tennis centre, a public swimming pool complex, squash courts, basketball courts, bowling greens, soccer pitches, a reflexology garden, two children's play areas, a jogging path, an exercise circuit, a model boat pool, an expansive lawn area, a refreshment kiosk, and a restaurant.

The park is so large that in order to get around and find your way, it is best to get the lay of the land before you arrive. If you picture the park area as a square it is fairly easy to navigate. The Causeway Bay entrance is at the west end of the park, Victoria Park Road (along the harbour) is the north end, Hing Fat Street is the east end and Causeway Road marks the south end. In the middle of the square is the centre lawn, a large grassy area that is the heart of the park. Around the perimeter of the lawn is a new jogging path which has shaded benches just off the trail every few feet. Also around the edge of the lawn is a fitness circuit. The circuit is comprised of six stations, each focusing on a different kind of exercise. Children will enjoy testing their skills on some of the apparatus. (Bear in mind though, these are not toys and therefore need to be used with caution.)

The first of the two children's play areas is located at the northwest end of the park. Though this play area is by far the smaller of the two, it is still worth a visit as it has a variety of jungle gyms and riding toys that children will enjoy. It is even partially shaded. Next door to this play area is the model boat pool which can be a fun stop. Unfortunately, there is no place to rent model boats to sail here, but people are welcome to bring their own. Even if you are not sporting a model boat in your back pocket, stop by the pool and see the intricate boats that some of the "children" (read "men") bring.

Move from here east toward the second children's play area, located at the northeast end of the park. Along the way you will find the reflexology garden. This rock garden will provide you with a lovely foot massage just by walking on its path of stones. Make sure to bring or wear socks as most people remove their shoes, but going barefoot is not allowed. Just northeast of the "foot paradise" is the second children's play area. This is an enormous playground divided into three sections. There are many swings, from the baby variety to those for older kids. There are also numerous riding toys, slides and jungle gyms. Some areas are designed for two- to five-year-old children and others are meant for five- to 12-year-olds. In the middle section of the play area is a wonderful climbing structure designed to look and feel like a suspension bridge. The very northeast corner is tailored specifically for toddlers.

Victoria Park comes alive at both Chinese New Year, when it hosts a large flower show, and at Mid-Autumn Festival, when the centre lawn is transformed into a lantern-filled carnival. There are also major international sporting events held here. On Sundays and public holidays the park hosts an "Art Corner" from 10:00am-6:00pm at the South Pavilion Plaza, where local artists come to show their work and demonstrate their craft. Check the website, the local paper or www.discoverhongkong. com for upcoming events at the park.

Seasons and Times
Park – Year-round, 24 hours
Model Boat Pool – 9:00am-9:00pm daily
Swimming Pool – 6:30am-10:00pm (April to October), 6:30am-6:30pm (November)
Tennis Courts – 6:00am-11:00pm (April to September), 7:00am-11:00pm (the rest of the year). Tel: 2570-6186
Basketball Courts and Bowling Greens – 7:00am-11:00pm daily
Victoria Park Swimming Pool Restaurant – 11:00am-11:00pm daily. Tel: 2838-9488

0-99

Admission
Free (though Tennis Courts, Swimming Pool and Bowling Greens require a small hourly fee to use and the Tennis Courts and Bowling Greens also require advanced booking).

The Best Ways of Getting There
By MTR
- From Central or Admiralty ride the blue line to **Causeway Bay** station and take exit "**E**".
- This exit puts you on **Great George Street**. Go left, walking along Great George Street for two blocks until you find the park directly in front of you.

↔ Travel time: 10 mins (MTR) + 5-10 mins (walk).

By City Tram
- From Central's **Des Voeux Road** or from Admiralty's Queensway to Causeway Bay, take the tram heading east. Stops are located in the middle of the road about every three blocks.
- Exit the tram at **Causeway Road**. You will know when to exit as you will see the park on your left hand side and the Central Public Library on your right (a large yellow gold coloured building).

↔ Travel time: 20 mins (tram) + 3 mins (walk).

By Car
There is very limited parking at Victoria Park, so don't try driving here during peak times.
- From Central: Connaught Road→Harcourt Road→ Gloucester Road→**Island Eastern Corridor.**
- Follow signs for **Causeway Bay** and then stay in the middle lane and look for the exit for **Causeway Bay**.
- Follow the road as it turns to the right and take the **Gloucester Road Flyover** and exit to the left onto **Causeway Road**.
- Go through the light and then make a left hand turn onto **Hing Fat Street**.

🅿 The metered parking lot will be on your left. From here it is a 5-10 minute walk to the library (heading south).

By Taxi
A taxi from Central will cost HK$35-$45 and take 10-15 mins.

Getting a Bite

There are two meal options in the park. For a light snack or drink there is a refreshment kiosk just off the central lawn area on the north side. Or if you are in need of something more substantial, visit the park's only sit-down style restaurant, **_Victoria Park Swimming Pool Restaurant,_** which serves local Chinese fare. Located above the park's pool complex, this restaurant serves lunch, tea and dinner either indoors or alfresco, overlooking the pool and park. Prices are reasonable and the outdoor terrace is particularly good for little ones. There are also two drink vending machines next to the Tennis Centre booking office if all you are looking for is a cold drink.

What's Close?

The Central Library, Toys R Us, and IKEA.

Comments

- Suitable for all ages.
- Plan to spend one to two hours here.
- This park is extremely crowded on weekends and public holidays.
- There are toilets at the larger children's playground that are sit-down style. There are also some toilets located at the southwest end of the park near the Great George Street exit.
- There is a baby-changing table in the ladies' bathroom at the playground.
- Stroller-friendly.

Word of Mouth

Some events held here are worth the trouble of dealing with the crowds, such as the Flower Market Show on Chinese New Year's Eve and the Lantern Carnival at Mid-Autumn Festival.

Paddle Boating – Wong Nai Chung Reservoir Park

Tai Tam Reservoir Road (off Wong Nai Chung Gap Road, on the way to Parkview)
Hong Kong Island

Tel: 2812-1252
Website: http://www.lcsd.gov.hk/lsb/en/facilities.php?ftid=13&did=11
For area map: Go to above website and click on 'Location Map'.

In a city like Hong Kong, where skyscrapers and roadways abound, it is always nice to find a little pocket of nature to enjoy with your kids. When you spend a few hours at this lovely reservoir park, city life will seem miles away.

Originally built in 1899, this basin once functioned as a water source for the city. Due to its relatively small size and the high cost of its use, the Government decided in 1986 to convert the reservoir into a recreational park.

Renting a pedal boat or rowboat and getting out on the water is this park's main attraction. The boats are easy to use and manoeuvre so the kids can do the 'driving,' provided their legs are long enough to reach the pedals. Once out on the water, prepare yourself for a treat, as the surrounding views are lush, green and peaceful. The water is stocked with turtles, geese, ducks and a plethora of enormous goldfish who are far from shy. The fish will swim open-mouthed right alongside your boat in the hopes of getting a meal. You will want to be ready with bread to feed the fish which you can either bring from home, or buy for HK$8 a loaf from the boat rental stand. Life vests are provided upon request, including appropriate child-sized vests for younger kids. After your boat ride you may want to stretch your legs and have a walk along the reservoir wall.

Be forewarned that once you introduce this venue to your children, you can expect them to be begging to come back!

Seasons and Times
9:00am to 6:00pm daily.

Admission

Park entrance is free.

Boat rental per hour:

Boat:	Mon-Fri	Sat, Sun & Public Holidays
4 seater pedal boat	$100	$120
2 seater pedal boat	$80	$100
Row Boat	$70	$90

The Best Ways of Getting There

By Bus

- From **Central Exchange Square Bus Terminus** take bus **#6** or **#66**.
- Alight the bus at the bus stop called **"Wong Nai Chung Reservoir Park"** on **Wong Nai Chung Gap Road**. This bus stop will actually leave you at a **petrol station**.
- From the petrol station you must **walk uphill** following the signs to **Parkview**. Look for **Tai Tam Reservoir Road** on your right side (this is a steep hill). There you will find the **Wong Nai Chung Reservoir Park** on your right as you head uphill.

↔ Travel time: 20-25 mins (bus) + 10 mins (walk).

By Car

- From Central, take **Des Voeux Road** to **Queensway**.
- At Queensway (near Pacific Place) get into the far right lane which will take you across the tramway tracks to the right onto **Queen's Road East**.

0-99

- Stay on **Queen's Road East** nearly to its end and you will find the right hand turnoff onto **Stubbs Road** heading up the hill. This right turn will be at a stop light. (If you get to the Happy Valley Racecourse you have gone too far).
- Take **Stubbs Road** all the way up until you get to the **roundabout**. Once on the roundabout you will take the **second left exit** which will be **Wong Nai Chung Gap Road**.
- Stay on **Wong Nai Chung Gap Road** until you see the fields of the **Hong Kong Cricket Club** on your left side. Just there you will find a right hand turnoff for Parkview (take the far right lane). Make the **right turn** and **head up the hill**. You are now on **Tai Tam Reservoir Road**.
- The park itself will be on your right side shortly after the turn.
P For parking, look for a small blue **"P"** sign which will be your first left once on **Tai Tam Reservoir Road** (before you see the park). Stop at the guard gate at the top of the hill to grab a parking stub before heading down into the covered car park.

147

From here, after you park, there will be a five-minute walk up the hill to the park entrance.

🅿 ***Alternatively, continue up **Tai Tam Reservoir Road** past the park (on the right) and look for a small car lot on your left. There is a small metered car park marked by the trailhead of the **Wilson/Hong Kong Hiking Trails** (though be aware there are only a few parking spaces here and they get full quickly at weekends).

By Taxi
A taxi from Central will cost HK$60-$65 and take 20 mins or less.

Getting a Bite
There are two places to purchase drinks and food in the park. *The Pier Café* is big on atmosphere, as it has tables overlooking the water, as well as hot and cold snacks and beverages. The second option is *The Beer House*, which is a small stall that sells hot drinks, cold drinks and hearty snacks like noodle soup and sandwiches. The Beer House is located on the stairs, near the entrance to the park, off Tai Tam Reservoir Road. Yet another option might be to pack your own snacks and have a bite out on the water with the fish. There are also vending machines stocked with bottled water and canned soft drinks down by the boat rental stand.

What's Close?
Tai Tam Country Park Walk and Black's Link Walk to the Police Museum and Coombe Road/Wanchai Gap Playgrounds.

Comments
- Suitable for all ages. (However, if you have toddlers, particularly very active ones, you may want to consider not bringing them on the boats. Although there are life vests available, falling in would be a very unpleasant and possibly very cold experience.)
- Plan to spend one to two hours here.
- This park can be crowded on Saturdays, Sundays and public holidays. You may have to wait for a boat to become available. When you arrive on the scene, check with the boat rental stand and they will give you your number on the waiting list.
- There are toilets at the entrance to the park which have sit-down style seats.

- There is a baby-changing station in the handicapped toilet.
- This is not a stroller-friendly park. The way to get down to the boats is by taking the stairs.

Word of Mouth

If feeding the fish is important to your kids, then you might consider going in the morning instead of the afternoon, because fish that have been feasting all day on the bread of others may not come up to your boat once their appetites have been satisfied.

Inspiration Lake
Penny's Bay, Lantau Island

Tel: 2983-6607 (Inspiration Lake Recreation Centre, ILRC)
Website: www.hongkongdisneyland.com – then click on "Plan your visit"
and then "Fun beyond the Park"
For printable map of the park: Go to www.googlemaps.com, click on
"My Maps", then write in "Inspiration Lake Hong Kong".

This beautifully landscaped park, built by Disney and just a stone's throw from the Disneyland resort hotels and theme park, is a wonderful place to spend a day with your kids. When you drive into the Disney area, you will immediately feel you have entered another dimension, as the foliage changes to palm trees and planted grass, and a feeling of peace and serenity prevails. While Inspiration Lake is not part of the Disney theme park, its creators have made every effort to keep the architecture in line with the Old Victorian theme which runs through Hong Kong Disney.

Inspiration Lake Recreation Centre opened in 2005 to serve the surrounding community as a recreation centre and an irrigation reservoir. Stretching over 30 hectares of land, the heart of the park is a 12-hectare picturesque manmade lake with an impressive geyser-like fountain in the centre. Kids will love that the water shoots more than eight metres into the air and lands back down in the water creating a refreshing splash. To get a little wet (or not), you will need to get them closer to the middle of the lake! That is easily done by the front entrance boat dock where you can rent two-seater and four-seater pedal boats, available by the half hour or by the hour. Pedal bikes, which look like covered surreys, can be hired to ride around the paved 1.6km lake loop. There is also an arboretum which can be reached by foot or by bike. The arboretum loop adds an additional 0.9km to the ride. The bikes have bench seats making them very family- friendly, so even if your child can't ride a bike or reach the pedals, they can steer and/or enjoy a ride as Mom and Dad do all the hard work. Two sizes of bikes are available by the hour, two-seaters or four-seaters, though you can easily squeeze a little one between you to make it three or five.

While the lake is not a swimming lake, make sure the kids are dressed in their suits, as the spotless and well equipped playground near the front entrance has a water feature with spouts coming up from the ground to cool the kids down on a hot day.

Even if you decide not to rent a bike or boat, the beautifully cut grass which lies all about the place is just begging to be used for a picnic or a ball toss. In Hong Kong it is absolutely lovely to have the opportunity to run barefoot and enjoy the feel of grass between your toes. You will not find "STAY OFF THE GRASS" signs here! Don't forget the bug spray as they love the grass and the lake as much as we do.

Seasons and Times
9:00am-7:00pm

Admission
Free

Surrey Bike Renting: two-seater: $100 per hour, 4-seater: $120 per hour
Pedal Boat Renting: two-seater: $70 for half hour, $120 for an hour, Four-seater: $85 per half hour, $150 per hour.

The Best Ways of Getting There
By MTR/Bus or Taxi
- From **Hong Kong Station** in **Central** (the one below the Airport Express Station) take the Yellow Line (Tung Chung Line) to **Sunny Bay Station**.
- At Sunny Bay Station transfer to **Disneyland Resort Line** and go one stop (end of the line) to **Disneyland Resort Station (Disneyland Resort Public Transport Interchange)**.
- Exit the MTR at exit "**A**" and look for the **public transport interchange** (bus station).
    By Bus
    • Look for bus #**R8**, a public bus, which runs from the **Disney MTR station** to **Inspiration Lake** every 20 minutes during the park's opening hours.
    By Taxi
    • It is often difficult to get a taxi, but if you can find one they can take you on a very short ride to the lake.

0-99

大嶼山　竹篙灣
迪欣湖

↔ Travel time: 35 mins (MTR) + 10 mins (bus) OR 3 mins (taxi).

By Car

There is very limited parking at Inspiration Lake, so if you are coming here on the weekend, try to arrive as early as possible, otherwise you will have to wait in a queue for a parking space. If you do run into a parking problem or you get tired of waiting, you can park in the Disney car park and take a bus or taxi back to Inspiration Lake from there.

- Take the **Western Harbour Tunnel** (HK$50); as you exit the toll booth you will be following the signs for **Lantau**, the **airport** and the **Mickey Mouse Ears**.
- Stay on this highway which is **Route 3**. This will take you over a bridge called **Stonecutter's Bridge** and through the **Nam Wan Tunnel**.
- Then take the **exit off of Route 3 to Route 8** (Lantau) which will take you over a long bridge called the **Tsing Ma Bridge**.
- Once over the bridge start looking for signs for **Disney** and **Penny's Bay**. The Mickey Mouse ears on the signs are a great guide.
- Take the **Disney and Penny's Bay Exit** off of the highway.
- Stay on this road, also called **Penny's Bay Highway**, until you reach the **roundabout**.
- At the roundabout you will choose the **exit for the Disneyland Resort**. You are now on **Magic Road**.
- At the **next roundabout** you will see the turn for **Inspiration Drive** and look for the sign that says **Inspiration Lake**.

🅿 The parking lot is on your left hand side as you enter the Inspiration Lake driveway. Parking is $25 per hour and can be paid for at the 7-Eleven just inside the entrance to the park.

By Taxi

A taxi from Central will cost HK$300-350+ and take 30-35 mins.

Getting a Bite

There is a 7-Eleven store in the park that is like no other 7-Eleven in Hong Kong. Housed in a beautiful blue-and-white Victorian style building, this 7-Eleven has a hot food kiosk which serves hot dogs, fish balls, beef balls, Chinese soup and a little bit of dim sum. They also have microwavable meals (and a microwave you can use), chips, candy, cookies, soft drinks, hot drinks, sun block, mosquito repellent, sunglasses, flip flops, magazines, beer and wine – everything you need for an impromptu picnic. Another thought would be to bring your own food and picnic blanket, find a spot of grass to call your own, and graze all day long as the kids frolic by the lake.

What's Close?
Hong Kong Disneyland and Disney Resort Hotels.

Comments
- Suitable for all ages.
- Plan to spend at least half a day here.
- This park is crowded on weekends and public holidays.
- There are lovely toilets at the entrance to the park and a few sprinkled around the bike loop as well. There is even a family toilet and a shower in the ladies' and men's rooms by the front entrance.
- While the bathrooms do not have baby-changing tables there are many benches that could be used for the purpose.
- Stroller-friendly.

Word of Mouth
Inspiration Lake is just a short drive or even walk away from the Hong Kong Disneyland Hotel and the Disney Hollywood Hotel. Both have multiple food outlets and amusements such as playgrounds, mazes, gardens, roaming Disney characters and other features that families can take advantage of when dining in one of the restaurants. These things are available to enjoy whether or not the guests are staying the night at the hotel. Either before or after your visit to the lake, you can add to your special day by visiting one of the hotels for a meal. Be aware though that the restaurant prices are higher than an average Hong Kong meal in town.

Victoria Peak Garden
Top of Mount Austin Road
(Opposite No. 40 Mt. Austin Road)
The Peak, Hong Kong Island

Tel: 2853-2566 (Leisure and Cultural Services Department)
Website with area map: http://www.lcsd.gov.hk/lsb/en/facilities.
php?ftid=47&did=1

Large patches of green grass, where children are allowed to scamper about, are a rarity in Hong Kong, which is why this picturesque garden is a good bet if you want a breath of fresh air and a place to let the kids run wild to their hearts' content. Located at the top of Victoria Peak, this garden is the remaining part of what was once the Governor's summer residence. Those Governors knew precisely what they were doing when they chose this spot for their retreats. Lovely and tranquil with welcoming breezes on a humid day, this garden is a place to unwind and get away from the city noise and heat.

The garden itself is a series of well maintained lawns connected by stone steps, each offering something slightly different, whether it be a stream, a wooded area or lovingly planted trees and flowers. Recently rejuvenated (in 2010), the tiered lawns now have Victorian-style gazebos which provide much-needed shade and are also a picturesque addition to the landscape. Benches, sundials and a stone pillared pavilion round out the new look. Numerous wooden picnic tables have also been added to accommodate those wanting to enjoy a meal in the great outdoors.

Arriving here is part of the fun! A designated stone pathway appropriately named Governor's Walk brings you from Mt. Austin Road up through the woods to the fields (see **Walking** below for explicit and detailed directions). Once you reach the very top, the path loops around to a lookout spot with fabulous views of Aberdeen and the South China Sea below. So, pack a blanket, a frisbee, some bubbles, a couple of balls to bat around and a picnic and head on up to this little-known sanctuary.

Seasons and Times
Year-round.

Admission
Free

The Best Ways of Getting There
Walking
- You can walk to **Victoria Peak Garden** from the **Peak Tram Terminus** at **The Peak** (see **Victoria Peak** chapter for information on riding the Peak Tram from Central) by following **Mt. Austin Road** all the way up to the top.
- Mt. Austin Road begins just next to the **Peak Lookout Restaurant** and ends at Victoria Peak Garden. (There is a black-and-white sign at the start of this walk right next to the restaurant that reads VICTORIA PEAK GARDEN and points you in the right direction _UP_ Mt. Austin Road.)
- Walk about five minutes **up Mt. Austin Road** and the road gives you no choice but to curve and **follow it to the right**.
- You will now see a nice little park on your left hand side called **Mount Austin Road Playground** (and garden). Keep the park to your left and continue straight ahead until again you have no option but to follow **Mt. Austin Road UP and this time to the left**.
- Shortly you will come to **a small traffic circle**. At 11 o'clock on the circle, you will find some **stone steps leading upwards** (they are NOT marked with any signs). Take these steps and walk uphill 10 minutes and you will dead-end into Victoria Peak Garden.

    (Tip: Don't be fooled into thinking the Mt. Austin Road Playground is Victoria Peak Garden; when you get to the playground you still have 15 minutes more to go... uphill!)
- The walk is a bit steep in parts but if instead of taking the steps up at the traffic circle, you stay on Mt. Austin Road all the way until it dead-ends into the park (the way a car would arrive there), the road is paved and therefore it is possible to push a stroller.

↔ Travel time: 20-30 mins (walk).

By Car
- From **Central** drive up **Garden Road** and follow the signs to **Magazine Gap Road** (it will be a left turn at the end of Garden Road).
- Stay on **Magazine Gap Road**; when you reach the **roundabout** at the top of **Magazine Gap Road**, make a **right onto Peak Road**.

香港 山頂
柯士甸山道

山頂公園

0-99

P

- Take **Peak Road** all the way up to the **Peak Galleria Building** and then make **a left onto Mount Austin Road**.
- Follow **Mount Austin Road** to the **right** until you see the **Mt. Austin Road Playground**.
- Then follow **Mt. Austin Road up to the left** and it will dead-end into the parking lot at **Victoria Peak Garden**.

  (Caution: The road on the way up is narrow and in places there is only room for one car to pass. Every few hundred feet though, there is a place to pull over so that two cars can pass each other. On Sundays and public holidays, Mt. Austin Road is blocked to all cars except taxis and residents of the area who sport a sticker in their windshield, so do not attempt to drive up here on a Sunday or a holiday as you will be turned away by the police. Park instead at the Peak Galleria car park and take the walking directions above to get there.)

P 2-hour metered parking is available in the car park.

By Taxi
- A taxi from the Peak Tram Terminus on the Peak or from the Peak Galleria building will cost HK$20-$24 and take 5-10 mins.
- A taxi from Central will cost HK$50-$60 and take 20-25 mins.

  (Tip: When you are ready to leave, you can walk down or you may have to telephone for a taxi as taxis do not wait up at Victoria Peak Garden for fares. Here are a few taxi numbers you can call for a ride: 2529-8822, 2574-7311, 2861-1011, 2861-1008, 2527-6324. Please note that there is an extra $5.00 fee which will be added to the fare for the call).

Other Ways
There are many modes of transport to Victoria Peak where you can start your walk or grab a taxi. See the **Victoria Peak** chapter – **The Best Ways of Getting There** for more information.

Getting a Bite
At the very top of the tiered garden, there is a refreshment kiosk which sells everything from cold drinks and snacks to kites and bubbles; however it is open only sporadically, generally when higher numbers of visitors are expected such as Sundays and public holidays. It would be wise to bring refreshments with you in case the kiosk is not open. Alternatively, plan to have a

meal at Victoria Peak (see **Getting a Bite** in the **Victoria Peak** chapter for details).

What's Close?
<u>Victoria Peak</u> and Mount Austin Road Playground.

Comments
- For all ages.
- Plan to spend at least one to two hours here.
- During the week, you will likely have this place all to yourselves and even if there are some crowds at the weekend, this place never feels crowded.
- There are toilets here near the kiosk and car park at the very top. Most are of the hole-in-the-ground kind but in the ladies' room there is a regular sit-down toilet.
- There is a baby-changing table in the ladies' bathroom.
- The garden itself is not a great place to push a stroller as there are many steps to navigate.

Extra Info
This garden is one of only a handful of places in Hong Kong where dogs are permitted. They must be leashed and of course cleaned up after, and there is a dog latrine to make that job easier. It is a lovely sight indeed to see families frolicking in the grass with their adored family pets.

Word of Mouth
It can be considerably cooler up on the top of the Peak, so even if it is temperate in Central, do bring some warmer outerwear with you especially in the cooler months.

Hong Kong Zoological and Botanical Gardens

Albany Road (pedestrian entrances also on Robinson Road, Garden Road and Glenealy – off Caine Road), Central, Hong Kong Island

Tel: 2530-0154
http://www.lcsd.gov.hk/LEISURE/LP/hkzbg/
For a printable map of the park: Go to the above website and click on
"Location Map"

This tranquil park and small zoo, located on a hill just south of the heart of Central Hong Kong, provides a welcome respite from the hustle and bustle of the city. Set on 5.4 hectares of land, the park has an impressive and varied horticultural life comprised of 1,000 different species as well as a modest 'city-style' zoo. Attractions at this park include: a large and well conceived children's playground; a green house which holds exotic blooms such as orchids and carnivorous plants; a piazza with an attractive fountain and rest area; mammal enclosures displaying a variety of primates including orangutans, gibbons and lemurs; a collection of birds from around the world; a small reptile house; and an education and exhibition centre.

The park is divided into two sections – east and west – connected by a pedestrian subway (which runs under Albany Road). The west side holds the mammal enclosures, the reptile house and the education centre, and the east side has all the rest, including the popular playground.

The entire park can be covered in an hour or two. A good plan might be to start on the west side to see the primates and reptiles, then pay a visit to the beautiful pink flamingos and other birds, see the green house, go on to the playground, and finally end your visit at the fountain piazza area to get a drink and snack at the refreshment kiosk in front of the lovely fountain and colourful blooms.

For those early risers arriving at the park near its opening time, it is very possible to find groups of people practicing Tai Chi in the piazza area. For the afternoon crowd, the fountain is lit with colourful lights that the kids will enjoy.

Seasons and Times
Fountain Terrace Garden – 6:00am-10:00pm daily.
Green House – 9:00am-4:30pm daily.
Other areas – 6:00am-7:00pm daily.

Admission
Free

The Best Ways of Getting There
By Bus
- From Central Star Ferry pier take bus **#13** or
- From City Hall bus **#3B** or
- From Jardine House bus **#12** or
- From Admiralty Bus Station take bus **#12A** or **#12M** or
- From right outside Pacific Place, on Queensway bus **#23**, **#23A**, **#23B**, or **#40**.
- Bus **#13**, **#3B**, **#12**, **#12M**, **#23**, **#23A**, **#23B**, or **#40** will drop you at **one of two stops** where you can access the park: **Kennedy Heights on Kennedy Road** or **Caritas Centre on Caine Road**.
- From **Kennedy Heights**, walk up the steps just to your left next to **Garden Road** until you see the pedestrian flyover on your right hand side just outside the commercial high-rise called **Coda Plaza**.
- If you alight the bus at **Caritas Centre**, the entrance to the park is just around the corner, on a road called **Glenealy**. You will have to walk back toward the traffic light and then make a right turn into a narrow lane (Glenealy). From there follow the signs to the park's entrance.
- If you take bus **#12A** you will alight at the **YWCA on MacDonnell Road** (the first stop on MacDonnell Road). From the MacDonnell Road bus stop, walk down **Garden Road** until you see the overpass to the park.
↔ Travel time: 10+ mins (bus) + 5 mins (walk).

By Car
- From Central take **Garden Road** up to **MacDonnell Road** (the first left off Garden Road).

0-99

P Make an **immediate left** (the first turn) once **on MacDonnell Road**, into a small road that dead-ends into metered parking on the right or two different car parks on the left. (From here walk across the Garden Road pedestrian flyover to access the park.)

By Taxi
A taxi from Central will cost HK$20 and take 5 mins.
   (Tip: You can either be dropped off at MacDonnell Road to begin at the east side of the park or Albany Road to begin on the west side of the park. At the MacDonnell Road taxi stand you will walk down Garden Road (around 40 feet) until you see the overpass to the park. At Albany Road, the taxi driver can take you directly to the entrance.)

Getting a Bite
The *kiosk* in the park has popular kids' snacks such as chips and ice cream as well as light fare such as noodles in soup and hot dogs. For something more substantial, take the sky bridge at the east side entrance to the park (near the greenhouse) over to the other side of Garden Road. Find Coda Plaza, a commercial building at 51 Garden Road. Inside is a large grocery store called *Fusion* where you can pick up what you might need for a park picnic. Also there are three *local Chinese restaurants* in the building that might be good for a casual meal.
Other options:
The Garden View International House Chinese Restaurant (a part of the YWCA) at 1 MacDonnell Road.
2 MacDonnell Road – Hotel coffee shop on the eighth floor of the building.

What's Close?
The Peak Tram Central Terminus (in the **Victoria Peak** chapter), Hong Kong Park and YWCA (on MacDonnell Road).

Comments
- Suitable for all ages but most enjoyable for ages nine and younger.
- Plan a one to two hour visit.
- There are three bathrooms in the park. One is in the playground, the second is just below the fountain/piazza area and the third is on the other side of the pedestrian tunnel.

- The bathroom in the playground has a baby-changing station in the handicapped toilet and the one near the fountain has a baby-changing station in the ladies' toilet.
- The park is stroller-friendly. You should bring one if you have little kids because the park is built on a steep hill and the kids might get tired of walking (especially uphill).

Extra Info

Baby animals are usually the highlight of any visit to this zoo. On a board next to the refreshment kiosk, right next to the guard gate on **Albany Road**, is a list of the baby animals that were recently born in the zoo. This same area also has free maps of the park. The only other place to get a map is the Education and Exhibition Centre.

For Educators

The park has an extensive zoo and horticultural educational program and is visited by 10,000 school children a year. For more information on the educational programs phone 2723-6080.

Word of Mouth

Remember to bring mosquito repellent, as there are more of them than animals at the zoo. Also don't forget sun block and umbrella because the park is very exposed to the elements.

Kowloon Park

22 Austin Road, Tsim Sha Tsui, Kowloon

Tel: 2724-3344
Swimming Pool Complex – Tel: 2724-3577
Kowloon Park Sports Centre – Tel: 2724-3120 or 2724-3494
Park website: http://www.lcsd.gov.hk/parks/kp/en/index.php
For a printable map of the park: http://www.lcsd.gov.hk/parks/kp/en/
layout.php
Health Education and Exhibition Resource Centre
Tel: 2377-9275
Website: http://www.fehd.gov.hk/english/research_education/heerc/info.
html
For a printable map of the Centre: http://www.fehd.gov.hk/english/
research_education/heerc/layout.html

Kowloon Park is one of the most popular and widely used parks in the city. Set on 13+ peaceful hectares of land in the middle of bustling Tsim Sha Tsui, this park is filled with exciting, fun and relaxing activities for every age group. Attractions here include: a large children's playground, a bird lake, a maze garden, an aviary, a swimming pool complex, a sports centre, a roof garden, a Chinese garden, a sculpture walk and garden, a colour garden, a discovery playground, a banyan tree court and the Health Education Exhibition and Resource Centre.

There are so many wonderful things to do here it may be hard to know how to begin your visit. At the centre of the park are the bird lake and the aviary. The bird lake is beautifully landscaped with a large flamingo pond, a small waterfowl pond and some bird shelters. There are more than 300 birds here from 29 species. The park has had unprecedented breeding success with some species and so you might very well see some ducklings, baby swans or other baby birds. Let your ears guide you to the aviary where you will first hear and then see the parrots, parakeets and macaws. The aviary, though small in size, has seven enclosures with over 160 birds from more than 40 species. Just next door is a large children's playground that is well equipped with jungle gyms and toys for both age groups two to five and five to twelve. Directly behind the children's playground is the discovery playground area which has a castle turret to explore and some old cannons too.

When you and the troops are ready to move onto something more peaceful, the park has a plethora of beautiful garden areas to offer. Across from the aviary is the Chinese Garden. Set in traditional Chinese landscape, this garden has a pond with turtles, pagodas and a covered walkway with benches where you can sit and have a picnic or enjoy the serenity. Next door is the maze. Challenge yourselves by finding the way in and the way out of this puzzle made of green shrubbery. When the game is over, take a walk through the sculpture garden. Several dozen striking pieces of art line this lovely pathway.

Before you leave, make sure to stop in at the Health Education Exhibition and Resource Centre. Though the name of the place may not excite the kids at first, once they get inside they will feel very differently. Set on two floors, this 1,100-square-metre air-conditioned exhibition centre offers dozens of interactive games and exhibits specially designed for kids on the topics of food safety and environmental hygiene. The topics, though a bit dry, are presented with the intent of arousing children's interest. This stop might actually be the highlight of your trip to the park.

Seasons and Times
Outdoor Areas – 5:00am-Midnight daily.
Discovery Playground – 6:30am-9:00pm daily.
Aviary – 6:30am-6:45pm (March to October), 6:30am-5:45pm (November to February).
Swimming Pool – (three sessions): 6:30am-12:00pm, 1:00pm-5:00pm and 6:00pm-10:00pm.
Sports Centre – 7:00am-11:00pm
Health Education Exhibition & Resource Centre – Tuesday, Wednesday, Friday and Saturday: 8:45am-6:15pm, Sunday 11:00am-9:00pm. Closed Monday, Thursday and Public Holidays.

Admission
Access to the park is free. There are nominal charges to use the pool and some activities in the indoor games hall.

The Best Ways of Getting There
By MTR
• From **Central** or **Admiralty** to **Tsim Sha Tsui station**, take the **red line**. Exit the MTR station at exit "**A1**".
• When you reach street level you will be directly across a side street from the park.

九龍　尖沙咀
柯士甸道22號　九龍公園

0-99

↔ Travel time: 10 mins (MTR) + 3 mins (walk).

By Star Ferry
- From **Central** to **Tsim Sha Tsui (TST)** take the **Star Ferry** from the **Star Ferry Central Pier**.
↔ Travel time: 10 mins (ferry).
*Once you exit the ferry in TST you can either walk or take a taxi to the park.

Walking
- Walk straight ahead from the TST Star Ferry Pier exit and you will be on **Salisbury Road**. Walk on Salisbury Road until you intersect **Kowloon Park Drive**. Make a left.
- Stay on Kowloon Park Drive until you see the entrance to the park. It will be on your right hand side.
↔ Travel time: 10-15 mins (walk).

By Taxi
- A taxi from right outside the TST Star Ferry Pier will cost HK$20-$24.
↔ Travel time: 5-10 mins (taxi).

By Car:
- From Central take the **Cross Harbour Tunnel**: Connaught Road→ Harcourt Road→Gloucester Road→ **Island Eastern Corridor.**
- In tunnel and tollbooths (HK$20) stay to **the far left**. Follow signs for **Tsim Sha Tsui and Kwai Chung**. From here there is **a series of three left hand turns** all marked for either **TST** or the **Hong Kong Coliseum/Railway Terminus**. These turns all lead you to **Chatham Road South**.
- Once you see the Polytechnic University on your left, get in the right lane to make a right turn onto **Austin Road**. Follow this road and you will pass the park on your left hand side.
- Look for **Scout Path**, a left turn after the park, where you will find the **Victoria Mall car park**.
🅿 Look for the blue signs with symbol "P". From here it is a two-minute walk to the park entrance.

By Taxi
A taxi from Central will cost HK$80-$90 and take 25-30 mins.

Getting a Bite

If your gang gets hungry or thirsty, there are three places to fix the problem in the park. One is the **McDonald's Restaurant** located next to the Indoor Games Hall. Another is the **McDonald's Ice Cream Stand** located across from the bird lake where for HK$2 you can get a soft serve cone. Just behind the McDonald's Ice Cream Stand are a few vending machines where you can get a snack or drink. If you would like to get a bite outside the park's perimeter, the Tsim Sha Tsui area is a diner's paradise. You will find many restaurants in the area that are great for kids. Your best bet might be to head to **Ocean Terminal** (a nearby shopping mall located on the water next to the Tsim Sha Tsui Star Ferry off of Salisbury Road or accessible through the Marco Polo Hotel on Canton Road), or **Harbour City** (on Canton Road near the park), where kids' dining options abound. Here is a small sample list of child-friendly possibilities in the area:

Dan Ryan's (kids' menu, crayons and balloons) – Ocean Terminal
BLT Burger (kids' menu, colouring, high chairs) – Harbour City
Pizza Hut (fast food pizza) – Ocean Terminal
Main Street Deli (American-style deli) – 8 Peking Road, the Langham Hotel
TGI Friday's (fun casual Western-style food and atmosphere) – 26 Nathan Road, Oterprise Square
Starbucks Coffee – Star House, opposite the Star Ferry Pier
McDonald's – Salisbury Road, opposite the Star Ferry Pier

What's Close?

Hong Kong Space Museum, Hong Kong Museum of Art, Ocean Terminal, Harbour City, and the Hong Kong Cultural Centre.

Comments

- Suitable for all ages.
- Plan a two to three hour visit.
- This park can get crowded on weekends and public holidays.
- There are seven bathrooms located around the park. All have sit-down style toilets.
- Three of the ladies' toilets have baby-changing areas. One is near the maze, one is near the discovery playground and the other is near the indoor games hall. The first two are cement, the last one is a proper pull-down table.
- Stroller-friendly.

Extra Info

Acquiring a map of the park is a good way to start your day here. If you do not have access to a computer to print the map (see above website) then try to get one from the Kowloon Park office located in the building next to the swimming pool complex and across from the Sports Centre, very near the Austin Road entrance. Though a little difficult to find, it may be worth the effort. The office is located on the first floor, not the ground floor, so you may need to ask one of the swimming pool staff to guide you. They are very helpful and friendly there. This is the only place you can get a hard copy of the park's map.

For Educators

If your school is covering or is going to cover material pertaining to hygiene and health, the Health Education Exhibition and Resource Centre is a great place to take them to supplement their learning. For more information call 2377-9275.

Word of Mouth

Kowloon Park hosts an Art Fun Fair every Sunday and public holiday from 1:00pm to 7:00pm in the area of the park very near the Mosque off of Nathan Road. Stalls with arts and crafts items, painters, sketchers, crafters all set up shop to create a small artsy fair for the public.

Tai Po Waterfront Park
Dai Fat Street, Tai Po, New Territories

Tel: 2664-2107
Website: http://www.lcsd.gov.hk/parks/tpwp/en/index.php
For printable map of the park: Go to the above website and click on
"Location Map".

新界　大埔
大發街　大埔
大埔海濱公園

0-99

This out-of-the-way spot may be a bit difficult to get to, but it is definitely worth the effort. Tai Po Waterfront Park covers 22 hectares of picturesque waterfront property at the edge of Tolo Harbour in the New Territories. More than HK$200 million was invested in its construction and the results are fantastic, particularly for children. Though there are many enjoyable and interesting facets to this lovely site, its most distinctive feature is the fact that you can rent bicycles here and ride them on a scenic path all the way around the park and beyond.

The park is beautifully landscaped and features three themed playgrounds, a model boat pool, an ecological garden, a western garden, a kite flying garden, bowling greens, an insect house, a pond filled with carp, a futuristic lookout tower and a seaside promenade. Make sure not to miss the 23-metre-high lookout tower which is this area's most famous landmark. This attraction resembles a rocket launching pad and from the top it offers 360-degree views of the park, Tolo Harbour and the surrounding mountainous countryside (which borders mainland China). The insect house is small but interesting and features all kinds of fun, hands-on activities which teach kids about bugs. The playgrounds are all named and feature special equipment related to their respective themes of science, technology and the senses.

Though all of the above activities will keep you busy for a morning or afternoon, save time for a bike ride along the 1000-metre promenade. There are three bike rental kiosks set up in the park, located just in front of the lookout tower. They have everything from bikes with training wheels and adult size bikes to three-wheelers that can fit three members of the family with a cover on top to protect you from the sun. If you have older kids or your kids are good riders, you have the option of riding the bicycles all the way to Sha Tin Park and returning them there. Along the way are great views of Tolo Harbour and the Shing

Mun River Channel (on the Sha Tin side). See Bike Riding in the New Territories chapter for more information on biking from this park to Sha Tin.

Seasons and Times
Tai Po Waterfront Park is open year-round.
Main area – 24 hours
Insect house – 8:00am-7:00pm
Spiral lookout tower – 7:00am-7:00pm
Bike kiosks – 9:30am-7:00pm

Admission
Park – Free
Bike Rentals – For bike rentals, use the following price list as a guideline ONLY as prices vary from vendor to vendor and from day to day*:
Kids' Bikes – 12"-16" wheels:
HK$15 per hour (Mon-Sat) + HK$5 (Sun & public holidays).
+ Training wheels: HK$20
Bikes 16"-20" wheels:
HK$20 per hour (Mon-Sat) + HK$5 (Sun & public holidays).
Bikes 24"-26" wheels:
HK$25 per hour (Mon-Sat) + HK$5 (Sun & public holidays).
Two Seaters (tandem bikes):
HK$40 per hour (Mon-Sat) + HK$5 (Sun & public holidays).
Family Bikes (three wheelers):
HK$60 per hour (Mon-Sat) + HK$5 (Sun & public holidays).
Quality speed bikes:
HK$40 per hour (Mon-Sat) + HK$5 (Sun & public holidays).
Basket/Seat: HK$5
Helmet or Bike Lock or Lights: All HK$10 per option
PLEASE NOTE: If you plan to ride only one way there will be a small surcharge to return the bikes in another location.
*Price by the day for ALL bikes is NEGOTIABLE.

The Best Ways of Getting There
By MTR
- From **Central** or **Admiralty** to **Kowloon Tong Station**, take the red line to **Mongkok**. Transfer to the green line (**across the platform at Mongkok Station**) to **Kowloon Tong**.
- In Kowloon Tong Station look for the **East Rail**. Ride it to **Tai Po Market Station**.
↔ Travel time: 20 mins (MTR) + 20-25 mins (East Rail).

From Tai Po Market Station you have two choices to get to the park:

By Bus

• Exit **Tai Po Market MTR Station** at exit **A3** and look for the bus terminus. Unfortunately there are only two buses that will take you directly to the park from here and they *run only on Sundays and Public Holidays*: KMB **#275R** and **#275S**. On **#275R** you will alight after only ONE STOP and exit at Yuen Shin Park which is adjacent to Tai Po Waterfront Park. **#275S** also takes you to Yuen Shin Park, but it will be your sixth stop on this bus.

↔ Travel time: 10-15 mins (bus) + 5 mins (walk).

By Taxi

• A taxi from Tai Po Market Station will cost HK$16.50.

↔ Travel time: 5 mins (taxi).

By Car

• From Central: Connaught Road→Harcourt Road→Gloucester Road→**Island Eastern Corridor (Route 4)→Cross Harbour Tunnel (Route 1)**:

• In tunnel stay in right lane. Once through tollbooth (HK$20) stay right and follow signs for **Ho Man Tin and Sha Tin**. **You are on Route 1**.

• Stay on Route 1 and follow signs for **Sha Tin and Kowloon Tong**. **Stay in centre lane**, you are now on **Princess Margaret Road**.

• Follow signs for **Lion Rock Tunnel**. Go through tunnel (HK$8). You are now **on Lion Rock Tunnel Road.**

• You are still on **Route 1**. Follow signs for **Sha Tin, Ma On Shan and Tai Po**.

• Then signs for **Ma On Shan and Tai Po**.

• You will **merge with Route 9** as you continue to follow signs for **Tai Po and Fanling**. You are now on **Route 9**.

• Now follow signs for Tai Po. You will be looking for the exit marked "**Tai Po Industrial Estate**".

• Once you take the rampway to exit the **road forks** and you will want to **stay to the right** and follow the signs for "**Tai Po Industrial Estate**".

• Now you will start to see **signs** for **Tai Po Waterfront Park**. Follow the signs for the park which will lead you to **Yuen Shin Road**.

• Follow Yuen Shin Road until you can make a right hand turn onto **Dai Fat Street**, the road the park entrance is on.

- The pedestrian entrance to the park will come up on your right hand side on Dai Fat Street, but to park your car you will want to turn left onto **Dai Wah Street** opposite the front entrance. P The car park is a private paid lot ($5 per hour) and will be a right turn into the lot off of Dai Wah Street.

By Taxi
A taxi from Central will cost HK$250-$300+ and take 50-55 mins.

Getting a Bite

There are four refreshment kiosks in the park. The first is located in the middle of the park near the amphitheatre. This kiosk sells hot and cold drinks, snacks, sandwiches, ice cream, insect repellent, kites, umbrellas, bubbles, and toys. There is also a small drink stand down by the waterfront adjacent to the bike kiosks. The third kiosk is indoors, on the ground floor of the lookout tower. There is also a fourth kiosk all the way down at the end of the promenade. This kiosk is only open periodically, most commonly during public holidays. Best not to count on this kiosk being open and be sure to take a drink with you when you go for your bike ride. Another great option is to pack a picnic from home as there are many lovely spots to set up an alfresco meal.

What's Close?

Hong Kong Railway Museum, Tai Po Market (see **Hong Kong Railway Museum** chapter for details), and **Biking in the New Territories**.

Comments

- Suitable for all ages.
- Plan to spend at least two hours here, more if you plan to go bike riding.
- This park is not crowded.
- There are six bathrooms located around the park which have both sit-down and squat style toilets.
- There are baby-changing stations in every ladies toilet in the park.
- Stroller-friendly.
-

Extra Info

For a hard copy of the park's map as well as the area's bike routes, stop in at the park's office located just off the Dai Fat Street entrance near the model boat pool.

Word of Mouth

Yes, it might require some effort to reach this park, but once you are out here you will be so glad you came.

Lai Chi Kok Park
(with Skateboard Grounds and Roller Rink)
1 Lai Wan Road, Lai Chi Kok, Kowloon

Tel: 2370-9187 or 2307-0429
Website: http://www.lcsd.gov.hk/parks/lckp/en/index.php
For area map: Go to above website and click on "Layout Map of the Park"

Lai Chi Kok's enormous recreation area is a truly unexpected find. Easy to get to by rail, car or bus, this 17+ hectare park in Kowloon has some unusual features that will make it a very big hit with active kids. Divided into three large stages, the park has all of the following features: a specialized skateboard arena, a roller skating rink, four playgrounds, basketball/volleyball courts, tennis courts, a swimming pool, two landscaped Chinese gardens, outdoor chess tables, a jogging trail, multiple fitness stations and an amphitheatre.

It is worth coming to Lai Chi Kok Park for the skateboard grounds alone. The arena has multiple structures and equipment, and also caters to BMX bike riders and in-line skaters (though sadly no scooters are allowed). There are a very limited number of places in Hong Kong that allow skateboarding, biking or roller blading (see **Extra Info** below for more information on other options), making this park a very unique attraction. Next door to the skateboard grounds is a small but clean and new roller-skating rink. The rink and the arena are both located in Stage 3. This section of the park is also where you can find Lingnan Garden, a large and beautiful landscaped walled park with water features, numerous pagodas, sculptures, ponds with turtles, carp and frogs and shaded paved walkways which are perfect for a stroll. Stage 3 also has two large playgrounds, one for toddlers and one for children ages 5-12.

Stage 1 of the park has two playgrounds, fitness stations, a podium garden, a refreshment kiosk, a swimming pool complex, a soccer pitch, outdoor covered chess tables and a pretty landscaped Chinese garden with fish-stocked ponds and water features. Stage 2 has the park's main office (a great place to go for information and a park map) and multiple tennis courts.

To help you navigate your way around this enormous place, it is useful to picture the park's shape which is an "L". Stage 1 is at the short side of the "L", Stage 2 is at the right angle in the centre and Stage 3 is the long side. Better yet, print a map from the park's website (above) before you head out; if you forget, there are plenty of posted maps inside the park to help guide you.

Seasons and Times
Most areas: Open 24 hours
Skateboard park: 7:00am-10:00pm
Roller Skating Rink, Lingnan Garden, Tennis Courts, Gateball Courts, Hard-surfaced Soccer Pitch, Basketball/Volleyball Courts: 7:00am-11:00pm
Swimming Pool: 6:30am-10:00pm (with two breaks from 12:00-1:00pm and from 6:00-7:00pm)

Admission
Free
Skateboard Grounds*: Please note that children must be eight years of age to use the skateboard arena. They must also be wearing protective gear including a helmet.*

The Best Ways of Getting There
By MTR
- From Central or Admiralty take the **Tsuen Wan Line** (red line) to **Mei Foo Station**.
- For the **skateboard park**, skating rink, Lingnan Garden and far set of playgrounds take exit **"D"**
- For the toddler and children's **playground** (on the short side/near side of the "L") take exit **"G"**
↔ Travel time: 25 mins (MTR) + 5-15 mins depending on where in the park you are going (walk).

By Bus
- From **Central** get Bus **#905** from **30-32 Des Voeux Road Central before Li Yuen Street East** and alight the bus at the **Nob Hill Bus Terminus** *(Note: This is the last stop for the bus).*
- Directly across the street is the entrance to **Lai Chi Kok Park**.
↔ Travel time: 60-70 mins (bus).

九龍　荔枝角　荔枝角公園
荔灣道1號

0-99

By Car

- Take the **Western Harbour Tunnel** (HK$50) staying to your left as you exit the toll booth.
- Take the **second exit** off the highway to your left which reads **Mongkok and Lai Chi Kok** (the first exit is not marked).
- You will be on a land bridge and driving over the motorway below. Once over it stay all the way left and **follow signs for Route 5 toward Kwai Chung**. There will be a sharp left **exit** (exit sign is largely concealed by trees).
- Keep following **Route 5 toward Kwai Chung**. Stay on Route 5 until you take a left off the highway labelled **Lai Chi Kok and Shatin**. Follow the signs when the road splits for **Lai Chi Kok**. There will also be signs for Mei Foo. You are now on **Lai Chi Kok Road**.
- Stay to your left and make a **left on Broadway Street**. Follow Broadway Street all the way to the end (many twists and turns) where you will come to a **roundabout** (road dead-ends here).
- Follow the **roundabout to the right** (essentially making a right hand turn off of Broadway Street). You are now on **Lai Wan Road**. You will see Lai Chi Kok Park on your left and the Mei Foo MTR on your right. Follow **Lai Wan Road**, you will pass a set of lights; at the **second set of traffic lights make a left,** with the left turn arrow. You are still on Lai Wan Road.
- On the very next block you will come to a traffic light. Make a **left at the light**, now you are on **King Lai Path**.
- You will see **Nob Hill** on your right.

P The parking garage is underground here at Nob Hill. Look for the big "**P**".

By Taxi:

A taxi from Central will cost HK$170-$220 and take around 20-25 minutes.

Getting a Bite

- The park has a refreshment kiosk at the toddler playground on the 'near' side (nearer to Nob Hill) of the park.
- At the base of the escalator of the Household Centre near the bus terminus are two bakeries which are good for a snack.
- The Household Centre also has a Chinese restaurant which is open for breakfast, lunch and dinner called *The Arch Banquet Hall*. English is not spoken here so you may need to get a bilingual customer to help you order your meal. The restaurant serves dim sum and other local Cantonese fare.

- Another option is to walk back to the Mei Foo MTR Exit C1 and above ground you will find a walking/shopping street called **Mount Sterling Mall**. Here you will find a variety of restaurants including many local noodle shops, *Ha-Ne Sushi* and a *McDonald's Restaurant*. There is also a *Pizza Hut* in the area on Lai Wan Road.

What's Close?
Dialogue in the Dark.

Comments
- Suitable for all ages, however children must be eight or older to play in the skateboard park.
- Plan to spend at least two hours here.
- Not generally crowded.
- There are toilets in the park, most have at least one sit-down style toilet, though sometimes that is located only in the handicapped toilet.
- There are baby-changing tables near the tennis courts as well as near the Lingnan Chinese Garden.
- This park is stroller-friendly.

Extra Info
Other popular places to skateboard in Hong Kong include: Tung Chung Park (North) in Tung Chung, Morrison Hill Road Playground in Wanchai, and Chai Wan Pool Side Garden in Chai Wan. For information on these venues and others go to the Leisure and Cultural Services Department website: http://www.lcsd.gov.hk/parks/, then click on "Leisure Facilities" and then "Other Facilities" and then "Skateboard Grounds."

Word of Mouth
This is a big park that covers a very large area. To walk from one end to the other takes time and patience. It might be best with small children to look at the map when you enter the park gates, pick one area of the park and head for it rather than wandering around. On the other hand, if you have a stroller or kids who love to walk, this is a lovely park to explore.

Noah's Ark and Ma Wan Park
33 Pak Yan Road, Ma Wan, Park Island
(an island under the Tsing Ma Bridge)

Ma Wan Park – the Nature Garden, Tel: 3446-1163
Ma Wan Park – the Nature Garden website: www.mawanpark.com
For area map: Go to the above website and click on "About Us" and
then click on "Park Map"
Noah's Ark Tel: 3411-8888
Noah's Ark website: www.noahsark.com.hk
For area map: Go to the above website and click on "Visit Noah's Ark"
and then click on "Park Map"
Ma Wan Ferry Service Tel: 2946-8888
Ma Wan Ferry Service website: http://www.pitcl.com.hk/eng/html/ferry.
htm

This new Hong Kong attraction, opened on Park Island in May
of 2009, boasts the world's only full-size replica of Noah's
Ark. It is also paired with a lush nature garden just next door
created to "calm and heal the mind and spirit". This privately
held enterprise is operated by some of Hong Kong's most well
known Christian charitable organizations including Chinese
YMCA of Hong Kong, Angela Luk's Education Foundation,
St. James Settlement, The Boys Brigade of Hong Kong and
The Media Evangelism. The goal here is to create universal
love and harmony, as well as respect for the planet, through
exposure to the experiences provided within the Ark and the
garden at Ma Wan Park.

Noah's Ark is both eclectic and interesting. This 'edutainment'
centre is actually rather difficult to describe. The Ark itself is a
four-story building which houses all of the following: Ark Expo
– a multimedia portrayal of nature and the earth's marvels;
Treasure House – an exhibit with 15 interactive galleries which
have titles such as 3D Fun, Robotic City Architecture and Music
Wonders; Ark Life Education House – interactive games area
which mirrors both the challenges and the happiness that is
reflected in life; Noah's Resort – holiday accommodation on
the top floor of the ark; Noah's Adventure Land – a physical
teambuilding area with a giant ladder, giant swings and other
games for group use which must be booked in advance; and
lastly, just outside the main structure, the Ark Garden – 67 pairs
of life-like animal sculptures in and around the ark, in a garden

setting, located in the open air facing the sea with a broad view of the Tsing Ma Bridge above.

It might be difficult to determine how to begin your adventure at Noah's Ark due to the somewhat unusual structure, layout and themes. The kids will enjoy the Ark Garden, so that might be a good place to start. The animal figures all have descriptive plaques with their names, pertinent information and maps with their countries of origin. This will be both educational and fun. Another part of the Ark Garden is an area called Two-Head Castle which has some very unusual exhibits. Here you will find two large live turtles and two live baby goats that the kids can hand-feed, a fish netting game where the kids can try their hand at catching fish (which they can take home), and a display of live animals that have genetic mutations such as two-headed turtles (conjoined twins), two-headed snake-turtles, a one-eyed fish, and conjoined fish. Some of these activities require the purchase of a ticket. From here head to Treasure House where the kids will be handed a "Student Passport" with a series of questions, one from each of the interactive galleries. If the children are able to complete the quiz, they are given a chop in their passport and can redeem a gift at the Kid's Deck gift shop on the Lower Ground Floor. This treasure hunt is meant for children ages 3-11. Ark Life Education House is all about love and has activities which revolve around helping others and demonstrating our appreciation for others. At the time of our visit, one of the activities was for the kids to make a cupcake out of small face towels and then write a card and give the cupcake to someone to show them how much they are loved. Other activities in this area included face painting (where one child paints another child), blackboard colouring and a game on a floor piano (much like the one in the movie "BIG").

If a full day at Noah's Ark still leaves you with more time, head across the way to Ma Wan Park's Nature Garden. This lovely mid-sized park consists of a series of tended gardens with names like Australian Garden, Sculpture Garden, Sunflower Garden, South American Garden, Forest Gully, Riverside Garden, and many more. The paths are beautifully and naturally done on wooden boardwalks that run through the centre of the park. One of the highlights here is the Hilltop Lookout, where there is a refreshment kiosk and tables and chairs where you can take a breather and enjoy the breeze, a cold drink and the view.

0-99

Seasons and Times
Ma Wan Park:
Mondays, Fridays, Saturdays 1:00pm-6:00pm (opens at
9:00am but until 1:00pm they offer only special pre-booked
programming)
Tuesdays, Wednesdays, Thursdays, Sundays and public
holidays: 8:00am-6:00pm (last entry at 5:00pm)
Noah's Ark: 10:00am-6:00pm daily

Admission
Ma Wan Park – Free
Noah's Ark – Tickets can be purchased online or at the Noah's
Ark entrance gate.
Ark Package = Ark Garden, Treasure House and Ark Life
Education House
Adults: HK$100, Children (3-11): HK$85
Noah's Package = Ark Garden and Ark Expo
Adults: HK$90, Children (3-11): HK$65
Rainbow Package = Treasure House and Ark Life Education
House
All tickets: HK$55 (Mondays-Fridays), HK$65 (Saturdays,
Sundays and public holidays)
Expo Special = Ark Expo Hall C, B and Two Head Castle
Adults: HK$65, Children (3-11): HK$50

The Best Ways of Getting There
By Ferry/Walk
- Take the **Ma Wan/Park Island Ferry** from the **Park Island
  Ferry Pier in Central**. This is a dedicated pier – **Central
  Pier #2**. The pier is located on the waterfront behind the IFC
  complex where the airport express train is located.
- The ferry takes 25 minutes and departs the Central Ferry Pier
  roughly every 15 to 30 minutes.
- Once you get to **Park Island** you will **walk** through a planned,
  no-vehicle community, following the path and **signs for
  Noah's Ark and Ma Wan Park**. Noah's Ark is on the left side
  of the path, Ma Wan Park is on the right.
↔ Travel time: 25 mins (ferry) + 10 mins (walk)

By MTR/Shuttle Bus Service
- From **Central** or **Admiralty** to **Prince Edward Station**, take
  the red line. Exit the station at exit **"B1"**.
- Come out onto the street, turn left and immediately left again
  and you are now on **Prince Edward Road West**. You will

walk right past the **Mongkok Police Station**, across **Tung Choi Street**, across **Fa Yuen Street**, and cross **Sai Yee Street**. You will see the Flower Market on your left and **Grand Century Place on your right**.

- Enter the mall and **find the ticketing office** in **Grand Century Place** on the first floor at the **customer service counter**.
- Once you purchase your roundtrip bus ticket, you will be directed from there to the bus port near the taxi stand to catch the shuttle bus.
- Shuttle bus departs from Grand Century Place every 30 minutes from 9:30am to 4:00pm. It returns from the park every 30 minutes from 1:00pm to 6:30pm.
- Cost of the bus is $38.00 roundtrip and **you must show proof of your purchased online ticket or buy a package ticket from the customer service counter before you purchase the bus ticket at Grand Century Place**.

↔ Travel time: 15 mins (MTR) + 10 mins (walk) + 20 mins (bus).

Getting a Bite

Noah's Ark has a restaurant on the premises called *Harvest Restaurant* with views overlooking the water. They serve international buffet as well as a la carte. Another great option are the restaurants and coffee shops along the Beach Commercial Complex which you will pass on your way to and from the parks to the Park Island Ferry Pier. Here you will find a 7-Eleven, a Park n Shop, several local Chinese restaurants, an Italian restaurant called *Café Roma* that serves pizza and pasta, and a bakery/coffee shop. They have some alfresco seating in some of the restaurants which is nice on a pretty day. Ma Wan Park has a refreshment kiosk located at the Hilltop Lookout.

Comments

- Suitable for all ages.
- Plan to spend a minimum of three hours.
- Noah's Ark can be crowded on weekends and public holidays.
- There are many toilets in both parks of the sit-down style.
- Noah's Ark has baby-changing tables in the disabled bathrooms. Ma Wan Park has two as well, one in the bus car park toilet and one near the Happy Days Centre.
- This is a stroller-friendly place.
- There are multiple gift shops that kids will love at Noah's Ark.

For Educators

Noah's Ark offers packages for kindergartens, primary and secondary schools to help children learn about "love and life". Contact them on their general number for more information. (Please note that buses can enter Park Island with a special permit, though private cars may not, which makes bringing a bus load of children to the park a possibility without having to use the public ferry.)

Word of Mouth

There are a series of films on offer at Ark Theatre which may not be suitable for all children. There are graphic scenes in some of them depicting events of religious significance. Please ask at the desk which films are being shown and their content so that you can make an informed decision based on your children's comfort levels.

Chapter 4

Fun in the Sand – Hong Kong's Beaches

It is sometimes easy to forget that Hong Kong is in fact an island in the South China Sea and as such is likely to have – beaches! Widely known as a metropolis filled with ultra-modern skyscrapers and crowded busy streets, Hong Kong is rarely thought of in terms of its sand, sea and surf. In fact, the Leisure and Cultural Services Department of Hong Kong maintains 41 beaches on Hong Kong Island, the New Territories and the Outlying Islands, many of which are well equipped with lifeguards, shark nets, changing facilities, showers and toilets. Some even have swim rafts stationed in the water, refreshment kiosks, children's playgrounds and barbeque pits. They are all generally well maintained and the majority have beautiful views of the sea and surrounding countryside. The ten beaches included in this chapter all have something extra special to offer kids and parents and therefore make wonderful family outings.

There are a few dangers that need to be mentioned before proceeding. The first pertains to pollution levels. Hong Kong's beaches are monitored very closely for levels of E. coli bacteria in the water. The rating system provides four different categories, each representing the count of E. coli present in 100mls of water: Good (less than 24), Fair (25-180), Poor (181-610) and Very Poor (more than 610). It is VERY IMPORTANT to check the water quality of the beach you intend to visit BEFORE you go there. This is easily done by either calling the beach directly (check at the top of each chapter's first page for the individual beach's telephone number) or by checking the website of Hong Kong's Environmental Protection Department (EPD) at http://www.epd.gov.hk/epd/ and looking up "Beach Water Quality" and then "Latest Beach Water Quality." You can also call EPD's dedicated water quality hotline on 2511-6666. Should you forget to call in advance, each beach's rating is posted near its lifeguard office. Try to swim only at a beach where the water quality level reads "Good." Illnesses at poor quality beaches range from skin irritations to stomach problems.

Shark attacks, though very rare, have occurred off Hong Kong's beaches. All beaches listed in this book have shark netting and are regularly monitored by helicopter beach patrol. Occasionally, there are also jellyfish, so be aware when you are in the water.

Make sure you pack the following three things in your beach bag: drinking water, sun block and mosquito repellent (though most beaches listed have refreshment kiosks that sell all of the above, it is important to carry those items with you at all times). Even if you are not comfortable with your kids swimming in the water, the beaches of Hong Kong are a nice way to spend some quality family time. Enjoy!

1. Deep Water Bay Beach

2. Repulse Bay Beach

3. South Bay Beach

4. Chung Hom Kok Beach

5. Shek O Beach & Village and Big Wave Bay Beach

6. Clear Water Bay Second Beach

7. Trio Beach

8. Pui O Beach

9. Cheung Sha Beach

Other chapters that include beaches:
Stanley Village – Stanley Main Beach and St. Stephen's Beach
Sai Kung Town and Hap Mun Bay Beach
Lamma Island: Sok Kwu Wan – Lo So Shing Beach
Lamma Island: Yung Shue Wan – Hung Shing Ye Beach
Cheung Chau Island – Tung Wan Beach
Bike Riding in Mui Wo – Silvermine Bay Beach
Discovery Bay Beach and Piazza

Deep Water Bay Beach
Island Road
Deep Water Bay, Hong Kong Island

香港 深水灣
香島道 深水灣
深水灣海灘

Tel: 2812-0228 or 2555-0103
Website: http://www.lcsd.gov.hk/beach/en/index.php
For area map: Click on above website and then click on "Location Map".

This scenic beach, set in a lovely bay on the South China Sea, has beautiful views and plenty of amenities. It also has the distinct advantage of being the nearest beach to Central, making it a good choice if you don't want to invest loads of time travelling to and fro, but still want to hit a Hong Kong Island southside beach.

It is easy for parents to relax here because most things you need for a fun day out at the beach are available without having to put your shoes back on. There is a recently renovated refreshment kiosk located on the east side of the beach offering umbrellas, beach chairs and lockers for rent. It also doubles as a Thai restaurant called Coco Thai, and serves a full menu of Thai food as well as kiddie favourites such as hot dogs, hamburgers, french fries and lasagne. This kiosk sits on the second floor of the changing room building which gives it excellent views of the bay below and is a very pleasant place to sit and enjoy the breeze at picnic tables shaded from the sun.

If the kids want to head out to one of the two swim rafts floating a short distance from shore, there are lifeguards on patrol all year round, which should make parents feel more comfortable. Other facilities include two sets of showers, both indoor and outdoor, changing rooms and a large (and popular) BBQ area.

0-99

If you want to go for a scenic walk, this beach has that too! On the far east side of the beach is the entrance to the Seaview Promenade, a scenic walkway which takes you along the sea from Deep Water Bay to Repulse Bay. This paved pathway has a guardrail and is a perfect place to take the kids for a stroll while taking in this area's breathtaking views. The walk takes about 20 minutes, or longer if you have very young children in tow. Bear in mind, it is not a loop and therefore you will wind up in Repulse Bay at the end of your walk.

Seasons and Times
Year-round. This beach is one of only five beaches in Hong Kong with year-round life guarding.

Admission
Free

The Best Ways of Getting There
By Bus
- From **Central Exchange Square Bus Terminus** take bus **#6A** (Mon to Sat only), **#6X**, or **#260** to Deep Water Bay Beach.
- Alight the bus at the **Deep Water Bay Beach bus stop**. The beach can be found immediately across the street.
  (Tip: Note that most buses are double deckers and are a great way to see the island if you sit on the top deck on the right hand side as you go toward the beach, left hand side as you head back to Central.)

↔ Travel time: 20-25 mins (bus).

By Car
- From Central: Connaught Road→Harcourt Road→Gloucester Road→**Island Eastern Corridor.**
- Once on the expressway, stay in the far right lane. It will be labelled **Happy Valley/Causeway Bay**. The far right lane will dead-end into a circular overpass. Here you will stay in the far right lane following the signs for the **Aberdeen Tunnel**.
- Once through the tunnel, take one of the tollbooths on the **left side** (HK$5) then get in the far left lane. This lane will force you to make a left turn. You will now be on **Island Road.**
- Follow Island Road until you reach **Deep Water Bay Beach** on your right side (you will see a golf course on your left).

P Metered parking is available right at the beach. There is also a private paid parking lot across the street to handle the overflow at busy times.

By Taxi
A taxi from Central will cost $65-$75 and take 20+ mins.

Getting a Bite
The refreshment kiosk serves the same menu as a restaurant that used to be located at the west end of the beach called *Coco Thai*. It serves tasty Thai food as well as comfort food that kids will like. Bare in mind that the prices are more similar

to what you would find at a restaurant in the city centre and not what you might find at a beach shack.

If you are feeling very ambitious and want to cook your own food, pack everything you need for a BBQ and make your own meal at one of the BBQ pits located near the road.

What's Close?
Repulse Bay Beach, **South Bay Beach** and Middle Bay Beach.

Comments
- Suitable for all ages.
- Plan to spend two to three hours here.
- This beach can get very crowded on the weekends during peak beach season from April to October and parking may be difficult.
- There are a few sit-down toilets on both sides of the beach.
- There is a baby-changing station in the handicapped toilet at the west end of the beach.
- Stroller-friendly, especially so if you plan a walk on the Seaview Promenade.

Word of Mouth
If you manage to get here before the crowd arrives, try to sit under one of the trees at the back of the beach to get some shade, which you will sorely need if you plan to spend the whole day here.

Repulse Bay Beach
Beach Road, Repulse Bay, Hong Kong Island

Tel: 2812-2483 or 2555-0103
Website: http://www.discoverhongkong.com/usa/attractions/hk-repulse-bay.html or
http://www.lcsd.gov.hk/beach/en/index.php

Magnificent views of the South China Sea and the mountainous islands jutting from its sea bed, coupled with the resort-like feel of this southside location, are the reasons why Repulse Bay is the number one beach destination in Hong Kong for locals and tourists.

Children and parents will both find things to love here. For starters, the beach itself is wide, clean and protected by lifeguard towers every few yards. There are three separate changing areas with toilets and showers, swim rafts in the water and a large BBQ area. On the beachfront is a stall selling everything from beach mats and towels to cold drinks and sand toys (just in case you have forgotten your pail and shovel). The stall also rents large beach umbrellas for HK$50 (with a HK$100 refundable deposit), a "must-have" item in the heat, as the beach does not offer many shaded areas. The beach stall also sells some hot snacks and has some shaded tables on a beachside patio where you can sit and take in the views. Just across Beach Road is a Pizza Hut restaurant and a 7-Eleven convenience store which should cover any other items that you might need or want.

When the kids have tired of sitting on their beach blankets or building sand castles, then head to the far eastern end of the beach where you will find an outdoor Chinese temple. The large statues of Tin Hau, the goddess of the sea, and Kwun Yum, the goddess of mercy, are fun and colourful, as is the wishing well where kids can throw coins, and the bridge of longevity which juts out into the sea and is said to add three days onto the lives of those who walk across its tiles.

Just near the Tin Hau shrine area, also on the east side of the beach, is a children's playground. There are a variety of climbing structures here as well as some covered pavilions if you need some shade. Some of the play areas are for two to five year olds, others are for five to 12 year olds.

On the far west side of the beach is the entrance to the Seaview Promenade, a scenic walkway that takes you along the sea from Repulse Bay to Deep Water Bay. This paved pedestrian pathway has a guardrail and is perfect for a breezy family stroll along the ultra-scenic South China Sea. This stroller-friendly walk takes about 20 minutes from one end to the other, 40 minutes round-trip, or longer if you have very young children in tow.

Seasons and Times
Year-round although lifeguards are only on duty from March to November.

Admission
Free

The Best Ways of Getting There
By Bus
- From **Central Exchange Square Bus Terminus** take bus **#6**, **#6A**, **#6X**, **#66** or **#260** to Repulse Bay Road just in front of the **Repulse Bay Complex** – an old colonial-looking building with shops and restaurants. (Look for a landmark blue residential building behind the complex with a hole in the middle of it.)
- From here, cross the street and head down a set of **steps** to the beach.
  (Tip: Note that bus numbers #6, #6A, #6X and #66 are double decker buses and are a great way to see the island if you sit on the top deck on the right hand side as you go toward the beach, left hand side as you head back to Central.)
↔ Travel time: 30+ mins (bus) + 5 mins (walk).

By Car
- From Central: Connaught Road→Harcourt Road→Gloucester Road→**Island Eastern Corridor.**
- Once on the expressway, stay in the far right lane. It will be labelled **Happy Valley/Causeway Bay**. The far right lane will dead-end into a circular overpass. Here you will stay in the far right lane following the signs for the **Aberdeen Tunnel**.

香港 淺水灣
海灘道 淺水灣
淺水灣海灘

0-99

- Once through the tunnel, take one of the tollbooths on the **left side** (HK$5) then get in the far left lane. This lane will force you to make a left turn. You will now be on **Island Road** which will automatically turn into **Repulse Bay Road**.
- Stay on Repulse Bay Road until you pass **Belleview Drive** on your left side.
- The next left turn will be **Beach Road** which is well marked with a blue "**Repulse Bay Beach**" sign with an arrow pointing toward Beach Road. Follow Beach Road until you find parking.

P There is both metered parking on the street at Beach Road and a paid parking lot just in front of the beach, which makes driving here a good option.

> *(Tip: Be forewarned that when the weather gets hot, the weekends here are very crowded and you may have to wait a long time for a parking space. There is also a covered paid parking lot in the Repulse Bay Complex on Repulse Bay Road which you can try if the Beach Road parking options are overcrowded.)*

By Taxi

A taxi from Central will cost HK$80-$100 and take 25-30 mins.

Getting a Bite

If you climb several flights of steps up from the middle of Beach Road (just across from the beach stalls), you will find Repulse Bay Road and a replica of the old Repulse Bay Hotel. (The original was demolished in 1982.) This lovely building houses some very upscale restaurants and a shopping galleria as well as a large grocery store. Should you wish to purchase some items for a picnic lunch, the grocery store called *Jason's Marketplace*, an upscale local chain, is a good bet. Two restaurants of note in the building are *The Verandah* which serves great afternoon tea and lovely weekend brunches (as well as lunch and dinner) and *Spices* which serves Asian fare and has a large covered outdoor area for alfresco dining. Keep in mind that both of these restaurants are quite posh and are priced accordingly. Other options in the complex would be *Pacific Coffee Company*, a coffee house that has sandwiches and desserts, and *Saffron Bakery,* a Western-style bakery and candy shop. There is even a homemade ice cream shop called *Ice Cream Gallery*. The courtyard of this complex has public outdoor shaded tables, and is a lovely child-friendly spot to enjoy your lunch or snack.

What's Close?
South Bay Beach, Deep Water Bay Beach and Middle Bay Beach.

Comments
- Suitable for all ages.
- Plan to spend two to three hours here or more.
- This beach can be very crowded during the summer. Thousands of people (literally) might be here on any given beautiful Saturday or Sunday in the summer months.
- There are toilets of both the hole-in-the-ground variety and the more modern sit-down style at the beach. There is even a toilet paper dispenser at the doorway so that you may take tissue in with you when you enter.
- There is a baby-changing station in the ladies' toilet near the playground. As well, the ladies' changing room is filled with benches that would do nicely for that purpose.
- Stroller-friendly, though if you are coming here by bus you will have to navigate a long set of steps to get to the beach.

Extra info
How much more fun can you have than a family picnic which includes hot pizza at the beach? At Repulse Bay this is very easily done. Simply call *Pizza Hut* (tel: 2812-6787) from the beach and order your meal. Then take the five-minute walk from the sand to the restaurant across the street to pick up your takeaway order and voila… instant happy picnic for parents and children.

Word of Mouth
If you would like to be on a southside beach but would rather avoid the crowds, you might try either South Bay Beach (see the **South Bay Beach** chapter) or Middle Bay Beach instead.

South Bay Beach
South Bay Road
South Bay, Hong Kong Island

Tel: 2812-2468 or 2555-0103
Website: http://www.lcsd.gov.hk/beach/en/index.php

There is a true Mediterranean feel to this lovely secluded beach. Its quiet nature and seclusion relative to its more popular neighbours (Repulse Bay Beach and Deep Water Bay Beach) make this spot a lovely place to spend a morning or afternoon with the kids. Set in a small cove away from traffic and noise, this beach is just big enough for the kids to run around like crazy, but not so big that you can't see them from your beach towel. The views of the South China Sea and the soft sand beneath your toes will make you feel like you are on a beach holiday. To improve on the vacation fantasy why not rent a large beach umbrella from the cafe? The going rate is HK$50 (with a HK$100 refundable deposit).

Taking in a meal at the South Bay Beach Club, a Mediterranean-style alfresco restaurant set above the changing rooms with stunning sea views, is a great way to start or end your visit. They have something for everyone here – kid fare as well as menu items the adults will enjoy. Even if you only stop in to have a cappuccino to go, take advantage of this lovely little gem.

This beach has a swimming platform offshore, shark nets around the large swimming area, and lifeguards on duty from April to October. Shower rooms, changing facilities and toilets are also available, making your beach "vacation" smooth sailing!

Seasons and Times
Year-round (although lifeguards are only on duty from April to October from 9am-6pm during the week and 8am-7pm on weekends and public holidays)

Admission
Free

The Best Ways of Getting There
By Bus/Taxi
- From **Central Exchange Square Bus Terminus** take bus **#6**, **#6A**, **#6X**, or **#260** to **Repulse Bay Road** just in front of the **Repulse Bay Complex** – an old colonial-looking building with shops and restaurants. (Look for a landmark blue residential building behind the complex with a hole in the middle of it.)
- Once you are in Repulse Bay hail a taxi for a quick 5-7 minute ride to **South Bay Beach**.
  (Tip: Note that bus numbers #6, #6A, #6X and #66 are double decker buses and are a great way to see the island if you sit on the top deck on the right hand side as you go toward the beach, left hand side as you head back to Central.)
↔ Travel time: 30+ mins (bus) + 5 mins (taxi).

By Car
- From Central: Connaught Road→Harcourt Road→Gloucester Road→**Island Eastern Corridor**.
- Once on the expressway, stay in the far right lane. It will be labelled **Happy Valley/Causeway Bay**. The far right lane will dead-end into a circular overpass. Here you will stay in the far right lane following the signs for the **Aberdeen Tunnel**.
- Once through the tunnel, take one of the tollbooths on the left side (HK$5) then get in the far left lane. This lane will force you to make a left turn. You will now be on **Island Road** which will automatically turn into **Repulse Bay Road**.
- Stay on **Repulse Bay Road** until you pass **The Repulse Bay complex** on your left side. Shortly thereafter you will come to a roundabout. Here you will turn left, past the gas station (on your left) and go to the next roundabout where you will turn right onto **South Bay Road**.
- Take **South Bay Road** all the way to the dead end.
 At the end you will find two metered parking areas for South Bay Beach. Once you have parked, walk down the stairway to get to the beach.
  (Tip: Though parking is available here, if you come on a weekend and don't get here early, you may have to wait a while for a spot.)

By Taxi
A taxi from Central will cost HK$80-$100 and take 25-30 mins.

0-99

Getting a Bite
South Bay Beach Club (2812-6015) – or if a beach barbeque is something you want to try, you will find a BBQ area here, but be forewarned you need to prepare in advance and arrive with all the equipment and food.

What's Close?
Repulse Bay Beach, Deep Water Bay Beach and Middle Bay Beach.

Comments
- Suitable for all ages.
- Plan to spend at least two hours here.
- This beach can be crowded on weekends.
- The toilets here have been recently renovated. There are two sit-down toilet stalls. Keep in mind that from the sand you have to walk back up some steps and on to the road to access the toilets.
- There is a baby-changing station in the ladies' toilet.
- This beach is not particularly stroller-friendly as you have to walk down steps to get to the sand from the parking lot.

Word of Mouth
During the summer months, beach outings are an especially popular thing to do for families in Hong Kong. Repulse Bay Beach, on weekends and holidays in particular, will be heaving with people due to its size, location and facilities. While the hordes of 25,000 or more struggle for a square foot of sand to call their own, why not beat most of the crowd and try South Bay Beach instead? **_BUT_** take a taxi because parking will be very tough!

Chung Hom Kok Beach
Off Chung Hom Kok Road
Chung Hom Kok, Hong Kong Island

香港　春坎角
春坎角道　春坎角
春坎角海灘

Tel: 2813-0454
Website: http://www.lcsd.gov.hk/beach/en/beach-address-south.php
For area map: go to the above website, scroll down to 'Chung Hom Kok
Beach' and then click on 'Location Map'.

For families with young children, the well-equipped and shaded playground attached to this lovely beach is what makes Chung Hom Kok a great choice for a seaside outing.

Located on the south side of Hong Kong Island, Chung Hom Kok sits on its own little peninsula just west of its larger and more popular neighbour – Stanley. It is accessible, but not widely used, making it a 'find' for families who want a little bit of peace without having to work too hard to get there.

Little kids will love having the choice of sand play or playground play, all in one location. The beach has good amenities including: toilets, changing rooms, outdoor showers, a swim raft, lifeguards, a first aid station, BBQ areas, picnic tables, and a refreshment kiosk. The playground has jungle gyms, riding toys and swings for the kids and also provides some restful features for adults, including good shade, padded flooring and benches for weary parents (also located in the shade).

If you have children under six, this may be the best choice for a beach outing on Hong Kong Island. The only downside here is the long series of steps that must be navigated before reaching the playground or the sand. It is worth the effort, but come prepared to work for it a little bit!

Seasons and Times
Year-round although lifeguards are only on duty from April to October.

Admission
Free

0-99

The Best Ways of Getting There

By Bus

- From **Central Exchange Square Bus Terminus** take bus **#6X**, or **#66** to **the roundabout** at the end of **Chung Hom Kok Road** (opposite 76 Chung Hom Kok Road). This is the Chung Hom Kok Beach bus stop.
- From here you will need to walk five minutes down the road directly opposite the bus stop (look for the alley offshoot of Chung Hom Kok Road.) At the end of the road on the left hand side you will find **some steps that lead down to the beach**.
- The path is well marked with a sign that says 'Welcome to Chung Hom Kok Beach'.

↔ Travel time: 30-35 mins (bus) + 10 mins (walk).

By Car

- From Central: Connaught Road→ Harcourt Road→ Gloucester Road→ **Island Eastern Corridor**.
- Once on the expressway, stay in the far right lane. It will be labelled **Happy Valley/Causeway Bay**. The far right lane will dead-end into a circular overpass. Here you will stay in the far right lane following the signs for the **Aberdeen Tunnel**.
- Once through the tunnel, take one of the tollbooths on the **left side** (HK$5) then get in the far left lane. This lane will force you to make a left turn. You will now be on **Wong Chuk Hang Road** which will turn into **Island Road**.
- Island Road changes names to **Repulse Bay Road** and then to **Stanley Gap Road**, though the road remains constant. Stay on Stanley Gap Road until you see the right hand turnoff for **Chung Hom Kok Road.**
- Follow Chung Hom Kok Road until you get to a **roundabout** where you will turn right. This road will **dead-end** into the cul-de-sac which leads to the beach.

P Free parking is available on the side of the road.

(Tip: This is not a very big parking area and on Sundays and public holidays it may be hard to find a space unless you get here early in the morning.)

By Taxi

A taxi from Central will cost HK$110-$120 and take around 30 minutes.

Getting a Bite

There is a refreshment kiosk at the beach that sells cold drinks and dry snacks. Alternatively pack a picnic lunch or bring the makings for a BBQ at the pits. If you would like to make a full day's outing out of your trip, visit Stanley Village (five minutes by taxi, 10 minutes by bus) and have a meal there before or after the beach (see the **Stanley Village** chapter for more details).

What's Close?

Stanley Village

Comments

- Suitable for all ages but will be most enjoyable for kids who still like playground play.
- Plan to spend half a day here.
- Generally not crowded.
- There are sit-down style toilets at the beach.
- There is a baby-changing station in the ladies' bathroom.
- This is NOT a great place to bring a stroller as there are many steps to navigate from the road to the beach.

Word of Mouth

This is a wonderful place to have an outdoor birthday party or event. The playground has two semi-covered pavilion type structures which make a great place to set up games and cake while the kids run around happily at either the playground or the beach or both! (The only downside will be transporting all your gear down the steps.)

Shek O Beach & Village and Big Wave Bay Beach

Shek O Road and Big Wave Bay Road
Shek O, Hong Kong Island South

Tel: (Shek O Beach): 2809-4557
Tel: (Big Wave Bay Beach): 2809-4558
Website: http://www.lcsd.gov.hk/beach/en/beach-address-south.php

Sometimes, the harder the journey, the more rewarding the destination. That certainly holds true for these two very lovely beaches at the far eastern end of Hong Kong Island. White soft sand, clean(er) water, fresh air and sea views reminiscent of the Mediterranean Sea, and fun dining options, are the reasons why these beaches are two of the most popular in Hong Kong.

Shek O Beach:
When you close your eyes and picture a beautiful unspoiled (but popular) beach on the South China Sea, this is it. Shek O's sleepy little fishing village, located just in front of the beach, completes the picture and offers everything to make this a great family day out. The beach itself has lifeguards, outdoor showers, a great BBQ area with benches, a fun playground with sand pit and digging toys, swimming rafts, a refreshment kiosk and best of all a miniature golf course at the beach's entrance (small fee per game). On the far north side of the beach is a cluster of rocks which you can climb on to get a better view of the sea ahead, and the cliffs and mountains behind. Directly in back of the beach parking lot, there is a row of stalls selling all sorts of items to make your day more fun: beach toys, swimsuits, mats, towels, umbrellas (rentals), inflatable floats, snacks, drinks and barbequing equipment such as charcoal, disposable grills and rods.

When you have had enough of the sand and surf, take a walk around town. The village itself is small but very picturesque and filled with quaint, tightly packed residences. Just down the narrow alleyway that intersects the village traffic circle is the town's Tin Hau Temple which is worth a stop. To explore more of the area, rent some bikes for an hour at the stalls that run parallel to the beach. Do plan to stay for lunch or dinner here and soak up the ambience in one of the outdoor restaurants. Some people come all the way here just for a meal.

Big Wave Bay Beach:

Big Wave Bay is completely off the beaten path and it makes you feel like you are a million miles away from the busy traffic and hectic lifestyle of the city. Smaller than Shek O, this beach offers a special feature unavailable anywhere else on Hong Kong Island – surf! (Beware though that occasionally the waves are so strong the lifeguards will raise the red flag and not allow you in the water, so make sure to call ahead or visit the website to check the swimming status before you venture out there.) To take maximum advantage, rent a boogie board or surf board (if you know how to surf) from the beach's kiosks. Amenities at this beach include showers, lifeguards, a first aid station, a café and changing rooms.

If the kids feel like going on an adventure, take them to see the Bronze Age rock carvings accessible by foot from the beach. Look for the trail entrance on the far north side of the beach (opposite from where you enter the beach). These prehistoric relics were declared a monument in 1978 and are one of eight ancient rock carvings found in the Hong Kong area.

On the way down to the beach from the parking lot/bus stop, you will pass a large grassy picnic area and playground. This is a great spot to bring the kids for a run around or a frisbee toss. There is also a small climbing wall for ages 5-12 and a foot reflexology stone garden to gingerly tread upon. The path to the beach is lined with shops that sell essentials such as towels, sun block, ice cream, cold and hot drinks and snacks.

How About Both?

If you are really adventurous, you can attempt both beaches in one day. Perhaps Big Wave Bay for the surf and Shek O for a meal? You can walk from Shek O Beach to Big Wave Bay Beach very easily. It takes around 30 minutes. From Big Wave Bay Beach parking lot, follow Big Wave Bay Road until you reach the traffic circle. Here you will go left and find yourself on Shek O Road. Follow Shek O Road until it dead-ends into the village.

0-99

Seasons and Times
Year-round, although lifeguards are only on duty from March to November.

Admission
Free

The Best Ways of Getting There
By City Tram/Bus
• From **Central's Des Voeux Road** or from **Admiralty's Queensway** to **Shau Kei Wan**, take the tram heading east. Stops are located in the middle of the road about every three blocks.
  *(Tip: Make sure the tram front reads "**Shau Kei Wan**" or it won't get you all the way to where you want to go.)*
↔ Travel time: 60+ mins (tram).
• Once you reach **Shau Kei Wan** take bus **#9** to **Shek O**. For **Big Wave Bay** the directions are the same except that **bus #9 only** *sometimes* **goes to Big Wave Bay**. If the bus is going to Big Wave Bay it should read "**Via Big Wave Bay**." If the bus you are on is not stopping there, you will have to first go to Shek O.
  (Tip: Do not wait exclusively for the bus that reads via "Big Wave Bay" as they come infrequently, just take the first bus that comes along.)
↔ Travel time: 30+ mins (bus).
> **From Shek O you have three options to get to Big Wave Bay:**
> **Walking**
> • Alight the bus at the traffic circle juncture of Big Wave Bay Road and Shek O Road and walk on Big Wave Bay Road to the beach.
> ↔ Travel time: 15 mins (walk).
> **Mini Bus**
> • In Shek O you can hail a small bus to Big Wave Bay.
> ↔ Travel time: 5 mins (bus).
> **Taxi**
> • In Shek O hail a taxi to Big Wave Bay.
> ↔ Travel time: 5 mins (taxi).

By MTR/Bus
• From **Central** or **Admiralty** take the blue line to **Shau Kei Wan Station**. Exit the station at exit "**A3**" which will put you above ground at the bus terminus.

- Follow directions above for bus **#9**.
- ↔ Travel time: 20 mins (MTR) + 30+ mins (bus).

By Car
- From Central: Connaught Road→ Harcourt Road→ Gloucester Road→ **Island Eastern Corridor**.

Option #1:
- Once on the expressway, stay in the far right lane. It will be labelled **Happy Valley/Causeway Bay**. The far right lane will dead-end into a circular overpass. Here you will stay in the far right lane following the signs for the **Aberdeen Tunnel**.
- Once through the tunnel, take one of the tollbooths on the **left side** (HK$5) then get in the far left lane. This lane will force you to make a left turn. You will now be on **Wong Chuk Hang Road** which will turn into **Island Road**.
- Island Road changes names to **Repulse Bay Road** and then to **Stanley Gap Road**, though the road remains constant.
- Once you reach the **Stanley traffic circle follow signs for Tai Tam** (straight ahead). You are now on **Tai Tam Road**.
- Keep following the road and you will cross **a narrow bridge over a reservoir**. Soon after you will come to a traffic circle with a large sign pointing to **the right for Shek O**. Make the right hand turn. You are now on **Shek O Road**. See * below.

Option #2:
(Tip: This is the faster option from Central but it is not as scenic a drive.)
- Once on the expressway you will stay in the **second lane from the right**. Follow signs for **North Point until you pass Causeway Bay** and later look for signs for **Chai Wan**.
- On the expressway you will pass signs and exits for North Point, Quarry Bay, Tai Koo Shing, Sai Wan Ho (among others). You are looking for signs for **Shek O and Shau Kei Wan**. Take the **exit marked "Shek O"**.
- After you exit the expressway you will be on **Chai Wan Road**. Look for the right hand turn to **Tai Tam Road and Shek O**. Follow Tai Tam Road until you reach the **Shek O traffic circle** where you will make a left onto **Shek O Road**. See * below.

* Follow the road all the way down until you come to a **second traffic circle**. **Shek O Road** will be a **right** at the circle. **Big Wave Bay Road** will be a **left**.

• For either beach, follow the road to its conclusion.

P Shek O Village parking lot will be on the right side directly in front of the beach. Parking is free here. Otherwise there is a private paid parking lot on your right side just before you get to the Shek O traffic circle.

P Big Wave Bay parking has two-hour meters and is a five-minute walk from the beach.

> *(Tip: Parking on weekends at either beach is **VERY** difficult. Try to avoid driving here on weekends and public holidays unless you get here very early in the morning.)*

By Taxi
A taxi from Central will cost HK$160+ and take 40-45 mins.

Getting a Bite
Shek O:
Shek O Village is a great place to have a meal. The two most popular spots for a bite are the ***Shek O Chinese & Thai Seafood Restaurant,*** No. 303 Shek O Village (tel: 2809-4426/2809-2202) and ***The Black Sheep,*** No. 330 Shek O Village (tel: 2809-2021). The seafood place is located just at the traffic circle in the centre of the village and is casual, open-air and inexpensive. The Black Sheep can be found by following the narrow lane located just in front of the seafood place, about a two-minute walk from the traffic circle. This pub serves very tasty international fare, is moderately priced and has something the kids cannot resist – pizza. There is also a lovely French bakery and light fare restaurant called ***Shining Stone,*** No. 452 Shek O Village (tel: 2809-2227) which is a perfect spot to have a light meal or a snack. To locate the Shining Stone follow the narrow street off of the traffic circle and veer right at the bend in the road. There are many snack stands and local restaurants that are right on or near the beach if you just want to grab something quickly and not stray too far from your beach towel.

Big Wave Bay:
Big Wave Bay has a great café right on the beach known as ***Eric's Kitchen***. This is a great spot for a weekend breakfast, brunch, lunch or supper. Opening hours are as follows: weekdays – 11:00am-7:00pm, weekends and holidays – 9:00am-7:00pm. Eric's serves Western food and kids' favourites such as pancakes, omelettes, burgers, hot dogs, sandwiches, wraps, pizza and for us weary parents – fresh ground coffee.

There are also a few local stalls selling noodles, soup and local Chinese fare on the path as you head down toward the beach from the parking lot.

What's Close?
Tai Tam Country Park.

Comments
- Suitable for all ages.
- Plan to spend at least half a day (as it is an effort to get here.)
- Both beaches are very crowded on weekends, particularly from April to October.
- There are toilets at both beaches. Shek O Beach has mostly squat-style but there are a few sit-down toilets at the very end of the stalls. Big Wave Bay has sit-down style toilets.
- There are no baby-changing tables at either beach, but there are benches in the changing rooms that could serve the purpose.
- Both beach areas are stroller-friendly.

Extra Info
The lane you must walk down in order to arrive at Big Wave Bay Beach is full of shops renting and selling gear. To give a rough sense of the pricing, the last stall on the left before you hit the sand is called *Lam Kee Store* and has the following prices for rentals:
Beach Chairs: HK$20 per day
Beach Umbrellas: HK$20 per day
Body Boards: HK$30 per day
Surfboards: HK$40-$90 per day

Word of Mouth
The mosquito population here is very high. Spray everyone in the family *BEFORE* you get out of the bus, car or taxi.

Clear Water Bay Second Beach
Tai Au Mun Road, Clear Water Bay
Sai Kung, New Territories

Tel: 2719-0351/2791-3100
Website: http://www.lcsd.gov.hk/beach/en/beach-address-sk.php
For area map: Click on above website and then click on "Location Map"

Sometimes the best way to find something great is to follow the crowd. Locals flock to the Clear Water Bay area when the weather warms up to soak up the sun and take in the soft white sand and beautiful scenery. Why not join them at Clear Water Bay Second Beach, the most popular and well-loved beach of them all?

There are good reasons why this one beach stands out above the rest, particularly for families. Amenities here include: changing rooms, indoor and outdoor shower facilities, proper toilets, swim rafts, lifeguards and a first aid station. There is also a fully stocked refreshment kiosk that sells everything from beach toys to sun block and will rent beach umbrellas, beach chairs, kick boards, rafts both big and small, and swimming rings and noodles. There is an atmosphere here that is different from other beaches, perhaps because you can hear the crash of the surf as it hits the shore. The waves are not large but they do come in and create that lovely sound that makes you feel as though you are on a beach holiday far away from the hectic pace of busy Hong Kong.

There is only one negative to report. The access to the beach is a flight of stairs from the parking lot or bus terminus down to the sand. This means that families will have to climb **UP** all those stairs on their way out. Still, it is well worth the effort.

Seasons and Times
Year-round. Lifeguards are on duty the whole year. It's one of only five Hong Kong beaches with year-round service.

Admission
Free

The Best Ways of Getting There

By MTR/Bus

- From Central or Admiralty to **Diamond Hill** station, take the red line to **Mongkok**. Transfer to the green line (across the platform at Mongkok Station) to Diamond Hill.
- Take exit "**C2**" to street level and look for KMB bus **#91** going to **Clear Water Bay**.
- You will alight the bus at the **last stop**, which will be the bus terminus for **Clear Water Bay Second Beach.**
- From here follow the steps leading down to the beach; they can be found to the left of the bus terminus as you face the water.

↔ Travel time: 25 mins (MTR) + 40-45 mins (bus) + 3 mins (walk).

By Car

- From Central: Connaught Road→Harcourt Road→Gloucester Road→**Island Eastern Corridor (Route 4)→Eastern Harbour Tunnel.**
- In **tunnel** (**Route 2**) stay in **far right lane**. Once through tollbooth (HK$25) look for **Kwun Tong/Tseung Kwan O Tunnel** to your **right**.
- Once past the first sign get to the **far left lane** and follow signs to **Kwun Tong/Tseung Kwan O, left to Exit 2A**. After the exit, the **road splits** and you will **stay right** following signs for **Route 7** and **Tseung Kwan O Tunnel**. Make a **right at the light** and follow signs for the tunnel. You are now on **Tseung Kwan O Road**. Go through the toll (HK$3) and **stay left in the tunnel**.
- You will take **Exit 2A** to the left with signs for **Po Lam, Hang Hau and Sai Kung**.
- Road will split again; **stay right** and follow signs for **Sai Kung and Hang Hau**.
- You will come to your first of MANY roundabouts.
- At the **1st roundabout**, follow the sign for **Sai Kung**.
- At **2nd roundabout** take the **1st left exit for Sai Kung**.
- At **3rd roundabout** take 1st exit with a sign marked "**Clear Water Bay**". You are now on Clear Water Bay Road.
- At the **4th roundabout** make a right turn out of the traffic circle following the signs for "**Clear Water Bay Golf and Country Club**". You are now on **Tai Au Mun Road**.
- Follow the road until you see the car park and the bus terminus on your left (about three minutes or less).
- P The parking here is free.

新界　西貢　清水灣

大坳門路　清水灣第二灣泳灘

0-99

By Taxi
A taxi from Central will cost HK$160-$190+ and take 40-45 mins, longer if you are travelling during peak hours.

Getting a Bite
The refreshment kiosk at the beach sells snacks, drinks and light fare such as noodles and sandwiches. If you think you would like to have something more substantial, then you may want to bring a picnic from home. There are covered sitting-out areas with tables and benches that are perfect for an outdoor lunch.

What's Close?
Clear Water Bay First Beach (see **Word of Mouth** below).

Comments
- Suitable for all ages.
- Plan to spend at least two to three hours here.
- This beach can be crowded on weekend and public holidays.
- There are two sets of toilets at the beach, one next to the parking lot and one right at the beach. Both have sit-down style toilets.
- There are baby-changing stations in the ladies' toilet near the parking lot as well as one down by the beach.
- This is not the best place to bring a stroller, as you must walk down a flight of stairs to get to the sand from the road.

Word of Mouth
A short 5-10 minute walk from Second Beach is Clear Water Bay First Beach. It is not as large or as scenic as Second Beach but it has a few good things going for it. First Beach has several BBQ sites which are nice if you have your heart set on a beach cookout, whereas you are not allowed to BBQ on Second Beach. Also, Second Beach can become quite crowded, so if you like this area but need some more room on the sand, First Beach is a good option. Be aware however that there are many, many steps leading down to First Beach. In fact, one might call it a hike! There is no way to get back to the road unless you are willing to climb back up the way you came. You will find an access to First Beach located up the road (Tai Au Mun Road) heading back toward the roundabout from Second Beach. Look for the sign that reads "Clear Water Bay First Beach" and an entry to a set of stairs leading down toward the water.

Trio Beach

Accessed from Hebe Haven Pier
(also called Pak Sha Wan)
Sai Kung, New Territories

新界　西貢
白沙灣　三星灣泳灘

Tel: 2792-3672
Website: http://www.lcsd.gov.hk/beach/en/beach-address-sk.php

This lovely, secluded beach in the Sai Kung area is a great combination of adventure and seaside fun. Beyond the beautiful surroundings in every direction, the sand here is soft and the water is a clear blue that is hard to find in Hong Kong. There is even enough visibility that some people snorkel. It is an effort to reach Trio Beach, and will involve a minimum of two forms of transport, but that is part of the fun of this experience.

0-99

To access the beach, you will need to begin your trip from Hebe Haven (also called Pak Sha Wan), a quaint little area just outside Sai Kung Town. This small village community is a congregating point for many locals and expats who enjoy boating, sailing and fishing, and therefore, despite the size of the place, it offers some lovely dining options including a few European cafés and a Thai restaurant. There is also a small Tin Hau temple in Hebe Haven, located opposite the pier, that is worth visiting. From the remodelled Hebe Haven pier you can hire a kaido (small private junk/ferry) to cross over to Trio Beach. The kaido ride is very pleasant and offers a chance to view all the pleasure boats as well as the cove from the water. The boat drops you off right at the pier next to the beach.

The beach itself is remote and relatively unspoiled. Though off the beaten path, it still has everything you will need to have a relaxing beach outing: Changing rooms, shower facilities, lifeguards, toilets, swim rafts, multiple BBQ areas, a well stocked refreshment kiosk that rents umbrellas, floats, inflatable rafts, swimming rings and lockers. They also sell flip flops, snorkel gear, goggles, and water guns. There is even a small shaded playground just behind the beach.

For even more adventure, it is possible to hike over to Trio Beach from just behind the Hong Kong Yacht Club located in Shelter Cove, just minutes from Hebe Haven (see "**Walking**" below). The hike itself takes around half an hour and is a great way to access the beach. Consider hiking to the beach and hiring a kaido to take you back. If you go to the Trio Beach pier you should be able to negotiate a one-way journey back to Hebe Haven or Shelter Cove.

Seasons and Times
Year-round although lifeguards are only on duty from April to October.

Admission
Free

The Best Ways of Getting There
To Hebe Haven
By MTR/Bus
- From Central or Admiralty to **Diamond Hill** Station, take the red line to **Mongkok**. Transfer to the green line (across the platform at Mongkok station) to Diamond Hill.
- Take exit "**C2**" and at street level catch KMB bus **#92**, going toward **Sai Kung**, or KMB bus **#96R** (only on Sundays and public holidays), going **toward Wong Shek Pier**.
- Alight the bus before Sai Kung in **Pak Sha Wan/Hebe Haven**. The bus stop is one block north of the pier on the opposite side of the street.

↔ Travel time: 25 mins (MTR) + 35-40 mins (bus) + 3 mins (walk to end of pier).

MTR/Mini Bus
- From Central or Admiralty to **Choi Hung** station, take the red line to **Mongkok**. Transfer to the green line (across the platform at Mongkok station) to Choi Hung.
- Use exit "**C2**" and at street level, catch minibus **#1A** or **#1M** going towards Sai Kung.
- Alight the bus when you see the **Hebe Haven Pier** on your right hand side.

↔ Travel time: 25 mins (MTR) + 30 mins (bus) + 3 mins (walk).

By Car
- From Central: Connaught Road→Harcourt Road→Gloucester Road→**Island Eastern Corridor (Route 4)→Eastern Harbour Tunnel.**

- In **tunnel** (**Route 2**) stay in **far right lane**. Once through tollbooth (HK$25) look for **Kwun Tong/Tseung Kwan O Tunnel** to your **right**.
- Once past the first sign get to the **far left lane,** follow signs to **Kwun Tong/Tseung Kwan O, left to <u>Exit 2A</u>**. After the exit, the **road splits** and you will **stay right** following signs for **Route 7** and **Tseung Kwan O Tunnel**. Make a **right at the light** and follow signs for the tunnel. You are now on **Tseung Kwan O Road**. Go through the toll (HK$3) and **stay left in the tunnel**.
- You will take **<u>Exit 2A</u>** to the left with signs for **Po Lam, Hang Hau and Sai Kung**.
- Road will split again, **stay right,** follow signs for **Sai Kung and Hang Hau**.
- You will come to your first of MANY roundabouts.
- At the **1st roundabout**, follow the sign for **Sai Kung**.
- At **2nd roundabout** take the **1st left exit for Sai Kung**.
- At **3rd roundabout** take 1st exit with a sign marked "**University, Kowloon, Sai Kung**". You are now on Hiram's Highway.
- At the **4th roundabout** take the first left marked "**Kowloon and Sai Kung**". **Stay right** and **follow signs to Sai Kung** when the road splits, you are still on **Hiram's Highway**.
- At the **5th roundabout**, follow signs for **Ho Chung and Sai Kung**. You will pass Marina Cove and Hebe Haven Marina then **Hebe Haven Pier** will be coming up shortly on your right hand side (note: if you hit Sai Kung Town you have gone too far).

  P There is metered parking on the road that leads to the pier as well as off the main road just past the pier in the Pak Sha Wan public car park. **Beware**: some, but not all, of the parking is two-hour parking meters only. If you need more time, consider parking in one of the Sai Kung Town garages (see **Sai Kung Town** chapter for details) or you will have to come back from the beach to feed the meter.

By Taxi
A taxi from Central will cost HK$200-$230+ and take 45-55 mins.

From Hebe Haven to Trio Beach
By Kaido (small ferry boat)
- From the **pier** in **Hebe Haven** take a **kaido** over to **Trio Beach**.

- You should **determine the fare** with your carrier **before** you leave the pier. (Prices should be roughly $10-$20 per round trip per person if you are in a group. The price is HK$20 or more per person round trip if your group is three or less people.) You will get a ticket with the colour flag that your boat will be flying; all of them fly different colours so you know which one is yours. Hang on to the ticket as it has the phone number of your service which you may need to arrange your return trip to Hebe Haven. Don't forget to bring a mobile phone! Alternatively, pre-arrange a pickup time.

↔ Travel time: 10 mins (kaido)

Hiking
- You can also **hike** to this beach from the **Hebe Haven area**.
- Take a **taxi** to **Shelter Cove** from **Hebe Haven** (home of the Hong Kong Yacht Club).
- Before you pass through the barrier gate on your left hand side you will see a set of cement steps near a group of residences which will lead you up to a road that dead-ends into the hiking trail which goes to Trio Beach.

↔ Travel time: 5 mins (taxi) + 30-40 mins (hike)

Getting a Bite

There is a refreshment kiosk above the changing rooms on the 2nd floor of the only building at the beach (so you cannot miss it!). The kiosk has cold drinks, snacks such as chips and ice cream as well as a small selection of hot food items including hot dogs, sausages, shao mai and fish balls. They also sell all the fixings you will need to use the BBQ pits that are at the beach, everything from the charcoal to the uncooked food itself. Another good option is to plan a meal either before or after your beach visit at one of the restaurants in Hebe Haven. There is a Thai restaurant called *Thai Thai Kitchen* at the pier (tel: 2719-8798) which has outdoor seating. Another option are the two European-style cafés across the street: *Hebe One O One* (tel: 2335-5515) which is child-friendly and has two roof terraces with great views of the sea, and *Chez Les Copains*, a small French restaurant (tel: 2243-1918). Make a booking at these popular spots to avoid disappointment.

What's Close?

Sai Kung Town/Hap Mun Bay Beach and Lion's Nature Education Centre.

Comments

- Suitable for all ages.
- Plan to spend at least half a day here.
- This beach is not usually crowded.
- There are sit-down style toilets at the beach.
- There is a baby-changing station in the ladies toilet on the 1st floor above the changing rooms.
- A stroller would not be very useful here. A baby backpack or infant carrier would be a better choice.

Extra Info

The refreshment kiosk at Trio Beach is very well stocked, however, there are a few things that are not available which should be brought from home such as sun block and mosquito repellent. Also, they do not sell hot drinks. If you would like a coffee or a hot tea bring a flask or thermos with you. The kiosk hours are: Mon-Fri – 9:00am-5:30pm, Sat, Sun and public holidays – 8:30am-6:30pm.

Word of Mouth

Sai Kung Town is very near Hebe Haven. It is a five-minute taxi ride or a quick bus trip. You could easily make a full day's outing out of a trip to Trio Beach by including a meal and a walk around Sai Kung Town (see **Sai Kung Town** chapter for more details).

Pui O Beach
and Oohlala Restaurant
Pui O Beach, Lantau Island

Oohlala Restaurant Tel: 2984-8710
Pui O Beach campsite (LCSD) Tel: 2984-1116 or 2852-3220
Pui O Beach Tel: 2984-7675 or 2852-3220
First Ferry Tel: 2131-8181
New Lantao Bus Company: 2984-9848
Website for Oohlala Restaurant: http://www.oohlala-hk.com/
Website for Pui O public campsite: http://www.lcsd.gov.hk/camp/en/p_ng_po.php
Website for Pui O beach: http://www.lcsd.gov.hk/beach/en/beach-address-is.php
Website for First Ferry: http://www.nwff.com.hk/
Website for New Lantao Bus Company: http://www.newlantaobus.com/nlb.html
For area map: Go to the website for Pui O Beach and then click on "Location Map".

Pui O is a "get away from it all" beach. Coming here for the day is like a pretend holiday. Apart from getting here – which though it sounds daunting, will only take an hour or so – everything you need for everyone is here and ready to be enjoyed. When you get home you will feel as though you had gotten away from it all and lowered your blood pressure.

Pui O Beach is a public beach with all the amenities one comes to expect from the Leisure and Cultural Services Department (which manages all of Hong Kong's public beaches). There are changing rooms, showers, toilets, a well stocked refreshment/fast food kiosk, lifeguards, BBQ areas and picnic tables. It is a lovely stretch of sand that is long enough that if you walked from one end to the other you would actually get some exercise.

This beach outing goes from lovely to magical when you add the presence of Oohlala Restaurant to the mix. If you book a table at this alfresco spot, the family can have a tasty and child-friendly meal and then afterwards the adults can stay on for coffee and/or wine while the kids enjoy the sand and frolic in the water just a step away. It is easy to watch them from the perch of this restaurant as it is literally built on the sand and everyone stays happy and gets a relaxing day out. The water is not deep for quite a few metres off shore as the shelf is out far enough that most kids are only up to their knees or chest, yet still out in the water. Oohlala also rents kayaks, boogie boards and surf boards by the hour. If your family is really keen on learning to surf or kayak you can even organize a private or group lesson. Just ask at the service desk located outside the entrance of the restaurant for more information. Oohlala will also set up beach sports for your group, either football or volleyball, right on the sand. Mountain bikes can also be rented from here with all the gear needed for a safe ride.

The restaurant succeeds admirably at creating a relaxed vacation atmosphere. Not only do they have alfresco dining but they also have a snack bar, outdoor seating under sun umbrellas, and couch areas with buckets of toys where sun-weary kids can still enjoy a play but get out of the heat. No one is rushed here and at the end of the day everyone will feel as though they have gotten away from it all and had a mini vacation.

If you want to extend the vacation beyond just a day, Oohlala offers an overnight camping package. They have a private, grassy site just a few metres away from the beach which includes a full equipment setup and everything needed to cook a do-it-yourself BBQ. They even throw in breakfast! If your family are seasoned camping professionals and have all the gear you need, another option is the Leisure and Cultural Services Department Pui O Public Campsite with 52 bays that can be used free of charge on a first-come, first-served basis. Each site faces the beach, has a picnic table and benches, a BBQ pit and is very much like camping right on the beach as every site's base consists of sand, instead of grass, and they all have beach views.

0-99

***Please be aware that the Pui O area is home to many water buffalo. They are normally gentle creatures but do not go up to them and do not feed them as they are wild animals and there was one recent report of someone being gored by one after it had been teased by a group of boys.

Seasons and Times
Beach – Year-round but lifeguards are only on duty from April to October.

Oolala Restaurant – 10:00am-10:00pm daily. Closed on Tuesday (unless Tuesday is a public holiday). Last order at 8:30pm.

Free

The Best Ways of Getting There
By Ferry/Bus or Taxi
- Catch the ferry from **Central Outlying Island Ferry Pier #6** going to Mui Wo, Lantau. The pier is located on the waterfront behind the IFC complex where the Airport Express Train is located.
- The Lantau ferry has its own **Pier (#6)** and is quite easy to find once you reach the harbour.
↔ Travel time: 30 mins ("fast" ferry) or 50 mins ("ordinary" ferry).
- Once you arrive in Mui Wo you can either take a bus or a taxi to Pui O Beach.

   By Bus
   • When you **exit the Mui Wo Pier** look for the **Mui Wo Bus Terminus** directly in front of the ferry terminus. You can either take bus **#1** or **#4** to **Pui O Beach**.
   • **When you get on the bus tell the bus driver that you are going to *Pui O Beach* so that you don't miss your stop**.
   • **Alight the bus at Pui O bus stop**. Pui O is a small village that has a good landmark to keep a lookout for – a building with large lettering at the top that reads "**BUI O SCHOOL**". The school is white with green-and-blue markings.
   • When you alight the bus you are on the main road, **South Lantau Road**. Walk past Bui O School, **following signs for Pui O Beach,** and this will take you down a small rural road called **Chi Ma Wan Road**. This road will take you past a playground, a small beach kiosk and a large field that is filled with water buffalo (please heed above warning).
   • At the end of this road you will find both **Oohlala Restaurant** dead ahead and **Pui O public beach** on your left.
   ↔ Travel time: 10-15 mins (bus) + 5-7 mins (walk)
   OR
   By Taxi

• A taxi from the Mui Wo Ferry Pier will cost HK$35-$45 and take 10-12 mins.

By MTR/Bus
• Take the MTR from **Hong Kong Station in Central** to **Tung Chung Station** on the Tung Chung Yellow Line.
• Get off the train at Tung Chung and **exit the station at e**xit **B**. When you get outdoors, walk straight ahead to the bus terminus.
   (Tip: The bus terminus is in the same direction as the cable car Ngong Ping 360.)
• Take Lantau Bus **#3M** or **#A35** to **Pui O**.
• When you get on the bus tell the bus driver that you are going to Pui O Beach so that you don't miss your stop.
• **Alight the bus at Pui O bus stop.** Pui O is a small village that has a good landmark to keep a lookout for – a building with large lettering at the top that reads "BUI O SCHOOL".
• When you alight the bus you are on the main road, **South Lantau Road**. Walk past Bui O school, **following signs for Pui O Beach,** and this will take you down a small rural road called **Chi Ma Wan Road**. This road will take you past a playground, a small beach kiosk and a large field that is filled with water buffalo.
• At the end of this road you will find both **Oohlala Restaurant** dead ahead and **Pui O public beach** on your left.
↔ Travel time: 35 mins (MTR) + 30 mins (bus) + 5-7 mins (walk)

Getting a Bite
Oohlala has a kids' menu and great meals for adults. They serve drinks, cocktails, snacks and ice cream. There is also a refreshment kiosk a few steps away from Oohlala on the public beach. Here they serve hot noodles, chips, candy, hot and cold drinks, ice cream, beach floats both for rent and for sale, inflatable boats both for rent and for sale, a complete set of everything you will need to do a BBQ at any of the pits at the beach, meat and other items to grill on your own BBQ. They are friendly and helpful and if you bring your own inflatable they will help you to use their electric pump to blow up your own float or boat.

What's Close?
Mui Wo and Bike Riding, **Cheung Sha Beach**, **The Giant Buddha, Po Lin Monastery and Tai O**.

Comments

- This beach is suitable for all ages.
- Plan to spend a minimum of three hours here.
- This beach is generally not crowded.
- The best toilets are located at Oohlala but there are also toilets at the Pui O Beach.
- There is no baby-changing station at Pui O Beach public toilet but there is a changing room with benches which could serve the purpose.
- You can bring your stroller here.

Extra Info

It might be very useful whether you are coming to the beach or leaving the beach to have taxi numbers on hand to get back to the ferry or the MTR. Here are two Lantau taxi numbers: 2984-1328 and 2984-1368.

Special Programs and Tours

Treasure Island Group, a children's camp company, runs their program off of Pui O Beach. They offer both surf camps and adventure camps throughout the summer as well as during other school holiday times such as spring break. For more information contact them:
Tel: 2546-3543
Website: www.treasureislandhk.com
Email: inquiries@treasureislandhk.com

Word of Mouth

On the way down to Pui O Beach from the main road, near the bus stop, there is a small playground. If your kids need a break from the beach this is a nice place to stop for a runaround.

Cheung Sha Beach
Lower Cheung Sha Village
Lantau Island

大嶼山 下長沙泳灘

Lower Cheung Sha Beach Tel: 2981-8389 or 2852-3220
The Stoep Tel: 2980-2699
High Tide (Thai restaurant) Tel: 2980-3002
News Bistro Tel: 2980-2233
Long Coast Seasports Tel: 8104-6222
Palm Beach Tel: 2980-4822
First Ferry Tel: 2131-8181
New Lantao Bus Company Tel: 2984-9848
Website for Cheung Sha Beach: http://www.lcsd.gov.hk/beach/en/beach-address-is.php
Website for The Stoep restaurant: http://thestoep.com/
Website for High Tide restaurant: http://www.hightidehk.com/
Website for News Bistro: http://newsbistro.com
Website for Long Coast Seasports: www.longcoast.hk
Website for Palm Beach: www.palmbeach.com.hk
Website: First Ferry: http://www.nwff.com.hk/
Website: New Lantao Bus Company: http://www.newlantaobus.com/nlb.html
For area map: Go to the website for Lower Cheung Sha Beach and then click on "Location Map".

0-99

South Lantau Island beaches are known to be among the most beautiful beaches in the territory. Lower Cheung Sha Beach offers a wonderful opportunity for families to spend a day relaxing beachside as every basic need for a fun day out at the beach is easily met here. Delicious family-friendly alfresco restaurant options are available right on the beach, as well as excellent watersport rental facilities and even the possibility of camping in luxury or in Native American teepees! This place is special and well worth a day trip or even an overnight visit.

The beach itself is a beautiful long stretch of sand, with outstanding views and facilities including toilets, changing rooms, outdoor showers, lifeguards, swimming designated areas and shark netting. It is unusual in Hong Kong to be able to take a meaningful stroll from one end of the beach to the other, as beaches are normally situated in small coves covering small sections of land; however Lower Cheung Sha affords everyone the luxury of a long walk down the beach.

215

Beyond the natural beauty of South Lantau, Cheung Sha is also well known for its dining. In fact junk boat day-trippers often make this their destination for lunch or dinner. The Stoep, a Mediterranean and South African restaurant, has been around for years and has developed a reputation for delicious food and excellent alfresco atmosphere right on the beach. Family-friendly, with high chairs, a small kids' menu and best of all its location on the sand, parents can sit back, relax and enjoy a great meal, a glass of wine or a coffee while kids frolic on the sand and in the water. You can see everything from your perch without having to get up! Other restaurant options include High Tide, a lovely alfresco Thai restaurant, and News Bistro, as well as two snack stands.

There are two outfits that rent a large variety of watersports equipment: Long Coast Seasports and Palm Beach. Both have boogie boards, wake boards, surf boards, kayaks, wind surfers, skim boards, body boards, paddle boards, sailboats, and floats for hire. They also have locker rentals and offer instruction if you or the kids want to try something for the first time.

If you simply cannot get enough of this lovely place, why not spend the night? There are several choices for accommodation. Long Coast Seasports offers something very interesting they call "Glamping", or glamorous camping. They own a spit of grassland behind their shop where they have set up two safari tents and have a gas BBQ grill that is easy to use. The tents can be rented out by families and the price of the rental includes the use of some of their watersports equipment the day of and the day after the tent rental. They also have four rooms to rent above their shop if camping is just not your thing. Another very interesting idea would be to camp out in the Native American teepees available for rent on the grounds of Palm Beach. Palm Beach has a lovely outdoor resort-like facility on the far end of Lower Cheung Sha Beach, similar to a Western-style campground with snack bar, rental equipment area, BBQ pits, bonfire pit and small, medium and large teepees for rent which thankfully are already pre-set on the grassy property.

Whether you come for a meal, the day or spend the weekend, Lower Cheung Sha Beach is a wonderful family getaway for all ages and if this is your visit time visiting, it will not be your last.

Seasons and Times
Beach – Year-round but lifeguards are only on duty from April to October.
The Stoep Restaurant – 11:00am-10:00pm Tuesday to Sundays. Closed Mondays, unless Monday is a public holiday.
High Tide Restaurant – 11:30am until last orders at 9:00pm daily, closed Tuesday unless it's a bank holiday.
News Bistro – Thursday-Monday and public holidays, 11:00am until late (kitchen closes at 9:00pm). Tuesday and Wednesday is by reservation only.
Long Coast Seasports – Open daily. Monday-Friday: 10:00am until sunset, Saturday, Sunday and Public Holidays: 9:00am until sunset.
Palm Beach – Open daily. Year-round: 9:30am-7:30pm.

Admission
Free.
Long Coast Seasports and Palm Beach both have watersports equipment and tents/teepees for hire and other exciting programs. Check their websites for details on pricing.

The Best Ways of Getting There
By Ferry/Bus or Taxi
- Catch the ferry from **Central Outlying Island Ferry Pier #6** going to Mui Wo, Lantau. The pier is located on the waterfront behind the IFC complex where the Airport Express Train is located.
- The Lantau ferry has its own **Pier (#6)** and is quite easy to find once you reach the harbour.
↔ Travel time: 30 mins ("fast" ferry) or 50 mins ("ordinary" ferry).
- Once you arrive in Mui Wo you can either take a bus or a taxi to Pui O Beach.
    #### *By Bus*
    - When you **exit the Mui Wo Pier** look for the **Mui Wo Bus Terminus** directly in front of the ferry terminus. You can either take bus **#1** or **#4** to **Lower Cheung Sha Beach**.
    - **When you get on the bus tell the bus driver that you are going to *Lower Cheung Sha Beach* so that you don't miss your stop**.
    - **Alight the bus at Lower Cheung Sha Beach Village bus stop**. En route you will **pass Pui O Beach** and then the next stretch of beach is Lower Cheung Sha. The bus

stop is labelled but there is no village on the road to use as a landmark.
• When you alight the bus you are on the main road, **South Lantau Road**. Walk straight ahead (uphill) 50 paces in the same direction as the bus was going and you will see the **sign pointing downhill** on a path to Lower Cheung Sha Beach. **Turn left**, walk down the driveway and it will lead you to Lower Cheung Sha Beach.
• At the end of this road you will find both **The Stoep Restaurant** on your right, **Long Coast Seasports** on your left and the **beach** dead ahead.
↔ Travel time: 12-15 mins (bus) + 3-5 mins (walk)
OR
By Taxi
• A taxi from the Mui Wo Ferry Pier will cost HK$50 and take 10-12 mins.

By MTR/Bus

- Take the MTR from **Hong Kong Station in Central** to **Tung Chung Station** on the Tung Chung Yellow Line.
- Get off the train at Tung Chung and exit the station at exit **B**. When you get outdoors, walk straight ahead to the bus terminus.
  (Tip: The bus terminus is in the same direction as the cable car Ngong Ping 360.)
- Take Lantao Bus **#11**, **#23** or **#A35** to **Lower Cheung Sha Beach Village**.
- **When you get on the bus tell the bus driver that you are going to *Lower Cheung Sha Beach* so that you don't miss your stop.**
- **Alight the bus at Lower Cheung Sha Beach Village bus stop**. Unfortunately there is no landmark or indeed a village on the road to use as a marker.
  (Tip: Sit near the front of the bus and make sure the bus driver knows that you need to get off at your stop.)
- When you alight the bus you are on the main road, **South Lantau Road**. Walk straight ahead (uphill) 50 paces in the same direction as the bus was going and you will see the **sign pointing downhill** on a path to Lower Cheung Sha Beach. **Turn left**, walk down the driveway and it will lead you to Lower Cheung Sha Beach.

- At the end of this road you will find both **The Stoep Restaurant** on your right, **Long Coast Seasports** on your left and the **beach** dead ahead.

↔ Travel time: 35 mins (MTR) + 30 mins (bus) + 3-5 mins (walk)

Getting a Bite

This is a wonderful place to have a meal; in fact many people come to Cheung Sha Beach for the alfresco and tasty dining experiences it provides. There are several options to chose from including The Stoep – Mediterranean and South African cuisine, High Tide – Thai cuisine, and News Bistro – Chinese, Thai, Western and vegetarian cuisine.

What's Close?

Mui Wo and Bike Riding, **Pui O Beach,** and **The Giant Buddha, Po Lin Monastery and Tai O**.

Comments

- This beach is suitable for all ages.
- Plan to spend a minimum of three hours here.
- This beach is not generally crowded.
- The best toilets are located at The Stoep but there are also toilets at the Cheung Sha Beach public area.
- There is no baby-changing station at Cheung Sha Beach public toilet but there is a changing room with benches which could serve the purpose.
- You can bring your stroller here.

Extra Info

It might be very useful whether you are coming to the beach or leaving the beach to have taxi numbers on hand to get back to the ferry or the MTR. Here are two Lantau taxi numbers: 2984-1328 and 2984-1368.

Special Programs and Tours

Palm Beach has a program called Lantau Kids Club. Their focus is on creating fun, adventure and developing friendship. Using their teepee village area as a base, they provide a lovely and natural setting for hosting outdoor functions such as birthday parties, family outings, various group celebrations and activities. In addition, they have put together some organized fun classes which kids/parents can participate in. Membership for the Kids Club is $800 per year and includes a welcome gift,

219

a free night in a *teepee* with one adult, enjoyment of all facilities in Palm Beach, entry to the outing activities and classes being organized by Palm Beach, and 20% off for birthday party at Palm Beach for the child. For more information on the Lantau Kids Club email: kidsclub@palmbeach.com.hk

Word of Mouth

It might be difficult to find Palm Beach the first time you try. Here are the directions to check it out. Stand with The Stoep at your back and the ocean in front of you. Look to your right and you will see a headland area with a pagoda on top. Walk in the direction of the headland. When you get to the base, you will see a path on your right hand side. Take the path through the headland and over to the other side. Once you reach the other side of the headland you will still be on the beach. Walk on the beach, keeping the water on your left, and within five minutes you will see the Palm Beach gates.

Chapter 5

Fun Shopping –
Hong Kong's Markets

Hong Kong is known around the world as a shopping mecca. Many are drawn here by the lure of inexpensive quality tailors, designer boutiques and Chinese antique shops, but the real bargains and all the fun are to be found at the open-air street markets. Even if you don't wish to make any purchases, take the family to see these narrow lanes and streets where the heart of the city beats. Absolutely everything is for sale in Hong Kong's markets – clothes, jewellery, computer games, music, movies, souvenirs, jade, pearls, birds, fish, flowers, beads… the list is endless. Culture is up for grabs too as children can take in everything from fortune tellers to Cantonese opera to flower arranging just by having a stroll through the stalls and shops.

Bargaining is a 'must-do' at all Hong Kong markets. It is, in fact, expected. For some kids this way of determining a price will be a learning experience in how Chinese merchants, and Asian merchants generally, have traditionally engaged in trade.

Whichever market you choose to visit, you and your kids will be in for a colourful and lively treat. Happy shopping!

1.   The Jade Market
2.   The Ladies' Market and the Goldfish Market
3.   Yuen Po Street Bird Garden and the Flower Market
4.   Sham Shui Po – Themed Street Shopping
5.   Temple Street Night Market

Other chapters that include markets:
Stanley Market – Stanley Village Chapter
Tai Po Market – Hong Kong Railway Museum Chapter

The Jade Market
Intersection of Kansu Street and Battery Street, Yaumatei, Kowloon

Tel: 2508-1234 (Hong Kong Tourism Board)
Website: http://www.discoverhongkong.com/eng/attractions/kln-jade-market.html
For area map: http://maps.google.com/ (then plug in Jade Market Hong Kong and zoom in for close-up)

This is a neat place! Hawkers gather together under one huge tent-like structure, selling all things jade and more. In this part of the world, jade is not only considered beautiful, it is believed to have mystical powers that can ward off evil spirits and protect wearers. Bracelets, necklaces, amulets, rings, pendants, carvings and loose stones, ranging in price from HK$15 to HK$1000+, can be bought here. Kids will enjoy pawing through the mounds of loose little carved pieces on offer for HK$15-$20. The stones come in just about every colour too: green naturally, but also yellow, brown, white, red, orange and purple.

The Jade Market offers a second commodity that is also very popular: pearls (fresh water, mostly). Kids can browse through hundreds of 'not-yet' strung strands of fresh water pearls in every shape, size and colour, choose one, and then have a necklace or bracelet, or both, custom-made before their very eyes. (Each piece starts at around HK$20, depending on the quality of the pearls chosen.) Make sure to bargain here – always with a smile and in good humour – but never settle for the first price offered. Bargaining is part of the fun and also necessary to get a fair price on jade or pearls. The atmosphere at the Jade Market is like no other place in Hong Kong, so go for the shopping and have a great cultural experience too.

Seasons and Times
Open daily 10:00am-3:30pm (some stalls stay open past 5:00pm depending on the whim of the stall owner).

Admission
Free

The Best Ways of Getting There
By MTR

- From Central or Admiralty to **Yaumatei** station take the red line. Exit the station at exit **"C"** marked "**Jade Hawker's Bazaar**".
- Once you get to street level you will be facing **Nathan Road** (a major thoroughfare). Make a right on Nathan Road and walk two blocks until you reach **Public Square Street** where you turn right.
- Stay on Public Square Street for a short block and turn left on **Shanghai Street,** walking past the **Leong Yaumatei Community Hall**. You will come to a small playground-cum-basketball court on your right. Stop outside and look behind it. A good marker to help you find the market is that it is painted red and blue on the sides and has a tarp-like structure as its roof.

    (Tip: If you pass the police station on Public Square Road, then you have gone too far.)

↔ Travel time: 10-15 mins (MTR) + 5-10 mins (walk).

By Star Ferry/Taxi
- From Central to **Tsim Sha Tsui (TST)** take the Star Ferry from the Star Ferry Central pier.
- Once you exit the ferry terminal in TST, go to the taxi stand directly in front of the pier and ask the taxi to take you to the **Jade Market** in **Yaumatei**. A taxi from TST will cost HK$30+.

↔ Travel time: 10 mins (ferry) + 15+ mins (taxi).

By Car
This is not an easy place to drive and I don't recommend it; however if you want to brave it, here are the directions:
- From Central take the **Cross Harbour Tunnel**: Connaught Road→Harcourt Road→Gloucester Road→**Island Eastern Corridor**.
- In tunnel and tollbooths (HK$20) stay to the far left. Follow signs for **Tsim Sha Tsui** and **Kwai Chung**.
- Make a left again at the turn marked **Hong Kong Coliseum/ Railway Terminus**. Keep to the middle lane, do **not** exit on Austin Road or Jordan Road to your left or go onto the overpass to your right. This middle lane will take you to **Gascoigne Road** which runs parallel to the overpass to your right.
- Follow this around as it veers left, you will be **crossing Nathan Road**. Once across Nathan Road the road name changes to **Kansu Street**.
- Take your first right turn onto **Temple Street**.

九龍　油麻地
甘肅街及炮台街交界　玉器市場

5+

P A paid parking garage can be found to your left on **Temple Street**. Look for the "Adams" car park sign. (The market is less than a block away on Kansu Street.)

By Taxi
A taxi from Central will cost HK$85-$100 and take around 25-30 mins. You can also request that the taxi travel through the Western Harbour Tunnel which will cut the time by half but will cost more (the Western toll is higher at $45 per crossing plus $15 return fee so you will have to add in $60 in tunnel fees).

Getting a Bite
There are no snack stands at the Jade Market. However, very nearby is a ***McDonald's Restaurant***. Walk back to Public Square Street and make a left. About half a block down on the right hand side, set back a few yards from the road, is a McDonald's. You will easily see their signature big yellow "M" from Public Square Street. Alternatively, if you don't mind walking a little bit, you can head up to Nathan Road where restaurants abound – everything from hotel coffee shops to Starbucks to a variety of local fare.

Comments
- Best suited to children aged five and above.
- Plan to spend one hour or more here.
- Can get busy on the weekends.
- The nearest toilet is in McDonald's. (See **Getting a Bite** section above.)
- There is no baby-changing station here but you could use the benches across the road in the small playground if you needed to.
- This is not a good place to bring a stroller, as the aisles are narrow and crowded.

Extra Info
Please note that not all things "jade" are real jade, so buyer beware!

Word of Mouth
Directly across the way from the Jade Market is a very small playground with a few riding toys and lots of benches. If you have toddlers along, you might want to take them to this little playground before or after your market visit.

The Ladies' Market and the Goldfish Market
Tung Choi Street, Mongkok, Kowloon

九龍　旺角
通菜街　女人街及金魚市場

Website: http://www.discoverhongkong.com/eng/shop/market/index2.jhtml
For area map: http://www.mtr.com.hk/jplanner/images/maps/mok.pdf

Do not be fooled by the name. Though called the 'Ladies' Market', there is really something for everyone here. Set in the middle of the most densely populated area in the world, Mongkok, this outdoor street market is a favourite among tourists and locals alike.

A shopper's paradise, Tung Choi Street will be an instant hit with your children. Stuff they want is for sale here and it is reasonably priced. Make sure to teach them how to bargain, a must-do if you want to get a good deal. Backpacks, rhinestone jewellery, toys, CDs, DVDs, purses, beaded hair clips, sunglasses, key rings, stickers, costumes, electronic products, T-shirts, beaded bags, and baseball caps are just a few things the kids might want to spend their allowance on. This market is more than an interesting shopping experience, it is a view into how some of the local population make their retail purchases and for many kids, who may be used to mall shopping, what they see will be eye-opening.

5+

If you keep walking on Tung Choi Street past the Argyle Street end of the Ladies' Market, you will find the Goldfish Market. This colourful market is filled with shops and stalls selling many varieties of fish and all that is needed to keep those fish happy, from food to aquarium supplies. The fish on offer include angelfish, koi, cichlids and, of course, goldfish. Inside the shops the fish are displayed in tanks, but there is no need to enter any establishment to view the fish as a good number of them are hanging outside the shops in plastic bags just waiting to be brought home. You will also spot some turtles for sale amongst the fish. The Goldfish Market is small and as such may not be a destination unto itself, but it is a good add-on when visiting the Ladies' Market.

Seasons and Times
Ladies' Market – Noon-11:30pm daily.
Goldfish Market – 10:30am-10:00pm daily.

Admission
Free

The Best Ways of Getting There
By MTR
- From Central or Admiralty to **Mongkok** station take the red line. Exit the station at exit "**D2**" marked "**Tung Choi Street – Ladies' Market**".
- Once you get to street level you will be on **Argyle Street**. Walk one block and you will intersect **Tung Choi Street** in the middle of the market. (Please note that exit "E2" will work as well to get you to the market. This exit puts you on Nelson Street. Walk straight ahead and you will dead-end into the market.)

The market runs in both directions from this point.

↔ Travel time: 15 mins (MTR) + 3 mins (walk).

By Star Ferry/Taxi
- From Central to **Tsim Sha Tsui (TST)** take the Star Ferry from the Star Ferry Central Pier.
- Once you exit the ferry terminal in TST go to the taxi stand directly in front of the pier and ask the taxi to take you to **Tung Choi Street** in **Mongkok**.
- A taxi from TST will cost HK$45+.

↔ Travel time: 10 mins (ferry) + 10-15 mins (taxi).

By Car
This is not an easy place to drive and I don't recommend it; however if you want to brave it, here are the directions:
- From Central take the **Cross Harbour Tunnel**: Connaught Road→Harcourt Road→Gloucester Road→**Island Eastern Corridor**.
- In tunnel stay in right lane. Once through tollbooth (HK$20) stay right and follow signs for **Ho Man Tin and Sha Tin**.
- Keep following the Ho Man Tin/Sha Tin route and stay left until you see the Wylie Road exit.
- Once you exit on **Wylie Road** you will eventually cross **Waterloo Road** and then make your first left shortly after onto **Soy Street**, then left again on **Fa Yuen Street** (first left).

- This will dead-end onto **Dundas Street** where you will make a right turn. You will pass the market as you cross **Tung Choi Street** on Dundas.

P There is a paid parking garage on your left, just past the market on **Dundas Street**. Look for the green car park sign.

By Taxi
A taxi from Central will cost HK$100+ and take 25-30 mins.

Getting a Bite
There are many snack stands and noodle vendors on Tung Choi Street. Look for them at street corners and behind the stalls. Otherwise Nathan Road is a major thoroughfare with hundreds of restaurants and coffee shops to choose from. Major hotels in the area also have coffee shops and restaurants.

What's Close?
Yuen Po Street Bird Garden and The Flower Market.

Comments
- Best suited to ages five and above.
- Plan to spend one to two hours here.
- Crowds are lightest early in the day and get very heavy by evening.
- The public toilets on the street here are not appealing. You may need to go to Nathan Road and look for a restaurant or a hotel to find a proper toilet.
- Tung Choi Street is not a good place to push a stroller as the markets are narrow and extremely crowded. If you have an infant or toddler and really want to go to these markets, it would be advisable to carry the child in a backpack or a baby carrier.

Word of Mouth
The stalls at the Ladies' Market do not open simultaneously. As the day progresses, more and more vendors are peddling their wares, so for the best shopping opportunities, it might be best to visit this market in mid-afternoon or evening.

Yuen Po Street Bird Garden and the Mongkok Flower Market

Yuen Po Street/Flower Market Road
Mongkok, Kowloon

Tel: 2302-1762 (Leisure and Cultural Services Department)
Website: http://www.lcsd.gov.hk/parks/ypsbg/en/index.php
For area map: Go to above website and click on "Location Map".

A trip to the bird garden is a great Hong Kong cultural experience that will be good fun for you and your kids. This is not an aviary or a bird sanctuary. It is a bird market located inside a garden, where bird enthusiasts gather, show off their birds and buy all kind of paraphernalia and live treats for their fine-feathered friends.

This market's presence is a part of Hong Kong's cultural heritage. Previously located in the centre of the action on a narrow old street in Mongkok, it was moved by the government in 1999 to its present location to make room for the gentrification of this old part of the city. What it lacks in historical surroundings, though, it makes up for with its spirit of old Hong Kong.

Birds are highly prized pets. This is particularly true for older Chinese men who bring their birds to the garden, in beautiful lacquered cages, to show off their plumage and vocal abilities. More than 70 shops are set up here to cater to these pet owners and their avian needs. There are of course birds for sale – loads of them – from colourful parrots to sparrows to Chinese songbirds. Perhaps even more interesting than the birds are all the things sold to make their lives more enjoyable, from bags of live crickets, live grasshoppers, and toasted seeds, to small porcelain feeders, bamboo cages and special honey drinks to help keep their voices in good working order.

There is a 'show'-like atmosphere in this garden. Some owners feed their birds live crickets or grasshoppers using chopsticks which they push through the bars of their birds' ornate cages.

Others parade their birds around so that their song will be heard and enjoyed. You may even find this garden a musical experience.

For a more visual and aromatic encounter, walk through the flower market on your way to or from the bird garden. This colourful place, which is home to more than 50 shops, is packed with hundreds of varieties of flowers and plants all arranged in traditional Cantonese style. The displays are both stunning and unusual and will be of interest to everyone in the family. Silk flowers, plastic plants, seeds, silk ribbons, coloured paper, glass beads and stones are just a few of the other items on offer. The prices here, particularly on flowers, are extremely reasonable, and therefore it will be hard to leave here without something in hand.

Seasons and Times
Mongkok Flower Market: 7:00am-7:00pm daily.
Yuen Po Street Bird Garden: 7:00am-8:00pm daily.

Admission
Free

The Best Ways of Getting There
By MTR
- From **Central** or **Admiralty** to **Prince Edward Station**, take the red line. Exit the station at exit **"B1"**.
- Come out onto the street, turn left and immediately left again and you are now on **Prince Edward Road West**. You will walk right past the **Mongkok Police Station**, across **Tung Choi Street**, across **Fa Yuen Street**, and come to **Sai Yee Street** (all the while still walking on Prince Edward Road West). Here you will make a left and then immediately afterwards a right on **Flower Market Road**.
- For the **Bird Garden** follow the directions above. Walk all the way down Flower Market Road until you can go no further (this is two blocks) and you will see **Yuen Po Street Garden** on your left.
↔ Travel time: 15 mins (MTR) + 5-10 mins (walk).

By Star Ferry/Taxi
- From **Central to Tsim Sha Tsui (TST)** take the Star Ferry from the **Star Ferry Central Pier**.

九龍　旺角　園圃街
園圃街雀鳥花園及花墟

0-99

- Once you exit the ferry terminal in TST go to the **taxi stand directly in front of the pier** and ask the taxi to take you to the **Yuen Po Street Bird Garden** near the **Mongkok Police Station** – or to the start of the Flower Market, ask to be taken to **Flower Market Road in Mongkok.**
- A taxi will cost HK$45-$50+
↔ Travel time: 10 mins (ferry) + 15 mins (taxi).

By Car
This is not an easy place to drive and I don't recommend it; however if you want to brave it, here are the directions:
- From Central: Connaught Road→Harcourt Road→Gloucester Road→Island Eastern Corridor **(Route 4)** to the **Cross Harbour Tunnel (Route 1)**.
- In tunnel stay in **right lane**. Once through tollbooth (HK$20) stay right and follow **signs** for **Ho Man Tin and Sha Tin,** you are on **Route 1**.
- Keep following the Ho Man Tin/Sha Tin route until you see signs for **Mongkok**. Do not get onto to the overpass and instead follow signs for Mongkok which will take you off to your left and you will find yourself on **Argyle Street** (which runs parallel to the overpass on your right hand side).
- Stay on **Argyle Street** until you get to **Waterloo Road** following the **exit to your left**.
- Take Waterloo Road until you see **Prince Edward Road West** and **make a left onto it**.
- On Prince Edward Road West, on your left hand side, you will see **Grand Century Place** (the Flower Market and the Bird Garden are across the road on your right).
P Grand Century Place has paid underground parking. This is the nearest car park to the markets.

By Taxi
A taxi from Central will cost HK$110+ and take 30-35 mins.

Getting a Bite
There is no snack stand inside the garden or the market but there is a soda vending machine by the toilets in the Bird Garden if you need a drink. If the kids are hungry, there are a few options. There are several local bakeries on Prince Edward Street West as you walk back toward the MTR (heading east). The *Supreme Bakery* on the corner of Sai Yee Street sells Chinese egg tarts (small yellow custard tarts which are a local specialty and almost always served warm – fabulous!) For a

more substantial meal try *The Prince Restaurant* (tel: 2393-3383) located in the heart of the flower market on the first floor of 162 Prince Edward Road. This is a local place that has English-language menus, a kids' menu and booster seats. There is also a *Pacific Coffee Company* at the corner of Sai Yee Street and Prince Edward Road West. Also, the *Grand Century Mall* across Prince Edward Road West from the Bird Garden has a dozen restaurant choices including Japanese, Korean, Indonesian, Chinese, Western, fast food and a food court.

What's Close?
Fa Yuen Street (shopping street and market) and **The Ladies' Market and Goldfish Market** (further down Tung Choi Street from the Flower Market).

Comments
- Suitable for all ages.
- Plan to spend one to two hours here.
- Both markets can be very crowded on weekends.
- There are a few sit-down style toilets in the Bird Garden.
- The ladies' toilet at the Bird Garden has a baby-changing table.
- This is a stroller-friendly place (provided the crowds are not too thick).

Extra Info
When the birds are fed crickets, some of the insects' limbs are first clipped off by the bird's owner or the shop owner, while the cricket is still alive. This might be hard for some sensitive children (and adults) to take.

Word of Mouth
Across the street from the flower market on Flower Market Road is a playground with a slide and a few riding toys. If your kids need a break from the markets, take them here for a run around.

Sham Shui Po – Themed Street Shopping
Sham Shui Po, Kowloon

Tel: 2508-1234 (Hong Kong Tourism Board)
Website (general information):
http://www.discoverhongkong.com/eng/shopping/theme-shopping-streets.html
For area map: http://www.mtr.com.hk/jplanner/images/maps/ssp.pdf
Dragon Centre Mall
37K Yen Chow Street, Sham Shui Po
Tel: 2360-0982 (general enquiry)
Website: http://www.dragoncentre.com.hk (most text is in Chinese)
Sky Rink (Ice Skating Rink)
8th Floor, Dragon Centre
Tel: 2307-9264 (for enquiries)

"Bead Street", "Button Street", "Ribbon Street" (crafts and more) – Yu Chau Street, Ki Lung Street and Nam Cheong Street

Many little girls and big girls too (read "women") will think they must have died and gone to heaven when they see this place. This is a crafter's paradise! Lining "Bead Street" are small shops, one after another, resembling old-fashioned candy stores, stocked with plastic jars from floor to ceiling filled with beads, beads and still more beads! The choices are as varied as they are plentiful. Maybe the most exciting part is how incredibly inexpensive the majority of stock is, which is due to the fact that these shops are primarily wholesale dealers. The area on Yu Chau Street which has the most bead shops is the 100-200 block. The same plethora of stock, but in buttons, can be found along Ki Lung Street; and Nam Cheong Street is full of ribbon rolls stacked row upon row, in every colour, shape and size imaginable. The largest craft shop in the area is located at 124-126 Cheung Sha Wan Road and is called **Tak Cheung Company** (located just off Nam Cheong Street). There are also many fabric sellers in the area, a large group of which are located on Wong Chuk Street (two blocks from Nam Cheong Street off Cheung Sha Wan Road passing Shek Kip Mei Street on the way).

"Fashion Street" – Cheung Sha Wan Road
In the heart of Sham Shui Po lies "Fashion Street," a collection of wholesale fashion outlet stores, many of which also sell retail. Shop after shop of the trendiest clothing is on sale here and young girls in particular will be interested in the styles. Bear in mind though that these stores are mostly for grown-up women. However, older girls will find something to fit them in the smaller sizes. Most of the shops are located on Cheung Sha Wan Road between Yen Chow Street and Wong Chuk Street.

"Men's Street" – Apliu Street Flea Market
This area of Sham Shui Po will appeal to the little boys and the big boys (read "men") in your group. The flea market is all about electrical devices, both new and used. Everything from audio-visual gear, to mobile phones, to home electrical products is for sale here and the prices are very much negotiable. You might also be able to find a few treasures here such as old coins, antique watches and LPs (vinyl records). Look for the outdoor stalls set up between Yen Chow Street and Nam Cheong Street on Apliu Street.

"Toy Street" – Fuk Wing Street
This "street" is only one block long but it is a great place to buy toys and other fun kiddie items such as erasers, pens, notebooks, gift bags, stuffed toys, mini games, whistles, balls, stickers, etc. If you are a planning a kid's birthday party, this makes for great one-stop shopping and it's extremely inexpensive as well, especially if you are buying in bulk.

Golden Computer Arcade and Golden Shopping Centre
The kids are going to love this place! This arcade is filled with shops that specialize in the sale of software, hardware, and all manner of accessories related to computers. This is a hot spot for local 'techies' and the prices are very competitive. Bargaining is a must and make sure to check out all the goods you are considering buying to be sure that they are exactly the make you are looking for. Be aware – pirated software, though illegal in Hong Kong, is still sold in some stores. This shopping plaza is located at the crossroads of Fuk Wa Street and Kweilin Street.

Dragon Centre
Dragon Centre Mall, a local hangout, has eight floors of shops, stalls, arcades, restaurants and a small indoor ice skating rink.

九龍 深水埗
深水埗 深水埗特色購物

5+

This is a great place to come for a bite to eat after you have wandered the many themed streets of Sham Shui Po. Choices include everything from local and international fast food chains to higher-end Asian restaurants. The ice skating rink is located on the eighth floor. Sky Rink, as it is called, has skate rentals and lockers are available for rent as well. The pricing here is very reasonable. The rink itself is not fancy, nor is it overly large, but the kids will still enjoy having a skate around. There are also two games arcades in the mall, one called Fantasia and the other Jumpin' Gym USA (a Hong Kong-based chain of amusement centres).

Seasons and Times

Sham Shui Po shops – Generally open during the week from late morning (times vary from shop to shop) until evening. Some wholesale shops are closed on weekends and public holidays.
Apliu Street Flea Market – Trading starts at around noon or before and goes until very late in the evening; some stalls stay open until 11:00pm or midnight.
Golden Computer Arcade and Golden Shopping Centre – 11:00am-10:00pm daily.
Dragon Centre – 10:00am-10:00pm daily.
Sky Rink – 9:00am-9:00pm Mon-Thurs, 9:00am-9:30pm Friday, 10:00am-9:00pm Saturday, 9:00am-6:00pm Sunday.

Admission
Free

The Best Ways of Getting There
By MTR
- From Central or Admiralty to **Sham Shui Po** station, take the red line.
- ↔ Travel time: 15 mins (MTR)
- For "Bead Street" – Yu Chau Street: Exit "**A2**". Walk directly ahead, cross **Apliu Street** (on Pei Ho Street), stay on **Pei Ho Street** one block until you cross **Yu Chau Street**. Make a left turn on Yu Chau Street. Both sides of the street are filled with bead shops.
- For "Button Street" – Ki Lung Street: Exit "**A2**". Walk directly in front of you, cross **Apliu Street** (on Pei Ho Street), stay on **Pei Ho Street** two blocks. You cross Yu Chau and the next block will be **Ki Lung Street**.
- For "Ribbon" Street – Nam Cheong Street: Exit "**A2**". Make a left (you are now on Apliu Street) and walk one block and

you will intersect **Nam Cheong Street**. Make a right on Nam Cheong and look for the shops on both sides of this large avenue.

- For "Fashion Street" – Cheung Sha Wan Road: Exit "**C1**" will put you right on **Cheung Sha Wan Road**. Both directions on this street have shops.
- For "Men's Street" – Apliu Street Flea Market: Exit "**C2**" puts you right on **Apliu Street**. Look for the market on your left.
- For "Toy Street" – Fuk Wing Street: Exit "**B2**". Walk straight ahead of you one block and then turn right looking for the sign that reads **"95A – 69B" Fuk Wing Street**.
- For Golden Computer Arcade and Golden Shopping Centre: Exit "**D2**." You will be at the intersection of **Fuk Wa Street and Kweilin Street**. The arcade is straight ahead.
- For Dragon's Centre: Exit "**C1**" marked "**Dragon Centre Mall**." When you get to street level turn left. You will be on **Cheung Sha Wan Road** (a major road). Walk north one block and turn left when you reach **Yen Chow Street**. Dragon Centre will be on your right side about halfway down the block.

By Car

This is not an easy place to drive and I don't recommend it; however if you want to brave it, here are the directions:

- From Central take the **Cross Harbour Tunnel**: Connaught Road→ Harcourt Road→ Gloucester Road→ **Island Eastern Corridor**.
- In tunnel stay in right lane. Once through tollbooth (HK$20) stay right and follow signs for **Ho Man Tin and Sha Tin**.
- Keep following the Ho Man Tin/Sha Tin route until you see signs for **Mongkok**. Do not get onto the overpass but instead follow signs for Mongkok which will take you off to your left and you will find yourself on **Argyle Street** (which runs parallel to the overpass on your right).
- Stay on Argyle Street until you get to **Waterloo Road** following the exit to your left. Take Waterloo Road until you see **Prince Edward Road West** and make a left onto it.
- Stay to your right and head for the overpass (around where you see Grand Century Place on your left and the flower market on your right). You are now on **Lai Chi Kok Road**.
- Go straight on this road and you will cross **Nam Cheong Street** and make the next left on **Pei Ho Street**. Cross Yee Kuk Street and make the next right onto Hai Tan Street and you will cross **Kweilin Street** and make a right on **Yen Chow Street**.

P To park, look for the large **Dragon Centre Shopping Plaza** on your left and make a left turn into the car park there.

(Tip: Apliu Street and Yu Chau Street are located directly across Yen Chow Street.)

By Taxi
A taxi from Central will cost HK$110-$130 and should take 30-35 mins.

Getting a Bite
Dragon Centre shopping plaza is the best place to get a snack or meal in the area. This is just a short walk from the themed shopping streets. There are some good restaurant options here for kids including two food courts, one with Asian fare, the other with more international options including *McDonald's* and *Kentucky Fried Chicken*. There are also candy shops and bakeries for snacks. Several of the more formal restaurants serve up tasty local food at reasonable prices.

What's Close?
Yuen Po Street Bird Garden, The Flower Market, Fa Yuen Shopping Street.

Comments
- Best suited for ages five and above (or younger if they don't mind shopping).
- Plan to spend a minimum of one hour here.
- This is a very crowded area generally, as many Hong Kongers live in this neighbourhood. But the crowds are part of the ambience in this case.
- The best toilets are located at the Dragon Centre Shopping Plaza.
- There are no baby-changing stations.
- You can push a stroller here on the streets but once inside the shops it will be hard to manoeuvre with one. A baby carrier or baby backpack would be a better choice.

Word of Mouth
Yu Chau Street and the surrounding area is a great place to get supplies for birthday parties, particularly for little girls. Jewellery making materials, crafts, even costume making supplies are all very easily acquired at reasonable prices. Don't forget to get the 'goodie' bag contents on Fuk Wing Street.

Temple Street Night Market
Temple Street
from Jordan to Yaumatei, Kowloon

Tel: 2508-1234 (Hong Kong Tourism Board)
Website: http://www.discoverhongkong.com/eng/shop/market/index2.
jhtml
For area map: http://www.mtr.com.hk/jplanner/images/maps/ymt.pdf
(Yaumatei)
or http://www.mtr.com.hk/jplanner/images/maps/jor.pdf (Jordan)

0-99

This market is among many top ten lists of "must-see" places.
A great spot for a fun night-time outing, this long street bazaar
runs from one colourful and interesting Kowloon neighbourhood
to another and is a great solution to what you can do with jet-
lagged kids or night owls.

The Temple Street Night Market is different from other markets
because it combines shopping with some interesting street
entertainment in traditional Hong Kong style. The market runs
from one end of Temple Street in Yaumatei to the other end
in Jordan. If you start your stroll at the Yaumatei end of the
market, you will more quickly come to the 'cultural' side of this
experience.

The first part of the market (near the Yaumatei MTR) is what
you might expect – stalls selling good tourist loot such as
T-shirts, jewellery, souvenirs, clothing (for kids and adults),
handbags, watches and traditional Chinese 'artifacts'. Once you
pass Public Square Street, things start to get more interesting.
Here you will find an area lined with fortune tellers where for
a small fee you can hear your future told by palm readers or
physiognomists (people who study the science of face reading).
Even if you aren't keen on commissioning these 'seers' for a
look into the future, this area is intriguing and visually interesting
with charts of palms and faces posted everywhere that attempt
to explain these special skills.

Once past the first line of fortune tellers, you will soon hear and
then see the area of the market where impromptu Cantonese
Opera is performed. Though the performers are not wearing
operatic costumes or face make-up, they are trained specialists
and their street theatre is free of charge. If you decide you want

to do more than just walk by and have a quick listen, there are some tables set up in the street where you can sit down and have a cup of tea and take in more of the performance, though this is not free of charge.

As you continue toward the Jordan end of the market, you will pass an area of Nepalese street-sellers set up on the ground on Kansu Street (a Temple Street crossroad). These vendors sell different wares from the rest of the market and are worth a look. As you carry on toward Jordan, the market becomes more conventional, selling the usual items. Keep a lookout on street corners for toy vendors demonstrating the latest gizmos, a little "show" kids will enjoy.

Seasons and Times
Year-round, starting at dusk (some stalls are open as early as 4:00pm) to 11:00pm daily. (The action is really at its peak from 8:00pm onward.)

Admission
Free

The Best Ways of Getting There
By MTR
- From Central or Admiralty to **Yaumatei** station, take the red line. Exit the station at exit "**C**".
- When you get to street level you will be on **Nathan Road**. Make a **U-turn** and head in the direction immediately **behind the MTR** exit. You are now on **Man Ming Lane**. Walk **past Arthur Street,** and **Temple Street** is the next left.
- You are now at the start of the Yaumatei end of the market.
↔ Travel time: 15 mins (MTR) + 5 mins (walk).
***Alternatively:
By MTR
- From **Central** or Admiralty to **Jordan** Station, take the red line. Exit the station at exit "**A**".
- When you get to street level you will be on **Jordan Road**. Turn right on Jordan Road heading west. **Temple Street** will be the third cross street on your right hand side. Look for a red brick paved road that is closed off to traffic.
  (Tip: The market really begins one block in from Jordan Road on Temple Street. Look down Temple Street and you will see the lights and stalls directly ahead of you.)

- You are now at the start of the Jordan Road end of the market.
- ↔ Travel time: 10-15 mins (MTR) + 5 mins (walk).

By Star Ferry/Taxi
- From Central to **Tsim Sha Tsui (TST)** take the Star Ferry from the Star Ferry Central Pier.
- Once you exit the ferry terminal in TST go to the taxi stand directly in front of the pier and ask the taxi to take you to the **Temple Street Night Market** in **Jordan**. A taxi from TST will cost HK$22-$25.
- ↔ Travel time: 15 mins (ferry) + 10 mins (taxi).

By Car
This is not an easy place to drive and I don't recommend it; however if you want to brave it, here are the directions:
- From Central take the **Cross Harbour Tunnel**: Connaught Road→Harcourt Road→Gloucester Road→**Island Eastern Corridor**.
- In tunnel and tollbooths (HK$20) stay to the far left. Follow signs for **Tsim Sha Tsui** and **Kwai Chung**.
- Make a left again at the turn marked **Hong Kong Coliseum/Railway Terminus**. Keep to the middle lane (you are now on **Chatham Road North** which will turn into Gascoigne Road), do not exit on Austin Road or Jordan Road to your left or go onto the overpass to your right. This middle lane will take you to **Gascoigne Road** which runs parallel to the overpass to your right.
- Follow this around as it veers left, you will be **crossing Nathan Road**. Once across Nathan Road the road name changes to **Kansu Street**.
- Take your first right turn onto **Temple Street**.
P A paid parking garage can be found to your left on **Temple Street**. Look for the car park sign. (The market is less than a block away on Kansu Street).

By Taxi
A taxi from Central will cost HK$95-$110 and take 25-30 mins.

Getting a Bite
There are many snack stands, noodle vendors and street side "impromptu" restaurants along Temple Street. Look for them at street corners and behind the stalls. Alternatively, there are two *McDonald's Restaurants* in the area. One is located one block

west of the Jordan MTR station as you head toward Temple Street. The other is located on Public Square Street, a road that intersects the market in the Yaumatei area. From the market on Temple Street, make a right turn on Public Square Street and you should see the big yellow "M" directly in front of you on the right a few blocks away.

What's Close?
The Jade Market (though it is only open until around 5:00pm).

Comments
- Suitable for all ages but best for older kids who stay up past 8:00pm.
- Plan to spend one to two hours here.
- This market gets crowded.
- The best toilets are located at the two McDonald's restaurants in the area (see the **Getting a Bite** section above).
- There is no baby-changing station here.
- This is not a great place to bring a stroller, as the street is narrow and crowded. If you have an infant in tow, a baby backpack or infant carrier would be a better option.

Word of Mouth
Be aware that there are a few stands set up in the market that are selling pornographic movies and paraphernalia. You will find them (for the most part) only if you are seeking them out, but you should be aware that they are there.

Chapter 6

Amusements Kids Will Love

When you want to treat your kids to an extra-special outing that is all about fun, try one of the options listed in this chapter. These amusements will keep kids enthralled for hours. Choices range from Hong Kong Disneyland to Hong Kong's own Ocean Park to the BMX Bike Park to indoor playrooms and much, much more.

Many of the options revolve around Hong Kong's large shopping centre complexes. Shopping is considered by many to be the local urbanites' favourite pastime. The many malls around the city reflect people's enthusiasm for shopping and are created as entertainment destinations for folks of all ages and interests. Many retails centres offer fun, child-friendly attractions such as ice cream parlours, movie theatres, ice skating rinks, bowling alleys, arcades, designated children's playrooms, and themed restaurants. They are therefore terrific places to take kids on rainy, hot or humid days. The five malls listed in this chapter are great choices but are not the only options. Other good alternatives include Festival Walk in Kowloon Tong (with indoor ice skating rink), Pacific Place in Admiralty, IFC shopping complex in Central, Maritime Square in Tsing Yi, Whampoa Garden in Hunghom and Ocean Terminal in Tsim Sha Tsui.

Before you head out to the malls, there are a few things to bear in mind: even in the dog days of summer the temperature in the shopping plazas will make you feel as though you are at the North Pole, so be sure to bring sweaters for the kids and maybe one for yourself too. Saturday is THE big shopping day in Hong Kong and Sunday is a close number two, so be prepared to deal with crowds on the weekends.

1. Hong Kong Disneyland
2. Ocean Park
3. City Plaza and Quarry Bay Park (Tai Koo Shing)
4. Hong Kong Central Library
5. Snoopy's World, Sha Tin New Town Plaza and the 10,000 Buddhas Monastery
6. West Kowloon – Elements Mall (ice skating), Sky100, DHL Balloon and West Kowloon Promenade (biking)
7. Bowling City, KITEC and E-Max Mall
8. Mega Box and Mega Ice
9. BMX Bike Park
10. Wise Kids Playrooms
11. Playtown
12. Bumble Tots
13. Open Topped Bus Tours – Big Bus Tours and Rickshaw Tours
14. Dialogue in the Dark

Hong Kong Disneyland
Penny's Bay, Lantau Island

Tel: 1-833-177 (Enquiry hotline)
Tel: 1-830-830 (Hotel reservation hotline)
Website: www.hongkongdisneyland.com or http://park.
hongkongdisneyland.com/hkdl/en_US/home/home?name=HomePage

For printable map of the park: Go to the above website, click on "Park" and then on "View Park Map". You can print a map of the park from your computer before you leave or pick up a free map at the main entrance to the park.

In 2005, Hong Kong Disneyland opened its doors, bringing the joy of the Magic Kingdom to Hong Kong. Having Disney in the territory has raised the level and profile of the city as a family-friendly destination. There is truly something special about entering a Disney theme park. From the moment you arrive, whether by car, by train or by bus, you know you are somewhere different. The landscape changes, the roads look different, the architecture of the buildings look otherworldly.

Built on reclaimed land in Penny's Bay, Lantau (very near the Hong Kong Airport), the whole resort – including the theme park, two themed hotels and a public park – covers 310 acres of land. For the time being the theme park has four lands (though there are plans to expand the park to include seven lands by 2014): Main Street USA, Adventureland, Fantasyland and Tomorrowland. There are also two Disney-themed hotels: Hong Kong Disneyland Hotel and Disney's Hollywood Hotel. Inspiration Lake, a public park built by Disney and located within their property is also part of the resort (for more information on this park see the **Inspiration Lake** chapter). Whether you come for half a day, a whole day or spend a night or a weekend, this is a wonderful family outing.

0-99

Your Disney experience starts before you even enter the park. If you ride the MTR you will ride from Sunny Bay to Disney on a special train with Mickey Mouse shaped windows and other Disney specialties. As you walk toward the entrance, no matter which way you arrive, you will find a large magical fountain with a bronze Mickey Mouse riding the top of a water spout on a skateboard. Great place for a photo! Buy your tickets at the booth (or online) and head on in.

The first land you come to will be **Main Street USA**. This land is a part of every Disney theme park worldwide. Architecturally this area looks like it could be Main Street anywhere in the United States during the early 1900s. The buildings are quaint and the street is tree-lined. Both sides of the road have shops and restaurants. This is where you can take in the Hong Kong Disneyland Railroad (which goes all the way around the park), Animation Academy, The Art of Animation, and Main Street Vehicles. This is also the area the parade passes through at 3:30pm daily (confirm schedule on the day you are going). Main Street USA dead-ends into Sleeping Beauty's Castle, another of Disney's iconic images.

> *Tip #1: Main Street USA is a good place to end your visit to Disney. After a full day out, it's nice to head into the air conditioning, and grab a bite as you peruse the shops. If you start with the shopping, it's hard to get out of there. Kids are mesmerized by everything in the stores. If you must go into the shop and buy something, an autograph book complete with large pen (for big hands like Mickey's) is a great purchase before you head in. You will come across many characters during your day and the kids love to get their autographs and pose for photos with them. Each page has a place for the character's signature and a spot to put the photograph of your child with that character. It makes a great keepsake and is not overly expensive.*

After Main Street USA you have a choice of heading in three directions from the front of Sleeping Beauty's Castle. Fantasyland is directly ahead, Tomorrowland will be on your right and Adventureland to your left. There is no right way or wrong way to go; however, the deeper you get into the park to begin with, the better, as people often go to the first thing they see, making the front part of the park the most crowded area early in the day. It might be best to head as deep as you can, and aim for one of the furthest rides from the entrance.

> *Tip #2: Get to the park early. If the park opens at 10:00am the day you are going, then get there at 9:30am. They often open the gates in advance of the opening time to help with the crowds. The park starts to get more and more*

busy as the day goes on. If you have rides that your kids are desperate to see and may want to do more than once, then head to those rides first, as there will be fewer people in the queue and the kids will be able to get their fill before the masses arrive at the park.

Tomorrowland has a futurist theme and includes the following attractions: Space Mountain – an indoor rollercoaster thrill ride in the dark, Orbitron – a flying saucer ride, Autopia – a futuristic electric car ride, Buzz Lightyear Astro Blasters – an interactive ride based on the movie Toy Story where you score points as you shoot bad guys, Stitch Encounter – a 'show' with Stitch from Lilo and Stitch, and UFO Zone – a water play area. There are also futuristic themed restaurants and snack stands.

> *Tip #3: It is not a bad idea to bring a bathing suit or a change of clothes for the kids if they like water play. The UFO Zone is like a water park playground and kids who play here are going to get very wet. On a hot day, this is a great way to cool them off, but it leaves you with soaking wet children, so don't forget to pack something extra for them to wear.*

Adventureland is exactly as it sounds, a place to go on an adventure. Here you will find: rafts to Tarzan's Treehouse (across a river), Tarzan's Treehouse – based on Disney's Tarzan movie, the Jungle River Cruise – a cruise down the Disney River with 'wild' animals to spot along the way, Liki Tikis – jungle rhythms made by dancing poles, and Festival of the Lion King – a live performance based on the Lion King movie. There are also adventure-themed restaurants and snack stands.

Fantasyland is all about the suspension of disbelief. If you have very young children this will be their favourite land. Sleeping Beauty's Castle, Dumbo the Flying Elephant Ride, Cinderella's Carousel, Mad Hatter Tea Cup Ride, Fantasy Gardens – where the characters do their meet and greet, It's a Small World cruise, The Many Adventures of Winnie the Pooh ride, Golden Mickey's Live Show and Mickey's Philharmagic – a magical 3-D film, can all be found here. There are also story-themed restaurants and snack stands.

Tip #4: Check the schedule for the times when your child's favourite character will be available for photos and autographs. If she or he has their heart set on meeting Snow White or Winnie the Pooh, it is easily done as long as you plan for it in advance and show up where the characters will make their appearance.

If you do manage to stay in the park until near closing time, don't miss the 8:00pm lighting of Sleeping Beauty's Castle and the nightly fireworks display over the park which starts at 8:30pm (check the schedule on the day you are going to be sure of the times). Being in the park after dark is as magical as during the day and should not be missed, especially if you have older children.

Tip #5: If you have very young children, come early and plan to end your day after the Main Street USA parade which starts at 3:30pm and ends before 4:00pm. Stop and get a snack for the way home at the bakery before you go, and don't forget to purchase a cold drink, because after running around all day, everyone will need to rehydrate.

Spending the night is a way to extend your time at Disney. There are two hotels to choose from. **Hong Kong Disneyland Hotel**, which is the larger of the two, is built in a Victorian theme and sits on the waterfront with views of the sea. This is not just about the kids! There are dining outlets, lounges, a spa, an indoor pool, an outdoor pool, a playground, a maze, live music in the foyer, character meet and greets, kids' planned activities and crafts, a pier, a garden and more.

Tip #6: Even if you do not wish to spend the night you can be a guest of the Hong Kong Disneyland Hotel by booking a meal at the Enchanted Garden Restaurant. This buffet meal is special because the characters come to your table all evening long and visit with you and your children. The kids can hug them and take photos with them, as you enjoy a meal together. Before or after your meal you can take in the outdoor amenities such as the maze, the gardens and the playground (some things are not permitted, for instance use of the pool). Even if you do not go into the park, this can be a wonderful way to spend some time as a family and soak up the Disney magic.

Great for birthday meals as a family, though please note that this is not an inexpensive treat.

Tip #7: The Disneyland Hotel has a program called "My Little Princess". For girls ages three to 10, this special treat will turn your little girl into her favourite Disney princess. Make-up, accessories, costumes and photos taken by a Disney photographer are included. This is not an inexpensive thing to do. Prices start at HK$350 per child.

Disney's Hollywood Hotel is another choice for a night in the resort. This hotel is built with an art deco theme and has several restaurants and lounges, a pool in the shape of a piano (complete with piano bar), vintage Californian cars, and daily planned activities for kids. This hotel is smaller than the Hong Kong Disneyland Hotel and slightly less expensive.

Tip #8: If you are staying at one of the hotels they can organize park tickets for you. As a hotel guest you can get a two-day ticket, which will enable you and your family to enter the park on the day of your stay, as well as the day after. There are often special package deals available at the Disney hotels, especially during non-holiday times, for overnight stays. There are also dining specials that are worth nothing. Check the website for details and more information to see what is on offer.

Seasons and Times

Most days the park is either open from 10:30am-8:30pm or from 10:00am-9:00pm. To find out the hours of the park on the day you intend to visit, go to the website and click on "Plan Your Visit" and then on "Park Hours and Calendar" to plan your day.

Admission

- One Day Tickets: Adults: HK$399, Children (3-11) HK$285.
- The Magic Access Pass has four tiers: Red, Silver, Gold and Platinum Cards.
- **Red**: Includes entry roughly 240 days within a year, most weekdays (including three designated weekends): Adults: HK$650, Students (ages 12-25, must be full time students): HK$ 460, Children (3-11): HK$460.
- **Silver**: Includes entry roughly 250 days within a year, most weekdays (including

- seven designated weekends): Adults: HK$850, Students (ages 12-25, must be full time students): HK$600, Children (3-11): HK$600.
- **Gold**: Includes entry more than 340 days most weekdays and weekends: Adults: HK$1,650, Students (ages 12-25, must be full time student): HK$1,180, Children (3-11): HK$1,180.
- **Platinum**: 365 days unlimited access on any days throughout the year: Adults: HK$2,400, Students (ages 12-25, must be full time students): HK$1,700, Children (3-11): HK$1,700.

The Best Ways of Getting There
By MTR
- From the **Hong Kong Station** in **Central** (the one below the Airport Express Station) take the Yellow Line (Tung Chung Line) to **Sunny Bay Station**.
- At Sunny Bay Station transfer to **Disneyland Resort Line** and go one stop (end of the line) to **Disneyland Resort Station (Disneyland Resort Public Transport Interchange)**.
- Exit the station at exit **"A"** and walk to the park following the signs.

↔ Travel time: 36 mins (MTR) + 10 mins walk to the entry gates and ticket booths (trains depart every 4-10 minutes).

NOTE: This is a great way of getting there as the ride from Sunny Bay to Disney is on a Disney train.

By Car
- Take the **Western Harbour Tunnel** (HK$50); as you exit the toll booth you will be following the signs for **Lantau**, the **airport** and the **Mickey Mouse Ears**.
- Stay on this highway which is **Route 3**. This will take you over a bridge called **Stonecutter's Bridge** and through the **Nam Wan Tunnel**.
- Then take the **exit off Route 3 to Route 8** (Lantau) which will take you over a long bridge called the **Tsing Ma Bridge**.
- Once over the bridge start looking for signs for **Disney** and **Penny's Bay**. The Mickey Mouse ears on the signs are a great guide.
- Take the **Disney and Penny's Bay exit** off the highway.
- Stay on this road, also called **Penny's Bay Highway**, until you reach the **roundabout**.
- At the roundabout you will choose the **exit for the Disneyland Resort**. You are now on **Magic Road**.

- At the **next roundabout** go left following the signs for Disneyland Park. You are now on **Fantasy Road. Follow Fantasy Road** all the way until you see the **private car parking** sign on your **right.**

P Turn into the car park and drive ahead as far as you can and get as close to the bus terminus as possible, as this is the nearest end to the entrance to the park. The parking cost is $120 a day.

By Taxi
A taxi from Central will cost HK$300-350+ and take 30-35 mins.

***Please note** that there will soon be a *ferry* that travels to the Disney Pier. At the time of printing of this book, it was not yet in operation, but check the website for more details.

Getting a Bite
The park is filled with restaurants and kiosks.

On **Main Street USA**:

There are two table services restaurants here. One is called *Corner Café* and serves a variety of food from both East and West in a Victorian-style setting. Their speciality is Mickey Mouse Waffles with chocolate and vanilla ice cream! You can also sit down and eat at *The Plaza Inn* whose décor is inspired by the Disney story "Mulan". Here they serve Cantonese-style fare including dim sum, and other Southern Chinese specialities. There is also quick service dining at the *Market House Bakery* which has great cinnamon buns, egg tarts, pizza, sandwiches and cakes. Kiosks are also available in this area and serve snacks such as hot dogs and waffles.

In **Fantasyland**:

There are two quick service restaurants. *Royal Banquet Hall* has various counters with different styles of food including: American grill, Japanese noodles, dim sum and rice dishes. You can also dine at *Clopin's Festival of Food*, inspired by the Disney movie "The Hunchback of Notre Dame," which serves traditional Chinese fare such as noodles in soup, wok-fried dishes and meat dishes with rice. There are also several food kiosks/carts around Fantasyland that serve chicken legs, chicken pies, fish balls and more.

In **Tomorrowland**:

There are two quick service restaurants: *Starliner Diner*, which has a space theme and serves American fare such as fried chicken, BBQ chicken wings and burgers, and *Comet Café* which serves Hong Kong dishes such as braised beef brisket curry, spiced chicken wings and noodles. Carts around the area sell snack foods such as hot dogs and Korean BBQ squid.

In **Adventureland**:

There is a table service restaurant called *Riverview Café* overlooking the river (where the Jungle Cruise ride is located) which serves dishes from around Southeast Asia. There is also a quick service restaurant of a tropical theme called *Tahitian Terrace* which serves Indian vegetarian dishes, Malaysian fare such as laksa noodle soup and Hainan chicken. Kiosks around this area serve snacks such as chicken legs and fishballs.

What's Close?
Inspiration Lake, Disneyland Resort Hotel and Disney's Hollywood Hotel.

Comments
- Suitable for all ages, though children under the age of 12 will be the most thrilled by a visit here.
- Plan to spend the whole day.
- Disney is crowded on weekends and public holidays.
- There are sit-down toilets throughout the park.
- The park has a baby care centre adjacent to the Main Street Corner Café on the Central Plaza. Parents can use this area to change diapers, warm bottles or find their children if they get separated from their parents in the park.
- The park is stroller-friendly. In fact strollers can be rented just inside the front gates at City Hall, at the guest relations and information centre.

Extra Info
What is a fast pass? A fast pass is an extra ticket that is given to you when you get your admission ticket. It is free of charge. It enables you to "book" a time for a particular ride and come back at that time, rather than wait in line. Simply go to the attraction and insert your fast pass ticket and it will give you information on when you can return to ride. When you do return, enter the "fast pass" line which is very quick. Only certain rides have this special fast pass. They include Buzz Lightyear Astro Blasters, Space Mountain and The Many Adventures of Winnie the Pooh. Save this fast pass for when the lines are really long. If it is the beginning of the day and the lines aren't too bad, then hang on to the pass until later in the day.

Special Programs and Tours

Star Pass: This is a special program, sometimes offered as an add-on to your admission fee, which enables you to get priority entrance to the most popular rides and attractions including: Mickey's PhilharMagic, The Golden Mickeys, The Many Adventures of Winnie the Pooh, Buzz Lightyear Astro Blasters and Space Mountain. Current Star Pass cost for the summer of 2011 is HK$198 for adults and children three and above.

Disney's Premium Tour/Disney's Supreme Tour: It is possible to hire a Disney Tour Host to help you plan your day and accompany you everywhere, though this is a very expensive option. Your host will arrange for you to see all the attractions you are interested in and set up your meals, parking and ticket arrangements. There are two tour types available:

The Premium Tour for up to six guests who are three and above: HK$2,400 for three hours (child under three is free) includes: Any three hours during your visit, priority entrance to all shows and attractions, park tour with customized itinerary, fun facts and stories of Hong Kong Disneyland, concierge services to pre-arrange priority parking, dining reservations and park tickets. (Note that admission is not included in this price.) You can also choose The Supreme Tour for up to six guests who are three and above: HK$3,200 for three hours (child under three is free) includes: Direct entrance to all attractions, reserved seating for theatre shows, exclusive viewing area for the parade, park tour with customized itinerary, fun facts and stories of Hong Kong Disneyland, concierge services to pre-arrange priority parking, dining reservations and park tickets.

Word of Mouth

There has been some talk about the fact that Hong Kong Disneyland is currently smaller than the other Disney parks and that it is geared more for younger children than for older ones. There are expansion plans currently underway. While it is true that at the present moment there are more rides for younger kids then for their older counterparts, even with the park as it stands today, everyone from babies to teenagers to grandparents can have a wonderful day out at Hong Kong Disneyland.

Ocean Park
Ocean Park Road, Aberdeen, Hong Kong Island

Tel: 3923-2323 (Guest relations)
Website: http://www.oceanpark.com.hk/html/en/home/
For area map: Go to the above website, click on "Plan Your Visit" and then "Park Map".

In years past, this amusement park was a nice local entertainment centre that was a hit with kids around Hong Kong. In the past several years it has morphed into an international, high-quality, ocean-themed amusement centre with a world-class aquarium, rides, games, restaurants and a multitude of animal exhibits. In fact it has become an *absolute* 'must-do' Hong Kong attraction.

Set at the foot of a mountain overlooking the beautiful South China Sea, this wonderful park offers a day of non-stop fun for children and adults alike. Built in the style of Western amusement centres, the spacious 870,000-square-metre park is a combination of an ocean-themed place like Sea World in San Diego and a traditional games-and-rides amusement park such as Coney Island in New York or the Six Flags Amusement Park chain in the US. It is so popular it has recently been voted "The World's Seventh Most Popular Amusement Park" and the "33rd Most Visited Tourist Attraction in the World" by Forbes. A large banner at the front gate announces it has surpassed five million visitors!

The park sits on either side of a mountain in Hong Kong's Southern District. It is divided into two very distinct areas: The Waterfront, which is on the 'front' side of the mountain, and The Summit which is at the top and 'back' side. As you enter the park you will find yourselves in a large open plaza called Aqua City Lagoon which has an enormous musical fountain at the centre, shops and restaurants around the outside and a large blue three story 'egg' which houses the walk-through aquarium. This aquarium was recently moved from the back side of the park to its new location and is a world-class facility. As you move through this specially designed building, you will see stingrays, sharks, tropical fish, starfish, sea horses and many more. It is quite amazing to walk under the tank, through a glass tunnel, as the fish swim above you. There are some hands-on exhibits as well, including one where you can pet live starfish.

When you exit the aquarium and head to explore the rest of the park at The Waterfront, you will find: the Giant Panda Habitat, Sky Fair where you can ride on a hot air balloon (at no extra charge), Gator Marsh, Panda Village, Goldfish Treasures, the Emerald Trail (a hike with bird watching), Amazing Bird Theatre and Whiskers Harbour. Whiskers Harbour is the "kiddie" area and will be your main destination if you have very little ones in tow. This area is home to: Toto the Loco (a kiddie train ride), Merry-go-Round, Motor Racing (mini cars), Balloon Up-up and Away (mini ferris wheel), a bouncy house, a playground with climbing wall, Clown-A-Round (a kiddie ride), Frog Hopper, games, food kiosks and Whiskers Theatre which hosts numerous shows daily with Whiskers the Sea Lion, produced just for the little ones.

If you want to head to the back side of the park, you have two options. The longer and more spectacular of the two is a 20-minute cable car ride which takes you over the top of the mountain, offering some of the most picturesque sea views in all of Hong Kong. Kids will love the ride and parents will love the photo op. Otherwise, a much faster option would be to ride the Ocean Express, a funicular railway in the theme of a submarine, which takes only four minutes to go from one side of the park to the other. (Be forewarned that this railway is more than just a lift to get to the other side, it is also a 'ride' and has a video that looks as though a giant squid is attacking the 'sub' that you are on. It is not particularly realistic, however some small children might become frightened, so it's best to warn them before you get on.)

If you have older children, this will be the side of the park they will want to come to. It is filled with thrill rides and attractions including all of the following: A large ferris wheel, a flying swing, The Dragon rollercoaster, Crazy Galleon – a swinging ship, The Abyss – a very high "drop" ride, The Eagle – a very high 'car' ride, The Mine Train – a rollercoaster, Raging River – a water flume ride, The Flash – a very high 'hammer' ride, Space Wheel – an upside-down ferris wheel of sorts, and Rainforest – a water rapids ride. There are also a few tamer things including: Ocean Park Tower – a slowly revolving lookout tower, Ocean Theatre, Chinese Sturgeon Aquarium, Sea Jelly Spectacular, Garden

0-99

P

253

of Joy, Pacific Pier which is home to the sea lions and harbour seals, games, restaurants, food kiosks and shops. Keep in mind that many of the thrill rides have height restrictions, so warn your kids that they may or may not be able to ride depending on how tall they are.

In the tradition of most theme parks of this calibre, Ocean Park has many shows on offer. There are animal shows featuring birds, sea lions, dolphins, and harbour seals. There are also entertaining performances by acrobats and live music around the park. If you are still at the park when it is dark, plan to stay for "Symbio", a light, water, fire and music show that is performed every night at 8:00pm. There are trainers' talks called "Animal Fun Talks" and feeding times for the animals which can be observed, as well as Mascot meet-and-greet schedules so you can get your photo taken with Whiskers or other Ocean Park pals. Check at the front gate for a printed schedule of show times so that you can plan accordingly.

Seasons and Times
Year-round.
Mondays-Saturdays: 10:00am-8:00pm
Sundays and public holidays: 9:30am-8:00pm
The park stays open later on certain holidays including Halloween and Christmas. Check local newspapers for more information or call the park directly.

Admission
Adults: HK$250; children (3-11): HK$125; under three: Free.
Annual memberships are called SmartFun Annual passes.
The gold pass entitles the holder access to the park 365 days a year. Prices – Adults: HK$695; children (3-1): HK$350.
The silver pass entitles the holder to entry Monday to Friday, and also Saturday before noon (excluding public holidays).
Prices – Adults: HK$545; children (3-11): HK$270. All major credit cards accepted.
Student Pass: Students ages 12 and above in Primary, Secondary, Post Secondary or Higher Education, with a student ID card, can purchase an unlimited pass for $485 per year.

The Best Ways of Getting There
By Bus
- Take **Citybus #629** from **Central Star Ferry Pier** (every 20-60 minutes) or **Admiralty Bus Terminus** (every 10 minutes). This is the most direct route and takes you to the front entrance of the park. The first bus departs Admiralty at 9:00am, last bus is at 4:00pm.

    (Tip: If you buy a package at the Citybus service counter that includes your bus fare and the entry ticket to the park, you can get up to 15% off on your entry fee!)

***Alternatively:
- From **Central Exchange Square Bus Terminus** you can take bus **#6A**, **#6X**, **#70**, **#75**, **#90**, **#97** or **#260** and **#590** and exit at the first stop after the Aberdeen Tunnel.
- From this stop it is a 15-minute walk to the park. There are signs to help guide you.

    (Tip: Every Saturday, Sunday & Public Holiday only, bus #90 will drop you off at the park's entrance from 1:00pm-7:00pm.)

By Car
- From Central: Connaught Road→Harcourt Road→Gloucester Road→**Island Eastern Corridor.**
- Once on the expressway, **stay in the far right lane**. It will be labelled **Happy Valley/Causeway Bay.**
- The far right lane will **lead into a circular overpass**. Here you will stay in the far right lane following **signs for the Aberdeen Tunnel**.
- Once through the tunnel, **take one of the tollbooths on the right side** (HK$5). Stay in the right lanes and follow **signs for Aberdeen**, you will be on **Wong Chuk Hang Road**.
- After you drive under the first overpass, go **all the way over to the left lane** and make a left onto **Ocean Park Road**, then another **left at the roundabout**, then a **left into the main entrance.**

P Here you will find a large parking lot (parking cost is HK$70 on weekdays and HK$80 on Sundays and public holidays). (Note: SmartFun pass holders get discounts on parking. Bring your pass to the Shroff before you leave to get the discount.)

By Taxi
A taxi from Central will cost HK$70-$90 and take 15-20 mins.

Getting a Bite

There are **many** choices for a bite to eat at Ocean Park. A large variety of kiosks serving all different fare are available in every area of the park. The kiosks normally have tables attached so you can sit down and enjoy your meal. The themes include all of the following: Hot dogs, fried chicken, ice cream, pizza, noodles and more. "Sit-down" style restaurants are listed below.

The Waterfront Area:

Aqua City Bakery – great place for a cup of coffee, breakfast, snack or light lunch. Indoor and outdoor seating.

Neptune's Restaurant – a variety of food is served including bento boxes, grilled fare and international dishes. The best part is the view of the aquarium from inside!

Panda Café – near the Panda exhibits, serves Asian dishes.

The Summit Area:

Bay View Restaurant – located next door to the cable car on the back side of the park. Great views, buffet-style fare.

Terrace Café – alfresco restaurant with views.

Café Ocean – located by the Abyss, serves local fare.

Middle Kingdom Restaurant – furthest restaurant from the main entrance. This large restaurant serves Cantonese cuisine including dim sum

McDonald's Restaurant (kiosk).

Comments

- Suitable for all ages.
- Plan a half-day or full-day visit. If you have small children, plan a half day on The Waterfront side of the park.
- Weekdays are much less crowded than weekends and summer is more crowded than winter.
- There are many nice, clean and sit-down style toilets located throughout the park.
- There are many baby-changing stations around the park. The one in Whiskers Harbour right next to Whiskers Theatre has a great nursing area too.
- Stroller-friendly.

Extra Info

Ocean Park offers a birthday party package which includes food, entertainment, gifts, and close encounters with the sea lions. This is a two-hour party that combines all of the following: A special appearance by Whiskers (the Ocean Park mascot), photo-taking sessions with a sea lion, a clown host, party favours and party hats, a two-pound birthday cake, a birthday present for the celebrant, electronic invitation cards, a sign at the park entrance and personalized banners at the private venue. You can also tailor-make a package if you want something different than the above. SmartFun annual pass holders are entitled to a discount. You must book at least seven days in advance and the minimum number must be 20. For booking call 3923-2743 or email: gr@oceanpark.com.hk

Special Programs and Tours

There are a multitude of fun and educational special activities for families to enjoy. The courses include all of the following: Honorary Panda Keeper Program, Lunch and Pandas, Dolphin Encounter, Behind-the-Scenes Tour Amazing Asian Animal Ed-venture, Behind-the-Scenes Tour Grand Aquarium Ed-venture, Sea Lion Snapshots, Sea Lion Feeding Frenzy and Night-time in the Ocean Depths. Some of the programs have a minimum age requirement of eight, others will take them as young as three. Application forms for these programs can be found on the Ocean Park website under "Unique Experiences". For more information contact 3923-2328.

Word of Mouth

Remember to bring mosquito repellent, sun block and a hat or an umbrella with you, as this park is very exposed to the elements and can be strangely sunny and hot even when the rest of Hong Kong Island is cloudy. Also, at the gate pick up a free map of the park so you can plan your day.

City Plaza (Tai Koo Shing) and Quarry Bay Park
with the Fireboat Alexander Grantham Exhibition Gallery

18 Tai Koo Shing Road
(Quarry Bay Park is just opposite City Plaza)
Tai Koo Shing, Hong Kong Island

Tel: 2513-8499
Website: http://www.lcsd.gov.hk/parks/qbp/en/index.html
Fireboat Alexander Grantham Exhibition Gallery Tel: 2367-7821
Website: http://www.lcsd.gov.hk/CE/Museum/History/en/fbag.php
For area map: Go to the above website and click on "Location Map"
City Plaza Tel: 2568-8665
Website: www.cityplaza.com.hk
For area map: Click on website above and then "Where is Cityplaza"
Ice Palace Tel: 2844-8633
Website: www.icepalace.com.hk
Jumpin' Gym USA Tel: 2560-0003
Website: www.jumpingym.com

The Tai Koo Shing/Quarry Bay area is filled with fun family-oriented activities that will work rain or shine. This cluster of apartment blocks, shopping plazas and office towers, also called Island East, is a popular residential choice for Hong Kong families with young children. As a result, family-friendly activities, shops, restaurants and amusements abound here and the general public is free to take advantage of all this area has to offer.

City Plaza:
This is a shopping plaza that truly caters to families. There are child-friendly restaurants, children's clothing shops, toy stores, a multi-screen movie theatre, an ice skating rink and a large children's amusement centre.

The Ice Palace skating rink, located on the first floor, can keep kids busy for hours and is conveniently located next to a restaurant with large glass walls so parents can have a drink or a meal while they watch their children skate (see **Getting a Bite** below). If your kids don't wish to get out on the ice or are too young to have a go, they might still enjoy watching the action from one of the benches provided in the viewing terraces on the floor above the rink. Private skating lessons and group lessons are both available. (Call the Ice Palace hotline for more details.)

The children's arcade, called Jumpin' Gym USA (a Hong Kong-based chain of amusement centres), is filled with games and rides for all ages and sizes. Here you will find a spinning cup ride, a mini bumper car ride, a ball pit with slides and tunnels, riding toys, games of skill, games of chance, and video games. Kids collect tickets from the games they play, which can then be redeemed for prizes. Admission is free but all amusements require the purchase of tokens to be played or ridden. Tokens cost HK$2 a piece but specials are always available for bulk purchases bringing the price down to HK$1 per token. Make sure you bring along a pair of socks for each child (and any accompanying adults as well), because the ball pit area requires each entrant to remove their shoes and cover their feet.

Quarry Bay Park:
Located just across the street from City Plaza, this lovely seaside urban park covers more than nine hectares of land and is filled with fun activities for kids. A seafront promenade, a full-size retired fireboat which can be boarded and toured, a cycling track, basketball courts, tennis courts, a tai chi garden, fitness stations, lookout towers and one of the largest playgrounds in Hong Kong can all be found here. Quarry Bay Park is divided into three distinct areas: The east side, the west side and the seafront, separated from one another by the Island Eastern Corridor (Hong Kong's east/west expressway). On the east side you will find the children's playground which is filled with all sorts of outdoor apparatus including swings, slides, bridges, riding toys and games. There are many benches and shaded areas in this part of the park for parents to relax while their kids explore and play.

From the playground, take the ramp up and across the pedestrian bridge to the seafront, where there is a long promenade with great views of the harbour. Just to your right, as you come over the bridge, is the *Alexander Grantham*

0-99

Exhibition Gallery. This hardworking fireboat, built in 1953, was decommissioned in 2002 and brought to the park to become a branch of the History Museum for the public to enjoy. Aboard, kids will find a number of interesting firefighting artifacts as well as multimedia displays on the boat's history – which is both a testament to marine safety as well a symbol of Hong Kong shipbuilding. Once you finish on the fireboat, have a stroll down the breezy promenade. Kids will enjoy observing the fishermen trying their luck all along the railing or watching the ships (big and small) as they head in or out of Victoria Harbour. Near the end of the promenade on the east side is a refreshment kiosk that sells snacks (see below) and also bubbles and kites. If you have little kids, these two sections of the park – the playground and the seafront promenade – can keep you very busy.

The west side is host to the sports area of the park and has basketball courts, tennis courts, football pitches, a jogging track and – best of all – a cycling track. Kids (and adults) can bring their bikes to this park and cycle around the designated pathway – a very unusual 'find' in Hong Kong. The courts are all available for public use but must first be reserved through the booking office. (Call Quarry Bay Park for more information.) To access the west side of the park from the seafront you must walk back over the pedestrian skyway (over the Island Eastern Corridor) and then walk west over another skyway (over the expressway's exit ramp) to the sports grounds.

Seasons and Times
Quarry Bay Park: 6:00am-11:00pm daily.
City Plaza: Most shops are open from 10:00am-9:00pm.
Ice Palace: Mondays-Fridays: 9:30am-10:00pm. Saturdays: 9:30am-10:00pm, Sundays: 9:30am-7:30pm, however on the weekends 9:30am to noon it is open only if you are registered for a class. Public holidays: 9:30am-10:00pm.
Jumpin' Gym USA: Mondays-Fridays: 10:00am-10:00pm. Saturdays: 9:30am-10:30pm, Sundays and public holidays: 10:00am-10:00pm.
Fireboat Alexander Grantham Exhibition Gallery: Monday and Wednesday to Sunday: 9:00am-5:00pm. Closed Tuesdays and the first two days of Chinese New Year.

Admission
Quarry Bay Park: Free
City Plaza: Free

Jumpin' Gym USA: Free entrance, though games and rides must be paid for by purchasing tokens.

Ice Palace:

Mondays-Thursdays: All-day skate HK$45.

Fridays: Morning sessions (9:30am-12:00pm) HK$45, afternoon/evening sessions (12:30pm-10:00pm) HK$50.

Saturdays and Sundays: Early sessions (12:30am-2:30pm) HK$60, midday sessions (2:30pm-5:00pm) HK$70, sunset sessions on Saturday (5:30pm-10:00pm) and on Sunday (5:30pm-7:30pm) both HK$60.

For holiday schedule pricing, check the website on the week of the holiday to get the schedule as it varies.

Fireboat Alexander Grantham Exhibition Gallery: Free

The Best Ways of Getting There

By MTR

- From **Central** or **Admiralty** take the blue line to **Tai Koo Shing Station** and take exit **"E1"** marked **"City Plaza"**.
- The exit will put you directly into **City Plaza** shopping mall on the **2nd floor**.
- ↔ Travel time: 15 mins (MTR).

Walking to Quarry Bay Park

- The entrance to **Quarry Bay Park** is a short **walk from the MTR** exit.
- Follow sign through the mall for "**City Plaza Three and City Plaza Four**" (these are both commercial office buildings).
- To reach the *east side* of the park follow signs for **City Plaza Four** then take the **escalator down two flights to street level.**
- Turn **left when you reach the street** and look for the entrance to the park next to the residential complex immediately next door to **City Plaza Four**.
- For the *west side* of the park follow signs for **City Plaza Three**. Once inside the building, head to the glass doors at the back of the lobby on the left hand side which **have a flight of steps** that take you down into the park.
- ↔ Travel time: 10-12 mins (walk from MTR exit)

By City Tram

- From **Central's Des Voeux Road** or from **Admiralty's Queensway** to **Tai Koo Shing/Kornhill,** take the tram heading **east**. Stops are located in the middle of the road about every three blocks.

(Tip: Make sure the tram front reads "Shau Kei Wan" or it won't get you all the way there.)

- Exit the tram at the juncture of **Kornhill Road and King's Road** (at Kornhill Plaza). From here **walk up King's Road (heading east)** to City Plaza. You will find the entrance on your **left** side.

↔ Travel time: 35-45 mins (tram) + 5-10 mins (walk).

(Tip: Keep in mind, this will be the "scenic" way to get there. Though the tram is by far the most time-consuming way to arrive at City Plaza, it may also be the most fun for your kids.)

By Bus

- From **Central Exchange Square Bus Terminus** take bus **#2** to **City Plaza** (King's Road side).

↔ Travel time: 30+ mins (bus).

By Car

- From Central: Connaught Road→Harcourt Road→Gloucester Road→**Island Eastern Corridor (Route 4)**.
- Follow signs for **North Point** until you pass Causeway Bay and later look for signs for **Chai Wan and Route 4**.

(Tip: Make sure though that you do not get into the tunnel lanes heading for Kowloon – the "C" Tunnel (Route 1) is the far left lanes and later the "E" Tunnel (Route 2) will be the far right lanes).

- On the highway you will pass signs and exits for North Point and Quarry Bay and then you will want to **stay left**. Take the **exit marked "Tai Koo Shing" – Exit 4.**
- The ramp off the highway will dead-end into **Tai Koo Wan Road** where you will make a left and then an immediate right following signs for **City Plaza** (just follow the road).

🅿 The underground parking garage is well marked on the right side with a blue "P" sign.

By Taxi

A taxi from Central will cost HK$70-$80 and take 15+ mins.

Getting a Bite
Quarry Bay Park

There is a refreshment kiosk which serves hot and cold drinks, sandwiches, snacks and ice cream at the far eastern side of the park.

Nearby Quarry Bay Park: If you walk on the promenade heading east and out of the park (the exit just behind the refreshment kiosk), you will find a street which runs parallel to the water called Tai Hong Street. This area of Hong Kong is called Sai Wan Ho and this street and its plethora of restaurants is now known as "*Soho East*". There are at least 20 restaurants, many of them open-air, to choose from. Kids will enjoy the **Wildfire Pizza** restaurant, but there are many other cuisines to choose from including German, French, Spanish, Italian, Thai, Chinese, Japanese, and more.

City Plaza

The mall and the surrounding area are filled with child-friendly eateries. Here is a short (but in no way comprehensive) list of choices:

City Plaza:

Ruby Tuesdays – Fun pub atmosphere with kids' menu and crayons.

Exp – Kid-friendly food with windows overlooking the ice skating rink.

Pizza Hut – Pizza.

McDonald's – Fast food.

Caffe Habitu – Coffee house and café.

Simply Life Bakery and Café – Wholesome fare.

The Spaghetti House

Mix – Sandwiches and wraps.

Pacific Coffee Company

Haagen Dazs Ice Cream Shop

Food Republic – 20 or more fast food outlets with choices of both Asian and Western fare; on the third floor.

Nearby City Plaza:

Pizza Express San Marzano – A fun pizza restaurant located two blocks from City Plaza (heading west) off Tai Koo Wan Road. Address: Shop 517, Ground Floor, Ko On Mansion, 9 Tai Yue Avenue, Taikoo Shing (in case you have trouble finding it, call them on 3150-8800).

What's Close?
Hong Kong Museum of Coastal Defence.

Comments
- Suitable for all ages.
- Plan to spend two to three hours here or more.

- This area, especially City Plaza, can get very crowded on weekends and public holidays.
- There are many toilets in the mall, several on each floor. They are all clean and offer sit-down style toilets. The park has two toilets, one located near the refreshment kiosk to the east, which has some sit-down style toilets, and one located near the sports grounds which has one sit-down style toilet. *(Note: There are no toilets in the playground area.)*
- There are six baby-changing stations located in six different ladies' toilets in City Plaza. One on the ground floor, two on the first floor (near the ice rink), two on the second floor (one near the Pacific Coffee) and one on the third floor. The park has one baby-changing table in the ladies' toilet near the refreshment kiosk.
- City Plaza and the park are both stroller-friendly.

Special Programs and Tours

City Plaza often has special exhibits or performances to draw shoppers. Many of these programs will be attractive to kids. One year the mall hosted a major dinosaur exhibit which drew thousands of people; this year there was a special touring Lego exhibit. At holiday times there are live performances. Check the mall website to find out what is currently on offer.

Word of Mouth

The Pacific Coffee Company shop is a great place to go for a break from shopping or playing especially if you are nursing a baby. Wide comfortable seats make nursing easier and more pleasant for mother and baby. Located on the 5th floor, opposite the UA Cinema, this coffee shop is particularly helpful if you have a toddler with you, as there is lots of open space for the kids to run around while parents take a much needed rest and load up on caffeine.

Hong Kong Central Library
(including the Toy Library)
66 Causeway Road, Causeway Bay, Hong Kong

Tel: 2921-0208 (Customer hotline)
Tel: 3150-1234 (Library enquiries)
Tel: 2921-0386 (Toy Library bookings)
Tel: 2921-0378 (Toy Library enquiries)
Tel: 2921-0375 (Children's Multimedia Room booking line)
Website for special events and program information:
http://www.hkpl.gov.hk/eindex.html – go to "Hong Kong Central Library"
then "Hong Kong Central Library Event Calendar of Exhibition Gallery
and Lecture Theatre."
For area map: Go to above website, click on "Location and Opening
Hours", then find "Wanchai District" then click on "Hong Kong Central
Library" then click on "Location Map".

香港 銅鑼灣 高士威道 66 號
香港中央圖書館

0-99

This is not the same library you went to as a kid! This one is bigger, better and is loads more fun. The entirety of the second floor of this beautiful library is about kids. Here you will find not only the traditional stacks of children's books for borrowing, but also a toy library, a children's multimedia room and an activities room where the library organizes all manner of children's entertainment – from readings to plays to puppet shows. There is also a lovely café that has an outdoor terrace perfect for little kids to run off the extra energy it takes to keep their voices down inside.

This main branch of the Hong Kong library system carries a wide selection of children's books in both English and Chinese. The area itself is smartly designed with shelves at munchkin level, and small chairs, tables and desks scattered about so that the little ones can peruse their selections. Children will respond well to this lovely space which was designed with them in mind.

In a glass-enclosed room, sandwiched between the stacks, is a slice of heaven for a little kid: the Toy Library. Inside, children between the ages of zero and eight are welcome to play with the myriad of amusements on offer, including puzzles, games, dress-up clothes, computers, a life-size doll house (which they can stand in and even take the stairs to the second floor) and a doctor's office. There is also a sectioned-off area for tiny tots aged three and below which is padded and mirrored and sprinkled with baby toys. But perhaps the best part of your experience here will be "checking out" a special toy for your child from one of the toy catalogues on display. Each page of the toy catalogue has a photograph and description of the toy on offer. Simply choose the toy you want, fill out a short form with your name or your child's name and either your library card number or your ID number. Your child will then be given that toy to play with for the duration of your visit to the toy library. The toys must be checked out one at a time and there is a limit of two toys per child per session, so if your child does not like his or her first selection, you may choose another. The only catch to using this lovely play area is that you must book a space at the Toy Library in advance, which means having to do some planning about a week ahead of your visit. (***See below for instructions on how to make a reservation***).

The Children's Multimedia Room is located next to the Toy Library. Filled with computers for children aged three to 12, here kids can choose between surfing the net or using CD-ROMs. Adults must accompany kids under six but the older kids can go in on their own. You should try to book in advance in order to ensure your child will have a computer to use. (***See below for instructions on how to make a reservation***).

In addition to all of the above, the Library has special events for children free of charge including exhibitions, readings and special presentations. Many of the events are in Cantonese, but there are some offered in English. It is best to call the library hotline on 2921-0208 to get the details on upcoming presentations.

Seasons and Times
Monday, Tuesday, Thursday-Sunday – 10:00am-9:00pm.
Wednesday – 1:00pm-9:00pm.
Public holidays – 10:00am-7:00pm.
Closed on New Year's Day, the first three days of the Chinese New Year, Good Friday, Christmas Day and Boxing Day.
Library closes at 5:00pm on New Year's Eve, Chinese New Year's Eve, Mid-Autumn Festival and Christmas Eve.

The Toy Library and the Children's Multimedia Room have the same hours as above except sessions on Tuesday mornings (10:00am-12:00pm) and Thursday afternoons (2:00pm-4:00pm) in the Toy Library are reserved for school and organization visits. It is also closed for cleaning daily (except Thursdays) from 2pm to 3pm and on Thursdays from 4pm to 5pm.

Admission
Free admission for the Library, the Children's Multimedia Room and the Toy Library.

Toy Library Booking Instructions
If you would like to have a session at the Toy Library you must book in advance by calling 2921-0386. Each session is 45 minutes and each child is allowed only one visit per day. You can book your session up to six days in advance. If for instance you wish to go on a Monday afternoon, then you should call the Tuesday before to book your place. You must turn up for your session 10 minutes before it is due to start and pick up your ticket, or your place will be forfeited. When the sessions are not full, they will give away the places to those who do not have a booking on a first-come, first-served basis. Do not count on being able to get in if you do not have a booking, as this is a very popular thing to do. Still it is worth checking at the desk just in case they have had a cancellation or a no-show. The maximum number of places you can reserve is six, which includes adults.

Children's Multimedia Room Booking Instructions
If you would like to book the multimedia room for your child, you can do so in advance by calling 2921-0375. Reservations are limited to two one-hour sessions each day. You must first register with the staff to enter (whether you have a booking or not). Reservations are taken within the week of the desired booking date. You must turn up within 10 minutes of your reserved time and you must not leave your seat for more than 15 minutes during your session or your place will be given away. If you do not have a reservation, you can check at the door to see if someone has cancelled.

The Best Ways of Getting There
- **By City Tram**
  From **Central's Des Voeux Road** or from **Admiralty's Queensway** to **Causeway Bay**, take the tram heading east. Stops are located in the middle of the road about every three blocks.

- Exit the tram at **Causeway Road**. You will know when to exit as you will see Victoria Park on your left side and the Central Public Library on your right.

  (Tip: The library is a 10-story gold-coloured building.)

↔ Travel time: 20 mins (tram) + 3 mins (walk).

By MTR
- From Central or Admiralty ride the blue line to **Tin Hau** station and take exit "**B**".
- Make a right on **Causeway Road** and walk directly ahead. Victoria Park will be on your right and you will see the library ahead on the left (across the street).

↔ Travel time: 12 mins (MTR) + 5 mins (walk).

By Car
There is no parking at the library. The nearest place to park is Victoria Park where there is only very limited parking. Don't try driving here during peak times.
- From Central: Connaught Road→Harcourt Road→Gloucester Road→**Island Eastern Corridor**.
- Follow signs for **Causeway Bay** and then stay in the middle lane and look for the exit for Causeway Bay.
- Follow the road as it turns to the right and take the **Gloucester Road Flyover** and exit to the left onto **Causeway Road**.
- Go through the light and then make a left hand turn onto **Hing Fat Street**.

P The metered parking lot will be on your left. From here it is a 5-10 minute walk to the library (heading south).

By Taxi
A taxi from Central will cost HK$35-$45 and take 10-15 mins.

Getting a Bite
If the kids need lunch or a snack, stop in at the ***Delifrance Restaurant*** on the ground floor. This international deli-style chain offers sandwiches, soups, pastas, fresh baked bread and desserts, and hot and cold beverages, all at reasonable prices. You can eat indoors or sit outside in the patio area.

What's Close?
Victoria Park, IKEA and Toys R Us (in the Causeway Bay shopping district).

Comments

- Suitable for all ages.
- Plan to spend one to two hours here.
- The library is least crowded during the week when kids are in school.
- There are sit-down style toilets here.
- There is a baby-changing station in the bathroom located next to the Toy Library.
- Stroller-friendly.
- The library has a gift shop that sells not only books but also souvenirs, stickers and CDs.

Extra Info

How do you apply for a Hong Kong library card? If you have a Hong Kong ID card you can bring it with you to the library along with some sort of proof of address (i.e. a bill addressed to you) and you can apply for and receive a library card on the spot. To apply for a card for your child, you will need to bring the above-mentioned items along with a copy of his/her birth certificate if they are not HKID holders. If you are a visitor, you can also apply for a card by having a friend who is a HKID holder guarantee your card, or you can leave a deposit in cash for each of the books you are borrowing. Stop in at the information booth on the ground level for more information.

Special Note:
List of All Public Libraries
There are more than 65 public libraries scattered throughout the territory. All branches carry children's books in English, but some have more than others. For a complete list of all the libraries and their locations, please go to www.hkpl.gov.hk.

For Educators

Special sessions at the Toy Library are available for schools and other organizations on Tuesday mornings and Thursday afternoons. There are also special tours of the Central Library available for school groups. Please call 2921-0208 for more information.

Word of Mouth

- Booking the Toy Library is a bit arduous but worth it. Young children visiting the library could be quite disappointed at not being able to go into the Toy Library if you have not booked a place. The Toy Library is enclosed with floor-to-ceiling glass walls and abuts the children's book lending section. This means that the kids on the outside choosing books have a full view of the kids on the inside playing with all sorts of toys, so be forewarned!

- If you have children of different age groups you might want to book the Toy Library for the younger ones at the same time as you book the Children's Multimedia Room for the older ones. They are next to each other so you can be in the Toy Library with the younger kids while the older ones are playing on the computers across the hall on their own.

Snoopy's World, Sha Tin New Town Plaza & 10,000 Buddhas Monastery

(New Town Plaza Phase I and III & Home Square, Grand Central Plaza)

Level Three, Phase I, Sha Tin New Town Plaza

Sha Tin Centre Street, Sha Tin,

New Territories

新界　沙田

新城市廣場　沙田正街

史諾比開心世界及萬佛寺

For Plaza and Snoopy's World – Tel: 2608-9329 (Phase I enquiry hotline) or 2691-6576 (Phase III enquiry hotline)
Website: www.newtownplaza.com.hk
For area map: Go to the above website and click on "Home" and then "How to Get There."
For 10,000 Buddhas Monastery: Off Pai Tau St., Sha Tin
Tel: 2691-1067 Website: www.10kbuddhas.org

Snoopy's World:
This little place can best be described as an outdoor themed playground. It is a fun outing for your children if you happen to be in the Sha Tin area. Decorated to the hilt with life-size figurines of Snoopy and his Peanut Gang pals, this is an amusing and colourful place to play.

The park has three main attractions. First, there is a big yellow traditional American school bus, which has been emptied of seats so that kids can run around inside and pretend to drive. There is also a vertical playground with a baseball theme which has many areas of discovery and fun, including a covered slide. And lastly, an amusement sure to be a hit with the kids, the electronically-run Snoopy canoe ride on a mini boating canal. The kids can sit on their own or with a parent in the canoe as they pass little vignettes of Snoopy stories such as "It's The Great Pumpkin, Charlie Brown" and others. There is a covered pavilion, complete with some benches and picnic tables, where Snoopy's World staff create balloon animals for children and run various arts and crafts events (normally around 3:00pm on weekends). Sometimes, there are performers doing various

0-99

271

tricks just in front of the pavilion. (When we were there, they were juggling yo-yos.)

Though the park is free of charge, there is one catch. The park is run by Sha Tin New Town Plaza and in order to have a go on the canoe ride, you must first present the ride supervisor with a same-day receipt showing at least HK$100 in purchases from any shop in the mall. The receipt entitles four people from your party to ride in two boats. If you have two kids, they can ride twice on the presentation of your receipt. They do adhere strictly to this requirement, so you may wish to do some shopping or perhaps have lunch or dinner at the mall before going to the park as restaurant receipts are also acceptable. Purchases made in the mall after 7:00pm will be honoured the following day, so make sure to hit the stores or restaurants before 7:00pm.

Sha Tin New Town Plaza:
Snoopy's World is a great place to play, but might only occupy your child's attention for an hour or so. The Sha Tin Mall area has other things to offer kids that can make your trip worthwhile. The mall is made up of three areas: Two connected buildings, New Town Plaza Phase I and New Town Plaza Phase III and a third unattached complex called Home Square at Grand Central Plaza, which is a short walk away.

New Town Plaza Phase I, where Snoopy's World is located, has a 10-plex movie theatre located on level LB, and outdoors on the 7th floor, a delightful roof garden with multiple porch swing chairs which face an impressive oval-shaped musical fountain. The fountain has 15-minute 'shows' several times a day where the water 'dances' to the beat of various tunes choreographed with light effects. If you are here in the evening (or even during the day time) this musical show is not to be missed; it is magical in the dark (ask at the customer care counter for a list of show times). New Town Plaza Phase III (Level One) boasts a children's shopping floor that includes a large Toys R Us and a variety of kids' clothing, book and toy shops.

On the other side of the MTR Station from the Plaza is Home Square, which has an IKEA store. The great thing about this IKEA is the kids' play area inside the store, which is a small kids' paradise. Moms and Dads can leave their children to play (free of charge) in this supervised play space while they shop. The sessions are 30 minutes long and children must be between 80cm and 120cm in height to be accepted. The playroom can accommodate up to 16 children at a time. The children's toy section of the store will also be of interest, as sample toys are left out on the floor for children to play with while parents peruse.

10,000 Buddhas Monastery:
Just around the corner from Grand Central Plaza is the entrance to the trail that leads to the 10,000 Buddhas Monastery. This is a very spiritual and interesting place. While monks don't really live here any more, there is certainly no inflation of the number of Buddha statues here. In fact there are more than 12,000 Buddhas of all different shapes and colours all around the temple.

Built in the 1950s on a hill overlooking Sha Tin, this lovely place will be a hit with adventurous kids. Reaching the temple is part of the experience and involves over 400 steps. The entire path is lined with life-size gilded statues, each of them with a different face and expression. This is more of a hike than a stroll and should be attempted with kids who are comfortable walking and do not need to be carried. If you do make the investment to reach the top, you will find a beautiful temple which houses thousands of miniature Buddhas, each holding a small light. The effect of these lights with the small statues is enchanting for kids and adults. To tempt the kids to climb on to the top, let them know that monkeys are often seen on the grounds (two were hanging out when we were there). It is best to do this visit in cool weather.

Seasons and Times
Snoopy's World: Year-round, 10:00am-8:00pm daily.
New Town Plaza: 11:00am-10:00pm daily (some shops are open earlier).
Grand Central Plaza: 10:30am-10:30pm daily.
10,000 Buddhas Monastery: 9:00am-5:30pm daily.

Admission
Free

The Best Way of Getting There
By MTR
- From **Central** or **Admiralty** to **Kowloon Tong Station**, take the red line to **Mongkok**. **Transfer to the green line** (across the platform at Mongkok Station) to **Kowloon Tong**.
- In Kowloon Tong Station look for the **East Rail**. Ride it to **Sha Tin**.
- When you exit the MTR station look for **exit "A"** marked **"New Town Plaza"**.

   (Tip: You will not have to go outdoors. The MTR "A" exit puts you right into Phase 1, Level 3 of the New Town Plaza Mall, the same level as Snoopy's World).
- Once in the mall look up and you will find a few Snoopy signs pointing the way to the park.

↔ Travel time: 20 mins (MTR) + 10-15 mins (East Rail)

Directions to Home Square, Grand Central Plaza, IKEA Store
- Exit the **Sha Tin MTR Station at e**xit **"B"** and follow the signs to "**Home Square, Grand Central Plaza**".
- Once you exit the station you will be outdoors and the bus terminus is all around. **Follow the crowd down the ramp** and walk directly ahead until you get to the corner.
- Home Square will be directly in front of you on **Pai Tau Street**. Cross the street at the crosswalk, **turn left** and enter the building.

↔ Travel time: 5-10 mins (walk from MTR exit).

Directions to 10,000 Buddhas Monastery
- **Follow the directions to Home Square above**. BUT instead of entering Home Square, keep **walking up Pai Tau Street** until you get to the **first right hand turn** which will be **Sheung Wo Che Road**.
- Walk one block and **the road will end**. The back of Grand Central Plaza will be on your right and Sha Tin Government Offices will be on your left.
- At the end of the road you will see a **sign to the Monastery** on your left, which will take you to a paved pathway. Follow the pathway and it will lead you to the steps up to the Monastery.
- **Do not turn left when the path forks**, instead keep steady and straight and you will shortly come upon the steps. (You will not have to wait to get to the top to see the Buddhas.

As soon as you start ascending you will see the golden statuettes.)

(Tip: If you do not make the right turn onto Sheung Wo Che Street, you will wind up at the dead end of Pai Tau Street. There is a temple-like structure there but this is NOT it. This is an ancestral hall. It's pretty, but it is NOT what you are looking for. It is tricky because it is also on a hill and looks like a temple. If you are not in an area that looks distinctly RURAL then you are not in the right place.)

↔ Travel time: 20 mins (walk from Home Square to the 10,000 Buddhas Monastery)

By Car

- From **Central**: Connaught Road→Harcourt Road→Gloucester Road→**Island Eastern Corridor (Route 4)**→ **Cross Harbour Tunnel (Route 1).**
- In tunnel stay in right lane. Once through tollbooth (HK$20) stay right and follow signs for **Ho Man Tin and Sha Tin**.
- Stay in centre lane, you are now on **Princess Margaret Road**. Follow signs for **Sha Tin** and **Lion Rock Tunnel (Route 1)**. Go through tunnel (HK$8); you are now on **Lion Rock Tunnel Road**.
- Take the **exit** on the left for "**Sha Tin Central**" **Exit 11A**. Follow this road across a small bridge over the **Shing Mun River Channel**.
- After you pass the **Heritage Museum on your left**, make a right turn on **Sha Tin Centre Street and this road will curve around to the left** and you will see the various phases of **New Town Plaza on both the right and the left**.

P There are many underground car parks in the nearby area to choose from; look for the **"P"** signs and park in any one of them.

By Taxi

A taxi from Central will cost HK$150-$170 and take 35-40 mins.

Getting a Bite

In New Town Plaza Phase I there is a myriad of kid-friendly eateries including an enormous variety of Asian restaurants plus *Ruby Tuesday*, *Shakey's Pizza*, *The Spaghetti House*, a *Haagen Dazs Ice Cream Store, Starbucks Coffee, Pacific Coffee Company, Triple O's by White Spot*, and *a McDonald's* and *McCafe*, to name just a few.

Phase III also has several restaurants for kids including a *Pizza Hut, Spaghetti 360, Ben and Jerry's Ice Cream* shop and *Kentucky Fried Chicken*.

IKEA has a bistro that is reasonably priced and there is also a *Starbucks* with an outdoor café in the building.

The 10,000 Buddhas Monastery has a place at the top where you can buy some drinks.

What's Close?

Hong Kong Heritage Museum and **Biking in the New Territories** (from Sha Tin Park).

Comments

- Suitable for all ages but Snoopy's World is best for little kids who still enjoy playgrounds. 10,000 Buddhas Monastery is best for kids who like to walk or hike.
- Plan to spend two to three hours here.
- Very crowded on weekends and public holidays. Mid-week you should be able to do everything without waiting in lines.
- There are toilets in the mall at the back exit to Snoopy's World. These are nice modern toilets.
- There is a baby-changing station on Level 1 in New Town Plaza Phase I and in Phase 3 on Levels 1 and 3. There are also nursing rooms at these same locations. IKEA has a baby-changing table in the toilet as well.
- Stroller-friendly (except 10,000 Buddhas – don't take a stroller there).

Word of Mouth

Snoopy's World is a good place to go if you plan to do more in Sha Tin beyond the mini park. If you are set on visiting Snoopy's World, plan some other Sha Tin activities as well.

West Kowloon: Elements Mall, Sky 100, DHL Hong Kong Balloon Ride & West Kowloon Waterfront Promenade (Park)

Tsim Sha Tsui, Kowloon

Elements Mall
1 Austin Road West, Tsim Sha Tsui Tel: 2735-5234
Website: www.elementshk.com

The Rink
Ground Floor, Elements Mall Tel: 2196-8016
Website: www.rink.com.hk

Sky 100
100/F, International Commerce Centre (ICC)
1 Austin Road West
(Sky100 ticket booth is on the 1st floor of Elements and the express lift entrance can be accessed through Metal Zone 2/F) Tel: 2613-3888
Website: www.sky100.com.hk

DHL Hong Kong Balloon
On the West Kowloon Waterfront Promenade (road leading to water from ICC) Tel: 2559-2983
Website: www.dhlhongkongballoon.com

West Kowloon Waterfront Promenade
On the road leading to the water from ICC Tel: 2302-1279
Website: www.lcsd.gov.hk/parks/wkwp/en/index.php
New Bike Shop (at West Kowloon Waterfront Promenade)
Tel: 6138-0070
Website: www.newbike.com.hk

0-99

West Kowloon is a relatively new area of Tsim Sha Tsui (West), built on reclaimed land and developed around Hong Kong's tallest skyscraper – the International Commerce Centre (ICC). This is a great place to come as a family and appreciate Hong Kong in all its splendour. The area is home to a high-end mall with indoor ice skating rink, movie theatres and restaurants, an observatory located on the 100th floor of the world's 5th-tallest building, a hot air balloon ride that floats above the harbour, and a park right at the water's edge which has a cycling track and a place where you can rent bikes! You can easily pass an entire day in this area whilst doing a variety of activities that all ages will enjoy.

Elements Mall:

This modern upscale mall is very conveniently located one MTR stop away from Central and right above the Kowloon MTR Station. It is large, clean and beautifully designed. It is divided into five 'zones' – Metal, Wood, Water, Fire and Earth. The Fire Zone is where you are most likely to spend your time with the kids. This is the "entertainment" area, where The Grand movie theatre, The Rink indoor ice skating rink, and Metrobooks, a 10,000-square-foot bookshop with a harbour-view Kids' Corner, can be found.

The Rink has a 'pay as you skate' concept using the Octopus card (see the **Introduction** for more info on Octopus), so skaters are not tied to fixed time sessions and are charged only for the time on the ice that they use. Parents are permitted to enter the rink area free of charge to watch their children. The front has a large glass wall which provides 180-degree views of the Harbour. The Rink rents fun, helpful, and cute upright penguin gliders, with handles, that help hold the kids up as they are learning how to skate. Check with the lesson desk for details. The Grand movie theatre is located two flights up from The Rink on Level 2. This is Hong Kong's largest cinema complex and is the world's first theatre built with infrasonic capabilities: a new technology installed in the theatre seats. You will not only see and hear the movie, you will feel it too (this is not available for all showings).

Sky 100:

This is Hong Kong's highest indoor observation deck, at 393 metres above sea level. Buy your ticket either online or at the ticket counter on the 1st floor of the Elements mall and ride the express lift directly up to the 100th floor of ICC. You will exit the elevator and enter a 360-degree circular observation deck with a bird's-eye view of Hong Kong's amazing city skyline below. Beyond the breathtaking sights, Sky 100 also has a large-scale interactive multimedia exhibit which covers local history and culture. Kids will enjoy playing with all the technology while the whole family learns more about Hong Kong's colourful history. Sky 100 also offers audio-visual devices in English, Cantonese, Putonghua and Japanese, which provide information about the city as you observe it from above. There are facilities on the deck including a café and a gift shop.

DHL Hong Kong Balloon:

This is a brand new attraction for Hong Kong: a tethered large yellow air balloon that takes passengers aboard and rises to 100 metres above the ground, giving passengers a 360-degree view of the incredible Hong Kong skyline and Victoria Harbour. Though the ride is only 15 minutes in length, the memories will last a lifetime. It is an absolute thrill to be floating high above Victoria Harbour, taking in one of the most iconic views in the world. The Balloon has both day rides and night rides which are equally stunning. Kids will love the adventure! The balloon is piloted by professionals and every precaution is taken. The opening hours are set (see below), however on occasion, depending on the wind and weather, the ride might be postponed. Children must be 1.2 metres or above in height and while there is no age limit per se, for safety reasons this requirement is not flexible.

West Kowloon Waterfront Promenade:

Just 10 minutes' walk from ICC is a waterfront park that until now has been a little-known Hong Kong "secret". Set on reclaimed land immediately next to the harbour waters, this promenade park, run by the Leisure and Cultural Services Department, is a great place to go for a bike ride while taking in the harbour views. The park covers more than 33,000 square metres of land, 1,500 of which is a cycling track which sits on some of the most scenic property in all of the city. Here you will find a young children's playground, a timber boardwalk, a bike rental stall, some vending machines and a flat cycling track. This is a great place to teach your young ones to ride a bike, provided it is not a super hot day, as there is very limited shade.

Rain, sun, heat, whatever the weather, there is fun to be had in West Kowloon. Views abound no matter where you go in this area, so don't forget your camera!

Seasons and Times

Elements Mall: 10:00am-9:00pm daily.
The Rink: Monday to Friday: 10:00am-10:00pm, Saturday, Sunday and public holidays: 9:00am-10:00pm.
Sky 100: 10:00am-10:00pm daily.

DHL Hong Kong Balloon: Daytime flights: 10:00am-6:45pm, Nighttime flights: 7:00pm-9:45pm.
West Kowloon Waterfront Promenade: 6:00am-11:00pm.
New Bike Shop: Monday to Friday – 3:00pm-8:00pm, Weekend and public holidays: 9:00am-8:00pm.

Admission
Elements Mall: Free
The Rink: Prices range from HK$0.60 to HK$1.00 per minute. There are also days during the week when you can buy a whole day pass for HK$30 for kids and HK$50 for adults.
Sky 100:
Advanced online booking (24 hours in advance of visit): Adults HK$125, Children 3-11 HK$90, Under-threes free, Family (two adults and one child) – HK$305
Same Day Walk in booking or same day on-line booking: Adults HK$150, Children 3-11 HK$105, Under-threes free, Family (two adults and one child) – HK$365
DHL Hong Kong Balloon:
Day Rides: 10:00am-6:45pm – Adults HK$150, Kids over 1.2 metres and 11 and under – HK$75
Night Rides: 7:00pm-9:45pm – Adults HK$250, Kids over 1.2 metres and 11 and under – HK$175.
West Kowloon Waterfront Promenade: Park is free. Bike riding charges are (roughly) as follows:
Kids' Bikes: HK$25
Adults' Bikes: HK$30
Family Bikes: HK$70

The Best Ways of Getting There
By MTR (then walk if you are going to DHL Balloon or the Promenade)
- From the **Hong Kong Station in Central** (the one below the Airport Express Station) take the Tung Chung Line to **Kowloon Station**.
- For Elements Mall or for Sky 100 exit the MTR at exit **"C1" or "D1."**
- For DHL Balloon or West Kowloon Promenade exit the MTR at exit **"D1"**.
    > *Walking – To access DHL Balloon or the Promenade:*
    > • Go out to the street from **Exit D1** and you will be on **Nga Cheung Road**.

- **Turn left and walk toward the water and the ICC Tower**. The road will dead-end onto **Austin Road West.**
- **Cross Austin Road West** (under the overpass) and look for the entrance which is signed for the **West Kowloon Waterfront Promenade**.
- Go **past the fencing and follow the road around**. The road has banners and will lead you right to the DHL Balloon launchpad on your left (you will see the balloon in the sky, just walk toward it).
- If you are heading to the Promenade pass the DHL launchpad and the car park and you will **see the park entrance around to your right**.

↔ Travel Time: 5 mins (MTR) to Elements or Sky 100 + 10-15 mins walk for DHL Balloon or for West Kowloon Promenade.

By Star Ferry + Free Shuttle Bus or City Bus

- From **Central** to **Tsim Sha Tsui (TST)** take the Star Ferry from the **Star Ferry Central Pier**.
- When you exit the ferry pier in TST walk straight ahead and you will see the **TST Star Ferry Bus Terminus.**
    By City Bus:
    - Take bus **#8** from **Star Ferry Bus Terminus** to **Kowloon Station Bus Terminus**.
    By Free Shuttle Bus:
    - From **TST on Peking Road**, right outside the duty free shop to **Elements Mall.**
    - Buses run every 20 minutes from 12:30pm-9:30pm.

↔ Travel time: 10 mins (ferry) + 10-12 mins (free bus or city bus).

By Car

- Take the **Western Harbour Tunnel – Route 3** (HK$50).
- Get in the left lane as you enter the tunnel and then when you exit the tunnel head to **the FARTHEST left hand lanes** marked for **Tsim Sha Tsui**.
- After you exit the toll booth you will **take the exit IMMEDIATELY to your left.**
- This exit will take a ramp to a traffic light; at this light you will make a left and cross a bridge overpass.
- After you cross the overpass you will come to **another light**. **Make a right** here (you will see the Elements Mall sign on your right). WARNING: At this light there are two rights.

The sharp right takes you back into the tunnel. Head for the Elements sign which is a soft right.

- You are now on **Nga Cheung Road**.

For Elements and for Sky 100:

P The Elements car park is an immediate left and is marked "**Elements North**".

Note: To access the DHL Balloon or the Promenade follow the "Walking" directions above; or for DHL Balloon and Western Kowloon Promenade:

- Stay on **Nga Cheung Road** and it will take you around past the ICC and will curve to the left, and down a ramp into a roundabout. Do a **U-turn at this roundabout** following the signs for the **West Kowloon Waterfront Promenade**. You are now on **Austin Road West**.
- Then **stay to your far left** following the signs for **Airport Express** and you will come to a **second roundabout**.
- At this roundabout make a left and enter the **West Kowloon Waterfront area.**
- The road will curve to the left (the road is lined with banners), just follow it around and you will see the **DHL Balloon on your left**. You cannot park there.

P Look for the public car park on your right just past the DHL Balloon entrance.

By Taxi

A taxi from Central to this area will cost HK$100-HK$120+ and take 10-12 mins.

Getting a Bite

Elements Mall **has many family-friendly eateries to choose from. Here are just a few:**

Wildfire – Pizza restaurant, kids' options.

Triple-O's – Burger place.

Inawira Udon Nabe – Japanese noodles and more.

Chips Republic – French fries and shakes.

Sen-Ryo – Sushi "train" restaurant.

Café Habitu – Coffee, snacks and lunch.

Caffe Vergnano 1882 – Coffee, snacks and lunch.

Haagen Dazs Ice Cream Shop

Starbucks Coffee

Elements – Civic Square – This is an area above the mall on a podium level with seven eateries, many of which have alfresco dining. The options here are upscale. The food is of high quality and is reflected in the price. Some of the options are child-friendly, especially if you sit outside.

Sky 100

Sky 100 has two cafes both called *Sky Café*. One is on the 2nd floor and serves a variety of Asian dishes as well as hot dogs, sandwiches and wraps. There is also a *Sky Café* on the 100th floor which serves drinks and bakery items. The 101st floor also has two restaurants, one serving Chinese fare, the other Japanese. This area is referred to as *Sky Dining 101*.

DHL Hong Kong Balloon

Currently there are no refreshments available at the DHL launch area, but plans are in place to have a *Pacific Coffee* stall on the premises to serve coffee and snacks.

West Kowloon Waterfront Promenade

There are no snack stands or restaurants here but there are cold drink and snack vending machines.

What's Close?

Hong Kong Space Museum, **Hong Kong Art Museum**, **Kowloon Park** and **Big Bus Tours**. *Please note that while you can walk to these locations, it would be a long walk (apart from Big Bus Tours), but all are only a short taxi ride away.

Comments

- Elements and Sky 100 are suitable for all ages. The DHL Balloon requires that children be 1.2 metres tall. West Kowloon Waterfront Promenade is best suited to kids who can ride bikes.
- Plan to spend a minimum of 2-3 hours in this area.
- None of these venues are generally crowded.
- There are nice toilets at Elements Mall and Sky 100. DHL has an 'outhouse' with sit-down style toilets. West Kowloon Waterfront Promenade has some sit-down toilets but they are not the nicest.
- There are two baby-changing and nursing facilities in Elements mall, one on Level 1 near shop #1048 and on Level 2 near shop #2010. There is also a baby-changing table at Sky 100. There are no baby-changing facilities at either DHL or at the Promenade.
- All of these places are stroller-friendly.

Extra Info
The Rink offers ice skating lessons. Check their website under "Skating School" for more information on courses for kids.

Special Programs and Tours
- DHL Hong Kong Balloon Ride has party packages which include: three hours rental of marquee, a bouncy castle, three tables and 20 chairs, use of AV system, and 50% off on the purchase of tickets for a ride to the balloon (minimum of 20 people). Please note that while this is an amazing party venue, it is quite pricey.
- Sky 100 has a special event venue area. Please call them to get more details if you would like to book a private event. This is a great venue but it is an expensive option.

Word of Mouth
Big Bus Tours has a hop-on/hop-off point at the DHL Hong Kong Balloon on their Kowloon Tour route.

Bowling City at E-Max (KITEC – Kowloonbay International Trade and Exhibition Centre)

九龍 九龍 九龍灣 九龍灣 九龍灣展貿中心

G/F, Emax, 1 Trademart Drive, Kowloon Bay

Tel: 2620-3010
Website: www.hkbowlingcity.com or www.emaxhk.com
For area map: Go to www.emaxhk.com/en/transport.html and click on "Location" and then on "Location Map"

Bowling is always a great family activity on a hot day, rainy day or an evening when you want to spend some quality time doing something everyone can enjoy. This is a great place to bowl! State-of-the-art automatic scoring systems, children's sized bowling shoes, children's bowling balls and special kids' ramps help to make this experience hassle free.

Bowling City is light and airy, some might even say cavernous. They have 48 international standard sized bowling lanes complete with 50-inch electronic score boards. There is also a great VIP room that can be used for kids' birthday parties, class parties and other functions (see **Special Programs and Tours** below). This bowling centre also has its own restaurant which serves customers all morning, afternoon and evening. There are numerous drink and snack vending machines, including one that dispenses Haagen Dazs ice cream. As in many bowling alleys in the West, this one also has some games beyond bowling to amuse kids, including air hockey, foosball (table football), electronic darts and electronic basketball.

This bowling mecca is located inside a mall called E-Max. The mall has several restaurants and coffee shops as well as a few younger-aged children's amusements. On the 5th floor there is a free-of-charge small toddler play area, complete with sofas so parents can relax while their kids play. There is also a small indoor playground on the ground floor which is only open on weekends and holidays. Children below 120cm in height are welcome to play inside after parents show a receipt of either a food or retail purchase from the mall or pay $5 for entry. This

5+

playground has three sessions a day (on those days when they are open): 2:00pm-3:30pm, 4:00pm-5:30pm and 6:00pm-7:30pm. If you have several children with you of varying ages, some of whom are too young to bowl, it's nice to have this play option for the little ones.

Keep in mind that the bowling alley can get crowded in the late afternoons when older children finish school and want to have a game. There is also free wireless internet access at Bowling City which adds to its popularity among local schoolkids who love to come here and hang out. Get out there and have a game, or two or three – the kids will love it!

Seasons and Times
Monday-Friday: 10:00am-1:00am
Saturday, Sunday, public holidays: 10:00am-2:00am.

Admission
Weekdays: 10:00am-6:00pm: Adults – HK$31, Students – HK$21
Weeknights: 6:00pm-1:00am: Adults – HK$38, Students – HK$38
Weekends: Adults and students – HK$42
Shoe rental: HK$4
Locker rental: HK$5

The Best Ways of Getting There
By MTR/Free Shuttle Bus
- From **Central** or **Admiralty** to **Kowloon Bay Station**, take the red line to **Mongkok**. **Transfer to the green line** (across the platform at Mongkok Station) to **Kowloon Bay Station**.
- Take exit **"A"** and look for the **free shuttle bus stop for E-Max/KITEC**. Buses run regularly and can be easily spotted as they are white with long yellow, purple and pink stripes running along the bottom side of the buses.
- ↔ Travel time 28 mins (MTR) + 5-7 mins (free shuttle bus).

By Car
- From Central take the **Eastern Harbour Tunnel**: Connaught Road→ Harcourt Road→ Gloucester Road→ **Island Eastern Corridor (Route 4).**
- In **tunnel (Route 2)** follow signs for **Kowloon Bay and Route 2** and **stay to your right.**

- The signs are well marked for Kowloon Bay. You will be on Route 2 for roughly **five kilometres** or less and then you will exit the expressway to your left at **Exit 2D** marked for **Kowloon Bay.**
- Stay to your right as the exit forks and continue following the signs for Kowloon Bay which will take you **down a ramp to a traffic light**.
- Turn **left at the first light** following the **signs** for **KITEC;** you are now on **Sheung Yee Road.**

   (Tip: You will now follow the blue-and-white signs for 'Kowloonbay International Trade and Exhibition Centre – KITEC' which will lead you right to the E-Max car park.)
- Follow **Sheung Yee Road** around **past Mega Box;** at the **next light make a left,** you are now on **Sheung Yuet Road.**
- Then **turn right at the light onto Wang Kwong Road** and then **your immediate first left on to Wang Chin Road**. Follow **Wang Chin Road** and it **will curve to the right**. You will see KITEC/E-Max on your left.
- Make your first left there on to **Trademart Drive**.

P The car park will be immediately in front of you on Trademart Drive.

   NOTE: These directions sound complicated but they are really very easy, as once you exit the expressway and get to the first traffic light, things are very well signposted.

By Taxi
A taxi from Central will cost HK$120-$150+ and take around 20 mins.

Getting a Bite
Bowling City:
Bowling City has its own restaurant called *301 Café* which serves breakfast, lunch and dinner. They have a small à la carte menu including noodles and sandwiches and many daily specials. There are also vending machines at Bowling City.

E-Max:
E-Max has many dining options including:
Starbucks Coffee
Pacific Coffee Company
Hot Dog Formula – Hot dog restaurant
Menu – An international buffet-style restaurant
Dong Sheng Organic Farms Restaurant – Organic Chinese food

Happiness Gastronomy – Chinese fare
Xi Shan – Traditional Chinese cooking
Roll N Dough – Bakery and hot dishes

What's Close?
Mega Box and Mega Ice

Comments
- Suitable for children five and up (or if they are strong enough to hold a bowling ball then younger).
- Plan to spend a few hours here.
- The lanes can get very crowded in the late afternoon when local schools get out.
- There are sit-down style toilets in Bowling City and in E-Max Mall.
- There is a baby-changing room on the ground floor near the play space, and also in the ladies' bathroom on the 4th floor.
- Bowling City and E-Max are both stroller-friendly.

Extra Info
Bowling City has a special private room that you can hire out to host birthday parties and special events. This large private area has four unique fluorescent bowling lanes, karaoke machines, and can fit up to 40 people. There are tables and chairs for all the party guests and there are special bowling ball ramps for kids to use so that young children can also comfortably have a turn. You must order your food from the canteen that is on the premises, but you may bring in your own cake. Café 301 has a special catering menu for parties which includes all of the following: spring rolls, fish fingers, sandwiches, pasta dishes, fried rice, salads, french fries, wraps and more. You must order three days in advance of your function and they require a 50% down payment. The room charge is by the hour and there is a two-hour minimum booking required.

Special Programs and Tours
You can become a member at Hong Kong Bowling City for HK$400 a year. Your membership includes being able to reserve a lane in advance (otherwise when you come out to Bowling City it is first come, first served), special discount pricing for every game you play, discounts for the VIP party room, free shoe rental for yourself and up to 10 companions,

discount on locker rentals, discounts at their pro-shop, and six special coupons which are "Buy 2 and get 1 free game."

Word of Mouth
If you want to make an all-day outing out of a trip to Kowloon Bay, it can be easily done by visiting both Bowling City and Mega Box Mall which are very near to one another.

Mega Box Mall and Mega Ice
Mega Box Shopping Plaza
38 Wang Chiu Road, Kowloon Bay

Tel: 2989-3000
Website: www.megabox.com.hk
For area map: Go to above website and click on "How to Get Here"
Mega Ice
Level 10, Mega Box
Tel: 2709-4020
Website: www.megaice.com.hk
UA Cinema & IMAX Theatre
Level 11, Mega Box
Tel: 3516-8811
Website: www.uacinemas.com.hk
Play House
Level 9, Shop 25, Mega Box
Tel: 2151-9761
Website: www.playhouse.com.hk
Flight Experience
Ground floor, Shop 20
Tel: 2359-0000
Website: http://www.flightexperience.com.hk

The 'Big Red Box,' as it is called, is an enormous vertical mall with an interesting modern design and LOTS of things to do with kids! Mega Box is host to Hong Kong's largest ice skating rink, a large cinema complex complete with an IMAX theatre, an indoor children's playroom, a children's shopping area decorated to delight children with play options sprinkled around, many child-friendly restaurants and a flight simulator school for those with a special interest in learning to pilot an airplane.

Mega Ice is Hong Kong's only international-sized ice skating rink, measuring 26 metres by 57 metres, and situated inside the enormous atrium of the mall next to 30-metre-tall glass windows with full Victoria Harbour views. The ice rink is open to the public most of the time for 'fun' skating sessions but occasionally is closed for hockey league practice, hockey games, figure skating lessons or events (check **Seasons and Times** below for more information on open skate times). This is a great place to skate. It is sunny and bright and offers parents bleacher seating rink-side, so that they can watch their kids glide around the ice.

290

The mall is also host to an IMAX theatre which has a five-story high screen and features the most technologically advanced sound and picture quality in the world. This United Artists Theatre complex also has seven regular movie screens and often has 3-D movies for kids. The complex can hold up to 900 moviegoers! The cinema is located on Level 11 and the ice rink on Level 10. These two floors have many restaurant options that are child-friendly (see **Getting a Bite** for more information).

Just below the rink on Level 9 of the mall is an area called Mega Kids. This floor is home to an indoor kids' playroom and a variety of children-centred shops including clothing, book, candy and toy stores. Decorated to the hilt in a jungle theme, this area has lots for kids to do and see. Mega Kids has an indoor slide and riding toys, colourful décor such as a life-size fish mobile, giant rotating flowers on the ceiling, chairs in the shape of wild mushrooms and life-size figurines of elephants and giraffes. The playroom located on this floor is called Play House and is sure to be a hit with kids 10 and under (though children 12 and under are welcome). The playroom has two different areas, one near the escalators which is their main facility and one near the shops in Mega Kids. The main area has two kids' mazes with tunnels, slides, foam-ball cannons, a ball pit, ride-on toys, a party area with small tables and chairs and some games. The second area has a bouncy castle in the shape of a bus and some kid-sized exercise equipment such as mini treadmills, mini rowing machines and mini exercise bikes. The playroom is well kept which is certainly helped by the requirement of all patrons to wear socks inside. If you forget yours, you can purchase them at Play House.

Last, but certainly not least, is Flight Experience, the flight simulator school located on the ground floor of Mega Box. For the child or adult who has always dreamed of being a pilot this is a special treat. A flight simulator, modelled after a Boeing 737 cockpit, is used to teach either a one-off course or a series of lessons to individuals, teens or families by licensed pilots. There are many packages to choose from which include anything from a 'Family Fun' experience to a three-year 'Young Cadet Program' for kids ages 12 to 18. This program is unique but be aware that is it also very expensive with prices starting at HK$700 and up.

0-99

Additional things worth noting at Mega Box are IKEA on Levels 3 and 4, Toys R Us on Level 8, a magic shop on Level 12, a Karaoke Club (called CEO) located on Level 17, and a Game Zone (for kids 16 and up) on Level 12. Children (and adults) of all ages will find something fun to enjoy at Mega Box!

Seasons and Times

Mega Box: 11:00-10:00pm weekdays, 11:00am-11:00pm weekends and holidays.

Mega Ice:

Monday and Wednesday: 10:00am-2:00pm, 2:30pm-5:00pm, 5:30pm-8:00pm, 8:30pm-10:30pm (open for Hong Kong Ice Hockey League only; welcome to watch).

Tuesday: 10:00-2:00pm, 2:30pm-5:00pm, 5:30pm-7:00pm, 7:30pm-10:30pm (Ice Hockey training).

Thursday: 10:00am-2:00pm, 2:30pm-6:00pm, 6:30pm-8:00pm, 8:30pm-10:30pm (open for Hong Kong Ice Hockey League only; welcome to watch).

Friday: 10:00am-2:00pm, 2:30pm-5:00pm, 5:30pm-8:00pm, 8:30pm-10:30pm (Mega Ice Skating School students only).

Saturday: 9:30am-11:00am, 11:30am-1:30pm. 2:00pm-4:30pm, 4:45pm-5:45pm (Main Event held), 6:00pm-9:00pm.

Sunday: 9:00am-11:00am (Hockey and Figure Skating training), 11:30am-1:30pm, 2:00-4:30pm, 5:00pm-7:00pm, 7:30pm-10:30pm (Ice Hockey training).

Play House: Monday-Thursday: 12:00-8:00pm.
Friday: 12:00-10:00pm, Saturday, Sunday and public holidays: 10:00am-10:00pm.

Admission

Mega Box: Free

Mega Ice: Open skating prices range from HK$40-HK$70 depending on the session that you choose. They also offer ice skating lessons, check website for details.

Play House: Monday-Friday: HK$45, after 6:00pm – HK$40. Saturday, Sunday and public holidays: HK$65, after 7:00pm – HK$50. Please note that the price is inclusive of one child and one adult. Children must be supervised at all times.

Flight Simulator: Package prices begin at HK$700 and go up significantly from there.

The Best Ways of Getting There
By MTR/Free Shuttle Bus or Walking

- From **Central** or **Admiralty** to **Kowloon Bay Station**, take the red line to **Mongkok**. **Transfer to the green line** (across the platform at Mongkok Station) to **Kowloon Bay Station**. *From here you can either take the free Mega Box shuttle bus or walk to Mega Box.*

> *Free Shuttle Bus*
> - Take **Exit "A"**, take several escalators up, **turn left past the bus terminus** (Circle K will be on your right) then head left **for Telford Plaza II** which you will see on your left. **After Telford Plaza II turn left and look for the taxi stand, free shuttle and mini bus stands**. <u>Buses run every 10 minutes</u>.
> ↔ Travel time 28 mins (MTR) + 5 mins (free shuttle bus).
>
> *Walking*
> - Take exit **"A"**, take several escalators up and then get on to street level and **walk up Telford Boulevard** (Circle K will be on your left). After one block you will be **looking straight ahead for a footbridge.**
> - **Take the footbridge** through Chevalier Engineering Service Centre and **make a right on Sheung Yuet Road.**
> - Walk one block and **turn left on to Wang Chiu Road**. You will see the big red Mega Box building **up and to your right**.
> ↔ Travel time 28 mins (MTR) + 10 mins (walk).
> *NOTE: Please go to the Mega Box website and have a look at their shuttle bus and walker's map before you head out so you can easily find the shuttle bus or walk there.*

By Car
- From Central take the **Eastern Harbour Tunnel**: Connaught Road→ Harcourt Road→ Gloucester Road→ **Island Eastern Corridor (Route 4).**
- In **tunnel (Route 2)** follow signs for **Kowloon Bay and Sha Tin and Route 2** and **stay to your right**.
- The signs are well marked for Kowloon Bay. You will be on Route 2 for roughly **5 km** or less and then you will exit the expressway to your left at **Exit 2D** marked for **Kowloon Bay.**
- Stay to your right as the exit forks, and continue following the signs for Kowloon Bay which will take you **down a ramp to a traffic light**.
- Go through the traffic light, you are now on **Wang Chiu Road. <u>Stay on this road until the next traffic light.</u>**

(NOTE: You will pass the big red Mega Box building on your left with what seems like a good left turn on Lam Fung Road, but it is <u>a one way street</u>, therefore you will need to go to the next turn and go around the block in order to access the car park.)

- At this light **make a left onto Sheung Yuet Road**.
- Go one block to the next light and **make a left on to Sheung Yee Road**.
- You will make the **next left onto Lam Fung Road**.

🅿 You will see Mega Box and car parking turn on your right hand side.

By Taxi
A taxi from Central will cost HK$120-$150+ and take around 20 mins.

Getting a Bite
There are many options for a meal at Mega Box, too many to name them all. Here are but a few:

California Pizza Kitchen – Pizza, kids' menu, high chairs and kids' booklet to entertain.

Studio City Bar and Café – Burger joint near the movie theatre, kid-friendly food, diner-like.

Naruto Sushi – Japanese restaurant with 'sushi train' going around with dishes ready made, as well as à la carte menu.

MOS Burger – Fast food burger joint.

Hachiban Ramen – Noodle joint.

Delifrance – Local French bakery chain with pastries and lunch and breakfast items.

Dressed – Salad place.

Starbucks Coffee

McDonald's and McCafe

Yogurt Time – Frozen yogurt place.

Chinese restaurants – Many on Level 13 and Level 14.

AND MANY MORE including Thai, Vietnamese, Portuguese, etc...

What's Close?
<u>Bowling City and E-Max Mall.</u>

Comments
- Suitable for all ages.
- Plan to spend two to three hours here.

- Mega Box can be very busy on weekends and public holidays.
- There are sit-down style toilets in every restroom.
- This mall has eight parents' rooms located on G, L1, L2, L5, L6, L7 and L9 with pleasant and spacious areas specially designed for baby care. There is even a baby food warmer on L9 in the parents' room!
- The mall is stroller-friendly. In fact they have a stroller lending service at the customer care counter.

Extra Info
It is rare to find pick-a-mix candy stores in Hong Kong. The Mega Kids area has one though and it is very reasonably priced.

Special Programs and Tours
Play House offers two monthly pass options, one for weekdays and one for any time. Prices start at HK$380 per month. They also have birthday party packages for 20 kids or more starting at HK$1,000 per party that include all of the following: Use of play area for guests, birthday party invitations, dining utensils, free use of the LCD TV and an electronic birthday banner for the birthday celebrant.

Word of Mouth
Make sure you bring socks for both you and your children for the Play House. All participants must be wearing them. Socks are also helpful to have in your bag if your kids would like to ice skate. For skaters, long sleeves, long pants, and a pair of gloves would also be helpful. Note that even if you are not skating, it is very cold in this mall, even in the middle of summer, so bring a sweater or jacket with you.

BMX Bike Park
91 Kwai Hei Street,
Gin Drinkers Bay, Kwai Chung

Tel: 2419-9613
Website: http://www.bmxpark.org.hk/
For area map: Go to above website and look for "Contact Us" and then click on "Location Map".

This is a cool place and a very welcome addition to the Hong Kong list of kid-friendly activities. Opened in 2009, this sports park was built by the Hong Kong Jockey Club but is privately operated. Kids and adults who enjoy adventure and sport can learn how to ride on BMX bikes or hone their skills if they are already practiced BMX riders. It is the only park of its kind in the territory.

Sometimes it's hard in Hong Kong for active sporty kids to let loose and find exciting things to do and experience. This BMX bike park is the perfect answer for those children and adults who crave the adrenaline rush that comes with trying something new and physically challenging. BMX biking is a rigorous sport, but it is offered here with good safety precautions and well thought-out training. Currently the park has three track levels – beginner, intermediate and advanced. In order to ride regularly on any of the three courses, you must first earn a license for each and every level to proceed to the next. While it might sound complicated it is easily done. Simply turn up at the park and let them know that you would like to pay for admission as well as licensing. Your kids will have the opportunity to practise on the track and then will have a 45-minute course with a trained instructor to earn their license. The license is a card that then can be brought back to the park at every visit to show the rider's current proficiency level. All riders must earn their license starting with beginner level even if they are experienced. The cost of the licensing, complete with the lesson, is HK$150 per person; this is in addition to the admission fee and rental gear fees if you need it, so bear in mind this is not an inexpensive outing, especially if you have multiple children riding and having to earn their licenses.

The BMX Bike Park is working on expanding their offerings. They are building a trail bike course as well as developing the surrounding grassy area into a mountain bike terrain. These new features will open sometime in late 2011 or 2012. They are also working on adding other features such as a canteen where they will offer meals for riders (see **Getting a Bite** for more information). There are also events held at the park that visitors are welcome to come and watch. Races and demonstrations are normally hosted here in the cooler and drier fall and winter months. They have some shaded stands where spectators can watch the advanced track riders.

Once you start coming to this park, if your kids like to ride, this may become a regular haunt. It would be best to get the licensing done on your first trip so your kids can get training, get their credentials and be ready to ride on subsequent visits. Parents, if you are not riding, take a hat, sunglasses, mosquito repellent, sun block and drinks or money/octopus card for the vending machines so that you can buy drinks. It can get brutally hot in the sun here and everyone should stay hydrated, riders and spectators alike.

***Please bear in mind that participating in this sport can result in injury. People DO get hurt. The BMX Park does not take responsibility for riders' injuries, so make sure you are insured and that you understand the risks involved.

新界　葵涌
醉酒灣　葵喜街
91號

8+

Seasons and Times
Mon, Tue, Wed and Fri: 2:00pm-6:00pm and 7:00pm-10:00pm
Sat and Sun: 9:00am-1:00pm and 2:00pm-6:00pm
Thur: Closed for scheduled maintenance
Pro Gate session: Night sessions on every Wed and Fri
Also closed on Chinese New Year holidays, red or black rainstorm warning, or when typhoon signal No. 3 or above is hoisted.
> *Please note:* The park management may also exercise discretion to close the park facilities when, in its sole opinion, the park facilities are unsuitable for use due to inclement weather, safety or operation reasons.

Admission
Standard: Adult admission charge – weekday: HK$100/session, Adult admission charge – weekend: HK$120/session, Student admission charge – HK$60/session

Bike & protection gear rental : HK$40/session
The BMX bike park offers special rates packages for people who will be frequent users.
Packages:
Adult Package (weekday): HK$140/session (included: Bike & protection gear rental, admission, locker)
Adult Package (weekend): HK$160/session (included: Bike & protection gear rental, admission, locker)
Student Package (weekend): HK$100/session (included: Bike & protection gear rental, admission, locker)
Monthly Pass:
License holder: HK$500/month (included: Bike & protection gear rental, admission, locker)
Student: HK$500/month (included: Bike & protection gear rental, admission, locker)
License test – (included Development Track, International Standard Track and Pro Gate)
Adult: HK$300, Student: HK$150
Bike locker: HK$600 per month or HK$1530 per quarter

The Best Ways of Getting There
By MTR then taxi or mini bus
- From **Hong Kong Station in Central** (under the Airport Express Terminal/IFC Mall) take the Yellow Line (Tung Chung Line) and alight the train at **Kwai Fong Station**.
- Take exit **"B" or "C" for taxi queue** or exit **"D" for mini bus** (please note that while there are walking directions from the MTR on the BMX Bike Park website, I don't recommend walking. It is too far with kids).
    By Taxi:
    • A taxi from Kwai Fong Station to the Bike Park should take around 5-7 mins.
    By Mini Bus *(Please note that taking <u>a taxi</u> is the best way to travel from the Kwai Fong MTR to the Bike Park)*:
    • Take mini bus **#404M**. Alight the bus at Riviera Gardens. Walk toward and then past Tsuen Wan Chinese Permanent Cemetery and walk to Kwai Hei Street. (Check out the map on the BMX website for more details. Print a google map and take it with you. HINT: Another way – Wing Shun Street if you keep following it will come to a fork, Kwai Hei Street will be a sharp left. Then look for the BMX gate on your right.)

↔ Travel time: 25 mins (MTR) + 5 mins taxi or 10 mins mini bus + 5-10 mins walk.

By Car
- Take the **Western Harbour Tunnel – Route 3** (HK$50); as you exit the toll booth you will follow signs for **Kwai Chung and Lantau** and subsequently for **Kwai Chung and Yuen Long** and all the while you remain on **Route 3.**
- Stay on **Route 3** for **7 to 8 km** until you see the exit for **Kwai Chung which is also labelled Exit 4B for Lantau, Tsing Yi and Route 5.**
- Take **Exit 4B, which immediately forks, stay to your right to Kwai Chung and follow the signs to Kwai Chung**.
- You are now on **Kwai Chung Road**. Follow this road and it will lead you **down a ramp**.
- At the bottom of the ramp you will **come to a light**, which is **your first left hand turn**. **Turn left** at this light. You are now on **Kwai Foo Road.**
- Stay on **Kwai Foo Road** and take the third left at a traffic light onto **Hing Fong Road** (Kwai Foo dead-ends and you must go right or go left).
- Then get in the far right lane and take the **1st right onto Kwai Fuk Road.**
- Then take the **1st left onto Kwai Hei Street**.
- **Follow Kwai Hei Street** along, winding your way around for 2-3 minutes. You will come to **a gate on your left hand side** just off the road to the left. This gate has the BMX marquee on it. Drive through the gate until you reach the guard gate where you will need to stop, get out of the car and get a parking stub and pay for admission.

P There is parking at the BMX Park ($8 per hour).

By Taxi
A taxi from Central will cost HK$250+ and take 30-35 mins.

Getting a Bite
On the premises there are half a dozen drinks vending machines. At present there is no canteen at the Bike Park but there are plans in the works to install one. In the drinks and resting room, there are menus posted for a local McDonald's Restaurant as well as a Pizza Hut. They also have the two restaurants' phone numbers posted. This is one option for having a meal at the park. Another is to bring a cooler with you and have a 'picnic' in the stands.

What's Close?
Dialogue in the Dark and **Lai Chi Kok Park**.
*Please note that none of these are very close, but in the same general area.

Comments
- Suitable for children who are already ***very comfortable*** riding a regular bicycle.
- Plan to spend at least one bike session here which is normally 3-4 hours.
- As of now, this bike park is not widely known, but my guess is that it might become crowded on weekends once the word is out. Right now though it is not crowded.
- There are clean sit-down toilets on the premises, as well as showers in both the ladies' and men's rooms.
- There are no baby-changing facilities here.
- This is a stroller-friendly place.

Extra Info
The BMX Bike Park welcomes kids to have their birthday parties on their premises. They offer a private activity room and will help you tailor-make a bike program based on your children's ages and ability levels. You can bring in your own food, or order from a restaurant. Call them to organize your event.

Special Programs and Tours
- The park offers special training courses for all levels, beyond the licensing practice. If your kids are serious about the sport, the training courses offered would be a great activity to pursue. Information on the coming six months of courses are available on the website by clicking on "BMX Training Course".
- The YMCA of Hong Kong occasionally organizes holiday camps for youngsters at this park. Another way to have your kids attend a holiday camp is to create one of your own. Get a group of kids together and talk to the BMX team about creating a youth camp for your group.

Word of Mouth
The best way to stay up to speed on all the happenings, offerings and changes at the bike park is to "friend" BMX Bike Park on Facebook. Their media department is very good at sending out notices using this medium.

Wise Kids

Cyberport Mall
Shop 101, The Arcade, Cyberport, Pokfulam Tel: 2989-6298
Causeway Bay
China Taiping Tower
1st Floor, 8 Sunning Road, Causeway Bay Tel: 2151-9968
Website: www.wisekidstoys.com
For area map of both Cyberport and Causeway Bay: Go to the above
website and click on "Shops" and a Google map will pop up.

香港　香港
薄扶林　銅鑼灣
數碼港商場101店　新寧道8號1樓

Having indoor play options with little kids in Hong Kong is important when the weather is rainy, too hot to go out to play or just muggy and unpleasant. Wise Kids is a great place to play indoors with your children. With two different locations to choose from, this lovely toy shop has created two colourful playspaces which are filled with fun and educational activities in a safe and clean environment, so everyone can relax and enjoy.

Cyberport: This enormous two-story toy shop is Wise Kids' franchise flagship store. On the second floor of the shop, you will find an 8,000-square-foot play area filled with fun and exciting activities for both babies from three to 30 months and older children up to eight years old. The play room has eight different areas that are all well designed and equipped with European toys, manufactured and recommended by specialists, to help in a child's development. The kids will not notice this of course, they will just be having fun!

0-99

There is a creative arts area where crafts are led by one of the staff members, a musical instruments area, a 'library' with books and bean bag chairs, a multi-sensory area with lights, sounds and textures led by a staff member, and a 'play house' area complete with a two-story pretend play house that kids can go up into and bring dolls or other toys with them. There is also a dress-up area, a face painting area, a trains and cars area and a kitchen area. The toys are of a very high quality and are all sold in the shop downstairs. At the end of each session the staff will lead the children in songs and games and parachute play with bubbles.

Causeway Bay: This lovely play space is similar to the one in Cyberport but much smaller. It has many of the same areas but on a smaller scale. The staff are delightful and during each and every session will do their best to ensure your kids are having fun. The crafts area, trains area, dress-up area, toddler area, kitchen and shopping area are all well designed. As with the Cyberport playroom, there is a limit to how many children can join each play session and therefore it is not overcrowded. At the end of each session, the staff will sing and dance with the kids and bring the session to a close.

Several special workshops are offered each month at Wise Kids in both venues. These workshops are normally held in Cantonese, however English speakers may find them worthwhile as the topics are very enticing for little ones including for example: Yummy Playdough, Wise Kids Kitchen and Creative Play. Check the website or call the shops for more details.

Seasons and Times
Cyberport
Shop Hours: 11:00am-8:00pm
Playroom Sessions: Though it varies, generally there are four sessions a day: 10:30am-12:00, 12:30pm-1:30pm, 2:00pm-3:30pm and 4:00pm-5:30pm. The playroom is closed on either Monday afternoons or Tuesday afternoons (after a public holiday) from 12:00 onward for cleaning.
Causeway Bay
Shop Hours: 10:30am-7:30pm (Sunday to Thursday), 10:30am-8:30pm (Friday and Saturday).
Playroom Sessions: There are five sessions a day from Sunday-Thursday and six sessions day on Fridays and Saturdays. 10:00am-11:15am, 11:30am-12:45pm, 1:00pm-2:15pm, 2:30pm-3:45pm, 4:00pm-5:15pm and 5:30pm-6:45pm (Friday and Saturday only).

Admission
Session fees: $120 per child (including two adults)
NOTE: Call in advance to reserve a space for your child in the session of your choice. Payment is not required at the time of phone booking, but if you don't book you could be turned away if they are full.
Monthly passes: $980 per month

The Best Ways of Getting There
To Cyberport:

By Bus
- From **Central Exchange Square Bus Terminus** to **Cyberport Bus Terminus** take bus **#30X**. Alight the bus at the **Cyberport Bus Terminus** and walk across the street to the **Wise Kids Shop.**
↔ Travel time: 20 mins (bus).

By Car
- From Central take **Route 4, Connaught Road** heading **West**.
- Exit Route 4, Connaught Road (a highway), take the **Pokfulam Exit** which will be to your **left.**
- Come down the ramp off the exit, you will **go through a stop light** and then will turn **left onto Pokfulam Road.**
- When you come to the next light **stay to your right and keep heading up Pokfulam Road.**
- **Follow Pokfulam Road's twists and turns for 2.5 kilometres** until you see the turnoff (exit) for **Bisney Road on your left**.
- **At the light make a sharp right**, go over the bridge and turn immediately left down Sassoon Road.**
- Follow Sassoon Road down to the **roundabout and then turn right onto Victoria Road.**
- At your next turn you will **make a left onto Sha Wan Drive**. Follow down the hill until you see the **Cyberport** (a big modern-looking structure with a spire facing the sea) ahead.
- Make **a left at the bottom of the hill roundabout**, you are now on **Cyberport Road**. First pass the Le Meridien Hotel on your right and then ISF (school) on your left.
P Follow the road around a curve and you will turn right into the car park.

By Taxi
A taxi to Cyberport from Central will cost HK$65-70 and take 15-20 mins.

<u>**To Causeway Bay:**</u>
By MTR
- From **Central** or **Admiralty Station** take the MTR to **Causeway Bay Station**. Exit the MTR at exit **"A"**.
- When you get to street level head for **Russell Street** ahead, and **make a right**.
- At the next block **make a right on to Percival Street**.

- Walk two blocks up on Percival Street (you will pass Lee Theatre Plaza on your right) and when you get to the first major intersection make a **left onto Hysan Avenue**.
- **Sunning Road** is three blocks up on your right hand side. Look for **#8** and go to the **first floor**.

↔ Travel time: 7 mins (MTR) + 10 mins (walk).

By Bus

- From **Central at Hang Seng Bank, 83 Des Voeux Road** or from **31-37 Des Voeux Road Central, outside United Chinese Bank Building** or from **93 Queensway outside Admiralty Garden / Queensway Plaza in Admiralty**, take bus **#10** to **Matheson Street** (Times Square Shopping Mall).
- Once you alight the bus follow the walking directions from the MTR above.

↔ Travel time: 10-15 mins (bus) + 10 mins (walk).

By City Tram

- From **Central's Des Voeux Road** or from **Admiralty's Queensway** to **Causeway Bay**, take the **tram heading east**. Stops are located in the middle of the road about every three blocks.

    (Tip: Make sure the tram front does not read "Happy Valley" or it won't get you all the way to where you want to go.)
- **Alight** the tram at the **first stop after passing Sogo Department Store** in Causeway Bay on Hennessy Road.
- Head **west on Hennessy Road toward Percival Street**. Turn **left on to Percival Street**, then **left on to Hysan Avenue**.
- Once on Hysan Avenue, count three streets on your right and **make a right** when you get to the third one called **Sunning Road**.

↔ Travel time: 15 mins (tram) + 10 mins (walk).

By Car

- From Central: Connaught Road→Harcourt Road→Gloucester Road→**Island Eastern Corridor.**
- Once on the expressway, stay in the far right lane. It will be labelled **Happy Valley/Causeway Bay**. The far right lane will dead-end into **a circular overpass**.
- **Stay in the far left lane on the overpass** as you will take the very **first left exit to Leighton Road.**
- Take the exit ramp down. You are now on **Canal Road East**. Follow it until you see the **left turn for Leighton Road**.

- Follow **Leighton Road** until you come to **an intersection** where in order to follow Leighton Road you will have to make a right. **DO NOT take the right turn from here to remain on Leighton Road**, **INSTEAD you will go straight ahead** and find yourself on **Hysan Road**.
- You will pass two streets on your right and at **the third one make a right hand turnoff from Hysan Avenue onto Sunning Road**.

P At the end of the block on the right is the car park marked with a large blue "P" sign.

By Taxi
A taxi from central will cost HK$50-$60 and take 15-20 mins (depending on traffic).

Getting a Bite
Cyberport:
While food is not permitted inside the playroom, there are plenty of places in the Cyberport mall that would be good for a snack or meal including:

Starbucks Coffee Shop
Kosmo Coffee Shop
Dynastie Chinese Restaurant – Chinese family-friendly restaurant, dim sum menu.
Oh Sushi and Tapas – reasonably priced sushi.
Tutti Bar and Restaurant – Italian fare, pizza for kids.
Le Meridien Hotel Cyberport – this high-end hotel has several food outlets:

> *Prompt* – international, buffet and à la carte, breakfast, lunch and dinner with alfresco seating.
> *Umami* – upscale Japanese with garden seating (goldfish pond to amuse the kids outside).
> *Nam Phong* – upscale Chinese, note: dim sum lunch at this spot on a Sunday is popular.
> *PSI* – bar and lounge, serves high tea.

Causeway Bay:
Causeway Bay is a district known for its shopping and dining and has lots of restaurants, bakeries, coffee shops, etc. The corner of Leighton Road and Hysan Avenue has a *Pacific Coffee* on one side and a *Starbucks* on the other for a quick snack and drink. Times Square Mall on Matheson Street has multiple floors dedicated to restaurants which they call "*Food Forum*". There are many, many others as well. If you want to be

adventurous, just walk around and find a place that appeals to your family.

What's Close?
From Cyberport Wisekids – **Pokfulam Country Park Walk** (a short taxi ride away).
From Causeway Bay Wisekids – Times Square Shopping Area, Happy Valley and the Hong Kong Racing Museum.

Comments
- Suitable for kids ages three months to eight years old.
- Sessions can be anywhere from 60 to 90 minutes.
- Not generally sold out during the week, but can become very busy during weekends and public holidays. Book in advance to avoid disappointment.
- There are sit-down style toilets in both malls.
- There are baby-changing stations at both venues right next to the playroom. This room has an unusual name: "The Cry Room".
- The buildings that house Wise Kids shops are stroller-friendly.
- Both play spaces are inside the toy shops.

Extra Info
Want to combine indoor play with outdoor play as well? At Cyberport, on the 4th floor, there is an outdoor grassy area that is perfect for children and their parents to have a relax and a run around. Though not a park, it is used as one by the people who live in and around Pokfulam. There is REAL grass here, a water feature, tables and chairs with sun umbrellas for shade and a *Starbucks Coffee* and *Kosmo* (café) on the same floor, so you can run in and get snacks and a coffee or tea. There is also a large ParknShop grocer on the ground floor where you can pick up items for a picnic. Bring some bubbles and a ball and you have the makings for an entire fun day out with the kids!

Special Programs and Tours
You can organize a kids' birthday party here at Wise Kids Playroom. The parties last two hours and 15 minutes and include one hour in the playroom and one hour and 15 minutes in the kids party area for food, cake, games, or anything else you want to do there. The party area will be decorated by Wise Kids with balloons and a banner. A host will be assigned to help

with the arrangements and execution of the event. 20 birthday party invites are included too. Keep in mind this is a great option, but is NOT inexpensive. Call the playroom for more details.

Word of Mouth

Each month Wise Kids offers a new theme. At the time of printing of this book, the themes were "Salon and Clinic" and "BBQ and Picnic". Special toys and projects are carefully matched to the monthly theme. The changing themes are very helpful to those who make this a regular place to come with their children, as it keeps the playtime material fresh and interesting for everyone. Holidays such as Valentine's Day, Easter, Mother's Day, Father's Day, Mid Autumn Festival and Christmas (to name just a few) are a great time to come to Wise Kids, as many of their creative activities centre around the holiday themes.

Playtown Candyland
Shop 121, Podium Level 1
The Westwood, 8 Belcher's Street,
Hong Kong Island

Tel: 2258-9558
Website: www.playtown.com.hk
For area map: www.ypmap.com.hk (plug in "Belcher's Street" and "8"
under "Street" search)

Parents rejoiced when in 2008 an indoor themed playground opened on Hong Kong Island. 10,000 square feet of great play structures in a clean, air-conditioned, and visually appealing indoor arena make for a great outing on an inclement weather day (or any day for that matter).

Playtown's designers considered parents' and children's' needs very carefully when they built this fabulous space. Babies and toddlers (ages 0-3) have an area all their own with slides, a ball pool, soft puzzle mats, multiple crawl-through tunnels and a wide variety of toys. Just outside this area are tables and chairs, couches and coffee tables complete with magazines for parents to read, and two baby-changing stations, all within a few feet of where the kids are playing. Oh and let's not forget WIFI!

The rest of the play space is devoted to children ages four to 12. The large play structures, all in the Candyland game theme, include slides, crawl-throughs, rope bridges, swinging vines, an entire soft room devoted to foam ball warfare (parents can play too), an interactive electronic floor game and a 'soft' sports zone which combines basketball and soccer in one area complete with electronic score boards. There are also private party rooms and a snack bar with more than enough tables for all the parents to find a place to relax. There is of course WIFI in the café too. Kids will be happily occupied here which makes for a great opportunity to surf the net or catch up on emails.

One of the ways they keep this play space so clean is by not permitting shoes to be worn inside. **Everyone, including adults, must wear socks in order to enter, so be sure to have socks with you when you go** (even in the height of summer). If you forget them, you can purchase socks from the front desk at HK$10 per pair. There are cubbies to store your shoes at the front entrance, but if you prefer you can also rent a locker for HK$10 per day from the front desk to stow your personal belongings.

Seasons and Times
Monday to Thursday: 10:00am to 7:00pm.
Friday-Sunday and public holidays: 10:00am to 9:00pm.

Admission
Monday to Thursday:
Two and below: HK$100*
Three to 12 years old: HK$120*
Extra adult: HK$50* (only one adult per child is permitted)

Friday to Sunday and public holidays:
Two and below: HK$120*
Three to 12 years old: HK$150*
Extra adult: HK$60* (only one adult per child is permitted)
*Note that the cost of admission is for the <u>whole day</u>. You can leave and come back, just make sure you keep your admission bracelet on.

Monthly Passes:
Two and under: HK$900
Three to 12 years old: HK$1,000

The Best Ways of Getting There
By Bus
- Take the **<u>M47</u>** from **Central Exchange Square Bus Terminus**. Alight the bus at the **Westwood Mall** on **Belcher's Street**.
    Or
- Take bus **<u>#5X</u>** (an express bus) from **26-29 Connaught Road Central** outside Wing Lung Bank Building. Alight the bus at **2 Sai Cheung Street** outside **Belcher Court**. From here walk the half block up to **Belcher's Street** and look for the **Westwood Mall** on the left hand side of the road.
- Buses **<u>#18P</u>** and **<u>#43X</u>** both depart from **26-29 Connaught Road Central**. Alighting point is slightly further from Belcher's Street at the **COSCO Hotel, 22 Kennedy Town Praya before Sai Cheung Street.** Follow directions from Sai Cheung Street as above.

0-12

↔ Travel time: 20-25 mins (bus) + 5-10 mins (walk).

By Car
- From Central take **Route 4/Connaught Road** heading **West**.
- Exit Route 4/Connaught Road (a highway) at **Kennedy Town exit**.
- Make a left on **Sai Cheung Street North** to the next intersection.
- Make a left here onto **Kennedy Town Praya Road**.
- Then make the immediate right onto **Collinson Street**.
- Then the next right onto **Belcher's Street**.
- The entrance to the **Westwood Mall** will be less than a block away on the left.

P There is a parking garage in the Westwood Mall; look for the guard post at the far end of the driveway to enter the upward ramp to the hourly car park.

By Taxi
A taxi from Central will cost HK$50-60 and take around 10-15 minutes.

By MTR – (starting in 2013/2014):
Soon the West Island Line will begin service. At that point, the Hong Kong University Station, Belcher's Street exit will be the closest MTR stop to Playtown and will likely take 8-10 minutes time to travel from Central. For more information on the opening of the West Island Line check www.mtr.com.hk.

Getting a Bite
Playtown has a snack bar on the premises which serves cold drinks, coffee and tea (for exhausted parents), snacks, baked goods, hot dogs and pancakes. If you are looking for more than a snack, the Westwood Mall, where the play space is housed, has many options including: ***McDonald's, Panash Bakery and Café*** (they have pizza and pasta here as well as bakery items), ***Chili n' Spice*** (Southeast Asian cuisine) and ***Victoria Harbour Restaurant*** (Hong Kong-style dim sum and Chinese hotpot).

What's Close?
Belcher Bay Park and Playground is about a five-minute walk from the Westwood Mall toward the harbour, just off Kennedy Town Praya (the road where the trams run).

Comments

- Suitable for ages 0-12.
- Plan to spend at least two hours here.
- Very crowded on weekends, public holidays and rainy afternoons.
- The toilets are sit-down style and they are clean.
- There are two baby-changing stations on the premises near the toddler play area.
- You can bring a stroller to the door but you won't be able to wheel it around the playroom.
- There is a snack bar here.

Extra Info

Fill out a frequent visitor card for your child at the door and earn a stamp for each visit and the eighth visit will be free.

Special Programs and Tours

This is a wonderful venue for a birthday party, though not inexpensive. They have private party rooms available and party packages designed for busy parents which include extras such as birthday invites, plates, cups, napkins, balloons, party hats and a large personalized banner for the birthday boy or girl.

Word of Mouth

In late 2010 Playtown opened a second space in Kwun Tong called Timegate, an Egyptian-themed indoor play arena. The address is: 9th Floor Crocodile Centre, 79 Hoi Yuen Road, Kwun Tong, Tel: 2258 9040. Check the Playtown website www.playtown.com.hk for more information on their new space.

Bumble Tots
The Waterside Mall
Unit 4-12, 1st Floor, 15 On Chun Street
Ma On Shan, New Territories

Tel: 2631-4001
Website: www.bumbletots.com.hk
For area map: Click on the above website, then click on "Contact" then click on "Here" for location map.

It can be hard in inclement weather to know where to take the kids to get out of the house and let them run off some of their boundless energy. Bumble Tots, opened in 2010, is a lovely, clean and bright 5,000-square-foot indoor play space which is a great alternative on a rainy day.

Designed for children 10 and under, little ones will have a ball here in the large play structure which has tunnels, slides, tubes, interactive games, a ball pit, firing cannons with soft foam balls, an enclosed trampoline, punching bags, a dance mat, ladders and spinning plates. There is also a climbing wall, a large selection of ride-on toys such as cars, bikes and scooters, a 'Bumble Babies' enclosed area for children two and under and mini tables and chairs covered in puzzles and games. There is even a coffee bar where moms and dads can have a latte, a snack and a well deserved rest while the kids amuse themselves with all Bumble Tots has to offer.

Admittedly, for those families who are coming from Hong Kong Island, it may be a bit far to come for a play. However, once you have made the journey, it is easy to make a half-day outing out of a trip to Ma On Shan by including a meal in the neighbourhood before heading home. It might be very exciting for the kids to play in a completely new space and make some new discoveries.

Seasons and Times
Monday-Thursday: 10:00am-7:00pm.
Friday, Saturday, and public holidays: 10:00am-8:00pm.
Closed on Wednesday except if Wednesday falls on a public holiday.

Admission

Monday-Thursday: HK$80 per child
Monday-Thursday (happy hour) 5:00pm-7:00pm: HK$50 per child
Friday-Sunday and public holidays: HK$100 per child
Friday-Sunday and public holidays (happy hour) 5:00-8:00pm: HK$80 per child
Monthly weekdays pass (Monday-Thursday excluding public holidays): HK$600
Monthly everyday pass, including public holidays: $800 per child
ALL TICKETS INCLUDE ONE ADULT ENTRY PER CHILD.
Extra adult (any day, any time): HK$40

The Best Ways of Getting There

By MTR

- From **Central** or **Admiralty** to **Kowloon Tong Station**, take the red line to **Mongkok. Transfer to the green line** (across the platform at Mongkok Station) to **Kowloon Tong**.
- In Kowloon Tong Station look for the **East Rail Line**. Ride it **one stop to Tai Wai** and transfer to the brown line (Ma On Shan Line) and exit the MTR at **Ma On Shan Station**.
- At **Ma On Shan Station** take exit **"A2"** (Horizon Suite Hotel).
- You will see a 7-Eleven on your right. Walk over to the other side of the mall atrium and **exit via the walkway** between the shops "I.P. Zone" and "Yves Rocher".
- Take **two flights of escalators down on your left** hand side. At street level, **walk left** (in the same direction as traffic on your side) **towards the green apartment blocks**.
- You will pass a public library and sports centre on your right.
- **Cross the road at traffic lights** and keep walking another 200 yards.
- Bumble Tots is directly above 7-Eleven at **The Waterside Mall**.

↔ Travel time: 50 mins (MTR) + 5-8 mins (walk)

By Car

- From **Central**: Connaught Road→Harcourt Road→Gloucester Road→**Island Eastern Corridor (Route 4)**→ **Cross Harbour Tunnel (Route 1).**
- In tunnel stay in right lane. Once through tollbooth (HK$20) stay right and follow signs for **Ho Man Tin and Sha Tin**.
- Stay in centre lane, you are now on **Princess Margaret Road**. Follow signs for **Sha Tin** and **Lion Rock Tunnel**

0-10

(Route 1). Go through tunnel (HK$8), you are now on **Lion Rock Tunnel Road**.

- After Lion Rock Tunnel you will follow the signs for **Ma On Shan and Tai Po** continuing to follow **Route 1**.
- Then take **Exit 11B** to **Ma On Shan**, you are now on **Route 2**.
- From **Route 2** you will be looking for **Exit 7** to **Ma On Shan and Sai Kung** and will take that **left exit.**
- Then you will find and follow the signs for **Kam Tin and Chung On**. Keep following signs for **Chung On** until you reach the roundabout.
- At the roundabout go straight through it, following signs for **Ma On Shan**. You are now on **Sai Sha Road**. You will pass one set of traffic lights; **at the second set of lights make a left** onto **On Yuen Street**.
- Then take the first left onto **On Chun Street** (note you will see a huge swimming pool complex on your right as you make the left hand turn and a primary school on your right after you turn). You will see **Bumble Tots** on your **left**.

P The parking "P" sign will be a left hand turn into **The Waterside (Mall) car park**.

By Taxi
A taxi to Ma On Shan from Central will cost HK$275-$300+ and take 45-55 mins

Getting a Bite
- Bumble Tots has a lovely little coffee and snacks bar for tired Moms and Dads to have a rest while their kids play. This is a great place for adults to hang out!
- If you are looking for a meal, head to *Sunshine Bazaar*, a surprisingly large mall just one block away from Bumble Tots. Exit the building on On Chun Street, turn right, walk up to the next main street which is On Yuen Street, cross at the crosswalk, turn right and halfway down the block you will find the Sunshine Bazaar entrance up a set of escalators to your left. Here is a sample of some of the dining options you will find here:
Pizza Hut, Ramen Noodle Shop, Chiu Chow Restaurant, A Sushi Restaurant, Kentucky Fried Chicken, McDonald's.

What's Close?
Tai Po Waterfront Park (this is in the same general area).

Comments

- Suitable for all kids under 10, including babies and toddlers.
- Plan to spend two hours or more in the play space.
- Not crowded during the week, but can become crowded on weekends and public holidays.
- There are sit-down style toilets on the same level of the mall as Bumble Tots (2 mins away).
- There are no baby-changing stations at the Waterside Mall (despite signs saying that there are).
- This area is stroller-friendly.

Extra Info

Bumble Tots gives out "frequent visitor" cards. After eight visits, your next is free of charge.

Special Programs and Tours

- Bumble Tots offer special party packages which include unlimited play at Bumble Tots, a decorated party room, personalized birthday banner, balloons and party accessories. The pricing does not include food, but they will help you organize the catering or you can bring your own. Contact the staff for more information.
- They also offer a discount for group bookings (that are not parties), such as playgroups. Full payment is required in advance to secure the discount.

Word of Mouth

Both adults and children must bring and wear socks in order to enter the facility. Make sure you don't forget them!

Open-Top Bus Tours

Big Bus Tours Hong Kong

Central Star Ferry Pier
1st floor, Pier #7, Central
OR:
TST East Promenade
End of Avenue of Stars (next to Starbucks)
Tel: 2167-8995
Website: www.bigbustours.com

Rickshaw Sightseeing Bus

Office: Admiralty (East) Bus Terminus, 95 Queensway, Hong Kong
Ticket Booth – Central Ferry Pier #6 (look for their kiosk and logo)
Tel: 2136-8888
Website: www.rickshawbus.com

This wonderful idea has finally made it to Hong Kong's shores! Previously the only open-topped bus we had in Hong Kong was for the short ride from the Ferry Pier in Central to the Peak Tram Terminus, also in Central. Now Hong Kong has not one, but *two* options for this excellent kid-friendly way to experience all this great city has to offer.

Choice is always a great thing when you are touring a city. Both of these tour operators offer the consumer something unique and cater to different needs and budgets. Though they both have similar open-topped double decker vehicles, provide air-conditioning on the lower deck and offer hop-on/hop-off service, that is where the similarities end.

Big Bus Tours is a comprehensive tour company that operates in London, Philadelphia, Shanghai, Dubai and Abu Dhabi. They offer three different routes in and around the territory: a Hong Kong Island City Tour, a Kowloon Tour, and a Stanley (South Side of Hong Kong Island) Tour. The passengers can get on and off as many times as they want and take as many tour routes as they like within a 24-hour period or a 48-hour period for only HK$60 more per ticket. The price of the ticket includes all of the following: Round-trip Peak Tram ride, Star Ferry round-trip ticket, free sampan ride, and a complimentary rewards booklet with discounts at retail outlets and restaurants around town. Big Bus Tours also offers a Night Tour in the Kowloon area (this is not part of the regular ticket price but a separate charge). Each tour has a running commentary in

10 languages available in each seat and provides individual headsets free of charge for every customer. This is a great way to experience all that Hong Kong has to offer in a fun way that kids will enjoy. The historical information that is shared will be interesting for everyone, adults too.

Rickshaw Sightseeing Tours is owned and operated by a local bus company called First Bus. They offer two different routes, both in and around the north side of Hong Kong Island covering the city centre. One route is called the Heritage Route (H1) and runs through the Central and Western Districts and the other is the Metropolis Route (H2) which covers Wanchai, Causeway Bay and Central. The biggest difference between this company and Big Bus is the length of the tour and the price charged. This company is simply offering transportation to fun places with a hop-on/hop-off option. There are no individual headsets but there is a recorded commentary in English and Chinese that plays over the PA system. They do not include any extras like tickets to other venues, however this can be a benefit when you consider that the price for the day is only HK$50 for adults and $25 for kids.

While these open-topped tours will likely appeal mostly to tourists and visitors, it is a very fun and enjoyable way to learn more about Hong Kong and get your bearings if you have just moved to the territory. It is also just a great fun thing to do on a hot day (there is always a breeze on top when the bus is moving) or with a child who loves riding in a fun vehicle. Even if you are a veteran Hong Kong resident, it can be lots of fun to be a tourist in your home town!

0-99

Seasons and Times
Big Bus Tours:
Hong Kong Island Tour – Service hours: 9:30am-6:00pm, runs every 30 minutes. Total tour time without getting off is 90 minutes.
Kowloon Tour – Service hours: 10:00am-6:15pm, runs every 45 minutes. Total tour time without getting off is 75 minutes.
Stanley Tour – Service hours: 9:45am-4:45pm, runs every hour. Total tour time without getting off is two hours.
Night Tour – Service hours: From Central Star Ferry at 6:15pm, from TST at 7:00pm, ends by 8:00pm (you can get off but there is no second bus to hop on to).

Rickshaw Bus Tours:
Route H1, Heritage Route – Service hours: 10:00am-5:30pm, runs every 30 minutes. Total tour time without getting off is 50 minutes.
Route H2, Metropolis Route – Service hours: 10:15am-6:45pm (Day scene), 7:15pm-9:45pm (Night scene), runs every 30 minutes. Total tour time without getting off is 50 minutes.

Admission
Big Bus Tours: Big Bus Tours (all) for 24 hours: HK$320 for adults, HK$180 for children (5-12); Night Tour or Single Route Tour (only one of their routes) HK$180 for adults and HK$120 for children (5-15). For HK$60 you can upgrade your pass so it's good for 48 hours instead of 24.
Rickshaw Bus: Hop-on/hop-off all-day pass: HK$50 for adults, HK$25 for children. Single trip fare: HK$17.40 for adults, HK$8.80 for kids (this is for going all the way around for 50 minutes and not getting off).

The Best Ways of Getting There
• Both tours can be taken from the heart of the Central District at the **Outlying Island Ferry Pier Terminus**. You will find **Big Bus Tours at Pier #7**, and **Rickshaw Sightseeing Bus at Pier #6**.

Getting a Bite
• The possibilities are endless as these buses go EVERYWHERE in Hong Kong. If you find yourself in one of the many areas that are covered by this book then have a look in the "**Getting a Bite**" section of that chapter for ideas.
• The Central Star Ferry Terminus has coffee shops, sandwich shops and restaurants if you get to the bus stop early and want a snack. Not a bad idea to take a snack with you on the bus for the kids, and a coffee for you?

What's Close?
Too many things to name.

Comments
• Suitable for all ages.
• Plan to spend a minimum of two hours for the Big Bus Tour and one hour for the Rickshaw Sightseeing Bus but with the

hop-on/hop-off option that both companies provide, this might be a whole day's outing.

- These tours normally do not sell out unless it is a public holiday.
- There are toilets at the Star Ferry Pier #7. It might be best to use them before you get on the bus.
- There is no baby-changing station in the area but there are lots of flat-top bench areas that could serve the purpose.
- Bring a stroller if you plan on hopping on and off or a baby carrier. If you are planning to stay on the bus for the round trip then maybe leave it at home.
- There are gift shops at nearly every stop the buses make.

Special Programs and Tours

Big Bus Tours offers excursion add-ons to their bus tours which include all of the following possibilities: Lantau and Monastery Tour, Madame Tussauds Hong Kong, Ocean Park, Afternoon Tea Set, The Peak Tram and Sky Terrace, Ngong Ping 360 and Hong Kong Dolphin Watch, Heliservices and DHL Balloon, Tasting in Hong Kong, Star Ferry Harbour Tour and Aberdeen Sampan Tour. Contact them on 2723-2108 for more information.

Word of Mouth

If you have very young children, it might be best to hop on and hop off a few times in different locations suggested in other chapters of this book that are child-friendly. It's probably best not to ride the whole way with young ones without getting off or they might get a bit bored.

Dialogue in the Dark – Experiential Exhibition

Shop 215, 2nd Floor
The Household Centre, Nob Hill
8 King Lai Path, Mei Foo, Kowloon

Tel: 2891-0438
Ticketing hotline: 2310-0833
Website: www.dialogue-in-the-dark.hk
For area map: Go to the website above and click on "Exhibition Address" and a map of the area will pop up.

In 1986 Dr. Andreas Heinecke, a German national, attempted to develop a rehabilitation program for his colleague who had lost his sight in a car accident. What he discovered in his efforts to assist his friend is that our modern society in general knows very little about blindness and because of this ignorance, discrimination against the sightless is unknowingly and unwittingly perpetuated. Inspired by the words of philosopher Martin Burber, "The only way to learn is through encounter", Dr. Heinecke opened his first Dialogue in the Dark exhibition in Hamburg in 1988. His goals were to lessen discrimination through empathy, to enhance the sighted person's experience through non-visual perception and to create a space where the sighted and blind could meet on neutral ground. By 1996, Dr. Heinecke had exported this unique exhibition around the world and today Dialogue in the Dark encounters exist in 150 cities across 25 countries.

In 2010, Dialogue-in-the-Dark Hong Kong opened its doors. This amazing 75-minute interactive exhibit takes the sighted person on a journey of discovery in a specially designed pitch-black 10,000-square-foot area which simulates for the sighted an experience in which for a short time they are completely blind. The tour is delivered by a blind guide who leads the visitors through each of the five different environments – a park, a sightless person's home, a market, a movie theatre and a café. Each of the areas is specifically created to enhance the sighted person's use of his or her other senses of touch, smell, sound and taste.

Dialogue in the Dark is a highly emotional experience for many; a worthwhile endeavour which is bound to inspire children as well as adults to spend some time contemplating the plight of others as well as grant them a greater understanding of the gifts we have all been given, which we invariably take for granted.

Seasons and Times
Tuesday-Thursday and Sunday: 10:00am-7:00pm
Friday and Saturday and public holidays: 10:00am-8:00pm
Monday: closed

Admission
Tuesday-Friday: Adults – HK$120, Students – HK$60
Saturday, Sunday and public holidays: Adults – HK$150, Students – HK$75

The Best Ways of Getting There
By MTR
- From Central or Admiralty take the **Tsuen Wan Line** (red line) to **Mei Foo station**.
- Take exit "**C1**", cross the street and turn right.
- Walk 50 metres and **take your next left**. Along the road there is the public library on your right, and you will pass a swimming pool on your left. Straight ahead of you is the **Household Centre**.
- Pass underneath the **bridge**, and enter the shopping mall via the **escalators**.
- ↔ Travel time: 25 mins (MTR) + 10 mins (walk).

By Bus
- From **Central** get bus **#905** from **30-32 Des Voeux Road Central before Li Yuen Street East** and alight the bus at the **Nob Hill Bus Terminus** directly beneath the **Household Centre Mall** where the exhibit is housed.
- ↔ Travel time: 60-70 mins (bus).

By Car
- Take the **Western Harbour Tunnel** (HK$50) staying to your left as you exit the toll booth.
- Take the **second exit** off the highway to your left which reads **Mongkok**, this is **Exit 2** (the first exit is not marked).
- The road will take you to the right and you will be on a land bridge and will be driving over the motorway below. Once

九龍 美孚 景荔徑8號

盈暉家居城2樓215號

8+

over it, stay all the way left and **follow signs for Route 5 toward Kwai Chung**. There will be a sharp left **exit** (exit sign is largely concealed by trees).

- Keep following **Route 5 toward Kwai Chung**. Stay on Route 5 until you take a left off the highway labelled **Lai Chi Kok and Shatin**. Follow the signs when the road splits for **Lai Chi Kok**. There will also be signs for Mei Foo. You are now on **Lai Chi Kok Road**.
- Stay to your left and make a **left on Broadway**. Follow Broadway all the way to the end (many twists and turns) where you will come to a **roundabout** (road dead-ends here).
- Follow the **roundabout to the right** (essentially making a right hand turn off of Broadway). You are now on **Lai Wan Road**. You will see Lai Chi Kok Park on your left and the Mei Foo MTR on your right. Follow **Lai Wan Road**, pass a set of lights, and at the **second set of traffic lights make a left** with the left turn arrow. You are still on Lai Wan Road.
- On the very next block you will come to a traffic light. Make a **left at the light**, now you are on **King Lai Path**.
- You will see **Nob Hill** on your right.
🅿 The parking garage is underground here at Nob Hill. Look for the big "**P**".

By Taxi
A taxi from Central will cost HK$170-$220 and take around 20-25 minutes.

Getting a Bite
- At the base of the escalator of the Household Centre are two bakeries which are a good place to get a snack or drink before or after your visit.
- The Household Centre also has a Chinese restaurant called *The Arch Banquet Hall* which is open for breakfast, lunch and dinner. English is not spoken here so you may need to get a bilingual customer to help you order your meal. The restaurant serves dim sum and other local Cantonese fare.
- Another option is to walk back to the Mei Foo MTR exit C1 and above ground you will find a walking/shopping street called **Mount Sterling Mall**. Here you will find a variety of restaurants including local noodle shops, *Ha-Ne Sushi* and a *McDonald's*. There is also a *Pizza Hut* on Lai Wan Road.

What's Close?
Lai Chi Kok Park.

Comments
- Suitable for ages eight and up (though it is something for each parent to consider as some eight to 12 year old children might feel anxious in this exhibit depending on their temperament).
- Plan to spend at least two hours here.
- Not crowded (they only take eight people at a time).
- There are nice toilets on the premises.
- There are no baby-changing tables here.
- The venue is not stroller-friendly though of course you can bring a stroller to the lobby area.

Special Programs and Tours
Birthday Party in the Dark, Dinner in the Dark, Wine Tasting in the Dark, Concert in the Dark, Executive Workshop in the Dark, and Dating in the Dark are just a sample of the other special experiences on offer at this very unique centre for learning.

For Educators
Dialogue in the Dark (DiD) runs special educational tours for school groups and other children's' groups. The founders and staff at DiD are committed to inspiring the next generation to understand the nature of diversity and explore their empathetic sides by creating programs which engage both their minds and their hearts and nurture understanding through personal experience. The three goals of their Educational Programs for students are:
- Discover their own potential
- Learn to appreciate diversity
- Learn to think innovatively

To apply for a special education tour, first complete the online application form from the website and send it to them three weeks in advance, via email (youth.edu@dialogue-in-the-dark. hk) or fax (2891 0136).
Teacher training sessions are also available.

Word of Mouth
Once your tour begins, you will be expected to stay with your guide in the dark until the journey concludes, unless there is an emergency. Going to the toilet in the dark is not one of the experiences that you will encounter in the exhibit so make sure you ALL go to the bathroom before you start your tour.

Chapter 7

Family Walks

Despite the fact that the majority of images that represent Hong Kong depict a modern sophisticated metropolis, in fact, three quarters of Hong Kong is still green! This wonderful city is a hikers' paradise with trails that lead through wooded areas, mountains, reservoirs and beaches, all with scenic vistas of the territory's natural beauty.

Though hiking opportunities abound in Hong Kong, young children and hiking do not always go hand in hand. The four walks covered in this chapter are the best ones for families because they are mostly flat, paved and offer attractions that young kids will enjoy. If you have older children who enjoy walking or hiking, Hong Kong has 24 country parks just waiting to be explored. For a list of all the parks and their respective trails, please check the Agriculture, Fisheries and Conservation Department (AFCD) website: http://www.afcd.gov.hk/eindex. html

No matter which walk or trail you choose, make sure that you follow normal safety precautions. Bring plenty of drinking water with you, always walk with a buddy, make sure to use mosquito repellent and sun block and bring a hat to guard against the sun. Plan your trip in advance so you know where you are going. Maps are always a good idea. For more tips on hiking safety, please see 'What's New/Highlights' and then scroll down to 'Hiking Safety' at the AFCD website above.

1. Bowen Road Walk
2. Pokfulam Country Park Walk
3. Tai Tam Country Park Walk
4. Sai Kung Country Park at Pak Tam Chung

Other chapters that include walks:

Victoria Peak
Stanley Village
Cheung Chau Island
Yung Shue Wan – Lamma Island
Sok Kwu Wan – Lamma Island
Peng Chau Island
Victoria Peak Garden
Inspiration Lake
Ma Wan Park and Noah's Ark
Deep Water Bay Beach
Repulse Bay Beach
Shek O Beach and Big Wave Bay Beach
Trio Beach
Hong Kong Wetland Park
Kadoorie Farm and Botanic Gardens
Lions Nature Education Centre
The Mai Po Wetlands

Bowen Road Walk
Bowen Road
(from Magazine Gap Road to Stubbs Road)
Mid Levels, Hong Kong

香港 牛山區 寶雲道
由馬己仙峽至司徒拔道

Tel: 2414-5555 (Leisure and Cultural Services Department)

Easy is the best word to describe a Bowen Road outing. This little walk is flat, fully paved and conveniently located, making it extremely popular for dog walkers and joggers, but also a fabulous spot for a family stroll.

Sandwiched between the buzz of Central and the tranquillity of the Peak, this Mid Levels walking trail is a breath of fresh air. Tree-lined and surrounded by the melodious sounds of birds singing (which are actually audible here) and little or no traffic, Bowen Road will make you feel like you are immersed in nature. Pretty views of Victoria Harbour, Central office towers, Admiralty and Wanchai residential buildings and the Happy Valley Racecourse are all part of the scenery, reminding you how close you are in fact to the heart of it all.

Bowen Road runs approximately five kilometres from Magazine Gap Road in Mid Levels all the way to Stubbs Road (near Adventist Hospital) in the Wanchai District. En route you will find a playground, a small park, a fitness trail, and two special places of worship – the Lover's Rock Garden and the Earth God Shrine.

If you can, begin your walk on the Mid Levels side. The first part of Bowen Road is residential, with traffic, but you will shortly come upon a paved trail at the intersection with Borrett Road (10 mins away). Once you pass the playground (another 10 mins), the rest of the trail narrows and is completely without vehicles. The next spot you come to is Bowen Road Park (10-15 mins away). This is more like a concrete sitting-out area with pavilions, stone tables and footbridges. If you are here in the early morning or late afternoon, look for tai chi practitioners perfecting their skills in the park. The first of 10 fitness trail stations starts here and more turn up periodically throughout the rest of the walk. Kids will enjoy having a go on the parallel bars, balance beams and other challenges.

0-99

Another 10-minute investment will get you to Lover's Rock, an interesting spot where locals come to give offerings related to love and romance. As you walk up the steps of this impromptu garden, you will find evidence of worshippers past and present, such as incense sticks, fruit, ceramic figures and decorated rocks. At the very top is the nine-metre-tall stone for which this garden is named. Much further down the trail, very close to the Stubbs Road exit, is another area of worship dedicated to the Earth God.

Seasons and Times
Year-round

Admission
Free

The Best Ways of Getting There
By Bus or Mini Bus:
- From **Central Exchange Square Bus Terminus** take bus **#15** going toward **The Peak**.
- Alight the bus at the **Adventist Hospital** bus stop and look for the **Stubbs Road entrance** to **Bowen Road** across the street from the hospital's driveway.

***Alternatively:
- From **Central Exchange Square** take green mini bus **#9** to **Magazine Gap Road** and exit at the mouth of **Bowen Road**.
- Look for Bowen Road on your left side shortly after the mini bus has made the turn onto Magazine Gap Road (the entrance is **just past the Peak Tramway tracks**).
↔ Travel time: 10+ mins (bus) + 3-5 mins (walk – to the entrance).

By Car
- From Central take **Garden Road** up to **Magazine Gap Road**. (Stay in the left lane on Garden Road until the road forces you to turn left. You are now on Magazine Gap Road.)
- You will make the first left off **Magazine Gap Road** and you will now be on **Bowen Road**. Bowen Road looks like it dead-ends onto a jogging path, but in fact you can drive here until you reach the playground.
    *(Tip: You must drive VERY SLOWLY as the road is only wide enough for one car to pass at once and it is **not** one way.)*
- Within 3-5 minutes you will reach the playground.

P There is limited metered parking at the playground.

By Taxi

A taxi from Central will cost HK$25+ and take 10 mins.
(Tip: Ask the driver to take you all the way to the playground area. This is where the pedestrian-only scheme begins.)

Getting a Bite

There are no snack stands or restaurants along Bowen Road. At minimum you will need to bring drinking water. If you would like to have a picnic, both the playground and the small park have tables that would be suitable.

What's Close?

Bowen Road Tennis Courts and <u>Police Museum and Coombe Road/Wanchai Gap Playgrounds</u>
*(Tip: You can walk from Bowen Road Park up a **very steep** path called Wanchai Gap Road, straight up to the Police Museum and adjoining playground. Look for the sign and the trail just next to the Bowen Road Park entrance; this path runs perpendicular to Bowen Road).*

Comments

- Suitable for all ages.
- Plan to spend a minimum of one hour here.
- There are two public toilets. One is at the playground (though these are of the hole-in-the-ground variety) and one at Bowen Road Park which has sit-down toilets.
- There is a baby-changing station at the Bowen Road Park toilets in the disabled bathroom.
- Stroller-friendly. (The only exception is the entrance on Stubbs Road where there are some steps to get down to the trail.)

Word of Mouth

If you are a jogger, this is a great place to come for a run. If you are with your partner or another mom and you both would like to have a run, why not take turns getting some exercise while the kids play merrily in the playground?

Pokfulam Country Park Walk
(From the Peak to Pokfulam Riding School)
Pokfulam Reservoir Road,
Hong Kong Island

Tel: 2508-1234 (Hong Kong Tourism Board)
Tel: #1823 (Agriculture, Fisheries and Conservation Department –
AFCD)
Website (with trail maps): http://www.hkwalkers.net/eng/trail_list/walkers_
companion/PokFuLam_Reservoir_to_the_Peak/Route_Map.htm

This trek is a great way to enjoy the great outdoors of Hong
Kong without committing yourself to a big day out. Butterflies,
turtles, fish, even horses are part of this gem of a walk that will
only take you about an hour to complete.

The entirety of the trail is paved and runs the length of the
mountainside that stretches between the Peak and Pokfulam
Road. The best option, if you have little kids in tow, is to start
up at the Peak and work your way downward. Look for the
trailhead, well marked on a tree stump labelled "Pokfulam
Country Park" (very near the Peak Lookout restaurant on Peak
Road) to begin. Within 20 paces of reaching the trail you will
have left the hustle and bustle behind.

The first half of the walk is a bit steep but very manageable,
even for little kids. Along the way you will spot a variety of
vegetation including many bamboo trees and some flowering
plants (in season). About 20 minutes into the trek, you will come
upon a fork in the road with posted signs and a trail map. You
will want to carry on to your right, following the arrows pointing
toward Pokfulam Reservoir and Pokfulam Road. As you
descend you will begin to notice streams and ponds on your
right side, all leading into the Pokfulam Reservoir (which you
will come upon about ¾ of the way into your walk). Once you
spot the reservoir, onwards from here the walk will be mostly
flat. Make sure to stop and look down into the water for fish and
turtle spotting.

Continue on the paved path. Once you exit the park, you will
be on Pokfulam Reservoir Road. Look for the Pokfulam Riding
School on your left side. Kids will enjoy going into the school

and having a look at horses being led around paddocks by children taking riding lessons.

There is another walk available here called the Pokfulam Country Park Family Walk. You will find the trailhead at the entrance to the park on the Pokfulam side. This is a nice flat walk that loops around the reservoir. The only issue here is that you must first climb a series of steps to get onto the loop. Look for the steps just near the trail map at the entrance to the park (on the Pokfulam side).

For older children or for more of a challenge, consider starting at Pokfulam Road and hiking uphill. The reward for your more strenuous effort will be that you finish your walk at the Peak where dining (and ice cream) options abound (see the **Getting a Bite** section in the **Victoria Peak** chapter for details).

Seasons and Times
Year-round, though the best time to hike in Hong Kong is from November to April when the weather is at its most temperate.

Admission
Free

The Best Ways of Getting There
For starting at the Peak
Please see **The Best Ways of Getting There** in the **Victoria Peak** chapter for options.

For starting at the Pokfulam Riding School, Pokfulam Reservoir Road
By Bus
- From **Central Outlying Island Ferry Pier Bus Terminus** (opposite Central Ferry Pier #6) or from **Central Exchange Square Bus Terminus** take bus **#7** going **toward Pokfulam**.
- Alight the bus at the juncture of **Pokfulam Reservoir Road** and **Pokfulam Road** (look for the sign for the Pokfulam Riding School on your left.)
***Alternatively:**
- From **Central Outlying Island Ferry Pier Bus Terminus** take bus **#91** or **#94** (which only runs Monday to Saturday peak hours but can also be picked up at **Central Exchange Square Bus Terminus)** to **Pokfulam Reservoir Road.**

0-99

香港　薄扶林水塘道

↔ Travel time: 15-20 mins (bus) + 5 mins (walk to the trailhead.)

By Car
- If you plan to make a round-trip journey of this trail starting at **the Peak** and returning to the Peak, then you can park in the **Peak Galleria** (please see **Victoria Peak** chapter, **By Car** section, for details).

By Taxi
A taxi from Central will cost HK$65-$85 and take 15-20 mins.

Getting a Bite
If you are starting from the Peak and walking down, a good option would be to pack a picnic. There are some benches in various places along the way where you can stop and have a bite. The Pokfulam Riding School has vending machines near the front entrance where you can buy drinks at the end of your walk. If you are walking up toward the Peak, there are many options to choose from (see **Getting a Bite** in the **Victoria Peak** chapter).

What's Close?
The Pokfulam Riding School and Pokfulam Family Walk.

Comments
- Suitable for all ages. If you have a child under the age of three, you will need to carry them on your back, in a backpack, in an infant carrier or in a stroller.
- The walk should take less than an hour going uphill, depending on your pace, and far less walking downhill.
- Not crowded.
- There is a public toilet on the walk near the section which abuts the reservoir. Though very clean, these toilets are the hole-in-the-ground variety. Try to use the toilets up at the Peak before you go.
- There are no baby-changing stations on the walk, but there are some benches along the way which could serve the purpose.
- You can push a stroller here as the entire walk is paved; however, the first half of the walk, from the Peak downward, is very steep and might be hard on your back. A backpack or baby carrier would be better options if you have an infant.

Extra Info
There are a few maps posted along the way to help guide you.

Word of Mouth
Bring some stale bread with you to feed the fish and turtles.

Tai Tam Country Park Walk
(From Parkview to Tai Tam Road)
Tai Tam Reservoir Road, Hong Kong Island

Tel: 2508-1234 (Hong Kong Tourism Board)
Tel: 1823 (Agriculture, Fisheries and Conservation Department – AFCD)
Website: http://www.hkwalkers.net/eng/trail_list/family_walk/Tai_Tam_
Family_Walk/introduction.htm
For area map: Go to the above website and click on "route map"

This tranquil trail requires a two-hour commitment (at least), but
it is worth every moment. Reservoirs, bridges, picnic and BBQ
areas, World War II relics and amazing vistas all await you on
this fully paved family-friendly walk.

You will begin your adventure up at Parkview, a large residential
community located on the eastern side of Hong Kong Island.
The trailhead will be easy to spot as Tai Tam Reservoir Road
leading to Parkview dead-ends into the starting point. You will
be looking for the signpost that reads "Tai Tam Country Park"
(but not the Wilson Trail, which is another trailhead). The walk
will take you from this eastern point, in a downward direction, to
the Tai Tam area on the south side of the island.

Tai Tam Country Park, of which this walk is but a small piece, is
named for the four lovely water basins within its borders: The
Tai Tam Upper, Byewash, Intermediate and Tuk Reservoirs.
Though the park itself covers a massive area (in fact it
encompasses a fifth of the area of Hong Kong Island), all of
the reservoirs are congregated along Tai Tam Reservoir Road
which is the route this trek follows.

The first third of the trail will bring you to Tai Tam Upper and
Byewash Reservoirs. Along the way, you will be treated to
beautiful views and many choices of picnic and BBQ areas that
were created with families in mind. These designated spots
are equipped with benches, tables and plenty of room to roam
about and explore or play for the little ones. Once you reach
the first reservoir, cross the dam and turn right. (Make sure
to ignore the signs for the Hong Kong Trail as it veers left.)
This next part of your walk takes you to Tai Tam Intermediate
Reservoir. The pavilion you will come to on your left side has a
great vantage point from which to view the largest of the four

basins: Tai Tam Tuk Reservoir. The last third of the trip takes you through some nice wooded areas and brings you out onto Tai Tam Road.

This large country park was a combat zone between Japanese and British forces during World War II. Relics from those engagements are still in evidence around the trail. Kids will enjoy the adventure of looking for military artifacts as you make your way down. They might also enjoy spotting the many fish and turtles that make their home in the reservoirs, so look out for them and consider taking along some bread for them or feeding them the remnants of your picnic.

Seasons and Times
Year-round, though the best time to hike in Hong Kong is from November to April when the weather is at its most temperate.

Admission
Free

The Best Ways of Getting There
By Bus
0-99
- From **Central Exchange Square Bus Terminus** take bus **#6** or **#66** to **Wong Nai Chung Gap**.
- Alight the bus at the **petrol station** and **walk uphill** following the signs to **Parkview** (you will pass Wong Nai Chung Reservoir Park on your right as you walk uphill).
  ↔ Travel time: 20-25 mins (bus) + 10-15 mins (walk uphill).

*****Alternatively:**
- Take the bus to the petrol station and then a **taxi** up to Parkview. A taxi from here will cost HK$20 and take three minutes.

By Car
The only reason to drive and park here would be if you are not planning to do the whole trail and will instead come out the same way you came in.
- From Central, take **Des Voeux Road** to **Queensway**.
- At Queensway (near Pacific Place) get into the far right lane which will take you across the tramway tracks to the right onto **Queen's Road East**.
- Stay on **Queen's Road East** nearly to its end and you will find the right hand turnoff onto **Stubbs Road** heading up the hill.

香港 大潭水塘道

This right turn will be at a stop light. (If you get to the Happy Valley Racecourse you have gone too far).

- Take **Stubbs Road** all the way up until you get to the **roundabout**. Once on the roundabout you will take the **second left exit** which will be **Wong Nai Chung Gap Road**.
- Stay on **Wong Nai Chung Gap Road** until you see the fields of the **Hong Kong Cricket Club** on your left side. Just there you will find a right hand turnoff for Parkview (take the far right lane). Make the **right turn** and **head up the hill**. You are now on **Tai Tam Reservoir Road**.
- The park itself will be on your right side shortly after the turn.

P For parking, look for a small blue "**P**" sign which will be your first left once on **Tai Tam Reservoir Road** (before you see the park). Stop at the guard gate at the top of the hill to grab a parking stub before heading down into the covered car park. From here, after you park, there will be a five-minute walk up the hill to the park entrance.

P ***Alternatively, continue up **Tai Tam Reservoir Road** past the park (on the right) and look for a small car lot on your left. There is a small metered car park marked by the trailhead of the **Wilson/Hong Kong Hiking Trails** (though be aware there are only a few parking spaces here and they get full quickly at weekends).

By Taxi
A taxi from Central will cost HK$50-$60 and take 20 minutes or less.

Getting a Bite
Packing a picnic or all the makings for a nice BBQ is a great meal option for this walk. If you decide you need provisions at the last minute, Parkview has a large ParknShop grocer on its premises. Another option would be to take a taxi or a bus at the end of the hike from Tai Tam Road to Stanley. There are many wonderful restaurants in Stanley to choose from (see the **Getting a Bite** section in the **Stanley Village** chapter). A taxi ride will take about five minutes and cost HK$20. You can also take a bus into Stanley. Bus **#314** runs to Stanley Beach Road from just outside Tai Tam Reservoir Road.

What's Close?
Paddle Boating – Wong Nai Chung Reservoir Park.

Comments

- Suitable for all ages.
- The walk will take you 90 minutes to two hours (or less with older kids) if you don't stop along the way.
- Not crowded.
- There are two toilets en route, one at the beginning and one at the end. The one near the beginning of the trail is brand new and has sit-down style toilets. There aren't any facilities in the middle of the trail so be sure to use the 'nice' toilet before you head out.
- There are no baby-changing stations on the walk, but there are many benches along the way that could serve the purpose.
- Stroller-friendly. If you have a child under the age of three, you will need to carry them on your back or in a backpack, infant carrier or stroller.

Extra Info

There are a few maps posted along the way to help guide you.

Word of Mouth

If you have very young children and you just want to go for a little walk and a picnic or BBQ, then consider walking a short distance into the park until you reach the first or second BBQ area. You can have a nice picnic there and turn around and walk back the way you came.

Sai Kung Country Park at Pak Tam Chung

(including the Sheung Yiu Folk Museum)
Tai Mong Tsai Road, Pak Tam Chung, Sai Kung Country Park, New Territories

Country Park Visitor Centre – Tel: 2792-7365
Website for Sai Kung Country Park:
http://www.afcd.gov.hk/english/country/cou_lea/cou_lea_ven/saikung.html
Website with printable map of Pak Tam Chung Nature Trail:
http://www.hkwalkers.net/eng/trail_list/nature_Trail/PakTam_Chung_Nature_Trail/Route_Map.htm
Website with printable map of Sheung Yiu Family Walk:
http://www.hkwalkers.net/eng/trail_list/family_walk/Sheung_Yiu_Family_Walk/Route_Map.htm
Sheung Yiu Folk Museum – Tel: 2792-6365
Website: www.heritagemuseum.gov.hk (under "Branch Museums")

When you enter the Sai Kung Country Park, you would never guess that the concrete jungle lies less than 20 minutes away. This area really is the true Hong Kong countryside and it is extremely family-friendly.

Located north of Sai Kung Town, Pak Tam Chung is an area inside the vast expanse of land (7,600 hectares) which makes up Sai Kung Country Parks East and West. Beyond simple enjoyment of the fresh air and peacefulness of this park, there are many fun things to see and experience for kids. All within a very short distance of one another are country trails, a playground, picnic and BBQ sites, a visitor centre complete with exhibits, and best of all a folk museum accessible only by hiking to it.

The Visitor Centre, conveniently located off the parking area and bus terminus, is a very good place to begin your outing. Your first order of business is to get a free map from the park rangers and ask them to help you determine a good hiking route for your kids, based on their ages and walking abilities. Have a look inside the centre while you are there and you will find exhibits that will educate the family on the Sai Kung region.

From the Visitor Centre, head out to do a walk or hike. You will need to walk down past the barrier gate which is the formal entrance to the park. You are now on a paved road called Pak Tam Road. On your right side you will come across a picnic and BBQ area which has a playground and is the entrance to the Pak Tam Chung Tree Walk. This easy 580-metre walk is a small loop peppered with various species of trees, most marked with interpretive plaques. This is a perfect walk for toddlers and small children.

For something slightly more challenging, continue walking past the playground on Pak Tam Road. You will shortly come to a refreshment kiosk just next to a bridge that crosses a stream. Here you will find the trailhead for the Pak Tam Chung Nature Trail, a 15 to 20-minute walk with an excellent payoff: the Sheung Yiu Folk Museum. Set on the grounds of a restored late 19th century Hakka village, this small museum (500 square metres) gives insight into the traditional home and work life of the villagers through the display of farming implements, an old lime kiln, pigsties, a cattle shed, kitchens, cooking utensils and furnishings of the times.

Once you have finished touring the museum, you can either return the way you came, or you can continue ahead and join another trail, the Sheung Yiu Family Walk. Along the way you will see the beautiful coastal scenery of the Sai Kung area. This trail will loop around past a portion of the Maclehose Trail to Pak Tam Road and back to the barrier gate.

There are many more hiking options in the immediate area. Check the map and then go exploring.

Seasons and Times
Country Park Visitor Centre – 9:30am-4:30pm daily, closed Tuesdays and the first two days of Chinese New Year.
Sheung Yiu Folk Museum – Monday, Wednesday to Sunday: 9:00am-4:00pm. Closed on Tuesdays, Christmas Day, Boxing Day, New Year's Day, and the first three days of the Chinese New Year.

Admission
Free

大網仔路　西貢郊野公園　北潭涌　新界

0-99

The Best Ways of Getting There

By MTR/Bus or Mini Bus

• From Central or Admiralty to **Diamond Hill** station, take the red line to **Mongkok**. Transfer to the green line (across the platform at Mongkok station) to Diamond Hill and take exit "**C2**".

↔ Travel time: 25 mins (MTR).

• From Diamond Hill you will have two options to get to **Pak Tam Chung**:

> #### Option #1
>
> • At street level, take bus **#96R** (ONLY on Sundays and public holidays). The bus will read **Wong Shek Pier** (via Pak Tam Chung).
>
> • Alight the bus at the **Pak Tam Chung Bus Terminus**
> ↔ Travel time: 45-55 mins (bus).
>
> #### Option #2
>
> • At street level take bus **#92** to **Sai Kung Town Bus Terminus**.
>
> • Once in Sai Kung you will alight the bus at the Sai Kung terminus and look for KMB bus **#94** going to **Wong Shek Pier** (via Pak Tam Chung), or mini bus **#7** going to **Hoi Ha** (via Pak Tam Chung), or mini bus **#9** going to **Lady Maclehose Holiday Village** (via Pak Tam Chung).
>
> • Alight the bus at the **Pak Tam Chung Bus Terminus**.
> ↔ Travel time: 35-40 mins (bus to Sai Kung) + 20 mins (bus to Pak Tam Chung).
>
> #### ***Alternatively:
>
> • Take a taxi from Sai Kung.

By MTR/Mini Bus

• From Central or Admiralty to **Choi Hung** station, take the red line to **Mongkok**. Transfer to the green line (across the platform at Mongkok station) to Choi Hung and take exit "**C2**".

• At street level, catch mini bus **#1A** (going toward Sai Kung) and alight the bus in **Sai Kung Town**.

• From here you can take a **taxi** to **Pak Tam Chung** or take bus **#94** as in *Option #2* above.

↔ Travel time: 25 mins (MTR) + 30 mins (mini bus) + 10 mins (taxi) **or** + 20 mins (bus).

By Car

- From Central: Connaught Road→Harcourt Road→Gloucester Road→**Island Eastern Corridor (Route 4)**→**Eastern Harbour Tunnel.**
- In **tunnel** (**Route 2**) stay in **far right lane**. Once through tollbooth (HK$25) look for **Kwun Tong/Tseung Kwan O Tunnel** to your **right**.
- Once past the first sign get to the **far left lane** and follow signs to **Kwun Tong/Tseung Kwan O, left to Exit 2A**. After the exit, the **road splits** and you will **stay right** following signs for **Route 7** and **Tseung Kwan O Tunnel**. Make a **right at the light** and follow signs for the tunnel. You are now on **Tseung Kwan O Road**. Go through the toll (HK$3) and **stay left in the tunnel**.
- You will take **Exit 2A** to the left with signs for **Po Lam, Hang Hau and Sai Kung**.
- Road will split again, **stay right** and follow signs for **Sai Kung and Hang Hau**.
- You will come to your first of MANY roundabouts.
- At the **1st roundabout**, follow the sign for **Sai Kung**.
- At **2nd roundabout** take the **1st left exit for Sai Kung**.
- At **3rd roundabout** take 1st exit with a sign marked "**University, Kowloon, Sai Kung**". You are now on Hiram's Highway.
- At the **4th roundabout** take the first left marked "**Kowloon and Sai Kung**". **Stay right** and **follow signs to Sai Kung** when the road splits; you are still on **Hiram's Highway**.
- At the **5th roundabout**, follow signs for **Ho Chung and Sai Kung**. You will pass Marina Cove and Hebe Haven Marina en route on your right. Hiram's Highway will turn into **Po Tung Road** which runs right into **Sai Kung Town**.
- Once you reach **Sai Kung**, continue through town. You are now on **Po Tung Road**.
- You will come to a **roundabout** (your **1st** after Sai Kung Town) where you will veer left. Keep following the signs to **Pak Tam Chung** and **Ma On Shan**.
- At the next roundabout (the **2nd** one counting from Sai Kung), veer left toward **Pak Tam Chung** and **Ma On Shan**.
- At the **3rd roundabout** you will see a wooden sign directly ahead that says "**Sai Kung Country Park**". You will bear right around the roundabout there heading toward **Pak Tam Chung**. You are now on **Tai Mong Tsai Road**.
- Stay on this road for 5-7 mins and then start looking for the signs for **Pak Tam Chung Visitor Centre** on your left.

P You will see a large parking lot next to the bus terminus. Parking is free.

By Taxi
A taxi from Central will cost $250-$290+ and take 60-75 mins.

Getting a Bite
There are several refreshment kiosks where you can purchase snacks and drinks in the park. The first is located at the car park and the second is located on Pak Tam Road at the trailhead for the Pak Tam Chung Nature Trail. If you want more of a meal, why not pack a picnic from home and have an alfresco lunch in one of the designated areas equipped with tables and benches. If you are really ambitious you can pack the makings for a BBQ, as there are BBQ pits available as well. If your kids don't want to rough it, head back to Sai Kung Town where there is an abundance of restaurant choices. (See **Getting a Bite** in the **Sai Kung Town and Hap Mun Bay Beach** chapter for details.)

What's Close?
Sai Kung Town and Hap Mun Bay Beach and Wong Shek Pier.

Comments
- Suitable for all ages.
- Plan to spend half a day here.
- The buses from Diamond Hill MTR and from Sai Kung can get crowded on Sundays and public holidays. You may have to wait in line to ride the bus.
- There are sit-down style toilets near the parking lot on the way to the Visitor Centre, and also in the playground area.
- There are no baby-changing tables.
- Stroller-friendly.

Extra Info
Should you wish to take a taxi from inside the country park to Sai Kung Town, you can call a Sai Kung taxi operator for a pick up: 2729-1199 or 2729-6600.

For Educators
The museum has guided tours available for schools and community groups. For details call the museum directly or fill out the booking form online. The Agriculture, Fisheries and Conservation Department provides conservation education

programs. For more information on guided walks, educational exhibits and video programs, contact the education unit on 2428-7137.

Word of Mouth

You may see some animal life here on your walks. We visited the first time in the summer and saw a snake on the path. If your kids are easily frightened by reptiles and bugs you may want to consider sticking to more open areas of the park.

Chapter 8

Hong Kong's Wild Side

Once you get outside the main urban areas of Hong Kong, a "wild" side of the territory emerges. Greenery is more prevalent than steel, and the wildlife that inhabits the countryside is available to be experienced by one and all. Whether you choose to see the rare pink dolphins or go bird watching in Mai Po, or simply take pleasure in the lush green landscape, natural wonders and creatures at other venues, an enjoyable day out will be in store for everyone. All of these outings require an investment of time and energy but are well worth the effort. Each provides educational opportunities for children which are always welcome, but above all they give kids a chance to see Hong Kong's creatures up close and in person.

1. Pink Dolphin Watching
2. Hong Kong Wetland Park
3. Kadoorie Farm and Botanic Garden
4. The Lavender Gardens
5. Tai Tong Lychee Valley Farm
6. Lion's Nature Education Centre
7. The Mai Po Wetlands (Bird Watching)

Other chapters with animals:
Ocean Park
Hong Kong Zoological and Botanical Gardens
Hong Kong Park
Paddle Boating at Wong Nai Chung Reservoir Park
Kowloon Park
Ma Wan Park and Noah's Ark
Yuen Po Street Bird Garden
The Goldfish Market

Pink Dolphin Watching
Hong Kong Dolphin Watch Ltd.
1528A Star House, Tsim Sha Tsui
(opposite Star Ferry Pier), Kowloon

Tel: 2984-1414
Website: www.hkdolphinwatch.com
Email bookings: booking@hkdolphinwatch.com
For printable maps: Go to website above, click on "Booking" then scroll
down to find the maps of the pickup points.

Yes, really, pink dolphins, and you and your kids can see them up close and in person. The more formal name for the animals is the Indo-Pacific Hump-Backed Dolphin, also known as the Chinese White Dolphin. Though no one knows precisely what makes the dolphins pink in colour, the theory is that they "blush" when they come to the surface of the water to cool their body temperature. Just grab a camera and a packed lunch for everyone and take a scenic boat ride to the waters off Lantau Island where you will observe these beautiful and graceful creatures in their natural habitat.

Hong Kong Dolphin Watch, a local tour operator, will take care of all the details for you. They will pick you up by air-conditioned coach at the Kowloon Hotel in Tsim Sha Tsui and drive you out to the Tung Chung New Development Pier in Lantau. En route you will be given an educational talk about these fascinating creatures. From the dock, a luxury cruiser will take you over to where the dolphins usually play and swim. The boat stays on the water for two-and-a-half hours so there is plenty of time to observe various pods of dolphins. On most trips you will be close enough to see the animals well and to take some memorable photographs. If you get lucky you might even see a mother and her baby.

The dolphins' habitat is right off the coast of Lantau Island, a stone's throw from Chek Lap Kok Airport. This provides a very interesting look at the coexistence of nature and modern technology. If you have not yet seen Hong Kong from the water this cruise will give you that opportunity. Just relaxing on board the top deck of the boat and taking in the sights around you can be nearly as rewarding as watching the dolphins.

This fun activity can also be a lesson in environmental protection for you and your children. These beautiful creatures are highly endangered. They face threats from pollution, habitat loss and boat traffic. Just by taking this day journey, your family will be helping to protect the dolphins, as Hong Kong Dolphin Watch supports World Wide Fund for Nature (HK) to support a dolphin research project and donates 10% of their profits to Friends of the Earth HK.

Seasons and Times

Tours depart from the Kowloon Hotel at 8:50am and return to the same location between 1:00pm and 1:30pm every Wednesday, Friday and Sunday. You can also meet the cruiser at the Tung Chung New Development Pier in Lantau at 9:30am.

Admission

Adults: HK$360; children (three to 11): HK$180; children under three are free.

Discounts: 50% off for local full-time students and 30% off for overseas students and seniors. You must pay for your trip at least one day in advance.

5+

Payment methods include: bank transfer to the Dolphin Watch account at HSBC bank; mailing in a crossed cheque; or going in person to the Dolphin Watch office in Tsim Sha Tsui to pay in cash or with a credit card at least one day in advance of your trip.

The Best Ways of Getting There

To take the tour bus:
- The bus will collect you at **the Kowloon Hotel** located on **Nathan Road** in **Tsim Sha Tsui.**

By MTR/Walk to the Kowloon Hotel
- Take the MTR red line from Central or Admiralty to **Tsim Sha Tsui station.** Exit the station at exit "**E.**"
- Come around the corner from the exit at street level to your right, looking for **Middle Road**, and you will easily find **the Kowloon Hotel** across the street from the back of the **Peninsula Hotel.**

↔ Travel time: 10 mins (MTR) + 2 mins (walk)

By Star Ferry/Walk to the Kowloon Hotel
- Take the Star Ferry from **Central** and walk from the **Tsim Shau Tsui Star Ferry Pier** to **the Kowloon Hotel.**

- After you exit the ferry walk straight ahead on **Salisbury Road** until you intersect **Hankow Road**.
- Make a **left** on **Hankow Road** and go one block until you find **Middle Road**.
- Make right on **Middle Road** and you will find the Kowloon Hotel on your left.

↔ Travel time 10 mins (ferry) + 10 mins (walk)

By Meeting the Cruiser at the Pier in Lantau
MTR/Walk
- **From Central station take the** Tung Chung Line to **Tung Chung Station**.
- Exit the station at exit "**B**" and walk toward **the pedestrian flyover next to the Ngong Ping 360 Cable Car station** to cross the road and follow the way to the seaside.
- Once you are facing the sea, **make a right** heading toward the pier on **Tung Chung Waterfront Road** until you reach the pier.

↔ Travel time: 36 mins (MTR) + 15 mins (walk).
(Tip: Another option, though I don't recommend it, is to take a taxi from the MTR station to the pier; however beware that while the taxi will only take a few minutes to arrive at the pier, taxis can sometimes be difficult to get and therefore you cannot predict the length of your journey which can be stressful as the tour will not wait for your party).

By Car
There is no parking at the pier and therefore this is not a great place to drive. It can be done however if you drive to Citygate Outlet Mall, park and walk (as above).
- From Central take the **Western Harbour Tunnel** following signs for **Lantau** and the airport, **Route 3**.
- Follow **Route 3** until it intersects with **Route 8** which is also the **North Lantau Highway**.
- Take the exit for **Tung Chung** and follow the signs for **Citygate Outlet Mall**.

P There is underground parking at the Citygate Mall.
↔ Travel time: 50 mins (car) + 15 mins (walk)

Getting a Bite
Lunch is not provided, though they do have tea, coffee and cookies on board. You should bring a bag lunch and some snacks and drinks.

Comments

- This trip is best suited to children aged five and above. Even for children over five, the trip can be long. The bus ride from the hotel is an hour or so in duration, and the boat ride is about two and a half hours. It would be a good idea to bring some crayons or a few toys for the little ones to help make the waiting time pass more quickly for them.
- This trip takes more than half a day.
- There is a sit-down style toilet on board the boat.
- There is no baby-changing station on board.
- Not stroller-friendly (though you will not have need for one on board).
- There is no formal gift shop. However, they do sell some souvenirs on board the boat.

Extra Info

Hong Kong Dolphin Watch spots dolphins on 97% of their trips, therefore there is a very slight chance you will return disappointed. If this happens, Dolphin Watch will take you again free of charge.

For Educators

Hong Kong Dolphin Watch can arrange exclusive charter trips for schools and other organizations. Contact them by email at: info@dolphinwatch.com for more information.

Word of Mouth

Most children who have seen dolphins before are accustomed to seeing them in aquariums and amusement parks where the atmosphere is "show" like. The dolphins you will see on this trip are in their natural habitat and do not perform any tricks. If these expectations are set in advance it might help to avoid any possible disappointment.

Hong Kong Wetland Park
Wetland Park Road
Tin Shui Wai, New Territories

Tel: 2708-8885

Website: www.wetlandpark.com

For area map: Go to the above website and click on "Ticketing and Admission" and then click on "Location Map."

With the world's focus on growth, industry and modernization, all opportunities to show our children a place that is completely about conservation and natural beauty are welcome, and perhaps some would even say – necessary. This 61-hectare wetlands park does an excellent job of demonstrating the diversity of Hong Kong's wetland ecosystem, as well as its peaceful beauty. In developing a place for us all to appreciate the natural wonders that exist right here in Hong Kong, the park's creators have hopes that we will all come away with a passion for conserving the natural habitats still left in Hong Kong and beyond.

There is much to do and see here, both indoors and out. A 10,000-square-metre Visitors' Centre which houses an interactive area called Wetlands Interactive World, as well as other interesting exhibits, and a 60-hectare Wetland Reserve, are the major centres in the park. If it is a beautiful day, start your visit out-of-doors and hit the Wetland Reserve. The grounds are easy to navigate and are set up in sections all meant to display a different area of wetland life.

(Tip: Due to the strong conservation message, the park will not provide a printed layout map at the park. Please go to the website in advance of your trip and print one out to take with you; or if you have an iphone or itouch, the app information is available at the information desk.)

It might be best to start your exploration by heading to the Wetland Discovery Centre which is only a few minutes' walk from the Visitors' Centre. This eco-friendly building is home to some pond life exhibits as well as the gathering point for a group of experts, called nature interpreters, who are on hand to direct you on your walks around the park as well as answer any burning questions. This building is also host to the park's free-of-charge workshops. From here you can pick one walk or several including: Stream Walk, Wildside Walk, Succession Walk, Mangrove Boardwalk or visit one of the three bird hides: Fishpond, Riverside or Mudflats. The paths are beautifully made using raised wooden planks and are as unobtrusively placed as possible, so that the animals are the least disturbed by our presence. Along the way you will see an enormous variety of birds, bats, butterflies, dragonflies, damselflies, fish, frogs, fiddler crabs, horseshoe crabs, and mudskippers. The hides are interesting and can be best described as buildings where humans "hide" to watch birds and other animals in their natural habitat without them knowing they are being watched. Bring binoculars along if you plan to go to one of the hides.

The Visitors' Centre is also filled with activities and exhibits kids will enjoy. Start in the exhibit area on the ground floor. These exhibits follow logically along and begin with "What are Wetlands?" There are real (but stuffed) animals from the frozen north to the tropical swamps, interactive screens, films, swamp community recreations which you walk through that include lots of live animals including crocodiles (don't worry – you are on the other side of the glass). The Living Wetlands exhibit is followed nicely by Human Culture which interprets our place in the wetland environment.

Once your party has a firm grasp on the answer to the question "What are Wetlands?" the exhibit cleverly moves you to a more interactive place called Wetland Interactive World. You begin your journey here by using the interactive computers to make a personal digital "entry" card complete with photo. Each of the interactive exhibits from here onward assumes that you and the children are reporters for Wetland Television. You will be gaining information as you move from one area to another on topics such as global warming, habitat loss, resources, pollution at the coast, mangrove destruction, coastal damage, coral reefs in danger, overfishing, etc. At every station there are games and other electronic tools which provide an education about each problem, disguised as fun. The reporter has to insert the card at each station and at the very end, the card is inserted into a final slot and the reporter sees how he or she has done in their 'work'. They can even email their results to themselves or to their friends.

0-99

新界 天水圍
香港濕地公園

The Centre also has a play area called "Swamp Adventure". This large double treehouse is full of climbing structures and tunnels for kids to play on. The downside here is that there is a strict height requirement to enter: No one is permitted who is over 1.25 metres or under 1.00 metre tall. Next to the play area, and just outside, is the home of Pui Pui, a famous crocodile that was found in the northwest New Territories in 2003 and proved very difficult to catch. Hong Kongers followed the story for days in the paper as the juvenile croc evaded capture. No one knows for certain where she came from but she is beloved by Hong Kong people for her tenacious spirit.

Before you leave, stop in the at canteen for a drink or a snack and take in the beautiful wetlands view from the floor-to-ceiling windows. Also, on your way out, you may want to visit the gift shop as it has several interesting scientific and educational games for kids that parents might not object to purchasing.

Seasons and Times
Park: Mondays, Wednesdays to Sundays, Public Holidays 10:00am-5:00pm
Closed on Tuesdays (except public holidays)
Ticket Office: 9:30am-4:00pm, closed every Tuesday (except public holidays)

Admission
Single Entry: Adults HK$30, Children (3-17) HK$15
Annual Pass: Adults HK$100, Children (3-17) HK$50
Half-year Pass: Adults HK$50, Children (3-17) HK$25
Annual Family Pass: HK$200

The Best Ways of Getting There
MTR/Light Rail
• From **Hong Kong Station in Central** (under the Airport Express Terminal/IFC Mall) take the Yellow Line (Tung Chung Line) and alight the train at **Mei Foo Station**.
• Transfer in **Mei Foo Station** for the **West Rail Line** to **Tin Shui Wai Station**.
• Alight at **Tin Shui Wai** and take exit **"E1"** or **"E3"** and catch the **Light Rail Train (LRT) #705** to **Wetland Park Station**.
↔ Travel time: 42 mins (MTR) + 10 mins (LRT)

By Bus

- From **Admiralty Bus Terminus** take the **#967 (Citybus)** to **Grandeur Terrace, Wetland Park Road.**
- From **Grandeur Terrace (housing estate)** walk to **Wetland Park Road**, turn right and follow the signs for the park.
- ↔ Travel time: 65 mins (bus) + 10 mins (walk).

By Car

- Take the **Western Harbour Tunnel – Route 3** (HK$50); as you exit the toll booth you will follow signs for **Kwai Chung and Lantau** and subsequently for **Kwai Chung and Yuen Long,** and all the while you remain on **Route 3 (West Kowloon Highway).**
- You will **stay on Route 3** from the tunnel for roughly **24.5 kilometres**
  (Tip: you will pass through the Tsing Yi Bridge, Cheung Tsing Tunnel and Ting Kau Bridge and then the Tai Lam Tunnel (toll $33)).
- Then look for the left hand **exit for Route 9**. This exit has no number but is labelled for "Airport Express Station, Yuen Long, Tin Shui Wai and **Wetland Park**".
- Stay on **Route 9 for 4.5+ kilometres**.
- Then take **Exit 15** marked for the "**Wetland Park**".
- Follow this road. **It will fork twice; both times stay to your right** following the signs for **Tin Shui Wai (N)**. This road is first called **Hung Tin Road**. As you bear left following these signs the road becomes **Tin Ying Road** which then becomes **Wetland Park Road**. From Exit 15 the Wetland Park is VERY WELL SIGNPOSTED, just **keep following all the signs**.
- The park **entrance will be a left hand turn off this road**, at this point called **Wetland Park Road**.
- P There is limited parking at the park ($8 per hour).

By Taxi

A taxi from Central will cost HK$300-$350+ and take 50-55 mins.

Getting a Bite

There is a canteen in the Visitors' Centre run by a local Chinese fast food chain called *Café de Coral*. They serve rice and noodle dishes as well as curries and grills, hot and cold drinks, ice cream and snacks such as chicken wings and spring rolls. Prices are very reasonable and the food hall has an incredible view of the wetlands. They also have high chairs available.

Vending machines with cold drinks are available in the Visitors' Centre as well as immediately outside the Wetland Discovery Centre.

What's Close?
Tai Tong Lychee Valley Farm is in the general Yuen Long area.

Comments
- Suitable for all ages.
  (Please note: Some of the large exhibits in the indoor area of the centre are best suited to those children who have already mastered reading).
- Plan to spend a half day here.
- This park can become very crowded on weekends and public holidays. Weekdays are the best time to visit this park.
- There are sit-down toilets throughout the park both inside and out.
- There is a mother's room for both baby-changing and for nursing near the information desk at the entrance to the Visitors' Centre.
- Stroller-friendly.

Special Programs and Tours
The park offers free-of-charge public workshops held at the Wetland Discovery Centre several times a day. They cover various topics and are normally 45 minutes in length and involve both a talk and a trip outside with your instructor to observe the things that you have learned. For instance, the one we attended was about "Pond Life". We learned all about the dragonflies and damselflies and their life cycles, as well as about frogs and toads and non-native Hong Kong snails and the havoc their alien status wreaks on the environment. After the powerpoint presentation, we went out to the pond to observe the animals. Most of the talks are given in Cantonese but roughly once a day during the week, the workshops are held in English. Check at the information counter when you arrive at the park to find out if and when an English tour will be offered.

For Educators
There are multiple programs set up for school children at the park, too many in fact to name. Go to the website and click on 'Learning at Wetlands' to get more information on what is available. The application forms are available online and

a response from the park administrators should arrive within seven working days.

Word of Mouth

The park is very strict about the height requirements for entry into the play area which they call Swamp Adventure. Your child must be between 1.0 m and 1.25 m to use the play facility. They must also remove their shoes and wear socks. There is a small slide in the area that is not part of the treehouse-like play structure where little ones under 1.0 metres can play while they wait. These restrictions create some upset for those children who do not fit the height requirements because they are either too big or too small, especially if their siblings or other accompanying children are able to play. Perhaps it is best to avoid this area if your children do not meet the height requirement.

Kadoorie Farm
and Botanic Garden
Lam Kam Road, Tai Po, New Territories

Tel: 2483-7200
Website: http://www.kfbg.org/
For area map: Go to above website, click on 'Visit Us' and then click on
the map provided.

There is no better way to learn about the natural beauty of Hong Kong, its native species and how to protect this beautiful land we inhabit, than to visit the Kadoorie's scenic mountainside farm and garden in the New Territories. Founded in 1951 by the Kadoorie brothers, the 148-hectare farm's original purpose was to help destitute war refugees earn a living through farming. It has since evolved into a privately run park whose stated mission is to "harmonize our relationship with the environment." The farm also has a stated vision: "A world in which people live sustainably with respect for each other and nature." It succeeds in its goals very admirably through the incredible job it has done preserving this site as an unspoiled piece of Hong Kong's mountainous countryside and through the animal conservation work it continues to promote and to foster.

The farm is full of sights to see that are especially appealing to kids, including all of the following: Pigsties, a wild boar display, a raptor aviary, a native mammals display, an amphibian and reptile house, a stream life display, an insect house, a parrot sanctuary, a flamingo enclosure, a wildlife pond, a chicken coop, a wildlife sanctuary with rescued deer, squirrels and wild boar, a monkey haven, an apiary, a butterfly garden, numerous greenhouses, an eco-farm which demonstrates organic farming methods, numerous nature walks, scenic gardens complete with waterfalls and pavilions, and a mountain peak lookout with incredible views.

There are also several permanent kid-friendly activities including an Art and Environment Workshop located in an area called Kwun Yum Garden, where children can create things using reusable materials. They will be helped by an instructor to make something they can take home with them such as a pencil holder made from old cardboard roll, a bookmark made of pressed flowers, an animal figure made from a toilet roll, a mobile made from recycled paper, etc. This activity is free of charge.

They also have a special treasure hunt set up for school-age children meant to teach the kids about the farm, demonstrate team spirit and make learning fun. At the reception area, one family, or group of 4-5, can have one treasure hunt map and booklet to use as a team. Together the team is meant to find 12 checkpoints around the lower area of the farm, do the tasks set out on the wooden treasure hunt boards, emboss the booklet at each checkpoint (to prove they were there), and bring the booklet back to the reception desk to be checked. After the team completes the activities the group will receive a certificate. The tasks are fun and educational. For instance, after walking through the eco-garden they are asked to name one good reason to eat organic food, or at a lookout spot they might be asked to write a poem about their surroundings, or to draw a flower which they see around them, etc. Kids will enjoy this challenge and learn something new along the way.

It is easy to navigate this huge farm if you have a mental picture of its structure. Built on the side of a mountain and running from street level all the way to the mountain's peak, the farm is divided into two distinct areas: the Lower Area and the Upper Area. The lower farm, as it is known, is the best spot to bring children. This is where the majority of the animals can be found, as well as the greenhouses, the eco-farm, the café and the Kwun Yam Garden which houses the Art and Environment Workshop. The lower area is also gently sloped, making it easier for little legs to get around without tiring too quickly. The middle and top of the hill have the butterfly garden, the firefly playhouse, the fern walk, the orchid sanctuary, several pavilions and the summit. To access the top of the park where the views are spectacular, you can either hike up (though this is a long and steep hike), take the free shuttle bus or arrange in advance for permission to drive your car up through the park. If you have kids who love to hike and commune with nature then head on up there, though most kids will be thoroughly satisfied with a day at the lower garden.

Bear in mind, this is not a petting zoo, nor is it a traditional "Western" style farm where you might find lots of grassy fields with cows to milk or sheep and pigs to pet. It is a fantastic

新界 大埔
林錦道 嘉道理農場

0-99

outing, but should be thought of as a conservation park with rescued animals and beautiful scenery. Preparing the children for this in advance will help avoid potential disappointment.

Season and Times
9:30am to 5:00pm daily. Entry not permitted after 4:00pm. Closed on Chinese New Year, Tuen Ng Festival and the day following Mid Autumn Festival. Closed early on Christmas Eve, New Year's Eve, Chinese New Year's Eve and 22nd of December (Winter Solstice).

Admission
$10 entry fee

The Best Ways of Getting There
MTR
- From **Central** or **Admiralty** to **Kowloon Tong Station**, take the red line to **Mongkok**. **Transfer to the green line** (across the platform at Mongkok Station) to **Kowloon Tong**.
- In Kowloon Tong Station look for the **East Rail Line**. Ride it to **Tai Po Market Station**. Take exit **"A3"** for the bus terminus or exit **"B"** for taxi rank.

↔ Travel time: 20 mins (MTR) + 20-25 mins (East Rail)

From Tai Wo Station you have two choices to get to Kadoorie Farm:

   By Bus
   - Take bus **#64K** (daily), **#64P** (Mon-Sat only) or **#65K** (Mon-Sat only) from outside the Tai Wo MTR Station to **Kadoorie Farm bus stop on Lam Kam Road**. The bus stops just outside the main entrance to the farm.
   ↔ Travel time: 20-30 mins (bus).

   By Taxi
   - A taxi from Tai Wo MTR Station will cost around HK$50-$60.
   ↔ Travel time: 15 mins (taxi).

By Car
- Take the **Western Harbour Tunnel – Route 3** (HK$50); as you exit the toll booth you will follow signs for **Kwai Chung and Lantau** and subsequently for **Kwai Chung and Yuen Long** and all the while you remain on **Route 3.**
- You will stay on **Route 3 for around 20 kilometres** until you see the signs for the **exit to Pat Heung** which will be

immediately *after* the toll booth for the **Tai Lam Tunnel** on your left.

(Tip: You must get in the far left lanes going through the toll booth or you will miss the exit.)

- Once you take the exit you are on **Pat Heung Road**. Follow the road over the overpass and it will shortly dead-end into **Kam Sheung Road**. Here you will make **a right turn onto Kam Sheung Road.**
- Stay on **Kam Sheung Road for 3-4 kilometres** and eventually it will **dead-end into a junction with Kam Tin Road**.
- You will be on **Kam Tin Road for about 15 seconds** when you come to a small **roundabout**. Stay all the way to the left and follow the leftmost road. Now you are on **Lam Kam Road.**
- Follow Lam Kam Road for several minutes and it will take you **up a fairly steep hill**. After you reach the top of the hill, and go over its crest, you will see **Kadoorie Farm on your right**.

P The car park is a right turn just after the main entrance. Parking is free of charge.

Please note: If you want to drive to Kadoorie Farm you must call them in advance to reserve a parking space. Also if you wish to drive your car up the mountain to explore other areas of the park that are not easily accessible by walking, then you must call them in advance to get permission to drive into the park.

By Taxi
A taxi from Central will cost HK$250+ and take 45-50 mins.

Getting a Bite
Kadoorie Farm now has a restaurant called *Sun Garden Café*. This is a beautiful place to sit and have a snack or lunch. This vegetarian, organic, alfresco eatery serves sandwiches, omelettes, soups, toasties, bakery items, hot and cold drinks and ice cream (they also have daily specials and when we were last there they served a pasta dish). You order at the counter and then take your food over to one of the lovely outdoor picnic tables complete with sun umbrella. The prices are reasonable and the food and the way it is served is environmentally aware. There are also vending machines around the property which sell drinks.

What's Close?
Hong Kong Railway Museum and Tai Po Market.

Comments
- Suitable for all ages.
- Plan to spend three or more hours here.
- The park can get very crowded on weekends and public holidays as well as on weekdays if a school is visiting.
- There are several sit-down style toilets around the farm. There is one very large one located up the stairs from the reception area. Everyone should use this toilet before proceeding onward as there are some great distances between toilets.
- There is a separate baby-changing room near the toilets that are up the steps from the reception area.
- This is not an ideal place to bring a stroller as the way to get from place to place is not always a paved path and quite often is a stairway. A baby carrier or a baby backpack would be a better choice.
- There is a farm store on the premises which sells some organic items as well as books on topics covered on the farm.

For Educators
Kadoorie Farm offers tours and programs for schools and organizations. Contact their Education Department on 2483-7110 or education@kfbg.org for details or fill out the PDF form for the program you are interested in by downloading it from their website.

Special Programs and Tours
The farm offers many tours and courses with families in mind. These tours need to be booked in advance of your visit and the programs normally require the purchase of a ticket unless the tour is for a school, then it is usually free of charge. Please visit their website for more information on planning a tour or event your children can take part in.

Extra Info
- The park offers regular daily shuttle bus service from the car park up to the top of the mountain and makes regular stops so people can alight and enjoy the scenery and then get back on the bus to explore another area of interest. The bus departs from the base of the mountain every 20 minutes from 9:40am to 3:40pm.

- There is no bottled drinking water for sale in the park. The farm is environmentally conscious and therefore while they are happy to provide visitors with water, guests must bring their own refillable bottles.

Word of Mouth
Stop at the reception desk and get a map (for a small fee of HK$5). This is a critical acquisition to get the most out of your visit.

The Lavender Garden and the Rainbow Organic Strawberry Farm

The Lavender Garden
DD76 Lot 655, Hok Tau Road, Fanling, New Territories

Tel: 2674-7822
Website: http://www.lavendergarden.com.hk
For area map: Go to above website and click on "Contact Us"
The Rainbow Organic Strawberry Farm
Next door to the Lavender Garden
Hok Tau Road, Fanling, New Territories
Tel: 9302-0258
Website: www.strawberry-farm.com.hk

There is *actually* a place in the Hong Kong countryside, near the Mainland border, where families can go and enjoy a walk though a small field of French lavender (also sweet lavender and others as well). This 160,000-square-foot garden offers a variety of down-to-earth activities that kids and parents will both enjoy. This is not a fancy place, in fact the beauty of coming to this lovely spot is to spend a few hours remembering what it's like to commune with nature and enjoy the simpler things in life.

The top draw here is of course the lavender, which parents will truly appreciate, as the photos you can take of your kids frolicking around these picturesque purple flowers is alone worth the trip out here. The Lavender Garden has many other activities beyond the lavender that kids will love, including: A very colourful kids playground with swings, slides and see-saws, a goat pen with adult and baby goats that you can feed, turtles and koi carp which can be fed, a goldfish game where you can take the fish home if you catch them, a candle-making stall, a water fun area with a few games, a fishing area with poles that you can rent (and if you catch a fish they will clean it and wrap it for you to take home), a plants stall where you can buy herbs such as mint, oregano, parsley, sage and more to start your own garden (very reasonably priced), and a farm right next door where you can pick strawberries (from December to April) and fresh vegetables year-round.

The Lavender Garden also has a large outdoor BBQ area which can be part of the experience. They have several marquee tents with individual BBQ pits and outdoor plastic tables and chairs where families can BBQ their own lunch or dinner. They sell several packages which include everything from the food to the charcoal to the plates and forks at very reasonable prices. Even if you don't have a meal here, the snack stand sells cold drinks and a wide array of ice cream which is a nice way to end your visit.

Right next door, and accessible through the back of the garden, is the Rainbow Organic Strawberry Farm. This large farm has strawberry picking from December to April as well as vegetable picking year-round. Organically grown produce such as watermelon, pumpkin, cucumber and zucchini can be picked by families and then taken home. Why not pick a bucket of strawberries and head home to make a pie or some jam? You will come home feeling like you connected once more with Mother Nature.

Seasons and Times
Lavender Garden
Monday-Friday: 10:00am to 6:00pm, Saturday, Sunday & public holidays: 10:00am to 10:00pm. Closed Chinese New Year Holidays, one week in July and others. Check the website for more details.
Rainbow Organic Strawberry Farm: 10:00am-6:00pm daily.

Admission
Lavender Garden – Monday-Sunday: HK$5 per person (under-threes free), public holidays: HK$10 (under-threes free).
Extras:
Fish, turtle and goat food: HK$5
Goldfish fishing: HK$10
Water fun games: HK$10
Candle making: HK$30-HK$40 depending on the size and style you choose. This activity is available only on Saturdays, Sundays and public holidays from 10:00am-6:00pm.
Fishing: HK$50 fishing pole rental with HK$50 deposit, plus if you catch something you can either BBQ it or they will clean it

新界 粉嶺 鶴藪路 香薰園
655地段

0-10+

P

for you, wrap it in fresh herbs from their garden, and you can take it home with you for HK$25.

Rainbow Organic Strawberry Farm
Entry fee: HK$10 per person, plus the fruit and vegetables you pick to take home will be weighed and priced separately.

The Best Ways of Getting There
By MTR
- From **Central** or **Admiralty** to **Kowloon Tong Station**, take the red line to **Mongkok**. Transfer to the green line (**across the platform at Mongkok Station**) to **Kowloon Tong**.
- In Kowloon Tong Station look for the **East Rail**. Ride it to **Fanling Station**.
↔ Travel time: 52 mins (MTR + East Rail).
- From **Fanling Station** you have two choices to get to the garden:

  By Mini Bus
  • From **Fanling Station** take exit **"C"** to the **#52B (Hok Tau) green mini bus**, which runs at 20-minute intervals. (The last bus is at 8:20pm).
  • Alight the mini bus before it turns right at the entry to **Hok Tau Village**. Walk straight along **Hok Tau Road for a couple of minutes** and you will see the Farm and the Garden on your left.

  By Taxi
  • From **Fanling Station** take exit **"C"** and catch a taxi to the Garden and the Farm. Just say "**Heung Fan Yuen**". A taxi from the MTR Station will cost around HK$40.
  ↔ Travel time: 15+ mins (mini bus) or 10 mins taxi.

By Car
- From Central take the **Eastern Harbour Tunnel**: Connaught Road→Harcourt Road→ Gloucester Road→**Island Eastern Corridor (Route 4).**
- In **tunnel** (**Route 2**) stay on Route 2 for **15.8 kilometres**. (You will go through the Tate's Cairn Tunnel).
- Then merge onto **Route 9** toward **Fanling** and stay on it for **13.5 kilometres.**
- Take **Exit 7** marked for **Sha Tau Kok** and **Fanling**. You are now on **Pak Wo Road** which will become **Jockey Club Road**.

- Follow the signs for **Sheung Shui** and **Sha Tau Kok** and this will take you through **two roundabouts**; both times you will choose the prong to **Sha Tau Kok Road**.
- Go straight along **Sha Tau Kok Road** until you get to the **third roundabout** where you will take the prong for **Lau Shui Heung Road**.
- You are now on **Lau Shui Heung Road**, go straight ahead until you reach the **top of the steep slope**, **veer left at the top of the hill** following the sign for **Hok Tau Road**.
- You are now on Hok Tau Road. The Rainbow Organic Strawberry Farm and the Lavender Garden are both at the end of this road on the left.

P There is free parking at the **Lavender Garden**. You can park there and see both venues.

Getting a Bite

The Lavender Garden has a large covered do-it-yourself BBQ area. You can purchase all of your food and drinks for your BBQ at their store. Their BBQ pavilion is fully equipped with tables, chairs and canopies which provide shade and they will provide the charcoal, paper plates, plastic forks, BBQ sticks and light the whole thing for you. All you have to do is cook your food. If you want to know about what they offer, have a look at the menu on their internet site. Call them on 2674-7822 if you wish to book your food and BBQ in advance (though this is not necessary). The stall also sells instant noodles, ice cream, cold drinks, snacks and a few toys. The fish food and the goat food can be purchased here as well.

What's Close?

Tai Po Waterfront Park is not far away. You will pass the Tai Po area on your way to or from the Lavender Garden from almost anywhere you might be coming from, whether it be Hong Kong Island, Kowloon, Sai Kung, etc.

Comments

- This outing is suitable for all ages, but will likely be enjoyed most by children who are 10 and younger.
- Plan to spend a minimum of two hours here.
- The site is not normally overcrowded though they do get tour buses that come through.
- There is only one sit-down style toilet at the Lavender Garden and it is located inside the handicapped bathroom near the snack stand. Make sure you bring your own tissues in

with you. You can purchase a pack from the snack stand in advance of your trip to the toilets for HK$1.

- There are no baby-changing stations here.
- The Lavender Garden is stroller-friendly, the Rainbow Farm is less so as you will be walking through fields.
- The Lavender Garden has a wide variety of plants and herbs for sale. You can purchase a lavender plant (of course) but also mint, oregano, parsley, sage and many more. The Rainbow Organic Strawberry Farm has strawberries (from December to April) and vegetables for sale that you can pick yourself.

Special Programs and Tours

If you are interested in growing lavender plants in your own home, the people at the Lavender Garden are happy to arrange instruction on how to grow lavender plants in Hong Kong. Ask at the snack stand for more details.

Extra Info

Please note that you cannot bring your own food or drink into the Lavender Garden. If you do not want to have a BBQ then why not pack a picnic and visit the Country Park just a few minutes' drive on the way to or from the park. You pass it on the way to the Farm and Garden. It is called Hok Tau Yuen Country Park.

Word of Mouth

This is very much a local Hong Kong experience. The people who run the Lavender Garden are lovely and friendly, but only a few speak English. This should not put anyone off coming, as most of what needs to be communicated can be done without language.

Tai Tong Lychee Valley (Farm)
No. 11 Tai Tong Shan Road
Tai Tong Tsuen, Yuen Long
New Territories

Tel: 2470-2201
Website: www.taitong.com.hk (though nearly the entire site
is in Chinese without English translation).

新界　元朗　十八鄉　大棠荔枝山莊
大棠山道11號

There is a place in Hong Kong where you can take your children to pick strawberries, ride ponies, pet and feed baby goats and rabbits and take an ox cart ride. Tai Tong Lychee Valley, located in the New Territories, offers families a wonderful day out in the countryside where kids can commune with nature and animals and take part in many enjoyable outdoor leisure activities.

It is important at the start to set expectations. If your children have been to petting zoos or organic farms in Australia, Europe, the US or Canada, this will be very different from those experiences. The farm, set on over one million square feet of land, was previously an abandoned piece of property which was resurrected by the Tai Tong villagers and is now a popular outing for the Hong Kong community. It is not fancy, nor does it cater to an expat crowd. The language, signs, food and general ambience are strictly local in feeling and flavour. When approaching this outing with an open mind, this can be a fantastic family day out!

Everything here is simple and down to earth. There is a small children's playground, a large goldfish pond, an elaborate climbing net made out of knotted rope with tunnels and bridges to climb and explore, a petting and feeding area which has goats and rabbits (food can be purchased for a small fee), an emu pen (you cannot feed them though), a Chinese sturgeon pond, a net fishing area where the kids can try their hand at catching goldfish (which they can take home), a lychee forest, a papaya forest, horse paddocks, short pony rides, a strawberry farm where you can pick your own berries (usually between November and April), an artist station where kids can paint an environmental bag or a small canvas (this area is open only on weekends and public holidays), a fruit tree education path, a

0-99

sightseeing tower, bullock cart rides, an organic products store, bike riding, war games (send an email for times and rules if your kids want to do this activity), three agricultural exhibition halls, a BBQ area and Chinese canteen.

There is enough here to keep everyone occupied for an entire day, after which the children will be begging for more. Don't forget mosquito repellent, sunscreen, a hat and sunglasses as there is not much shade to be found around the farm. The best time to visit is between November and April when the weather is more temperate.

Seasons and Times
Open daily: 9:00am-6:00pm
Closed only on Chinese New Year

Admission
Entrance fee to farm: HK$20 per person
Combo ticket: HK$80 per person which includes entrance and three tickets to use on any of the following: Food for petting zoo, pony rides or goldfish catching (net fishing)
Pony rides: HK$40/two rounds
Bullock cart rides: HK$20 a ride per person
Four-wheel bicycle: HK$50 for 30 minutes
Bicycle: HK$30 per hour
Strawberry picking: HK$80 per basket (entry of one child and one adult to the fields)
Painting environmental bag or canvas: HK$45 per person

The Best Ways of Getting There
By MTR/Taxi:
- From **Central** take the **red line** to **Mei Foo Station** and transfer there to the **MTR West Rail**, the **purple line** to **Yuen Long Station**.
- Alight the MTR at **Yuen Long Station** and take exit **"G1"** to the taxi queue.
- Take a taxi from Yuen Long Station to Tai Tong Lychee Valley.
↔ Travel time: 40 mins (MTR) + 10-15 mins (taxi).

By Taxi
A taxi from Central will cost HK$300-$350 and take 45-55 mins.

By Car

This can be a very difficult place to find; however, if you follow the directions below very carefully you will hopefully be able to avoid any frustration.

- Take the **Western Harbour Tunnel** (HK$50), **Route 3,** staying to your left as you exit the toll booth.
- After the toll booth follow signs for **Kwai Chung and Lantau**. This is **Route 3** which you will stay on for **24.6 kilometres**, following the signs for **Route 3 and Yuen Long** and as they appear. *(Note: you will travel through a tunnel and a bridge en route)*.
- **Exit Route 3 onto Route 9**. This exit will be on your **left**. The exit sign will read "**Yuen Long, Tin Shui Wai, Wetland Park, Shenzhen Bay.**"
- Once on Route 9, you will stay on this road for only **1.3 kilometres before taking Exit 13A** which reads "**Yuen Long**".
- At the **first traffic circle** you come to, take the **SECOND spur/exit which reads "Tin Shui Wai"**. You are still on Route 9 at this point.
- At the **second traffic circle** take the **SECOND spur/exit which reads "Yuen Long (S)". AS SOON AS YOU TAKE THIS SPUR/EXIT PUT YOUR LEFT TRAFFIC SIGNAL ON**, as you will take **an immediate left** which has a blue sign reading "**Tai Tong**". You will go over an aqueduct.
- Then you will come to a **junction at a traffic light**. Behind the light you will see a huge billboard advertising **Tai Tong Lychee Valley – 3.5km**. Here you will turn **LEFT**. You are now on **Tai Tong Road**, but there are few if any signposts (you will know you are on it because every few metres there is a bus stop which reads K66 and has an MTR symbol at the top of the post).
- About a kilometre later you will make a **LEFT turn onto Kiu Hing Road** at another billboard that says **Tai Tong Lychee Valley – 2.0km**.
- You will be on **Kiu Hing Road** for only about **30 metres** before you make a **left onto Tai Tong Shan Road**, where there is another billboard for Tai Tong Lychee Valley Farm.
- Shortly you will come to the **driveway of the farm**. You cannot miss it if you look for the **GIANT billboard with strawberries on it**. This is a **right turn into the driveway**. You will pass a military war games training centre on your left.

P Head up the driveway and follow the gravel road until you reach the car park. Parking is free of charge.

Getting a Bite

There are several options for lunch at the farm. There is a large covered BBQ area which has tables and individual-use BBQs. To do your own BBQing, simply purchase a BBQ buffet ticket at the counter and then go and get your gear and food and start cooking it all up! The BBQ ticket includes one drink per person, someone coming to light your fire, forks, tissues, a jar of honey and a brush to marinate your meat, plastic gloves, styrofoam plates, and plastic cutlery. There are many food options which are all-you-can-eat: steak, pork, chicken, chicken wings, hot dogs, fresh corn, vegetables, sweet potatoes wrapped in foil to stick into your fire, shao mai, bread (for toasting), honey.

(Tip: Start to BBQ before your kids get hungry as it takes a while to cook everything.)

Another option for a meal is the very casual Chinese restaurant right next to the BBQ area. They serve traditional Chinese fare in an alfresco setting. There are no other restaurant options in the vicinity so if Chinese fare or BBQ does not appeal to your kids, consider bringing a picnic of your own along.

What's Close?

Yuen Long Town

Comments

- Suitable for all ages though it will likely be a bigger hit with the younger kids.
- Plan to spend at least three hours here.
- The farm can get crowded on weekends and public holidays and even during the week when schools are visiting.
- The best toilets are located on the other side of the playground ropes course. They are all sit-down style but they are made for little kids. The kids won't have any problem, but they are small for adults.
- There are no baby-changing stations.
- Stroller-friendly.

For Educators

Tai Tong Lychee Valley is a popular trip for schools, particularly when students are studying farming or botany. Scouting organizations also find this farm a wonderful trip out to the countryside. For information on school group tours and visits go to the website and send an enquiry by clicking on "Contact Us" and sending them an email.

Extra Info

If you regularly use Google Maps to get around, please be aware that for this area the road names on Google Maps don't match the current road names. The maps are helpful to get only very general directions, East, West, etc… but the street names do not tie in and therefore trying to follow the names Google provides will get you lost and frustrated.

Word of Mouth

While the website is almost all in Chinese, on site the farm does provide a map/guide in English. When you arrive, head to the ticketing office and ask for an English map.

Lions Nature Education Centre
Hiram's Highway
(on the road to Sai Kung Town)
Sai Kung, New Territories

Tel: 2792-2234
Website: http://www.hknature.net/lnec/eng/index.htm
For area map: Go to the above website and click on "Location Map."

Visiting the Lions Nature Education Centre is a wonderful way to spend a day in the countryside with your children. Established to encourage the public to experience the beauty of nature and to promote environmental conservation, this lovely centre succeeds admirably at both.

Located on a 16-acre parcel of land very near the coastal village of Sai Kung, the Lions Centre offers a plethora of things to see, experience and enjoy. The exhibitions are many and varied and include: An agricultural hall about the life and work of Hong Kong's farming community, a fisheries hall which describes the marine resources of Hong Kong, the Hong Kong Geopark Visitors' Centre which introduces the geological features of Hong Kong, a countryside hall, an insectarium which reveals the habits of insects, a shell house with a very large collection of sea shells, a Chinese herbal garden with over 500 herbs, a field crops exhibition, a rock and mineral corner, a bamboo grove, a specimen orchard with over 30 species of local fruit trees, an arboretum, a fernery, a butterfly valley, a dragonfly pond, a fish pond, a banana grove and the Tsui Hang Nature Trail (a 0.8km loop) peppered with signs about the local vegetation. There is also a VMO (Vegetable Marketing Organization) stall at the Centre, where locally grown premium and organic vegetables are sold.

Start your day off here by stopping in at the information booth to arm yourself with a map. The grounds are laid out very logically. The exhibits are all located around a paved loop which is very easy to navigate and can be completed within a couple of hours. If you are short on time, 'must-see' highlights for the children would be the insectarium, the shell house and the exhibition halls. Don't forget to stop at the small playground and picnic area for a play!

Seasons and Times

Park: 9:30am-5:00pm daily.
Exhibition Halls: 9:30am-4:30pm daily.
Closed on Tuesdays and the first two days of Chinese New Year.

Admission

Free

The Best Ways of Getting There

MTR/Bus

- From **Central** or **Admiralty** to **Diamond Hill Station**, take the **red line** to **Mongkok,** transfer to the **green line** (across the platform at **Mongkok Station**) to **Diamond Hill,** exit "**C2**".
- Catch **KMB bus #92** going toward **Sai Kung**, or **KMB bus #96R** going toward Wong Shek Pier (this bus is only available on Sundays and public holidays).
- Alight the bus at **Pak Kong bus stop** on **Hiram's Highway** and **walk from there** to the Lions Centre following the signs.
↔ Travel time: 25 mins (MTR) + 30 mins (bus) + 10 mins (walk).

MTR/Mini Bus

- From **Central** or **Admiralty** to **Choi Hung Station**, take the **red line** to **Mongkok,** transfer to the **green line** (across the platform at **Mongkok Station**) to **Choi Hung,** exit "**C2**".
- Catch **mini bus #1A** going towards **Sai Kung**.
- Alight the bus at **Pak Kong on Hiram's Highway** and **walk** to the Lions Centre following the signs.
↔ Travel time: 25 mins (MTR) + 20-25 mins (bus) + 10 mins (walk).

By Car

- From Central: Connaught Road→Harcourt Road→Gloucester Road→**Island Eastern Corridor (Route 4)**→**Eastern Harbour Tunnel.**
- In **tunnel** (**Route 2**) stay in **far right lane**. Once through tollbooth (HK$25) look for **Kwun Tong/Tseung Kwan O Tunnel** to your **right**.
- Once past the first sign get to the **far left lane** and follow signs to **Kwun Tong/Tseung Kwan O, left to** <u>Exit 2A</u>. After the exit, the **road splits** and you will **stay right** following signs for **Route 7** and **Tseung Kwan O Tunnel**. Make a **right at the light** and follow signs for the tunnel. You are now on

西頁公路　西貢　新界
獅子會自然教育中心

0-12

Tseung Kwan O Road. Go through the toll (HK$3) and **stay left in the tunnel**.

- You will take <u>Exit 2A</u> to the left with signs for **Po Lam, Hang Hau and Sai Kung**.
- Road will split again, **stay right** and follow signs for **Sai Kung and Hang Hau**.
- You will come to your first of MANY roundabouts.
- At the **1st roundabout**, follow the sign for **Sai Kung**.
- At **2nd roundabout** take the **1st left exit for Sai Kung**.
- At **3rd roundabout** take 1st exit with a sign marked "**University, Kowloon, Sai Kung**". You are now on Hiram's Highway.
- At the **4th roundabout** take the first left marked "**Kowloon and Sai Kung**". **Stay right** and **follow signs to Sai Kung** when the road splits, you are still on **Hiram's Highway**.
- At the **5th roundabout**, follow signs for **Ho Chung and Sai Kung**. You will pass Marina Cove and Hebe Haven Marina en route on your right.
- Then start looking for **a large blue sign** on the left that reads "**Lions Nature Education Centre**." The arrow on the sign will be pointing to the right. **Make the right turn here**. You are now on a little road heading for the centre.
- There will be another sign asking you **to turn left into the parking lot**.

    (Tip: If you find yourself in the village of Sai Kung, you have gone too far and will need to turn back.)

🅿 There is free but limited parking at the Lions Centre.

By Taxi
A taxi from Central will cost HK$190-$220 and take 45+ mins

Getting a Bite
There is a cafeteria on the premises, run by the society for the deaf and operated by people who are hearing-impaired, which has a wide-ranging menu including spaghetti, sandwiches and noodles as well as a variety of snacks kids will enjoy. Be aware though that on a busy day the queues at the restaurant can be very long. Another option would be to bring your own packed lunch. There is a lovely picnic area which abuts the small playground, a perfect spot for enjoying a meal in the great outdoors.

What's Close?

Sai Kung Village and Hap Mun Bay Beach, Sai Kung Country Park and Trio Beach and Hebe Haven.

Comments

- Suitable for ages 0-12.
- Plan to spend two to three hours here.
- This park can become very crowded because many schools visit the Centre for field trips during the week and on Saturdays.

  (Tip: To avoid large crowds, call ahead to ask about the number of schools that have planned a visit on the day you intend to go there. School holiday periods are an excellent time to see this park.)

- The toilets near the parking lots and the ones near the Geopark Exhibition Hall have sit-down style toilets.
- There is no baby-changing station here but there are many benches around which can be used for the purpose.
- Stroller-friendly.

For Educators

The Lions Nature Education Centre offers guided walks for school groups. Contact the general line on 2792-2234 for more information.

Word of Mouth

You can bring dogs to this park! There is even a dog exercise area that your dog can play in.

The Mai Po Nature Reserve (Wetlands)
(Managed by WWF Hong Kong)
Mai Po, Yuen Long, New Territories

Tel: 2526-1011 or 2482-0369 (Public visit hotline)
Website: www.wwf.org.hk
For area maps: Go to the above website and click on "Mai Po" and then
choose either a map of the Mai Po Wetlands area or a directions map
on how to get to Mai Po.
For private tours:Martin Williams Tel: 2981-3523
Website: www.hkoutdoors.com
Email: martin@drmartinwilliams.com

Located in the northwest New Territories, sandwiched between modern Hong Kong and the bustling special economic zone of Shenzhen in Mainland China, the Mai Po Wetlands is one of Hong Kong best-kept secrets. An area of uncommon natural beauty, the World Wildlife Fund (WWF) site is known to be the winter home and migration stopover area for thousands of birds. In 1976, the wetlands were designated as an area of scientific interest and since then enormous effort has been made to safeguard this site for the preservation of the fragile ecosystem that thrives here, as well as for the enjoyment and education of the people of Hong Kong and its visitors.

The 1,500-hectare site is made up of a series of flat trails that lead you through shrimp ponds, fish ponds and mangrove forests where you can take in the beautiful surroundings while you spot various species of birds along the way.

Please note that the only way to access this natural wonderland is with a tour. There are several ways to do this. The WWF runs two different tours for the general public on Saturdays, Sundays and public holidays. One is called Exploring Mai Po and the other is Mangrove Boardwalk. Exploring Mai Po will take children ages four and up, Mangrove Boardwalk requires that they be 12 and older. Highlights of the Exploring Mai Po tour include taking in fishponds, bird hides, and a visit to the Education Centre all guided by an English-speaking nature interpreter. The Mangrove Boardwalk tour features the unique experience of walking on the floating boardwalks through the mangrove forest and stopping at a floating bird hide with a great view of Inner Deep Bay (the body of water between Hong Kong and Shenzhen), accompanied by a nature expert.

The other choice is a private tour with expert Martin Williams. You can expect to walk the trails and visit the tower bird watching hide as well as the floating hide on Deep Bay. He carries along with him a very high-powered scope that will enable bird watchers to get great close-up views of the birds as they wind their way through the marshes.

Seasons and Times
The Wetlands – Mondays, Tuesdays, Thursdays, and Fridays: 9:00am-5:00pm
Saturdays, Sundays and Public Holidays: 9:00am-6:00pm
Closed on Wednesdays.
WWF Tours: Saturdays, Sundays and public holidays (except the Chinese New Year holidays)
Exploring Mai Po: 9:30am, 10:00am, 2:00pm, 2:30pm (this tour will only permit children ages four and up)
Mangrove Boardwalk: 9:00am and 1:30pm (this tour will only permit children ages 12 and up).

5+

Admission
WWF Tours
Exploring Mai Po: HK$70 per person
Mangrove Boardwalk: HK$180 per person
*You must apply for these tours online by filling out the online forms and submitting them for each person in your party.
Private Tours
HK$2,300 guide fee for a full day per group. (This price is for guide fee only and does not include the cost of permits or mini bus rental.)

The Best Ways of Getting There
- If you take a private tour, your tour guide can arrange a mini bus for your group from the Tsim Sha Tsui area in Kowloon.
- If you take the WWF tour you will have to meet your tour in the parking lot of the Mai Po Marshes Reserve in the New Territories. The best way of getting there is to take public transportation.

By MTR/Taxi
- From **Central** or **Admiralty** take the red line to **Mongkok**, transfer to the green line (across the platform at Mongkok Station) to **Kowloon Tong**.
- In Kowloon Tong station look for the **East Rail**. Ride it to **Sheung Shui Station.**
- At street level, get a taxi to the **WWF parking lot in Mai Po** which will cost around HK$$70.
↔ Travel time: 20 mins (MTR) + 30-35 mins (East Rail) + 20 mins (taxi).

By Car
Be forewarned that if you are not familiar with the area, it is very easy to get lost. Directions and a map are available by calling the Mai Po Nature Reserve directly on 2471-8272.
- Take the **Western Harbour Tunnel** (HK$50), **Route 3,** staying to your left as you exit the toll booth.
- After the toll booth follow signs for **Kwai Chung and Lantau**; this is **Route 3** which you will stay on for **24.6 kilometres** continuing to follow the signs for **Route 3 and Yuen Long** as they appear. *(Note: you will travel through a tunnel and a bridge en route).*
- **Route 3 will merge onto Route 9 (San Tin Highway).** The signposts will read "**Yuen Long, Tin Shui Wai, Wetland Park and Shenzhen Bay**."
- From here you will be following signs for **Lok Ma Chau and Sheung Shui**.
- **Exit for Mai Po** is marked by a large sign for "**Fairview Park**".
- After the exit you will come to a roundabout where you will turn off following the **signs for Mai Po.** You are now on **Castle Peak Road**.
- Follow this road until you see the sign for the **Mai Po Nature Reserve** where you will **turn left and follow this narrow road to the WWF car park**.
P There is free but limited parking.

By Taxi
A taxi from Central will cost HK$280-$350+ and take 45-50 minutes. There are taxi directions in Chinese that you can print out when you fill out the online form for the WWF tours.

Getting a Bite
There are no restaurants anywhere near this area so be sure to bring your own lunch and snacks with you. However, there are

vending machines and a small snack kiosk at the visitors' centre near the parking lot.

Comments
- These tours are best suited to children aged five or older.
- Whichever tour you choose, this is a big day out involving lots of walking.
- The area will not be crowded, but the WWF tours do sell out.
- There is a toilet in the parking lot near the visitors' centre which everyone should use before departing, as there are no other toilets along the way. Bring your own toilet paper or some tissue with you as there may not be any in the toilet.
- There is no baby-changing facility.
- This is not a good place to bring a stroller; a baby backpack or baby carrier would be a much better choice.

Extra Info
Binoculars are available for rent at the visitors' centre for HK$20 each.

For Educators
Tailor-made programs for young students, both of primary and secondary school age, are available here. More than 400 school groups visit this area each year. Please contact a WWF education officer for more details.

Word of Mouth
Make sure you bring a pair of binoculars, plenty of drinking water, sun block and mosquito repellent. If your children get tired easily or get spooked by insects or reptiles, this is not a good place for them. Though the reptiles (like snakes) are not often seen, they do live in these marshes and there are bugs.

Table of Maps

Table of Maps

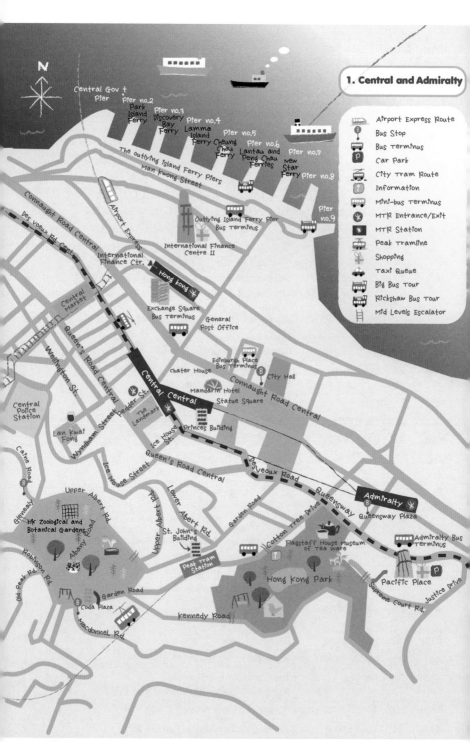

Airport Express Route
Bus Stop
Bus Terminus
Car Park
City Tram Route
Information
Mini-bus Terminus
MTR Entrance/Exit
MTR Station
Peak Tramline
Shopping
Taxi Queue
Big Bus Tour
Rickshaw Bus Tour
Mid Levels Escalator

Central Gov t Pier
Pier no.2
Park Island Ferry
Pier no.3
Discovery Bay Ferry
Lamma Island Ferry
Pier no.4
Cheung Chau Ferry
Pier no.5
Lantau and Peng Chau Ferries
Pier no.6
Pier no.7
New Star Ferry
Pier no.8
Pier no.9

The outlying island Ferry Piers
Man kwong Street

Connaught Road Central
Des voeux Rd Central
Airport Express
International Finance Ctr.
International Finance Centre II
Outlying Island Ferry Pier Bus Terminus
Hong kong
Central Market
Exchange Square Bus Terminus
General Post Office
Queen's Road Central
Chater House
Edinburgh Place Bus Terminus
City Hall
Connaught Road Central
Wellington St.
Central Central
Mandarin Hotel
Statue Square
Central Police Station
Pedder St.
The Landmark
Lan Kwai Fong
Wyndham Street
Ice House St.
Princes Building
Ice House Street
Queen's Road Central
Deveoux Road
Admiralty
Queensway
Queensway Plaza
Cathe Road
Glenealy
Upper Albert Rd.
Rd Lower Albert Rd.
St. John's Building
Garden Road
Cotton Tree Drive
Flagstaff House Museum of Tea Ware
Admiralty Bus Terminus
HK Zoological and Botanical Gardens
Albany Road
Peak Tram Station
Hong kong Park
Pacific Place
Robinson Rd.
Old Peak Rd.
Garden Road
Coda Plaza
Macdonnel Rd.
kennedy Road
Supreme Court Rd.
Justice Drive

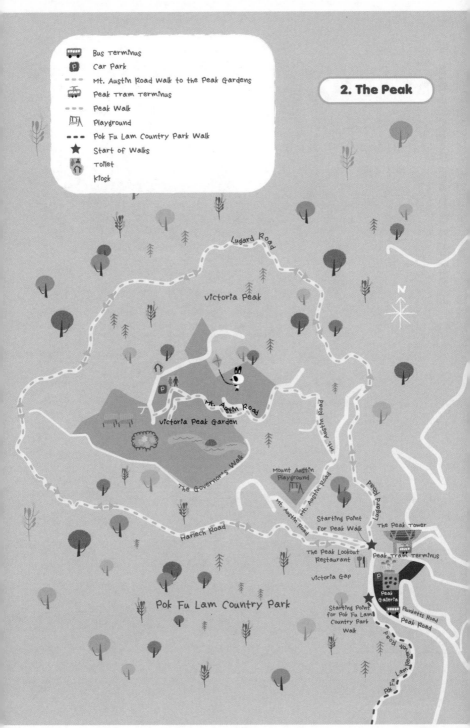

Legend

- Bus Terminus
- Car Park
- Mt. Austin Road Walk to the Peak Gardens
- Peak Tram Terminus
- Peak Walk
- Playground
- Pok Fu Lam Country Park Walk
- Start of Walks
- Toilet
- Kiosk

2. The Peak

Lugard Road

Victoria Peak

Mt. Austin Road

Mt. Austin Road

Victoria Peak Garden

The Governor's Walk

Mount Austin Playground

Mt. Austin Road

Mt. Austin Road

Starting Point for Peak Walk

The Peak Tower

Findlay Road

Harlech Road

The Peak Lookout Restaurant

Victoria Gap

Peak Tram Terminus

Pok Fu Lam Country Park

Peak Galleria

Starting Point for Pok Fu Lam Country Park Walk

Plunketts Road

Peak Road

Pok Fu Lam Reservoir Road

N

Legend:
- Bus Stop
- Cars are allowed
- Car Park
- For Pedestrians Only
- Peak tram
- Peak tramway
- Playground
- Steps

Garden Road

Magazine Gap Road

Borrett Rd.
Bowen Road
Borrett Rd.

Bowen Drive

Tennis Court

Bowen Road

Kennedy Road

Bowen Road

Peak Road

Peak Road

Magazine Gap Road

Coombe Road Playground

Coombe Road

Police Museum

Magazine Gap

Peak Road

Aberdeen Country Park

Wanchai Gap Playground

Mount Cameron Road

Middle Gap Road

Coombe Rd.

Wan Chai Gap

Wanchai Gap

Stubbs Road

Black's Link

Aberdeen Country Park

Wan Chai Gap Rd.

Bowen Road Park

Bowen Road

Lover's Rock

Bowen Road

Kennedy Road

Stubbs Road

Earth God Shrine

Lower Stubbs Road

Mt. Nicholson Road

Black's Link

Stubbs Road

Bowen Rd. Road

Stubbs Road

Hong Kong Adventist Hospital

Tai Hang Road

Wong Nai Chung Rd.

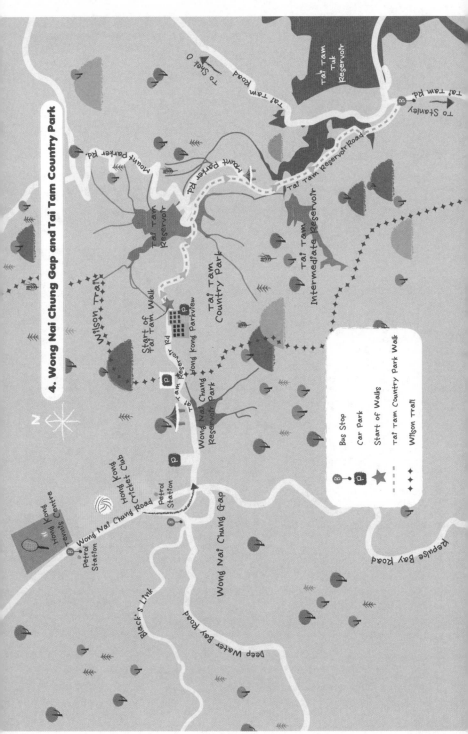

4. Wong Nai Chung Gap and Tai Tam Country Park

Tai Tam Tuk Reservoir

Tai Tam Road

To Shek O

Tai Tam Rd

To Stanley

Tai Tam Reservoir Road

Mount Parker Rd.

Mount Parker Rd.

Tai Tam Reservoir

Wilson Trail

Start of Tai Tam Walk

Tai Tam Road

Hong Kong Parkview

Tai Tam Country Park

Tai Tam Intermediate Reservoir

Tai Tam Reservoir Rd

Wong Nai Chung Reservoir Park

Hong Kong Cricket Club

Hong Kong Centre

Tennis Centre

Petrol Station

Wong Nai Chung Road

Petrol Station

Wong Nai Chung Gap

Black's Link

Deep Water Bay Road

Repulse Bay Road

Legend

B	Bus Stop
P	Car Park
★	Start of Walks
- - -	Tai Tam Country Park Walk
+ + +	Wilson Trail

N

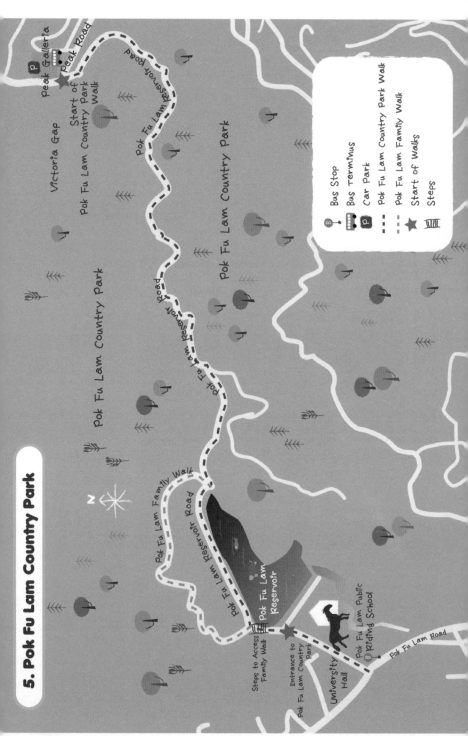

Peak Galleria

Peak Road

Reservoir Road

Victoria Gap

Start of
Pok Fu Lam Country Park Walk

Pok Fu Lam Country Park

Pok Fu Lam Country Park

Pok Fu Lam Country Park

Pok Fu Lam Reservoir Road

Pok Fu Lam Family Walk

Pok Fu Lam Reservoir Road

Pok Fu Lam Reservoir

Steps to Access Family Walk

Entrance to
Pok Fu Lam Country Park

Pok Fu Lam Family Walk

University Hall

Pok Fu Lam Public Riding School

Pok Fu Lam Road

N

Bus Stop
Bus Terminus
Car Park
Pok Fu Lam Country Park Walk
Pok Fu Lam Family Walk
Start of Walks
Steps

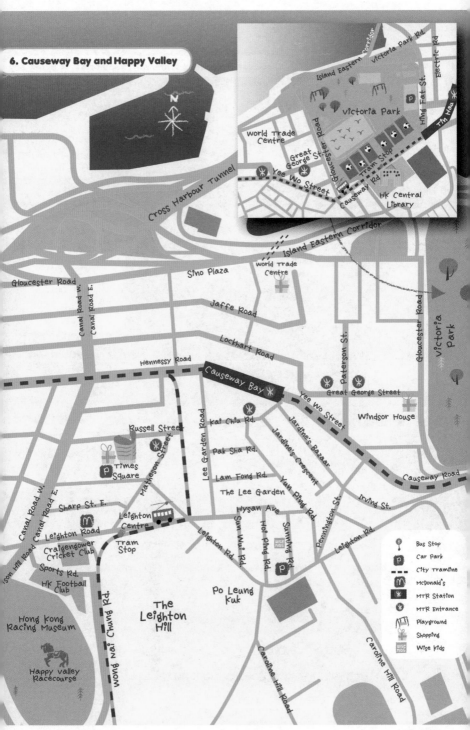

Island Eastern Corridor

Victoria Park Rd.

Electric Rd.

World Trade Centre

Great George St. Centre

Gloucester Road

Tram Stop

Hing Fat St.

Tin Hau

Victoria Park

P

HK Central Library

Yee Wo Street

Causeway Rd.

Cross Harbour Tunnel

Island Eastern Corridor

Gloucester Road W.

Canal Road E.
Canal Road E.

Sino Plaza

World Trade Centre

Jaffe Road

Lockhart Road

Paterson St.

Gloucester Road

Victoria Park

Hennessy Road

Causeway Bay

Yee Wo Street

Great George Street

Windsor House

Kai Chiu Rd.

Russell Street

Lee Garden Road

Matheson Street

Pak Sha Rd.

Jardine's Bazaar

Jardine's Crescent

Causeway Road

P
Times Square

Lam Fong Rd.

The Lee Garden

Yun Ping Rd.

Irving St.

Pennington St.

Sharp St. E.

Canal Road W.
Canal Road E.

Leighton Centre

Hysan Ave.

Sun Wui Rd.

Hoi Ping Rd.

Sunning Rd.

Leighton Rd.

M
Leighton Road

Tram Stop

Leighton Rd.

P

Leighton Rd.

Craigengower Cricket Club

Son Hill Road

Sports Rd.

HK Football Club

Po Leung Kuk

Wong Nai Chung Rd.

The Leighton Hill

Hong Kong Racing Museum

Happy Valley Racecourse

Caroline Hill Road

Caroline Hill Road

🚌	Bus Stop
P	Car Park
- - -	City Tramline
M	McDonald's
🚇	MTR Station
Ⓜ	MTR Entrance
⛩	Playground
🎁	Shopping
WISE KIDS	Wise Kids

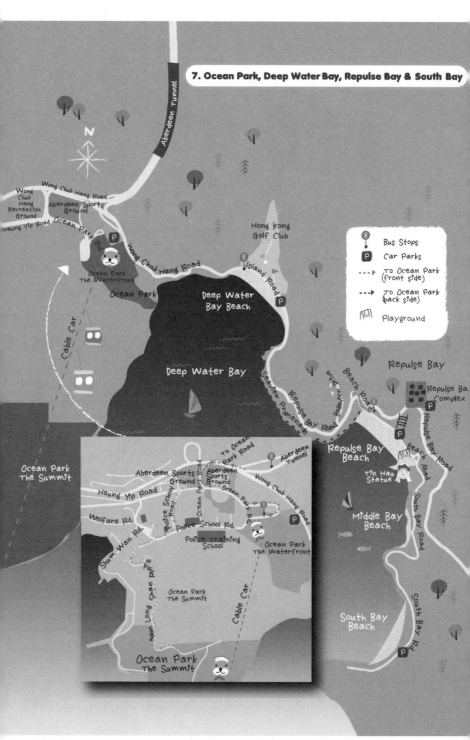

7. Ocean Park, Deep Water Bay, Repulse Bay & South Bay

N

Aberdeen Tunnel

Wong Chuk Hang Road
Wong Chuk Hang Recreation Ground
Aberdeen Sports Ground
Heung Yip Road   Ocean Park

Wong Chuk Hang Road

Ocean Park The Waterfront
Ocean Park

Hong Kong Golf Club

Island Road

Deep Water Bay Beach

Cable Car

Deep Water Bay

Ocean Park The Summit

Bus Stops
Car Parks
To Ocean Park (front side)
To Ocean Park (back side)
Playground

Repulse Bay

Repulse Bay Complex

Seaview Promenade
Repulse Bay Road
Belleview Drive
Beach Road

Repulse Bay Beach

Tin Hau Statue

Middle Bay Beach

Beach Road
Repulse Bay Road
South Bay Road

To Ocean Park Road
Aberdeen Sports Ground
Aberdeen Sports Ground
Aberdeen Tunnel
Wong Chuk Hang Road
Ocean Park Rd.
Ocean Park Road
Police School Road
Heung Yip Road
Welfare Rd.
Shum Wan Rd.
Police School Rd.
Police Training School
Ocean Park The Waterfront
Man Long Shan Road
Ocean Park The Summit
Cable Car
Ocean Park The Summit

South Bay Beach

South Bay Rd.

388

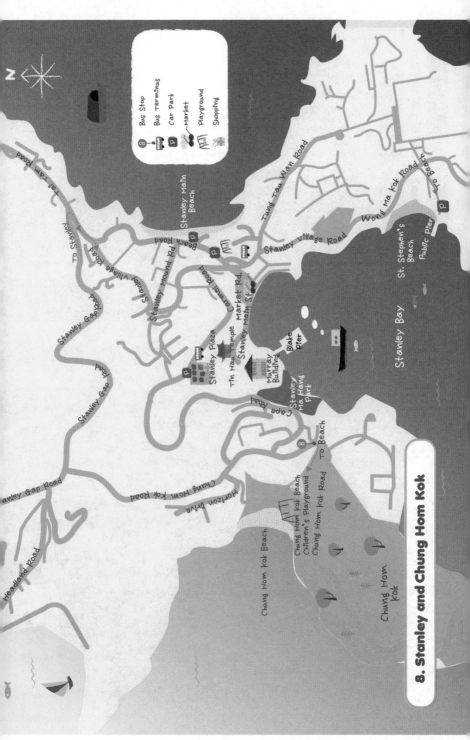

Legend:
- B — Bus Stop
- Bus Terminus
- P — Car Park
- Market
- Playground
- Shopping

Tai Tam Road

To St

Stanley Village Road

Stanley Gap Road

Road

Stanley Gap

Stanley Gap Road

Headland Road

Stanley Village Road

Stanley Mound Rd

Beach Road

Carmel Road

Stanley Main Beach

Stanley Village Road

Tung-Tau Wan Road

Wong Ma Kok Road

To Beach

St. Stephen's Beach

Public Pier

Stanley Bay

Stanley Market Rd

Stanley Main St

Stanley Plaza

Tin Hau Temple

Murray Building

Blake Pier

Stanley Ma Hang Park

Cape Road

Road

Horizon Drive

Chung Hom Kok Road

To Beach

Chung Hom Kok Beach

Chung Hom Kok Beach

Children's Playground

Chung Hom Kok Road

Chung Hom Kok

Chung Hom Kok

8. Stanley and Chung Hom Kok

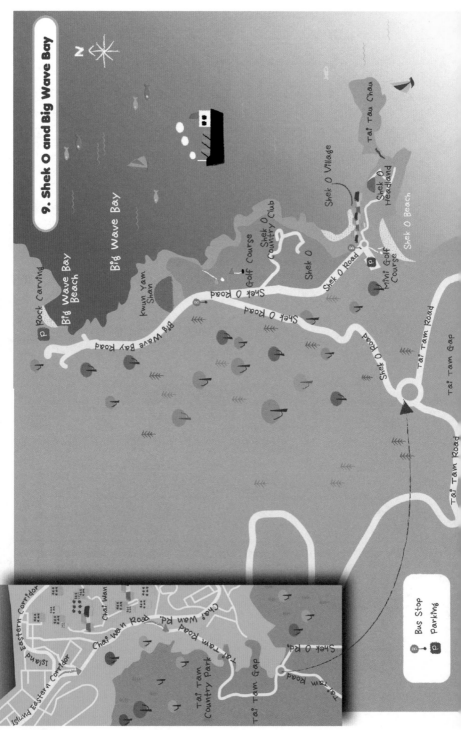

Rock Carving

Big Wave Bay Beach

Big Wave Bay

Kwun Yam Shan

Shek O Golf Course

Shek O Country Club

Shek O

Shek O Village

Shek O Headland

Shek O Beach

Mini Golf Course

Big Wave Bay Road

Shek O Road

Shek O Road

Shek O Road

Tai Tam Road

Tai Tam Gap

Tai Tam Road

Tai Tau Chau

Island Eastern Corridor

Island Eastern Corridor

Chai Wan

Chai Wan

Chai Wan Road

Chai Wan Road Rd.

Tai Tam Road

Tai Tam Country Park

Tai Tam Gap

Shek O Rd.

Tai Tam Road

Tai Tam Road

Bus Stop

Parking

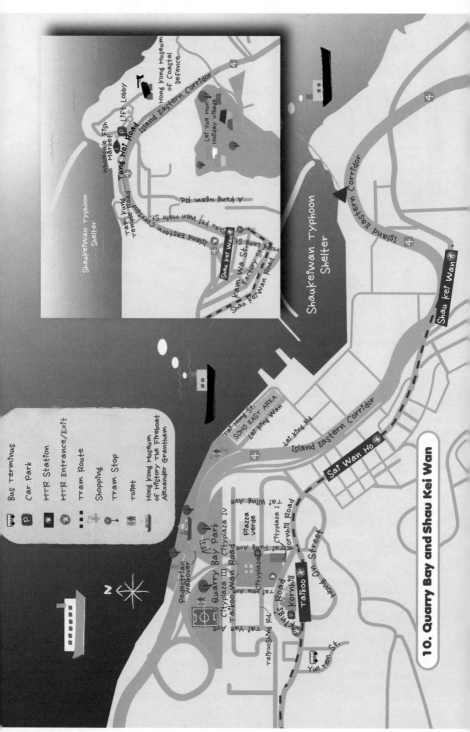

10. Quarry Bay and Shau Kei Wan

Legend:
- Bus Terminus
- Car Park
- MTR Station
- MTR Entrance/Exit
- Tram Route
- Shopping
- Tram Stop
- Toilet
- Hong Kong Museum of History the Fireboat Alexander Grantham

N

Ferry

Shaukei'wan Typhoon Shelter

Wholesale Fish Market
Tung Hei Road
P Lift Lobby
Tam Kung Temple Road
Island Eastern Corridor
Hong Kong Museum of Coastal Defence
Lei Yue Mun Holiday Village
A Kung Ngam Rd.
Island Eastern Corridor
Shau Kei Wan Main St.
Shau Kei Wan
Kam Wa St.
Factory St.
Shau Kei Wan Road

Shaukei'wan Typhoon Shelter
Shau Kei Wan
Island Eastern Corridor
Island Eastern Corridor

Tai Hong St.
SOHO EAST AREA
Lei King Wan
Lei King Rd.
Island Eastern Corridor
Sai Wan Ho

Pedestrian Walkover
Quarry Bay Park
Cityplaza III
Cityplaza IV
Cityplaza Road
Taikoo Wan Road
Tai Koo Shing Rd.
King's Road
Cityplaza Ave
Tai Wing Ave
Plaza Verde
Tai Koo Ave
Tai Fung Ave
Taikoo
Kornhill Road
Kornhill
Taikoo
Hong On Street
Yue Man St.

391

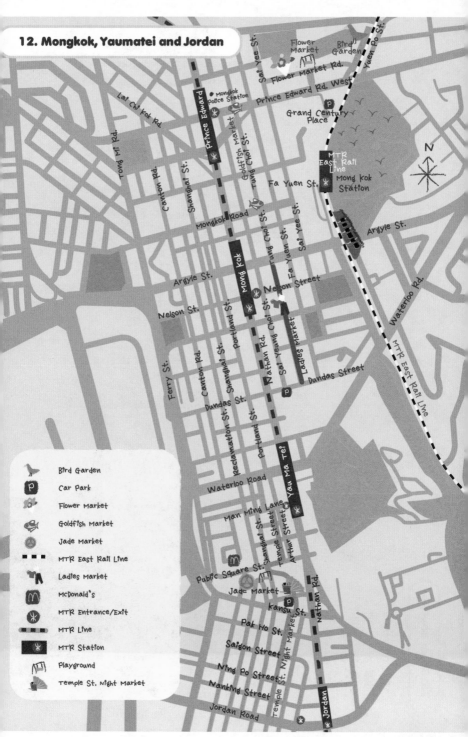

Flower Market
Bird Garden
Sai Yee St.
Flower Market Rd.
Yuen Po St.
Lai Chi Kok Rd.
Mongkok Police Station
Prince Edward Rd. West
Grand Century Place
Tong Mi Rd.
Canton Rd.
Shanghai St.
Prince Edward
Goldfish Market
Tung Choi St.
MTR East Rail Line
Mong Kok Station
Mongkok Road
Fa Yuen St.
Sai Yee St.
Argyle St.
Mong Kok
Tung Choi St.
Fa Yuen St.
Argyle St.
Nelson St.
Nelson Street
Ladies Market
Waterloo Rd.
Ferry St.
Canton Rd.
Dundas St.
Shanghai St.
Portland St.
Nathan Rd.
Sai Yeung Choi St.
Dundas Street
MTR East Rail Line
Reclamation St.
Shanghai St.
Dundas St.
Portland St.
Waterloo Road
Yau Ma Tei
Man Ming Lane

Legend

- Bird Garden
- P Car Park
- Flower Market
- Goldfish Market
- Jade Market
- MTR East Rail Line
- Ladies Market
- M McDonald's
- MTR Entrance/Exit
- MTR Line
- MTR Station
- Playground
- Temple St. Night Market

Public Square St.
Shanghai St.
Temple Street
Arthur Street
Jade Market
Kansu St.
Nathan Rd.
Pak Ho St.
Saigon Street
Temple St. Night Market
Ning Po Street
Nanking Street
Jordan Road
Jordan

N

13. Sham Shui Po

Car Park
MTR Station
MTR Entrance/Exit
MTR Route
Shopping

Shek Kip Mei

Shek Kip Mei St.
Tai Po Road
Nam Cheong St.
Cheung Sha Wan Road
Ap Liu St.
Yu Chau St.
Ki Lung St.
Lai Chi Kok Road
Mong Chut St.
Boundary Street
Lai Chi Kok Road

Tai Po Road
Kowloon Road
Fuk Wing St.
Fuk Wa St.
Sham Shui Po
Nam Cheong St.
Pei Ho St.
Kweilin St.
Yen Chow St.
Dragon Centre
Fuk Wa St.
Cheung Sha Wan Road
Kiu Kiang St.

Tai Nam St.
Yee Kuk St.
Hai Tan St.
Tung Chau St.
Tung Chau Street Park

Tonkin St.
Lai Chi Kok Road Park
Sham Shui Po Park

Sham Shui Po

Golden Computer Arcade
Fuk Wing St.
Fuk Wa St.
Nam Cheong St.
Cheung Sha Wan Rd.
B2
Sham Shui Po
A1
Ap Liu St.
Kweilin Street
D2
C1
C2
Yu Chau St.
Ki Lung St.
Pei Ho St.
Government Offices
Dragon Centre
Yen Chow Street

N

394

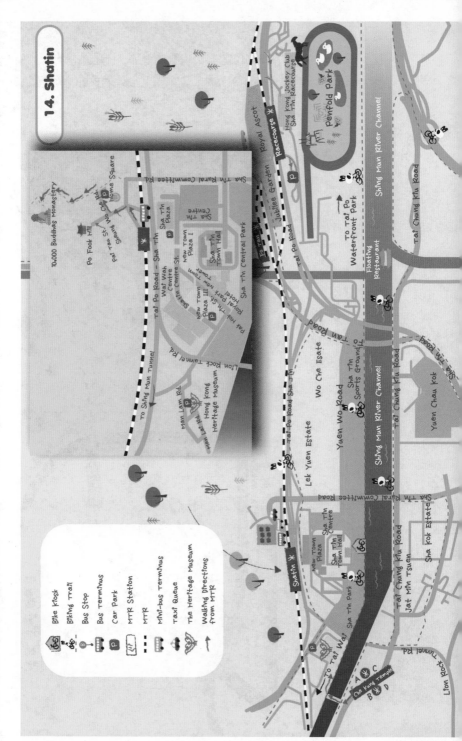

395

15. Tai Po 1

396

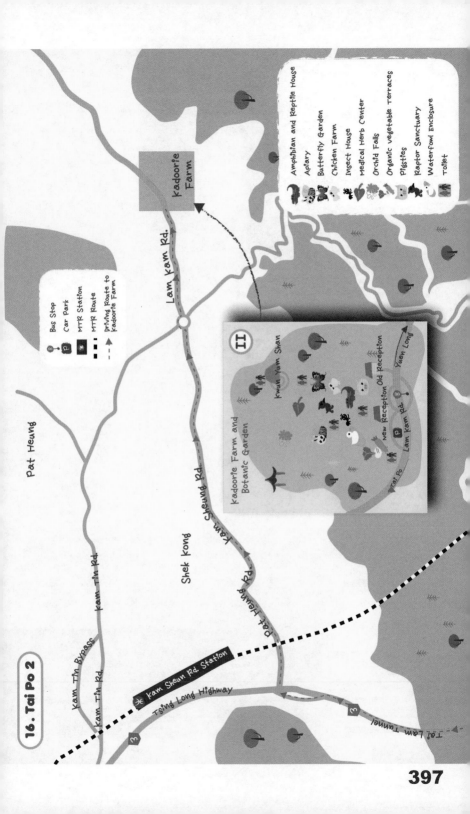

16. Tai Po 2

Legend

- 🅑 Bus Stop
- 🅟 Car Park
- ✳ MTR Station
- ▪▪▪ MTR Route
- ---→ Driving Route to Kadoorie Farm

Kadoorie Farm and Botanic Garden

II

- Kwun Yum Shan
- New Reception
- Old Reception
- Yuen Long
- Lam Kam Rd.
- Tai Po

Index

- Amphibian and Reptile House
- Apiary
- Butterfly Garden
- Chicken Farm
- Insect House
- Medical Herb Center
- Orchid Falls
- Organic vegetable terraces
- Pigsties
- Raptor Sanctuary
- Waterfowl Enclosure
- Toilet

Place names

- Pat Heung
- Kadoorie Farm
- Lam Kam Rd.
- Shek Kong
- Kam Tin Rd.
- Kam Tin Bypass
- Kam Tin Rd.
- Kam Sheung Rd.
- Pat Heung Rd.
- Kam Sheung Rd. Station
- Tsing Long Highway
- Tai Lam Tunnel
- 3

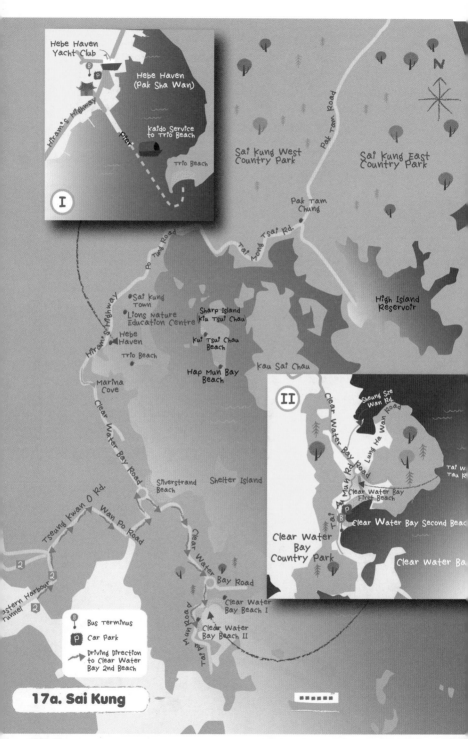

I

Hebe Haven Yacht Club

Hebe Haven (Pak Sha Wan)

Hiram's Highway

Pier

Kaido Service to Trio Beach

Trio Beach

Pak Tam Road

Sai Kung West Country Park

Sai Kung East Country Park

N

Po Tung Road

Tai Mong Tsai Rd.

Pak Tam Chung

Hiram's Highway

Sai Kung Town

Lions Nature Education Centre

Sharp Island (Kiu Tsui Chau)

Hebe Haven

Kui Tsui Chau Beach

Trio Beach

Hap Mun Bay Beach

Kau Sai Chau

High Island Reservoir

Marina Cove

Clear Water Bay Road

II

Clear Water Bay Road

Sheung Sze Wan Rd.

Lung Ha Wan Road

Tai W. Tau R

Clear Water Bay First Beach

Clear Water Bay Second Beach

Clear Water Bay Country Park

Clear Water Ba

Silverstrand Beach

Shelter Island

Tseung Kwan O Rd.

Wan Po Road

Clear Water Bay Road

2

2

Eastern Harbour Tunnel

2

Tai Au Mun Road

Clear Water Bay Beach I

Clear Water Bay Beach II

B Bus Terminus

P Car Park

Driving Direction to Clear Water Bay 2nd Beach

17a. Sai Kung

17b. Sai Kung

Pak Tam Chung

🚏	Bus Stop
	Bus Terminus
P	Car Park
	Mini-bus Terminus
	Pak Tam Chung Tree Walk
	Pak Tam Chung nature Trail
	Pak Tam Chung Family Walk
	Playground
	Restaurant
	Sheung Yiu Family Walk
	Temple
	Toilet
V	Visitor Centre

Sai Kung Country Park

Sheung Yiu Folk Museum

Sheung Yiu

To Sai Kung

Port Shelter

Tai Mong Tsai Road

Sha Sha Road

Sai Kung Tang Shiu Kin Sports Ground

Tai Mong Tsai Road

Pak Mann Rd.

Po Tung Rd.

Sai Kung Village

Sai Kung Promenade

Yi Chun St.

Pak Tam Road

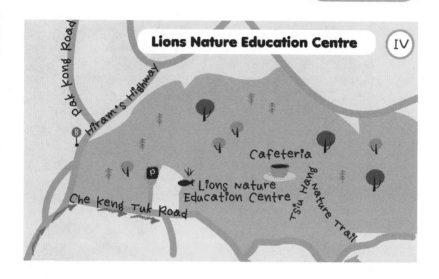

Lions Nature Education Centre IV

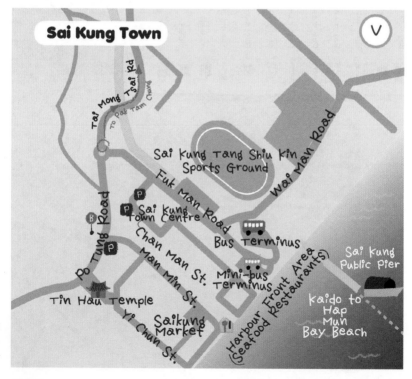

Sai Kung Town V

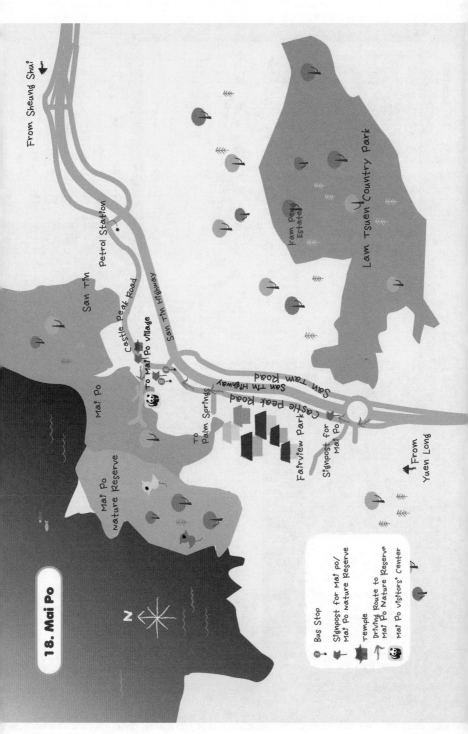

18. Mai Po

From Sheung Shui

San Tin

Petrol Station

Castle Peak Road

San Tin Highway

To Mai Po Village

Mai Po

Mai Po nature Reserve

To Palm Springs

Fairview park

Castle Peak Road

San Tin Highway

San Tam Road

Signpost for Mai Po

Kam Pong Estate

Lam Tsuen Country Park

From Yuen Long

N

Bus Stop

Signpost for Mai Po/ Mai Po nature Reserve

temple

Driving Route to Mai Po Nature Reserve

Mai Po Visitors' Center

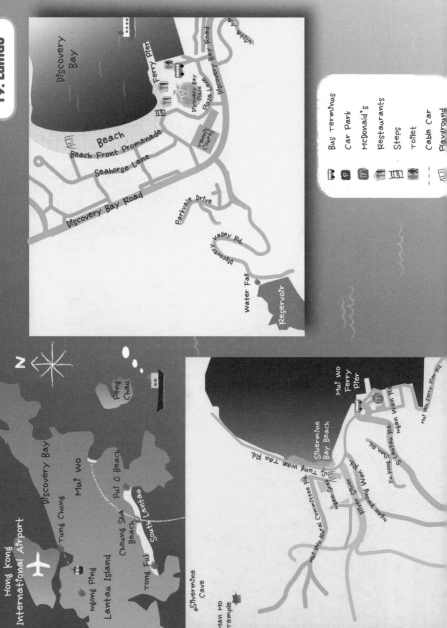

Discovery Bay

Discovery Bay

Beach
Beach Front Promenade
Seahorse Lane
Discovery Bay Road

Ferry Pier
Discovery Bay Plaza
Plaza Lane
Discovery Bay Road
Vista Ave.
Tennis Courts

Parkvale Drive

Discovery Valley Rd.
Valley Rd.
Water Fall
Reservoir

Bus Terminus
Car Park
McDonald's
Restaurants
Steps
Toilet
Cable Car
Playground

N

Hong Kong
International Airport

Peng Chau

Discovery Bay
Tung Chung
Mui Wo
Pui O Beach
Cheung Sha Beach
South Lantau
Tong Fuk
Ngong Ping
Lantau Island
Tai O
Shek Pik

Mui Wo Ferry Pier

Silvermine Bay Beach
Tung Wan Tau Rd.
River Silver
Mui Wo Rural Committee Rd.
Ngan Shek St.
Ngan Wan Rd.
S. Lantau Rd.
Chi Kong St.
Ngan Kwong Wan Rd.
Mui Wo Ferry Pier Rd.

Silvermine Cave
Man Mo Temple

402

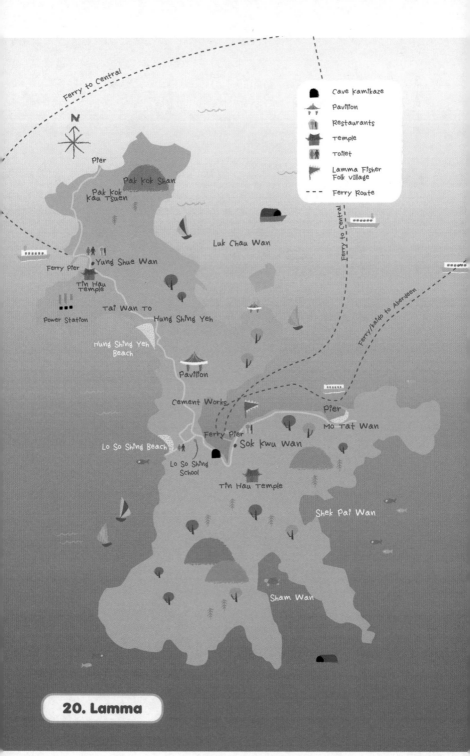

Cave kamikaze
Pavilion
Restaurants
Temple
Toilet
Lamma Fisher Folk village
Ferry Route

Ferry to Central

N

Pier

Pak Kok Shan

Pak Kok Kau Tsuen

Luk Chau Wan

Ferry to Central

Ferry Pier

Yung Shue Wan

Tin Hau Temple

Power Station

Tai Wan To

Hung Shing Yeh

Hung Shing Yeh Beach

Pavilion

Ferry/kaido to Aberdeen

Cement Works

Pier

Mo Tat Wan

Ferry Pier

Lo So Shing Beach

Sok Kwu Wan

Lo So Shing School

Tin Hau Temple

Shek Pai Wan

Sham Wan

20. Lamma

403

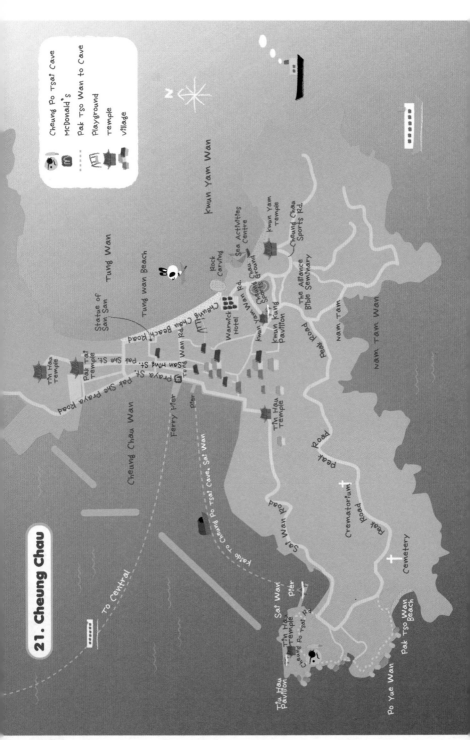

Legend:
- Cheung Po Tsai Cave
- McDonald's
- Pak Tso Wan to Cave
- Playground
- Temple
- Village

To Central

Cheung Chau Wan

Ferry Pier

Pier

To Cheung Po Tsai Cave, Sai Wan

Pak Tai Temple
Tin Hau Temple

Pak She St.
Praya St.
Pak She Praya Road
San Hing St.
Tung Wan Road

Statue of San San

Tung Wan Beach

Tung Wan

Cheung Chau Beach Road

Warwick Hotel

Rock Carving

Kwun Yam Wan Rd.

Kwun Yam Wan

Cheung Chau Sports Club

Sea Activities Centre

Kwun Yam Temple

Cheung Chau Sports Rd.

Kwun Kung Pavilion

The Alliance Bible Seminary

Tin Hau Temple

Peak Road

Nam Tam

Nam Tam Wan

Sai Wan Road

Peak Road

Crematorium

Peak Road

Cemetery

Tin Hau Temple
Sai Wan

Pier

Cheung Po Tsai Rd.

Tin Hau Pavilion

Po Yue Wan

Pak Tso Wan Beach

Pak Tso Wan

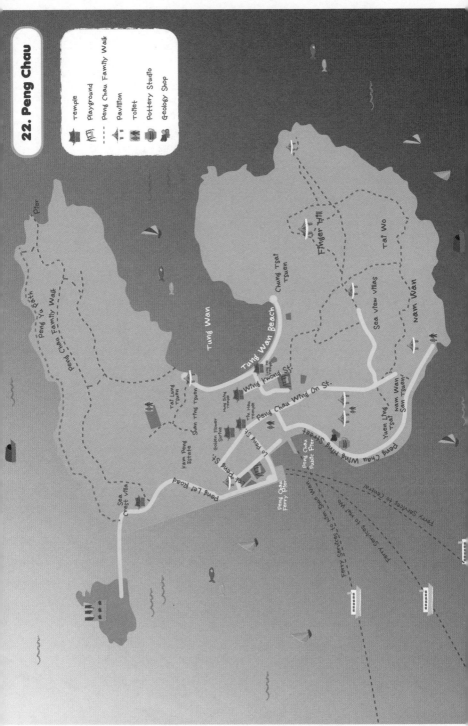

22. Peng Chau

Temple
Playground
Peng Chau Family Walk
Pavilion
Toilet
Pottery Studio
Geology Shop

Pier
Peng Yu Path
Peng Chau Family Walk
Tai Lung Tsuen
Sun Ying Tsuen
Kam Peng Estate
Sea Crest Villas
Peng Lei Road
Wing Hing Street
Lo Peng St.
Golden Flower Surihai
Tin Hau Temple
Peng Chau Wing On St.
Wing Kwong St.
Tung Wan
Tung Wan Beach
Chung Tsai Tsuen
Finger Hill
Tai Wo
Sea View Villas
Nam Wan
Yuen Ling Tsai
Nam Wan San Tsuen
Peng Chau Wing Hing Street
Peng Chau Public Pier
Peng Chau Ferry Pier

Ferry Services to Central
Ferry Services to Mui Wo
Ferry Services to Hei Ling Chau

405

23. Penny's Bay/Disney

Legend:
- Hotel
- Parking
- MTR Station
- MTR Tung Chung Line
- Disney Resort Line
- Disneyland Park
- Bus Terminus
- Bus Stop

Sunny Bay

North Lantau Highway

Sunny Bay

Penny's Bay Highway

Sunny Bay Road

Inspiration Lake

Inspiration Drive

Penny's Bay

Fantasy Road

Disneyland Resort

Tomorrowland

Main Street USA

Fantasyland

Hong Kong Disneyland

Adventureland

Magic Road

Park Promenade

Disney's Hollywood Hotel

Hong Kong Disneyland Hotel

Promenade

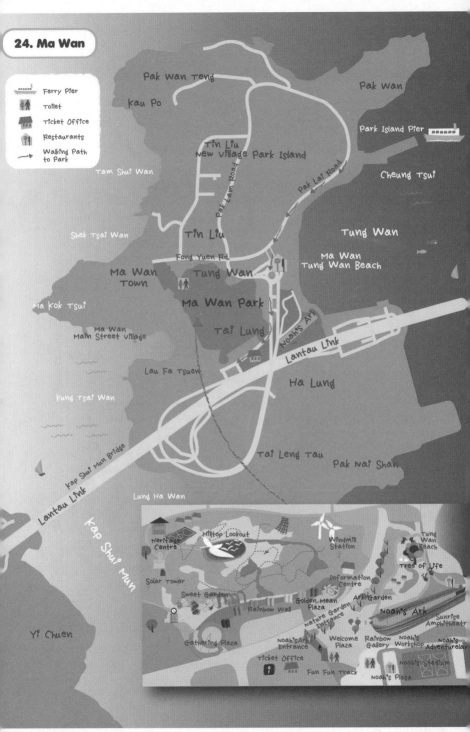

24. Ma Wan

Legend:
- Ferry Pier
- Toilet
- Ticket Office
- Restaurants
- Walking Path to Park

Pak Wan Teng

Kau Po

Pak Wan

Park Island Pier

Tin Liu New Village Park Island

Pak Lam Road

Pak Lai Road

Cheung Tsui

Tam Shui Wan

Shek Tsai Wan

Tin Liu

Tung Wan

Fong Yuen Rd.

Ma Wan Town

Tung Wan

Ma Wan Tung Wan Beach

Ma Kok Tsui

Ma Wan Park

Ma Wan Main Street Village

Tai Lung

Noah's Ark

Lantau Link

Lau Fa Tsuen

Ha Lung

Kung Tsai Wan

Tai Leng Tau

Pak Nai Shan

Kap Shui Mun Bridge

Lantau Link

Lung Ha Wan

Kap Shui Mun

Yi Chuen

Park detail map:

Heritage Centre

Hilltop Lookout

Windmill Station

Tung Wan Beach

Solar Tower

Tree of Life

Sweet Garden

Information Centre

Rainbow Wall

Golden Mean Plaza

Ark Garden

Nature Garden Entrance

Noah's Ark

Sunrise Amphitheatr

Gathering Plaza

Noah's Ark Entrance

Welcome Plaza

Rainbow Gallery

Noah's Workshop

Noah's Adventurelan

Ticket Office

Fun Fun Track

Noah's Plaza

Noah's Stadium

Consort Rise

Bisney Rd

Queen Mar
Hospital

Scenic Villa Drive

Bisney Rd

Sassoon Rd.

Pok Fu Lam Road

Rodrigues Court

Northcote Close

Sha Wan Drive

Victoria Road

HKU Li ka Shing Faculty of Medicine

Stanley Ho Sports Centre

Tam Villas

Sassoon Rd.

Carrianna Sassoon

Carrianna Sassoon

Victoria Road

Seascape

Kong Sin Wan Road

Magnolia Villa

The Independent Schools Foundation Academy

Aegean Terrace

Information Crescent

Cyberport

1

P

2

H

3

Cyberport Road

Cybercentre

WISE KIDS

Cyberport

Cyberport Road

	Parking
	Route to Cyberport
	Movie Theatre
	Le Meridien Hotel
	Grassy Area
	Wise Kids Toy Shop
	Bus Terminus

Cyberport Waterfront Park

Bel-air rise

Residence Bel-Air

25. Pokfulam & Cyberport

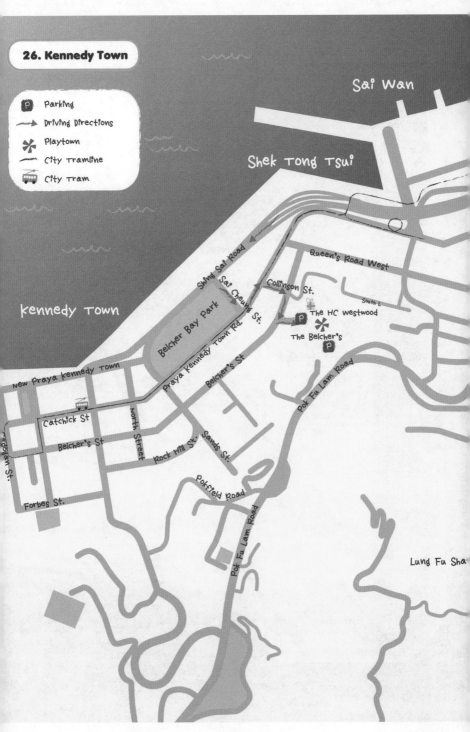

26. Kennedy Town

P Parking

→ Driving Directions

✳ Playtown

— City Tramline

🚋 City Tram

Sai Wan

Shek Tong Tsui

Queen's Road West

Kennedy Town

Collinson St.

South L

The HC Westwood

The Belcher's

Shing Sai Road

Sai Cheung St.

Belcher Bay Park

Praya Kennedy Town Rd.

New Praya Kennedy Town

Belcher's St.

Catchick St

North Street

Belcher's St

Rock Hill St.

Sands St.

Forbes St.

Pok Fu Lam Road

Pokfield Road

Pok Fu Lam Road

Lung Fu Sha

409

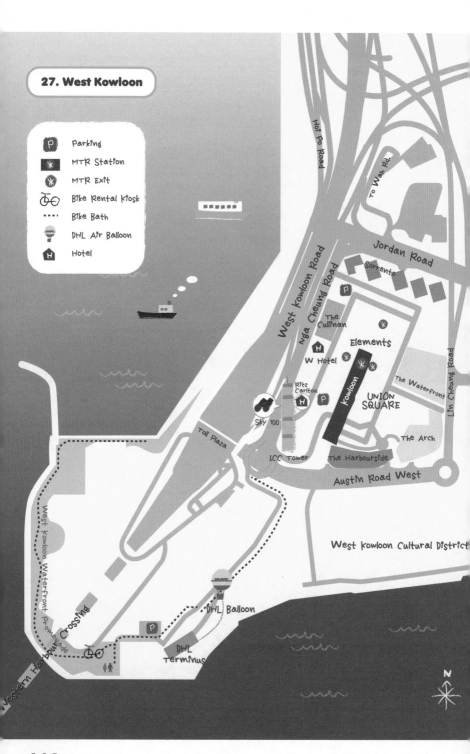

27. West Kowloon

Legend:

- P — Parking
- ✳ — MTR Station
- ❋ — MTR Exit
- 🚲 — Bike Rental Kiosk
- ···· — Bike Bath
- 🎈 — DHL Air Balloon
- H — Hotel

Hoi Po Road

To Wah Rd.

Jordan Road

West Kowloon Road

Nga Cheung Road

Lin Cheung Road

Sorrento

The Cullinan

Elements

W Hotel

Ritz Carlton

Kowloon

UNION SQUARE

The Waterfront

Sky 100

The Arch

ICC Tower

The Harbourside

Austin Road West

Toll Plaza

West Kowloon Cultural District

Western Harbourfront Crossing

West Kowloon Waterfront Promenade

P

DHL Balloon

DHL Terminus

N

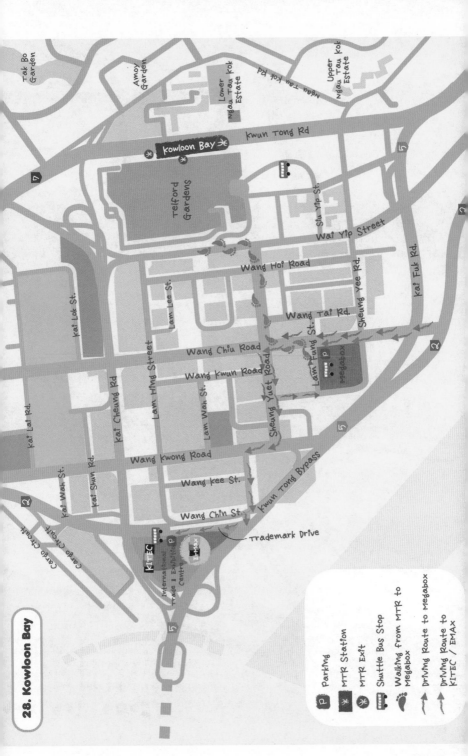

28. Kowloon Bay

Tak Bo Garden

Amoy Garden

Lower Ngau Tau Kok Estate

Upper Ngau Tau Kok Estate

Ngau Tau Kok Rd.

Kwun Tong Rd

Kowloon Bay

Telford Gardens

Sta Yip St.

Wai Yip Street

Kai Fuk Rd.

Kai Lok St.

Wang Hoi Road

Wang Tai Rd.

Sheung Yee Rd.

Lam Lee St.

Lam Tung St.

Megabox

Wang Chiu Road

Wang Kwun Road

Sheung Yuet Road

Kai Cheung Rd

Lam Hing Street

Lam Wai St.

Kai Lai Rd.

Wang kwong Road

Kai Shun Rd.

Wang kee St.

Kwun Tong Bypass

Kai Wan St.

Wang Chin St.

Trademark Drive

Cargo Circuit

KITEC

International Trade & Exhibition Centre

E-MAX

Legend

P Parking
✳ MTR Station
✳ MTR Exit
🚌 Shuttle Bus Stop
👣 Walking from MTR to Megabox
↑ Driving Route to Megabox
↑ Driving Route to KITEC / EMAX

411

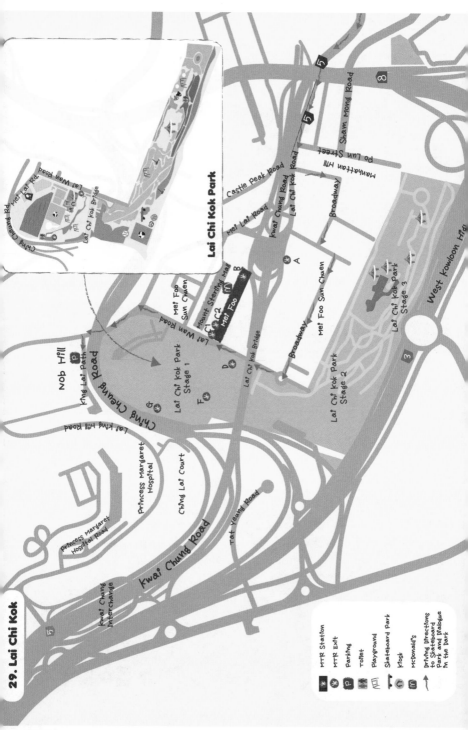

Lai Chi Kok Park

Chung Cheung Rd/ Mei Lai Road
Lai Wan Road
Lai Chi Kok Bridge

Castle Peak Road
Mei Lai Road
Kwai Chung Road
Lai Chi Kok Road
Broadway
Po Lun Street
Sham Mong Road
Manhattan Hill

Mei Foo Sun Chuen
Mount Sterling Mall
A
B
C2
C1
Mei Foo
Lai Wan Road

Lai Chi Kok Bridge
Broadway
Mei Foo Sun Chuen
Lai Chi Kok Park Stage 2
Lai Chi Kok Park Stage 3
West Kowloon Highway

Nob Hill
King Lai Path
Ching Cheung Road
Lai King Hill Road
D
F
E

Lai Chi Kok Park Stage 1
Lai Chi Kok Path

Princess Margaret Hospital
Ching Lai Court
Princess Margaret Hospital Road
Kwai Chung Road
Lai Yeung Road

Kwai Chung Interchange

Legend

- MTR Station
- MTR Exit
- Parking
- Toilet
- Playground
- Skateboard Park
- Kiosk
- McDonald's
- Driving Directions to Skateboard Park and Dialogue in the Dark

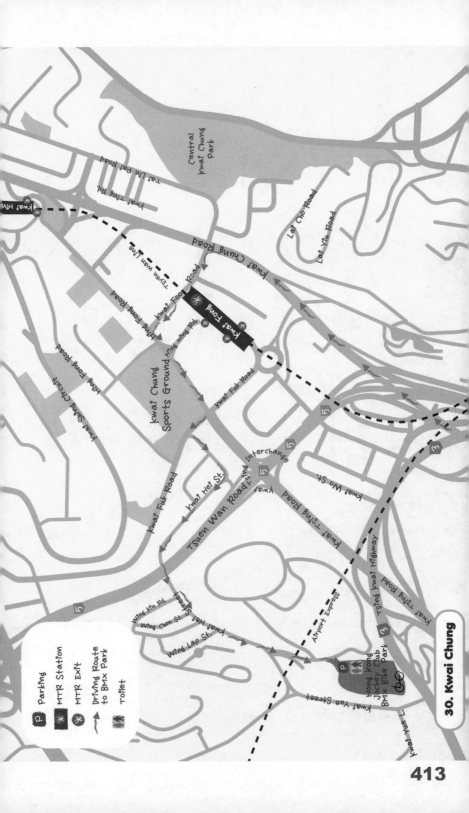

30. Kwai Chung

413

On Chun Street

Sai Sha Road

Saddle Ridge Garden

Kam Ying Road

Kam Ying Court

Ma On Shan Bypass

Ma On Shan Road

Park Belvedere

On Chun Street

Ma On Shan Centre

Fu Fai Garden

Bayshore Towers

Ma On Shan

Sunshine City

On Shing St.

On Luk Street

Ma On Shan Park

Hang Hong St.

On Yuen Street

Kam Hay Court

Yiu On Estate

Horizon Suite Hotel

Bumble Tots

The Waterside

Ma On Shan Sports Ground

Ma On Shan Recreation Ground

Heng On Estate

Chung On Estate

Sai Sha Road

Ma On Shan Promenade

Heng On

Hang Ming St.

Parking

Hotel

MTR Station

MTR Exit

Directions to Bumble Tots

Restaurant

Bus terminus

Playground

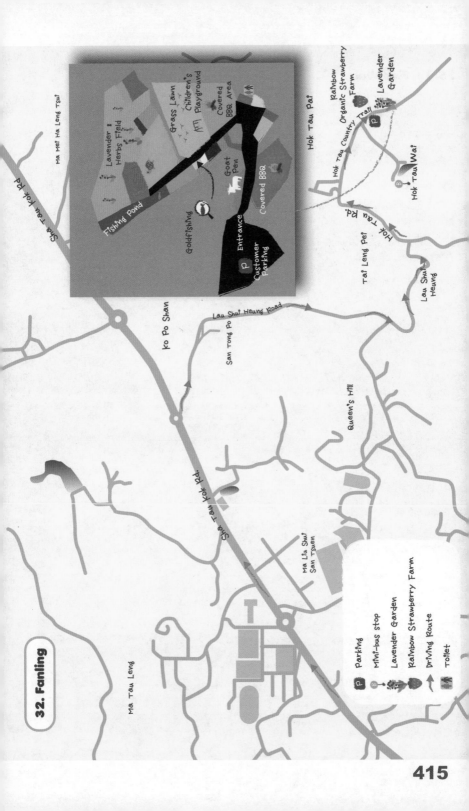

Ma Mei Ha Leng Tsui

Sha Tau Kok Rd.

Lavender & Herbs Field

Grass Lawn

Children's Playground

Covered BBQ Area

Fishing Pond

Goat Pen

Goldfishing

Entrance

Customer Parking

Covered BBQ

Hok Tau Pai

Rainbow Organic Strawberry Farm

Lavender Garden

Hok Tau Country Trail

Hok Tau Wai

Hok Tau Rd.

Tai Leng Pei

Lau Shui Heung

Ko Po Shan

Lau Shui Heung Road

San Tong Po

Sha Tau Kok Rd.

Queen's Hill

Ma Liu Shui San Tsuen

Ma Tau Leng

Parking

Mini-bus stop

Lavender Garden

Rainbow Strawberry Farm

Driving Route

Toilet

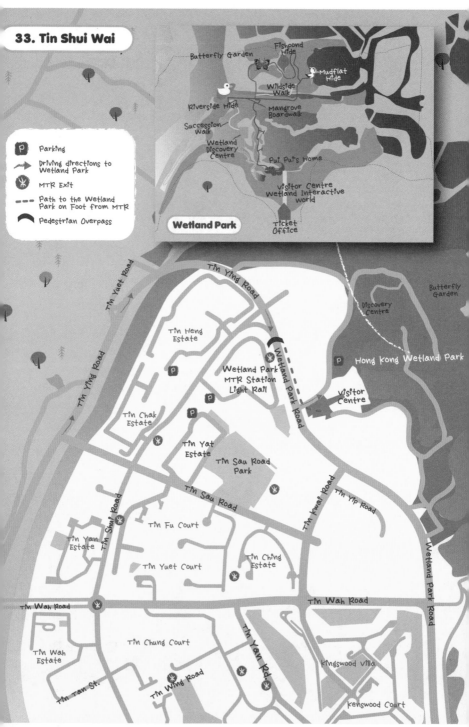

P Parking

Driving directions to Wetland Park

MTR Exit

Path to the Wetland Park on Foot from MTR

Pedestrian Overpass

Wetland Park

Butterfly Garden

Fishpond Hide

Mudflat Hide

Wildside Walk

Riverside Hide

Mangrove Boardwalk

Succession Walk

Wetland Discovery Centre

Pui Pui's Home

Visitor Centre Wetland Interactive world

Ticket Office

Tin Ying Road

Tin Yuet Road

Tin Ying Road

Tin Heng Estate

Wetland Park MTR Station Light Rail

Wetland Park Road

Discovery Centre

Butterfly Garden

Hong Kong Wetland Park

Visitor Centre

Tin Chak Estate

Tin Yat Estate

Tin Sau Road Park

Tin Sau Road

Tin Kwai Road

Tin Yip Road

Tin Shui Road

Tin Fu Court

Tin Yan Estate

Tin Yuet Court

Tin Ching Estate

Wetland Park Road

Tin Wah Road

Tin Wah Road

Tin Wah Estate

Tin Chung Court

Tin Yan Rd.

Kingswood Villa

Tin Tan St.

Tin Wing Road

Kenswood Court

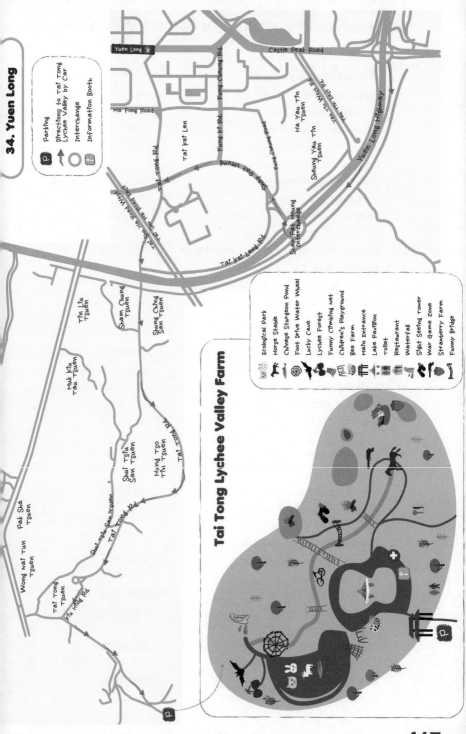

Useful Phone Numbers and Websites

GENERAL INFORMATION:

Hong Kong emergency number	999
Telephone directory (English)	1081
Telephone directory (Chinese)	1083
Hong Kong Tourism Board	2508-1234
www.discoverhongkong.com	
Hong Kong Government Information	1823
www.gov.hk	
Community Advice Bureau (CAB)	2815-5444
www.cab.org.hk	
Maps of Hong Kong – Internet Yellow Pages	2828-2033
www.ypmap.com	
Hong Kong buildings, street names and maps – Centamap	
www.centamap.com	
Environmental Protection Department	2838-3111
www.epd.gov.hk/epd/	
Leisure and Cultural Services Dept. (parks, beaches & swimming pools)	
www.lcsd.gov.hk/en/home.php	2414-5555
Agriculture, Fisheries and Conservation Department (country parks)	
www.afcd.gov.hk	2708-8885
Hong Kong Public Libraries	2921-0208
www.hkpl.gov.hk	
World Wildlife Fund Hong Kong	2526-1011
www.wwf.org.hk	
Hong Kong Eco-tours	2981-3523
www.hkecotours.com	

TRANSPORT INFORMATION:

Transport Department enquiries	2804-2600
www.td.gov.hk	
Transport Complaints Unit hotline	2889-9999
Octopus Cards	2266-2222
www.octopuscards.com	
The Peak – Hong Kong	2522-0922
www.thepeak.com.hk	
MTR Corporation	2881-8888
www.mtr.com.hk	

Citybus	2873-0818
www.citybus.com.hk	
Kowloon Motor Bus Company	2745-4466
www.kmb.com.hk	
New Lantao Bus Co. Ltd.	2984-9848
www.newlantaobus.com	
Hong Kong & Kowloon Ferry	2815-6063
www.hkkf.com.hk	
New World First Ferry	2131-8181
www.nwff.com.hk	
The "Star" Ferry Co. Ltd.	2367-7065
www.starferry.com.hk	
Chuen Kee Ferry Co. (Aberdeen-Sok Kwu Wan)	2982-8225
www.ferry.com.hk	
Tram information line (Hong Kong Tramways)	2548-7102
www.hktramways.com	
Airport Authority/Airport Express Train	2181-8888
www.hongkongairport.com	

TAXI INFORMATION:

Taxi – lost property hotline	1872-920
To call HK or Kowloon red taxi – Wai Fat Co.	2861-1008
To call HK or Kowloon red taxi – Yau Luen Co.	2527-6324
To call New Territories green taxi	2457-2266
To call Lantau Taxi Service blue taxi	2984-1328

CHILD CARE SERVICES/BABY CARE CONSULTANTS:

Rent-a-Mum – childcare solutions	2523-4868
www.rent-a-mum.com	
The Nanny Experts – childcare services	2574-7473
www.thenannyexperts.com	
Baby Bloom – baby planning and greenproofing	9167-2737
www.babybloom.com.hk	
Annerley – maternity and early childhood professionals	
www.annerley.com.hk	2983-1558

PARENT WEBSITES:

Hong Kong for Kids	www.hongkongforkids.net
Little Steps Asia	www.littlestepsasia.com
Yummy Mummy	www.yummymummyasia.com
GeoBaby	www.geobaby.com

EMERGENCY MEDICAL CARE:

(not a complete list of hospitals in Hong Kong)

Private Hospitals with 24-Hour Urgent Care:

Matilda Hospital (on the Peak, Hong Kong Island) 2849-0111
www.matilda.org
Adventist Hospital (Stubbs Rd., Hong Kong Island)3651-8888
www.hkah.org.hk
Canossa Hospital (Old Peak Rd., Mid Levels, Hong Kong Island)
www.canossahospital.org.hk   2522-2181
Baptist Hospital (Waterloo Road, Kowloon)   2339-8888
www.hkbh.org.hk
St. Teresa's Hospital (Pentland Street, Kowloon)   2200-3434
www.sth.org.hk
Union Hospital (Sha Tin, New Territories)   2608-3388
www.union.org

Public Hospitals with 24-Hour Urgent Care:

Queen Mary Hospital (Pokfulam, Hong Kong Island) 2255-3838
http://www3.ha.org.hk/qmh/index.htm
Queen Elizabeth Hospital (Gascoigne Rd., Kowloon) 2958-8888
http://www.qeh.org.hk
Kwong Wah Hospital (Waterloo Road, Kowloon)   2332-2311
http://www.ha.org.hk/kwh
Princess Margaret (Lai Chi Kok, Kowloon)   2990-1111
http://www.ha.org.hk/pmh/index800.htm
Prince of Wales (Sha Tin, New Territories)   2632-2415
http://www.ha.org.hk/pwh

CAR RENTAL INFORMATION:

Avis International   2620-0586
www.avis.com.hk
Crown Motors – Rent-a-car   2880-1515
www.crown-motors.com
Hertz   2525-1313
www.hertz.com.hk
Hong Kong Car Rental   6734-8515
www.CarRental.com.hk

About the Author

Cindy Miller Stephens has lived in Hong Kong for 15 years. Cindy was born in Miami, Florida, and moved to Paris, France as a young child. She travelled Europe widely, and lived between France and the U.S. before enrolling in high school in Rochester, Minnesota. She later graduated from Colgate University and moved to New York City in the late 1980s where  she pursued a career as a country music recording artist. She moved to Hong Kong in 1996 with her husband Chris and had three children, Lara (13), Hailey (10) and Audrey (six).

In Hong Kong, beyond raising a family, Cindy earned her Hong Kong corporate real estate license and worked as a relocation agent, advising clients on living in and relocating to Hong Kong. Cindy spent a number of years meticulously documenting information on parks, museums, beaches, markets, hikes/walks and other venues and activities throughout Hong Kong. She has always enjoyed referring friends and business acquaintances to unusual or far-flung outings to enjoy with their children. After being encouraged by a publisher to compile all of her information into a book she started the long process in 2003. The result was *Hong Kong for Kids*, first published in 2004.

Cindy hopes that this book will be a tool to get your family out there, enjoying all that Hong Kong has to offer. If you have ideas you would like to share about places to take kids in Hong Kong, she would love to hear from you. Please contact her through the book's website: www.hongkongforkids.net.

EXPLORE ASIA WITH BLACKSMITH BOOKS

From retailers around the world or from *www.blacksmithbooks.com*